Enlightenment and Reform in Eighteenth-century Europe

Enlightenment and Reform in Eighteenth-century Europe

DEREK BEALES

I.B. TAURIS

LONDON · NEW YORK

Reprinted in 2(... by I.B. Tauris & Co Ltd
6 Salem Road, London W2 4BU
175 Fifth Aven ... New York NY 10010
www.ibtauris.

In the United States of America and ... re
Macmillan, a division of St Martin's Press, 175 Fifth Avenue, New York
NY 10010

First published in 2005 by I.B.Tauris & Co. Ltd

International Library of Historical Studies 29

ISBN 978 1 86064 949 3
       978 1 86064 950 9

A full CIP record for this book is available from the British Library
A full CIP record for this book is available from the Library of
Congress
Library of Congress catalog card: available

Set in Monotype Dante by Ewan Smith, London
Printed and bound in Great Britain by
CPI Antony Rowe, Chippenham, Wiltshire

Contents

*To Tim Blanning, in gratitude, friendship
and admiration*

Acknowledgements

I owe thanks to Dr Lester Crook and Professor Hamish Scott for making possible the publication of this book; to the Master and Fellows of Sidney Sussex College, Cambridge for a grant towards the cost of transferring to a computer articles written in the 1970s and early 1980s; to Ms Wendy Hedley for undertaking this task; and to Ms Janet Law for intelligent and resourceful copy-editing. Acknowledgements for help with individual articles will be found at the end of the relevant text. As always, I have been encouraged and sustained by my wife Sally.

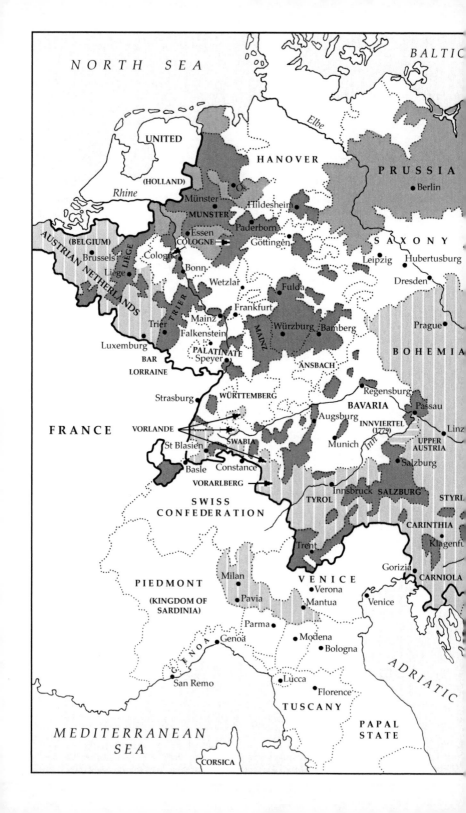

The Austrian Monarchy in the Eighteenth Century

Legend:
- Generally accepted boundary of the Empire (Reich)
- Principal Ecclesiastical states
- Prussian gains by partition of Poland in 1772
- Prussia from the 1740s
- The Monarchy from the 1740s
- The Monarchy's gains in the 1770s
- Military frontier regions

Danzig

EAST PRUSSIA

Vistula

Warsaw

P O L A N D

LESIA
Breslau

Neisse

SILESIA
Olmütz
Wieliczka
Teschen

MORAVIA
Brünn

ZIPS (1770)

Lemberg

G A L I C I A (1772)

Dniester

Sereth

Sbruts

Pruth

BUKOVINA (1775)

MOLDAVIA

VER
elk
Klosterneuburg
Vienna
Pressburg
nfeld
RIA
Danube
Vác
Pannonhalma
Buda
Pest
az

H U N G A R Y

TRANSYLVANIA

Hermannstadt

Temesvar

B A N A T

WALLACHIA

Carlstadt

Belgrade
Save
Passarowitz
Old Orsova
LITTLE WALLACHIA

BOSNIA

SERBIA

Danube

DALMATIA (to Venice)

O T T O M A N   E M P I R E

MONTENEGRO

EA

0   100   200 miles
0   100   200   300 kilometres

Introduction

No period can outmatch the catalogue of fundamental changes that came to pass during the eighteenth century. Britain conquered India and much of North America; it then lost what became the United States, as a result of the American Revolution. Russia expanded vastly to the west, the south and the east. The continent of Australasia was discovered. As knowledge of the Scientific Revolution of the seventeenth century was diffused, the Enlightenment and the growth of the 'public sphere' transformed the attitudes of the elite in nearly all European countries, sapping the power and credit of the Christian Churches and their theology. The Roman Catholic Church was most affected, as it had preserved many of the beliefs and practices long abandoned in Protestant countries. The fact that it had a head, the pope, who claimed to exercise authority within all Catholic states, aroused growing opposition from their secular rulers, whose own power was increasing. Their first target was the Jesuits, who took a special vow of obedience to the pope. After a long campaign by the Catholic Powers, the pope was forced to suppress them in 1773. The French Revolution not only brought down the old regime in France; the revolutionary armies removed most Catholic rulers from power, including the pope, and brought about the abolition of monasteries and the seizure of all Church property in France, Belgium and Catholic Germany, and of nearly all of it in Italy.

It was during the eighteenth century that the great surge of world population growth began, that western technology eclipsed that of the East, and that the beginnings of rapid industrialisation became visible in Britain. The later decades of the century saw the birth of the theory of nationalism and its revival or first appearance in many countries. German, Czech, Hungarian and Italian feeling and languages were revivified; among others, Flemish, Slovak, Romanian and Croatian made a tentative appearance.

All these changes, and many others only less spectacular, had effects that are still acutely felt in the twenty-first century. To give only a few examples, it is to the British conquest of India and North America that the hegemony of the English language is due; Russia's western and southern neighbours cannot efface roughly two centuries of its rule or feel confident that they can prevent its return; the American and French Revolutions changed political theory and practice for ever; though Catholicism and the papacy have regained some of their influence, they have never recovered their lands. Nationalism flourishes almost everywhere in the world; population growth remains out of control; economically backward countries still seek to learn from the Industrial Revolution; and opponents of repressive regimes still look to the examples of the American and French Revolutions.

Yet in Britain, at least at school level, the eighteenth century has never been a widely taught period. Once, most schools seemed to favour starting sixth-form work around 1500, which meant that few pupils ever reached the eighteenth century. Now Hitler and Stalin are the staple diet, and the stultifying effects of the National Curriculum include the extrusion of much of the eighteenth century from the syllabus altogether. Up to now, however, neglect in the schools has been compensated by enthusiasm in the universities. Few periods have attracted a galaxy of historians to compare with Tim Blanning, John Brewer, Owen Chadwick, Peter Dickson, Robert Evans, Olwen Hufton, John McManners, Isabel de Madariaga, the late Roy Porter, Simon Schama, Hamish Scott and Tony Wrigley – to name only some of the fine British historians whose work has transformed our knowledge of the century and, incidentally, influenced my own research and writing. These historians have illuminated, among other things, the development of states, bureaucracies and armies; the character and causes of economic development; the nature and diversity of the Enlightenment and its influence on governments; the complex interplay between Enlightenment, religion and the churches; related developments in the visual arts and music; and the connection of all these phenomena to Revolution.

This book brings together most of the essays, articles and special lectures I have written on eighteenth-century Europe, in some cases revised, in one case translated into English. Some of them are concerned with the whole Continent ('Social Forces and Enlightened Policies'; 'Christians and "Philosophes"'). Most form part of, or arise out of, my research on Joseph II, Holy Roman Emperor from 1765 to 1790 and ruler of the Austrian Monarchy from 1780 to 1790. Anyone who works on him and on the Austrian Monarchy in the eighteenth century is in effect studying the history of the modern states of Austria, Belgium, Croatia, the Czech Republic, Germany, Hungary,

Italy, Luxembourg, Poland, Romania, Serbia, Slovakia, Slovenia and Ukraine. Joseph was a dedicated and tireless reformer, often credited with effecting from above enough changes to justify describing him as 'the Revolution in a single man' – or, at least, enough changes to stave off in his territories upheavals such as occurred in France.

Since his work affected such a huge area, it is particularly important to establish what precisely his ideas, aims and achievements were. It happens that the nature of his 'revolution from above' has commonly been characterised by historians with the use of historical sources that turn out to be spurious. Detailed research was required to peel away from his image the ideas erroneously attributed to him by these much-used sources ('The False Joseph II'). On the other hand, his remarkably radical early *Rêveries* had never before been published complete and are now translated into English for the first time (see Chapter 6). These reassessments necessarily go with a reconsideration of the role of the Catholic Church, which was not only, in many aspects, an obstacle in the way of his reforms but also, in other aspects, their inspiration: he drew on the ideas of a 'Catholic Enlightenment' very different in tone from the French, was not in fact an enemy of the Jesuits, and saw himself as a Catholic reformer, inspired by God to purify the Church ('Maria Theresa, Joseph II and the Suppression of the Jesuits'; 'Joseph II and the Monasteries of Austria and Hungary'; 'The Origins of the Pope's Visit to Joseph II in 1782'; 'Joseph II and Josephism'). The findings of these studies alter our view of his relationship to the Enlightenment, particularly the French Enlightenment ('Christians and *"Philosophes"*'; 'Was Joseph II an Enlightened Despot?'). The nature of his collaboration with his mother as her co-regent, and of their differences over policy, is also illuminated ('Love and the Empire'; 'Maria Theresa, Joseph II and the Suppression of the Jesuits', 'Joseph II and Josephism'). An appraisal of his 'Enlightened despotism', together with a detailed study of his legislation on monasteries and its implementation in Austria and Hungary, shows both what problems of enforcement he faced, and also how hopeless it was to try to apply the same policies and expect to achieve the same results in disparate provinces ('Joseph II and the Monasteries of Austria and Hungary'; 'Was Joseph II an Enlightened Despot?'). Finally, Joseph – contrary to the common view, disseminated by the play and film *Amadeus* – turns out to have been Mozart's appreciative patron, thus significantly enhancing his role in cultural history ('Mozart and the Habsburgs').

Pietro Verri, one of his Italian officials, wrote of Joseph's 'great project'. The emperor himself talked of his 'mission'. To understand his aims it is necessary to consider what he owed to the Enlightenment. But it is also necessary to grasp what the project and the mission amounted to in order to understand the Enlightenment as it manifested itself in his vast territories. To appraise properly the Enlightened absolutism or despotism characteristic of central and eastern Europe in the second half of the eighteenth century, the policies of Joseph, the most radical of all the rulers concerned, have to be properly assessed. They were certainly too radical for most of his subjects, and in some provinces provoked actual revolution against him. Although there was a strong reaction against his programme at his death, much of it survived – for example, religious toleration, the abolition of personal servitude, the suppression of nearly half of all monasteries. Those houses that survived mostly lasted until the Second World War, and in Austria many still exist. His linguistic policies, making German the language of nearly all the Monarchy, both encouraged the use of German, by Jews for example, and fostered the other vernaculars of his provinces and the nationalisms associated with them. In the age of Reaction after 1815, his heritage so dominated the countries he had ruled that the term 'Josephism' was invented to describe it by those in the 1830s, including Metternich, who wanted to pursue policies more friendly to the pope and Catholicism ('Joseph II and Josephism'). His great project was revolutionary enough to attract both the enthusiastic support of reformers and the violent opposition of conservatives.

PART ONE

Contexts: European and Austrian

CHAPTER I

Social Forces and Enlightened Policies

Enlightened ideas and attitudes, and the policies influenced by them, are commonly explained by twentieth-century historians as in some sense the product of social forces – perhaps as the result of pressure exerted from below by a class or classes or groups, perhaps as the outcome of less easily identified but more fundamental economic and social tendencies. To take a distinguished example, Albert Soboul, one of the most notable Marxist historians of the French Revolution, which he saw as the triumph of the bourgeoisie, was equally convinced that the *Encyclopédie*, the central text of the French Enlightenment, published between 1751 and 1765, should be regarded as a manifesto of the bourgeois spirit.[1] He conceived 'Enlightened absolutism' as the characteristic product of those eastern European societies which experienced in the early modern period 'the second enserfment', that is, a strengthening of landlord domination over the peasantry.[2] Other historians have explained Enlightened absolutism as an effect or a concomitant of industrialisation – or of 'proto-industrialisation'.[3]

Eighteenth-century writers themselves, however, seldom discussed such social forces, and particularly rarely – perhaps never – when explaining the spread of Enlightenment. They did not, that is, see Enlightened ideas and the policies influenced by them as the transient products of contemporary social structure or of particular social and economic – or even political – pressures. On the contrary, these authors imagined, as for example d'Alembert maintained in the *Discours préliminaire* of the *Encyclopédie*, that Enlightened views, strengthened by scientific and other discoveries, had been spreading remorselessly through European society at least since the time of the Renaissance, essentially by their own force as ideas.[4] Voltaire in his innovative history of the world, the *Essai sur les moeurs* (1756), declared that, apart from war, *opinion* had proved the most powerful force in modern history; and by *opinion* he clearly meant the prevailing attitudes of the educated rather than any form of active pressure from below.[5] The chief contributory factor mentioned, as for example by Beccaria in his *Crimes and Punishments* of 1764, was the invention and agency of printing.[6] It was Enlightened writers who originated the notion of a seventeenth-century Scientific Revolution; they saw themselves as its heirs, and they conceived the spread of Enlightenment to be essentially its consequence.[7] For some authors it was merely or largely a question of the triumph of reason or of self-evidence − *évidence* as the French economic theorists known as the physiocrats called it[8] − or of an unquestionable good. It was supposed that when rulers and their advisers adopted an Enlightened programme, their personal intellectual convictions had much to do with it. The more optimistic writers believed that, once governments embarked on such policies, and especially wherever a measure of religious toleration and some freedom of expression existed, the spread of Enlightenment would gather momentum, and so promote further cognate legislation.[9]

Even those writers in the tradition of Montesquieu who related many of men's varying attitudes and customs to the nature of the particular society they lived in, and condoned practices such as polygamy if they were characteristic of a civilisation remote in time or place, did not treat the central ideas and policies of the Enlightenment in the same way, but saw them as absolutely and universally valid. Montesquieu himself was obviously torn between description and prescription. Here are some of his remarks in *De l'esprit des lois* (1748) on the subject of punishments:

> The severity of punishments is fitter for despotic governments, whose principle is terror, than for a monarchy or a republic … It would be an easy matter to prove that in all, or almost all, the governments of Europe, penalties have increased or diminished in proportion as those governments favoured or encouraged liberty … I was going to say that [torture] might suit despotic states … but nature cries out aloud and asserts her rights.[10]

Adam Ferguson put forward in his historical writings the strikingly modern view that each age should be judged on its own terms, but he still did not make connections in the twentieth-century manner between Enlightened attitudes and contemporary social forces.[11] Contemporary critics of Enlightenment also missed this trick.

Rousseau himself, in all his denunciations of civilisation, inequality, cosmopolitanism, rationalism and Enlightenment, did not suggest that they were the product of social forces as modern historians use the term.[12] A still more virulent critic of the *philosophes*, Linguet, particularly criticised their readiness to attack the institution of slavery, claiming that civilisation, and Enlightenment itself, rested on the subjection of the majority of men. In other words, he was exceptionally aware of social forces and constraints, so much so that he ranks as an inspirer and precursor of Marx.[13] Yet he believed that Enlightenment, far from arising out of the existing state of society and furthering the self-interest of the Enlightened, challenged the former and contradicted the latter. Even for him, therefore, ideas had a life of their own, and purely intellectual developments might have powerful, if often baleful, effects in practice. Herder came nearest to dismissing the Enlightenment as time-bound, but he too saw it as a movement of thought divorced from social forces and deserving of criticism precisely for that reason.[14]

So far as there was awareness that social forces were related to Enlightened policies, it was the hostile rather than the friendly forces that were noticed. Frederick and Voltaire talked obsessively of their battle against the *infâme*, that is, 'superstition' and 'fanaticism', the Church, theology and religion, especially in their Roman Catholic versions. Monks and nuns in general, and Jesuits in particular, were very commonly seen as obstructing the progress of Enlightenment.[15] So were more secular vested interests like the *parlements* in France and the Estates in other continental countries, or guilds and universities.[16] With regard to serfdom, three of the more radical men of the Enlightenment, Frederick II of Prussia and Joseph II of Austria for their own dominions, and Rousseau for Poland, were all agreed in the 1770s, despite their widely differing standpoints, that, however desirable its abolition might be in principle, no rapid or radical reform could safely be attempted, given the strength of aristocratic resistance and the fact that the institution had to be seen as part of the constitution.[17]

As for the people at large, all thinkers admitted them to be in general hostile to Enlightenment.[18] True, there were occasions when pressure for certain Enlightened policies was seen to come from below. As Joseph II travelled round his territories, he made himself available to all his subjects of whatever class, and thus collected tens of thousands of petitions. Of these, though many were protests against change, some advocated measures of an Enlightened character, such as the abolition of tax-farming – though generally on grounds of personal hardship rather than intellectual persuasion.[19] Some of the demands made in the great peasant revolts of the 1770s in Bohemia and Russia may be classed as Enlightened.[20] More specific cases of pressure for Enlightened reform include the petition of the medical faculty of the University of Vienna in 1773 against too severe torture, and the request from a group of Moravian Protestants in 1777 for religious toleration.[21] But it was notorious that, even in the relatively tolerant intellectual climate of Britain, popular outcry in the shape of the Gordon riots prevented mitigation of the anti-Catholic code in 1780; and the same had happened with the relaxation of laws against the Jews in 1753.[22] Petitioning was a weapon that could be used by opponents as well as supporters of Enlightenment, as the Duke of Parma showed when he deployed it in his campaign to get rid of his Enlightened minister, Du Tillot, in 1771.[23] Within months of freeing the Danish press, Struensee saw it join in hounding him from office.[24] The rebellions of the period could be wildly reactionary: the Belgian insurgents of 1787 asked for a return to the position of two hundred years before, and the Hungarians in 1790 insisted on the restoration of Latin as the language of administration.[25] Even the majority of the French Third Estate's *cahiers* of 1789 have been described as profoundly conservative.[26]

Further, it was always a question whether a government was right to give in to pressure, and especially to rebellion, whatever the nature of the opposition's demands.[27] Joseph's accessibility to his subjects was deplored by an Enlightened minister like Count Firmian in Milan, and even by an advanced ruler like Leopold of Tuscany who claimed to favour the introduction of representative government everywhere.[28] Joseph's aim in soliciting petitions was not to find out what his subjects wanted and then do it. The hostility he found to the tax-farm in Milan only strengthened his hand to impose on a reluctant bureaucracy a policy he was already advocating. Though in the 1770s he had bowed to aristocratic pressure on the question of abolishing serfdom, in the 1780s he tried after all to undermine the institution. And he told the recalcitrant Estates of Brabant in 1789: 'I do not require your permission for doing good.'[29]

Contemporaries, then, had some conception of the relation between Enlightened policies and such social forces as opinion groups and even classes. But their awareness of general social and economic tendencies was minimal, and often mistaken. To take a classic case, population was rising in most places most of the time in the eighteenth century. Yet it was well into the century before observers realised it. They were simply ill-informed; they could not know better before the days of full and regular censuses.[30] The physiocrats and other early economic theorists were convinced that only agriculture among economic activities could create wealth. Here such experts had much justification, given the state of many contemporary economies. The first classical economists, Adam Smith included, not merely failed to predict an industrial revolution, they thought such a development impossible. Again, their mistake is understandable. Among other things, they could not be expected to foresee the massive exploitation of mineral fuel and power resources. Moreover, recent writing about 'the first Industrial Revolution', the British Industrial Revolution, has shown how little impact industrialisation actually made, even in the country most affected, until far into the nineteenth century.[31] But the track record of eighteenth-century thinkers in dealing with economic developments is not impressive. So, although contemporary discussion must always be taken seriously, and its apparent shortcomings explained rather than condemned, historians must plainly go beyond it in their attempts to analyse the relationship between social forces and Enlightened policies.

I shall now try to throw light on the problem by considering certain examples of Enlightened policies on the basis both of contemporary and modern analysis.

Voltaire, the arch-priest of the French Enlightenment, agreed with Kant, the greatest figure of the German *Aufklärung*, that at the heart of Enlightenment lay questions of religion; and the great rulers who are known as Enlightened shared their opinion.[32] To enlarge religious toleration, to reduce the influence of the clergy and Churches generally, to exclude it altogether from a growing range of affairs now conceived to be purely secular, to control the study of theology, to attack what was seen as 'superstition' and 'fanaticism' – these were always and everywhere aspects of Enlightened statesmanship. Since this is almost the only generalisation that can validly be made about Enlightened policies across the whole of Europe, this seems to be the best area to take for discussion. How far, then, did social forces contribute to the adoption and implementation of such policies? I shall take certain crucial instances which happen to have been well studied: the Calas case in France, the progress of toleration in Hamburg,

Joseph II's toleration edicts of 1781–82, and the position in Britain's North American colonies.

Jean Calas, a Protestant citizen of Toulouse, was executed there in 1762 by the barbarous method of being broken on the wheel, having been convicted of the murder of his son. The motive for his alleged crime was said to have been that his son was on the point of converting to Roman Catholicism. Voltaire took up the case, made it into a great public issue in France and elsewhere, and was largely responsible for the quashing of the verdict in 1765.[33]

The case is best approached through Voltaire's writings. In the *Traité sur la tolérance* of 1763 he castigates the bigotry of the Roman Catholics of Toulouse, which he declares responsible for Calas's unjust condemnation and cruel punishment. But, whatever had happened in the time of persecution under Louis XIV before and after he had revoked the toleration Edict of Nantes in 1685, during the decades immediately before the Calas case relations between the Protestants and Catholics of the city were generally easy, even cordial; the penalties of the laws against Protestants were seldom invoked; Catholic 'fanaticism' appeared to be diminishing; and although religious prejudice played a part in the judgment of the court against Calas, it has to be recognised that legal procedure was weighted against a defendant of any faith, especially if (as Calas did) he changed his story from one implausible version to another; and the barbarity of the punishment had nothing to do with the victim's creed. Such religious hysteria as was aroused by the case in Toulouse seems explicable largely as a transient product of the hardships and defeats experienced in the war that France happened to be waging against Protestant Powers. As a witch-hunt, the short-lived and localised campaign against the Protestants around Toulouse paled into insignificance beside the exactly contemporary crusade against the Jesuits, who were expelled from France on the initiative of the *parlements* with scant regard for truth and justice, to the applause of the *philosophes*.[34] Within a decade after the reversal of the verdict against Calas by the *parlement* of Paris, the *parlement* of Toulouse itself was leading the way in bending the law in the interests of Protestants. Prejudice such as Calas encountered seemed to be becoming rarer. Over the whole of France in the eighteenth century, down to the Revolution, with occasional setbacks, religious tolerance appeared to be growing, as part of a general tendency towards greater rationality and secularism and away from 'superstition' and 'fanaticism'.[35]

Some of the chapters in Voltaire's *Traité* appear to argue for virtually complete toleration of all religious or irreligious opinions that are not themselves actively intolerant and politically subversive – including those of Buddhists, Deists and Jews. When it comes to specific demands, though, he does not venture to ask for civil equality even for French Protestants. He proposes merely the introduction of a measure resembling the restricted toleration extended by the Act of 1689 to some Nonconformists in England, that is, the right to worship and teach and practise some professions, but not the right to any public office. He does not even go so far as to advocate the introduction of a French version of the Indemnity Acts which had further eased the position of English Dissenters, the first of which was passed when Voltaire was in England in 1727.[36] This tension within his argument is revealing. He evidently realised that his own view, that a man's private and peaceable opinions and religious practices were a matter of indifference to the state, had no prospect of commanding general support in France. The Protestants themselves hesitated to put forward demands on their own account, for fear of provoking a reaction and making their actual position worse. Public opinion as a whole had certainly not adopted the views of radical figures of the early Enlightenment like Bayle and Locke, or of Voltaire himself. Nevertheless, opinion had moved significantly since the days of Louis XIV's *dragonnades*. It was a question of the slow defusing of religious issues, of a growing acknowledgement, found among clergy as well as laity, that some matters once thought to be matters of earthly as well as spiritual life and death need not be taken quite so seriously, of a slow and very incomplete approach to secularisation. Ultimately, in 1787, encouraged by Joseph II's measures, Louis XVI issued an edict of toleration that gave some legal recognition to this limited but momentous change of spirit and behaviour.[37] During the Revolution, however, it soon became clear that to take toleration further, to give Protestants civil equality, was too strong a step for many Catholics to accept.[38]

In the Lutheran imperial city of Hamburg, as compared with France, a greater, though still very small, degree of legal toleration existed even at the beginning of the eighteenth century, as a result of the struggles of the Reformation, the Thirty Years' War and the terms of the Peace of Westphalia of 1648. Some non-Lutherans were allowed to worship publicly and to enjoy certain rights of citizenship. The city became the centre of German-language Enlightenment in the second half of the eighteenth century. A movement to extend toleration started in the 1760s – at almost the same moment as the Calas case – involving a Patriotic Society and pamphlet and pulpit warfare. Eventually a small concession was made to the Calvinists in 1785. In all the debates on the subject no one seems so much as to have mentioned Calas or Voltaire. Equally, the long-standing and wide-ranging toleration notoriously practised by Frederick II seems to have exerted no influence. The admiration felt for Frederick by most German Protestants was tempered in the case of Hamburg by the bullying attitude he adopted towards the city for political and commercial reasons. It was of some importance that an adjoining territory, the port of Altona, controlled by Denmark, enjoyed a much wider measure of toleration, designed to attract trade and inhabitants away from Hamburg. The economic disruption caused by the Seven Years' War may have promoted change. Unlike in France, some of the non-tolerated Churches themselves dared to campaign for relief. But the most effective forces seemed to be, first, a slow decay of religious ardour and strife, associated with a diminution in the perceived role of religion and the clergy – as in Toulouse and, more widely, in France – and secondly the impact of the toleration edicts of Joseph II, who as Holy Roman Emperor was Hamburg's nominal sovereign.[39]

Joseph had very little power as emperor, though what influence he could exert over the largely independent German states was used to extend religious toleration.[40] However, from 1780 to 1790 he exercised more or less absolute power as ruler of an enormous collection of inherited lands, including all of modern Austria, Slovakia, Slovenia, Croatia and Hungary, most of what are now Belgium, Luxembourg and the Czech Republic, and substantial portions of present-day Poland, Romania, Serbia, Ukraine and Italy. His mother and predecessor, Maria Theresa, though she gave up trying to convert Protestants and others to Roman Catholicism by force, continued to exclude them from office in nearly all her territories, allowed non-Catholic worship only where treaties required her to do so, and, when heretics were discovered in her relatively prosperous central provinces, had them transported as colonists to inhospitable parts of Transylvania and the Banat of Temesvar. Joseph told her that her policy was 'unjust, impious, impossible, harmful, ridiculous'.[41] His own edicts varied a little from province to province, they were not in all cases fully publicised, and the resounding principles of their preambles were belied by the limitations of their detailed provisions: in most of his territories, among Christians other than those in communion with Rome, only the Greek Orthodox, Lutherans and Calvinists were affected; and they were allowed merely to build meeting-houses that did not too closely resemble churches, in certain circumstances to run their own schools, to engage in hitherto restricted occupations, and to hold office. But these provisions, restricted though they seem, went much further than any other legislation then operative in Catholic states, and further than most Protestant countries. Joseph's treatment of the Jews, permitting them to enter a wider range of employments and to set up their own schools, although it was directed towards assimilating them into the German-speaking population at large, was far more sympathetic than any other ruler's. The introduction of civil marriage in 1783 made the legal position of non-Catholics better still.[42]

The emperor himself sometimes expressed views on toleration that sounded as radical as Voltaire's, though they derived as much from German and Italian writers such as Thomasius and Muratori as from French. He maintained that, within certain limits, an individual's religious beliefs and observances should not concern the state. At other times, however, he talked of toleration as a means to recover dissenters for Catholicism. He was much influenced by the desire to encourage immigration into the remoter and sparsely inhabited parts of the Monarchy, partly with a view to enlarging his army, and partly from the conviction, instilled into him by his tutor, Beck, that states which persecuted and drove into exile worthy and industrious subjects, as France had done in 1685 and Salzburg in 1731, were bound to suffer economically.[43]

Some religious groups had ventured to put pressure on him and on the government, particularly the Greek Orthodox of Transylvania and the Protestants of Moravia. When some of the latter requested toleration at the end of Maria Theresa's reign, Kaunitz, her chief minister, told her that it was 'quite impossible in the present state of affairs for her not to grant it to the dissenters of Moravia, as [will be the case] elsewhere when sooner or later the same state of affairs comes to pass'. She rejected this advice, and she did not live long enough for its validity to be tested.[44] 'Fanaticism' had somewhat diminished in the Habsburg lands: for example, executions for witchcraft at last died out even in Hungary in the 1760s, when 'the belated sea-change of an enlightenment mentality among the educated anticipated radical legal reforms under Maria Theresa'.[45] But in several parts of the Monarchy, such as Belgium,[46] it is plain that any pressure from Protestants in favour of toleration was more than balanced by hostility to it on the part of Catholics. Joseph's toleration edicts clearly went far beyond what public opinion in his lands would have demanded. He had the support, it is true, of a small party among the nobility and clergy and of many government officials, some of whom had studied in Protestant universities and most of whom had been influenced by the writings of the 'cameralists', theorists whose rationalistic manuals on statecraft were widely used in the training of the army of bureaucrats required to run the more than three hundred German states.[47] His radical relaxation of the Viennese censorship in 1781 led to the *Broschürenflut* ('flood of pamphlets') of the next few years and most of the pamphleteers supported him on religious issues.[48] Since his toleration edicts survived the débâcle of the rest of his policies at the end of his reign, it would appear that the pamphleteers had by then persuaded opinion to accept them. One of the writers claimed as much: 'This whole Reformation, the introduction of toleration, would never have been brought to pass so easily if the pamphleteers hadn't bombarded the people's minds with so many booklets, and said ... exactly what the people needed to know.'[49] But the initiative of the emperor himself was fundamental. The Moravian Protestants only put forward their demands because of his known sympathy for them.[50] If the social conditions of the big city made possible the *Broschürenflut* once the censorship had been relaxed, the history of Austria before and after the reign of Joseph II makes it clear that the forces in favour of liberalisation could be contained with ease if the government so wished. Indeed, Joseph himself learned from the Belgian revolt and Hungarian opposition that in the end he did need – and would be unlikely to receive – his subjects' 'permission to do good'.

It is almost as though social forces were operating at one remove. In certain countries – Britain, Holland and parts of Germany – social forces in the sense of religious groups and associated political factions, with *some* relation, though an equivocal one, to social classes and economic development, had played a part in promoting what came to be regarded as Enlightened policies, or in creating a situation favourable to toleration – but this had happened in the sixteenth and seventeenth centuries, before the days of so-called Enlightenment. Then, later, self-consciously Enlightened rulers in other countries – without much encouragement from indigenous social forces, because religious dissidents were weak and economic and social development was less advanced – carried such policies further than they had been taken in their original homes.[51] In some cases, paradoxically or ironically, these initiatives in turn exerted influence back on more developed and yet apparently more conservative countries, as Joseph's edicts did in Belgium, France and Hamburg.

At least that seems to be the pattern until one looks across the Atlantic. Several of the colonies that became part of the United States had been founded by religious groups not tolerated in the mother country. Though there were established Churches in some colonies, they did not compare in power, status and wealth with those of Europe. By the end of the seventeenth century some states were already exceptionally tolerant, and the Quaker foundation, Pennsylvania, accorded full religious liberty. Hostility to Church establishments in all their aspects was naturally strengthened in the struggle against Britain, especially since most of the religious conservatives were also loyalists and many of them emigrated during and after the Revolution. It proved easy to make the new United States, by their constitution of 1787, officially secular; and something approaching complete religious freedom was achieved. Here social forces – among the whites, that is – can be said to have made possible the realisation in the New World of a programme of Enlightenment devised in the old. But the forces concerned included the obscurantist demands of rigid Puritans; it was a question of sect and religion rather than of class and *philosophie*; and it owed nothing whatever to industrialisation.[52]

The story of toleration has something in common with the story of numerous other issues that were seen as related to religion. Many of the great men of the Enlightenment attacked, to take some examples, the judicial use of torture, the indiscriminate application of the death penalty, the penalties imposed on the corpses and families of suicides; and belief in the authenticity and efficacy of religious relics, in witchcraft, diabolic possession, exorcism and so on and so forth. In many states these practices and attitudes were decaying slowly, though unevenly, without the direct influence of abstract thinkers being easily discernible, and without much legislative encouragement. This happened with the treatment of suicide and suicides, and with the exaction of the death penalty, in both France and England. In England, indeed, the strange situation prevailed that Parliament, if less bloodthirsty than has sometimes been claimed, was none the less continually making more and more offences capital, supported by at least some elements of public opinion, while fewer and fewer executions were actually taking place, presumably in response to

growing humanitarianism.[53] The root-and-branch proposals for criminal law reform made by Beccaria can be seen as extreme extensions
of tendencies already operating, for example in Frederick's Prussia,
and his ideas owed much to the progressive circle in which he moved.
But they cannot be said to have had a very rapid effect on his own
country: in the 1770s Maria Theresa and Joseph abolished torture in
their central lands, but could not induce the legal authorities in Milan
to do the same; and Beccaria himself was never given much scope as
a government servant.[54] In Russia, on the other hand, Catherine the
Great tried, and with a degree of success, to impose some of Beccaria's
recommendations from above, thus creating or much extending a
body of sympathetic opinion. The main social force on her side was
a section of the aristocracy, seeking recognition of their own civil
rights.[55] So, in many parts of Europe, a growing 'social force' favouring Enlightened policies was visible, a movement towards rationality,
secularisation, humanitarianism and sentimentality – a movement
supported by, but wider than, such institutions as reading societies
and Freemasons' lodges. Among its sympathisers were Enlightened
clergy, aristocrats and bourgeois, but it was opposed by many, probably
most, members of the same classes.[56] It sometimes gave Enlightened
rulers and writers a fair wind. They in turn, by proposing and enact-
ing stronger measures, could cause it to blow more strongly. But if
they went only a little too far, they would suddenly find themselves
caught up in a reactionary hurricane.

Toleration is unusual among Enlightened policies in that war,
diplomacy and international contacts played a large part in its history. The degree of toleration found in the model states of England,
Holland and the United States was to a large extent the outcome
of armed struggle. Many German states were only as tolerant as
the Peace of Westphalia required. It was the terms under which the
Habsburgs acquired Hungary and Transylvania that ensured their
grudging toleration of Protestantism in both provinces before 1781,
even extending to Unitarianism in the case of the latter. In late eighteenth-century Poland, the land of 'second enserfment' *par excellence*,
Roman Catholicism was gaining ground, and the limited toleration
previously established was threatened. Its survival largely depended on
the intervention of Russia and on the dismemberment of the country
in successive partitions after 1772, a fact which Voltaire adduced in
lending his support to Catherine's Polish annexations.[57] Suppression
of the Jesuits was another policy whose success owed much to con-

siderations of power-politics: it was adopted by Maria Theresa chiefly to please her Bourbon allies, and without her acquiescence the pope would not have dissolved the Society.[58]

In most fields, though, war and diplomacy mattered little, but there remained an important element at least of international imitation. The south and east of Europe commonly lagged behind the west and north, especially in the early stages, though later Prussia and Russia, and then America, were set up as examples to more conservative regimes. Study of each policy, of course, reveals a somewhat different pattern. An exceptionally interesting instance is inoculation against smallpox, the only major advance of eighteenth-century medicine, The method adopted was 'variolation', infection of the subject with smallpox itself. This practice appears to have begun in Europe within the purview of folk medicine, that is among the superstitions that the Enlightenment derided, though it had also been known in the more respected ambiences of China and the Near East. The first European country in which it became acceptable among the upper classes was the England of the 1720s, and Voltaire backed it after seeing its opera-tion there. The medical profession generally considered it dangerous and of doubtful benefit, and an otherwise progressive doctor like the elder Van Swieten in Austria stubbornly opposed it. Many Jesuits were in favour, while some radicals were against. The English example continued to be important at later stages of its diffusion. Probably nothing did more to commend it in Austria, apart from the frightful death-rate from the disease, than the patronage of English royalty. Maria Theresa, after nearly dying of it herself and losing several of her close relatives to it, in 1768 accepted from George III the loan of the services of Dr John Ingenhousz, had her family inoculated and arranged an inoculation feast at Schönbrunn for a group of sixty-five children. This ceremony – highly utilitarian compared with the usual Habsburg round of pilgrimages, retreats, crib-blessings and foot-wash-ings – owed little either to the great Enlightenment thinkers or to any social force other than the broad movement of opinion already discussed. In the same year Catherine II had herself inoculated by another Englishman, Dr Thomas Dimsdale.[59]

Outside the range of the battle for some measure of religious tolera-tion and against the more obvious superstitions, most issues divided the Enlightened. The disunity of the *philosophes* and the *Aufklärer* is particularly obvious in the realm of economic policy. If there could be broad agreement on the abolition of guilds and impediments to internal trade, support for international commercial freedom, a policy passionately advocated by the physiocrats, was not unanimous. The numerous attempts to impose free trade in grain, made by those who believed in its manifest rightness, were generally frustrated in the end by opposition and riot. In so far as this policy was recommended as a result of economic and social pressure rather than as the fruit of new economic theory, it favoured and was favoured by the large capitalist, probably noble, agriculturalist rather than by the peasant, industrialist, merchant or consumer. The classic case is the French: in 1763 free trade in grain was enacted as part of a radical new departure in economic policy made acceptable by the indebtedness of the country at the end of the Seven Years' War. After a brief honeymoon period, the shortage of corn in a succession of bad years aroused the fury of the consumers and awoke the scepticism of the Enlightened. The measure had to be repealed in 1770.[60]

Attempts have been made to establish a close linkage between 'proto-industrialisation' and certain Enlightened policies in the Habsburg Monarchy.[61] Both Maria Theresa and her son, in common with other Catholic rulers, succeeded in reducing the very large number of saints' days which workmen were allowed to treat as holidays. The two rulers also introduced in and after 1774 a scheme to establish enough schools to make possible universal primary education in their dominions. It has been argued that both these reforms arose from the necessity to discipline the growing number of industrial workers, mainly engaged in manufacturing textiles, especially in Bohemia. So far as the reduction of saints' days is concerned, it is certainly true that the principal motive of the government was to extract more work from its subjects. But the measure was not designed with special reference to industrial workers; the problem was conceived to be universal, which meant that in the Monarchy it primarily concerned agriculture. As for education, the motives were much more complex. The ignorance of the mass of the population alarmed the rulers for many reasons, because it handicapped the development of industry no doubt, but much more because it hampered agricultural and commercial development, more still because it made the vast conscript army less efficient and narrowed the state's choice of servants, and perhaps most of all because it implied a lack of knowledge of Christianity, and particularly of Catholic doctrine, among the ordinary people of the Monarchy.[62]

In the context of this discussion, it is a striking fact that most *philosophes* and *Aufklärer* were against universal education precisely because they thought it hopeless to expect Enlightenment to permeate a whole nation.[63] Some writers, it is true, believed that universal education could create an enlightened nation. One such, probably Baron Holbach, proclaimed this belief in his *Essai sur les préjugés* of 1769: truth is made for Man and should always be uttered; the multitude can and should be rescued from superstition; society can and should become more equal. Frederick the Great was stung to publish a reply: 'prejudices', he declares, 'are the reason of the people'; it is unsafe to tell the people the whole truth; the clergy will always have more power than the *philosophes*; the first essential is to maintain respect for the ruler and the aristocracy. The view that Enlightenment must necessarily be confined to the elite was widely shared, if seldom so brutally stated. Diderot denounced the king's assault on the *Essai*, but not in print.[64]

There is, though, a sense in which Enlightened policies were actually embodied in what could reasonably be regarded as a social force. I am thinking of the bureaucracy, especially in what Marc Raeff calls 'the well-ordered police state', 'police' in this context being an attempt to translate *Polizei* or *police* as used in the eighteenth century, when it almost meant 'civilisation' or 'ordered society'. The states of Germany and in the German tradition, with Prussia at their head, developed relatively large bureaucracies which spawned and tried to enforce vast codes of regulation, often restrictive, sometimes ridiculous, not always effective, but at least in part justified on theoretical grounds by cameralist principles taught in state-controlled universities, and tending to order, rationalise and secularise society in the name of a ruler who had identified himself with an impersonal state. They developed a 'bureaucratic ethic', sometimes obstructive and tradition-bound, but at its best or most creative uncorrupt, selfless, benevolent, progressive and meritocratic.[65] The notion and practice of 'the career open to the talents' have been too little studied. How does it come about that Joseph II could write in 1763: 'Everything to personal merit – if this rule is inviolably observed, what geniuses will not emerge who are now hidden through slackness or noble oppression!'[66] Such sentiments were appearing in English radical circles at the same time, but they can hardly be imagined yet in the mouths of England's or France's monarchs – or even in Frederick the Great's, despite his introduction of competitive examinations for the civil service in 1770.[67] The article

Génie in the *Encyclopédie* contains nothing so subversive. It is difficult to see how Joseph's ideas can be products of 'the second enserfment', or of bourgeois influence, or of proto-industrialisation.

Historians could not get very far in discussing the relationship between social forces and Enlightened policies if they acquiesced in the more extreme criticisms sometimes made of any historical analysis that uses modern concepts. It is only too evident that contemporaries failed to grasp fully what was really going on.[68] Not only were they at sea about economic developments. I am not sure that any eighteenth-century discussion of the suppression of the Jesuits gave much weight to such a basic factor as the self-interested hostility of other religious orders. I should be surprised to learn that anti-clericalism was an eighteenth-century concept, yet we can hardly doubt that it was an eighteenth-century force. But it is possible to go too far from contemporary explanations. The Enlightenment was by definition an intellectual movement, and intellectual history possesses a degree of autonomy. Sometimes Enlightened policies were imposed from above that were more advanced than were being demanded by, or were appropriate to, the balance of social forces in the society concerned; and this happened essentially because of intellectual development at the top of society, perhaps among the elite as a whole, more commonly among a limited group, and in some cases largely because of the ruler's own attitude. Below that level, but not among the uneducated, a much more dilute and generalised Enlightenment was slowly and unevenly seeping though society and affecting policy, and that too represented a partly autonomous change of attitudes. That both movements, which were of course interrelated, were limited in scope, at least in Europe, was shown by the numerous bouts of popular hostility aroused when Enlightened measures were hastily or inopportunely introduced. The Enlightenment seems actually to have widened the intellectual gap between educated and uneducated, rulers and people.[69]

Education does not always lead to Enlightenment, but without education there can be no Enlightenment. The fact that the mass education of the people so often resisted Enlightened measures reflected the limitations of eighteenth-century popular education. In all European countries it was necessarily in the hands of the clergy, Catholic or Protestant. When an Austrian minister, Count Pergen, fought to exclude monks at least from secondary teaching, Maria Theresa, Joseph and Kaunitz all agreed that the thing was impossible.[70]

When the Society of Jesus was dissolved in 1773, the Catholic states lost their best teaching instrument. Afterwards, individual ex-Jesuits remained indispensable to their educational systems, though the rulers of Prussia and Russia enticed as many of them away as they could.[71] The alternative to monks and nuns as teachers was not lay men or women, but non-monastic clergy. The pessimism of so many *philosophes* about the possibility of mass Enlightenment becomes more comprehensible against this background. It was virtually impossible in the eighteenth century to imagine a society capable of establishing, let alone affording, any kind of secularised system of universal education. Yet, with education in the hands of the clergy, there seemed no hope of enlightening the masses.

Notes

This chapter is a substantially revised and enlarged version of a paper which appeared under the same title in *Seventh International Congress on the Enlightenment: Introductory Papers. Budapest, 26 July–2 August 1987* (Voltaire Foundation, Oxford, 1987), pp. 33–43. It was republished in H. M. Scott (ed.), *Enlightened Absolutism* (1990). I am most grateful to Dr Andrew Brown and to the editor of the conference proceedings, Professor Haydn Mason, and to Palgrave for permission to reprint this article here.

I acknowledge generous help from Professors J. Black and T. C. W. Blanning.

1 See A. Soboul and P. Goujard, *L'Encyclopédie ou Dictionnaire raisonné des Sciences, des Arts et des Métiers: Textes choisis* (Paris, 1984), incorporating the essence of Soboul's edition of 1952. Goujard's (later) contributions often take a different line. Cf. Soboul's own essay 'Les philosophes et la révolution', in J. Le Goff and B. Köpeczi (eds), *Intellectuels français, intellectuels hongrois, XIII–XXe siècles* (Budapest, 1985), pp. 113–32.

2 See especially his contributions to B. Köpeczi, E. Bene and I. Kovacs (eds), *Les Lumières en Hongrie, en Europe centrale et en Europe orientale. Actes du troisième Colloque de Mátrafüred 28 septembre–2 octobre 1975* (Budapest, 1977) and to B. Köpeczi, A. Soboul, E. H. Balázs and D. Kosáry (eds), *L'absolutisme éclairé* (Budapest, 1985).

3 E.g. J. V. H. Melton, 'Arbeitsprobleme des aufgeklärten Absolutismus in Preußen und Österreich', *Mitteilungen des Instituts für österreichische Geschichtsforschung* [hereafter *MIÖG*], 90 (1982): 49–75.

4 For the content and importance of the *Discours préliminaire* see e.g. E. Cassirer, *The Philosophy of the Enlightenment* (Boston, 1955), pp. 8, 223–5; A. M. Wilson, *Diderot* (Oxford, 1957), pp. 131–4; R. Grimsley, *Jean d'Alembert (1717–1783)* (Oxford, 1963), pp. 18–22; B. Cohen, 'The Eighteenth-century Origins of the Concept of the Scientific Revolution', *Journal of the History of Ideas* [hereafter *JHI*], 27 (1976): 270–3.

5 The bibliography of Voltaire's *Essai sur les moeurs* is extremely complicated, but it was in 1756 that his account of general history first appeared in 'its full development' with *Essai sur les moeurs* as part of its title. See R. Pomeau (ed.) (2 vols, Paris, 1963), esp. vol. I, p. xvi; vol. II, pp. 904–6, 910–18.

6 C. Beccaria, *Dei delitti e delle pene* (1764; facsimile edn, Turin, 1964), p. 4.

7 See Cohen, *JHI*, 27 (1976): 257–88. Among other writers of the Enlightenment who take this line are Chastellux in *De la félicité publique* (1772) and Condorcet in his *Esquisse d'un tableau historique des progrès de l'esprit humain* (1793).

8 E.g. Le Mercier de la Rivière, *L'ordre naturel et essentiel des sociétés politiques* (1767), ed. E. Depitre (Paris, 1910), esp. ch. IX.

9 E.g. Holbach (see n. 64 below) in *Essai sur les préjugés* (1769).

10 Montesquieu, *The Spirit of the Laws*, trans. T. Nugent (London, 1949), pp. 81, 91.

11 A. Ferguson, *An Essay on the History of Civil Society*, ed. D. Forbes (Edinburgh, 1966). On the general issue see Cassirer, *Philosophy of the Enlightenment*, ch. V.

12 It is difficult to footnote a negative, but I believe that what I say in the text is borne out by Rousseau's works, esp. *A Discourse on Inequality*, trans. M. Cranston (Harmondsworth, 1984).

13 S. N. H. Linguet, *Théorie des lois civiles* (1767) (Paris, 1984), esp. Book V. H.-U. Thamer, *Revolution und Reaktion in der französischen Sozialkritik des 18. Jahrhunderts. Linguet, Mably, Babeuf* (Frankfurt-am-Main, 1973), esp. p. 275.

14 F. M. Barnard (ed.), *J. G. Herder on Social and Political Culture* (Cambridge, 1969), e.g. pp. 4–5, 34–45, 201–5.

15 A vast bibliography could be compiled on this subject. I will refer only to Voltaire's frequent discussions, esp. in the *Essai sur les moeurs*, and to O. Chadwick, *The Popes and European Revolution* (Oxford, 1981), esp. chs 3 and 5.

16 Another vast theme. See P. Gay, *Voltaire's Politics* (Princeton, 1959); D. Dakin, *Turgot and the Ancien Régime in France* (London, 1939); H. E. Strakosch, *State Absolutism and the Rule of Law* (Sydney, 1967); F. Diaz, *Filosofia e politica nel Settecento francese* (2nd edn, Turin, 1962).

17 Frédéric II, *Essai sur les formes de gouvernement* (1777) in J. D. E. Preuss (ed.), *Oeuvres de Frédéric le Grand* (31 vols, Berlin, 1846–57), vol. IX, pp. 205–6; D. Beales, *Joseph II. I: In the Shadow of Maria Theresa, 1741–1780* (Cambridge, 1987), ch. XI; J. J. Rousseau, *Considérations sur le gouvernement de Pologne* (1771) in C. E. Vaughan, *The Political Writings of Jean Jacques Rousseau* (2 vols, Cambridge, 1915), vol. II, pp. 497–9.

18 Cf. P. Gay, *The Enlightenment: An Interpretation* (2 vols, London, 1967, 1970), vol. II: *The Science of Freedom*, esp. ch. X; H. Chisick, *The Limits of Reform in the Enlightenment* (Princeton, 1981).

19 See Beales, *Joseph II*, chs 8, 11 and 12.

20 Some of the most interesting recent discussion of these rebellions can be found in F. Venturi, *Settecento riformatore* (5 vols, 1969–2002), vol. III, chs V and VI; vol. IV, tome 2, ch. VIII.

21 See Beales, *Joseph II*, pp. 237, 267–8, 350, 466.

22 T. W. Perry, *Public Opinion, Propaganda, and Politics in Eighteenth Century England: A Study of the Jew Bill of 1753* (Cambridge, MA, 1962); J. Stevenson, *Popular Disturbances in England, 1700–1870* (London, 1979), esp. pp. 76–90.

23 U. Benassi, 'Guglielmo du Tillot', ch. VIII, 'Il commercio', in *Archivio storico per le province parmensi*, new series, vol. XXIII (1923), p. 112.

24 K. Tønnesson, 'Les exemples scandinaves: le Danemark', in Köpeczi et al., *L'absolutisme éclairé*, pp. 301–2.

25 P. A. F. Gérard, *Ferdinand Rapedius de Berg* (2 vols, Brussels, 1842–43), vol. I, pp. 228–9; C. A. Macartney, *The Habsburg Empire, 1790–1918* (London, 1968), p. 137.

26 G. V. Taylor cited in W. Doyle, *Origins of the French Revolution* (Oxford, 1980), p. 20. But see G. Chaussinand-Nogaret, *The French Nobility in the Eighteenth Century* (Cambridge, 1985), chs 7 and 8, where the emphasis is on the relative radicalism of the nobles or their willingness to join the Third Estate in radical demands.

27 See the discussion in Vienna on how to deal with the Bohemian revolt of 1775 reported in Beales, *Joseph II*, pp. 350–8.

28 Ibid., pp. 197–8, 267.

29 Ibid. esp. ch. 8; Gérard, *F. Rapedius de Berg*, vol. II, p. 210.

30 See e.g. M. D. George, *England in Transition* (London, 1953), p. 77; J. McManners, *Death and the Enlightenment* (Oxford, 1981) pp. 105–11; P. G. M. Dickson, *Finance and Government under Maria Theresia, 1740–1780* (2 vols, Oxford, 1987).

31 Cf. E. A. Wrigley, 'The Classical Economists and the Industrial Revolution', in his *People, Cities and Wealth* (London, 1987) and D. N. Cannadine, 'The Present and the Past in the English Industrial Revolution, 1880–1980', *Past and Present*, 103 (1984): 131–72.

32 R. Pomeau, *La religon de Voltaire* (Paris, 1956); Kant, 'What is Enlightenment?' (1784) in H. Reiss (ed.), *Kant's Political Writings* (Cambridge, 1971), p. 59. Cf. Gay, *The Enlightenment: An Interpretation*.

33 This section is based on D. D. Bien, *The Calas Affair* (Princeton, 1960) and on Voltaire, *Traité sur la tolérance*, in J. Van den Heuvel (ed.), *L'affaire Calas* (Paris, 1975), esp. pp. 90–8.

34 See e.g. D. V. Kley, *The Jansenists and the Expulsion of the Jesuits from France, 1757–1765* (London, 1975).

35 The general point is powerfully supported in McManners, *Death and the Enlightenment*.

36 As Besterman points out (*Voltaire*, p. 110); *L'affaire Calas*, p. 106.

37 McManners, *Death and the Enlightenment*; the chapters on France in R. Crahay (ed.), *La tolérance civile* (Brussels, 1982).

38 G. Lewis, *The Second Vendée* (Oxford, 1978), esp. ch. II.

39 This paragraph is based on J. Whaley, *Religious Toleration and Social Change in Hamburg, 1529–1819* (Cambridge, 1985) and F. Kopitzsch, *Grundzüge*

einer Sozialgeschichte der Aufklärung in Hamburg und Altona (2 vols, Hamburg, 1982).

40 Cf. Beales, *Joseph II*, p. 131.

41 Ibid., p. 470 and n.106.

42 C. H. O'Brien, 'Ideas of Religious Toleration at the time of Joseph II', *Transactions of the American Philosophical Society*, new series, vol. LIX, pt 7 (1969); Crahay, *La tolérance civile*, esp. the article by H. Hasquin on marriage.

43 Beales, *Joseph II*, pp. 58, 61, 465–73.

44 Ibid., p. 472.

45 R. J. W. Evans, *The Making of the Habsburg Monarchy, 1550–1700* (Oxford, 1979), p. 405.

46 Articles on Belgium in Crahay, *La tolérance civile*.

47 As well as O'Brien's study, see A. W. Small, *The Cameralists* (Chicago, 1909); R. A. Kann, *A Study in Austrian Intellectual History* (New York, 1973); K.-H. Osterloh, *Joseph von Sonnenfels und die österreichische Reformbewegung im Zeitalter des aufgeklärten Absolutismus* (Lübeck, 1970).

48 G. Bodi, *Tauwetter in Wein* (Frankfurt-am-Main, 1977).

49 L. A. Hoffmann(?), *Zehn Briefe aus Oesterreich an den Verfasser der Briefe aus Berlin* (3rd edn, 1784), p. 160: 'Ich will nun sagen, daß diese ganze Reformation, die Einführung der Toleranz … u.s.w. nie so leicht würde seyn zu Stande gebracht worden, wenn die Broschürenmacher nicht die Köpfe des Volks mit so vielen kleinen Büchelchen belagert, und auf einigen Boden gerade das gesagt hätten, was das Volk zu wissen brauchte.'

50 Beales, *Joseph II*, pp. 470–1.

51 Cf. the thesis of R. Mandrou, *La raison du prince: l'Europe Absolutiste, 1649–1775* (Verviers, 1980). Professor D. Kosáry, in his introductory address to the Budapest conference for which this paper was originally written, made a similar distinction between the 'centre', i.e. England, France and Holland, and the 'periphery'.

52 E.g. H. S. Commager, *Jefferson, Nationalism, and the Enlightenment* (New York, 1975); more critical, J. R. Pole, 'Enlightenment and the Politics of American Nature', in that generally useful collection, R. Porter and M. Teich (eds), *The Enlightenment in National Context* (Cambridge, 1981), pp. 192–214; S. E. Ahlstrom, *A Religious History of the American People* (London, 1972), esp. ch. 23; J. G. A. Pocock, 'Enlightenment and Revolution: The Case of English-speaking North America', in *Seventh International Congress on the Enlightenment: Introductory Papers*, pp. 45–57. The late Dr M. D. Kaplanoff gave me some guidance here.

53 McManners, *Death and the Enlightenment*, chs XI and XII; M. MacDonald, 'The Secularization of Suicide in England, 1660–1800', *Past and Present*, 111 (1986): 50–97, and 119 (1988): 158–70 (with D. T. Andrew); J. Innes and J. Styles, 'The Crime Wave: Recent Writing on Crime and Criminal Justice in Eighteenth-century England', *Journal of British Studies*, 25 (1986): 380–435.

54 The great authority of course, as for so much else, is Venturi, *Settecento*

riformatore. Cf. C. Capra, 'Il "Mosé della Lombardia": la mission di Carlo Antonio Martini a Milano, 1785–1786', in C. Mozzarelli and G. Olmi, *Il Trentino nel Settecento fra Sacro Romano Impero e antichi stati italiani* (Bologna, 1985).

55 Among recent discussions of Russian Enlightenment see W. J. Gleason, *Moral Idealists, Bureaucracy, and Catherine the Great* (New Brunswick, NJ, 1981) and J. P. LeDonne, *Ruling Russia: Politics and Administration in the Age of Absolutism, 1762–1796* (Princeton, 1984).

56 This point of view has recently been argued strongly in the case of England by J. C. D. Clark, *English Society, 1688–1832* (Cambridge, 1985).

57 See the works by O'Brien and Whaley cited above and L. R. Lewitter, 'The Partitions of Poland', in *New Cambridge Modern History*, vol. VIII (Cambridge, 1965), esp. pp. 338–9, 344.

58 This factor is seldom stressed in modern accounts, but seems overwhelming in the case of the Austrian Monarchy. See A. Ritter von Arneth, *Geschichte Maria Theresias* (10 vols, Vienna, 1863–79), vol. IX, esp. ch. 4. See ch. 8 below.

59 W. H. McNeill, *Plagues and Peoples* (Harmondsworth, 1979), pp. 229–38; P. Razzell, *The Conquest of Smallpox* (Firle, 1977); D. Baxby, *Jenner's Smallpox Vaccine* (London, 1981); McManners, *Death and the Enlightenment*, pp. 46–7; Beales, *Joseph II*, p. 158.

60 C. B. A. Behrens, *Society, Government and the Enlightenment: The Experiences of Eighteenth-century France and Prussia* (London, 1985), esp. pp. 128–40, 152–75. See also the classic study by S. L. Kaplan, *Bread, Politics and Political Economy in the Reign of Louis XV* (2 vols, The Hague, 1976).

61 Melton, *MIÖG*, 90 (1982).

62 Cf. Beales, *Joseph II*, pp. 455–60.

63 Chisick, *The Limits of Reform in the Enlightenment*.

64 Frédéric II, *Examen de l'essai sur les préjugés* (1770) in *Œuvres philosophiques* (Paris, 1985), pp. 361–85. Diderot, *Pages contre un tyran* (1771) in *Œuvres politiques*, ed. P. Vernière (Paris, 1963), pp. 135–48. J. Vercruysse, *Bibliographie descriptive des écrits du Baron d'Holbach* (Paris, 1971) accepts the *Essai* as Holbach's, but it is impossible to be sure.

65 See esp. M. Raeff, *The Well-Ordered Police State* (London, 1983).

66 D. Beales (ed.), 'Joseph II's "Rêveries"', *MIÖG*, 33 (1980): 156. See p. 171 below.

67 See W. Bleek, *Von der Kameralausbildung zum Juristenprivileg: Studium, Prüfung and Ausbildung der höheren Beamten des allgemeinen Verwaltungdienstes im 18. und 19. Jahrhundert* (Berlin, 1972), esp. p. 76.

68 See A. Ryan, 'The Marx Problem Book', *The Times Literary Supplement*, 25 April 1986.

69 Cf. K. V. Thomas, *Religion and the Decline of Magic* (London, 1971).

70 Beales, *Joseph II*, pp. 456–7.

71 Chadwick, *The Popes and European Revolution*, pp. 374–90.

CHAPTER 2

Philosophical Kingship and Enlightened Despotism

The idea of the philosopher king in the eighteenth century[1]

The notion of the philosopher king comes from Plato's *Republic*. Plato's influence declined after the Renaissance, and none of the authors writing about the late sixteenth and seventeenth centuries in the relevant volume of the *Cambridge History of Political Thought* found it necessary to mention this notion at all. But Hobbes concluded the second part of *Leviathan*, in a characteristically sardonic passage, by placing the concept at the very heart of his political philosophy:

> considering how different this Doctrine is, from the practise of the greatest part of the world ... and how much depth of Morall Philosophy is required, in them that have the Administration of the Soveraign power; I am at the point of believing this my labour, as uselesse, as the Common-wealth of *Plato*; For he also is of opinion that it is impossible for the disorders of State, and change of Governments by Civill Warre, ever to be taken away, till Soveraigns be Philosophers. But when I consider again, that the Science of Naturall Justice, is the onely Science necessary for Soveraigns, and their principall Ministers; and that they need not be charged with the Sciences Mathematicall, (as by *Plato* they are,) ... and that neither *Plato*, nor any other Philosopher hitherto, hath put into order, and sufficiently, or probably proved all the Theoremes of Morall doctrine, that men may learn thereby, both how to govern, and how to obey; I recover some hope, that one time or other, this writing of mine, may fall into the hands of a Soveraign, who will consider it himselfe, (for it is short, and I think clear,) without the help of any interested, or envious Interpreter; and by the exercise of entire Soveraignty, in protecting the Publique teaching of it, convert this Truth of Speculation, into the Utility of Practice.[2]

So Hobbes in the middle of the seventeenth century, with an elaborate if back-handed acknowledgement to Plato, looked forward to the enthronement of a philosopher sovereign, asserting that only such a ruler, armed both with absolute power and with the certainty of acquired wisdom, could rescue society from disorder and establish a state on true principles. But Hobbes's imagined philosopher was to be trained very differently from Plato's. It was not simply that he could do without a mathematical education. What distinguished Plato's philosopher more than anything else was his supposed ability to see behind the evidence of the senses and the superficial realities of life and politics to a deeper reality of ideal 'forms'. This was an example of the metaphysical, quasi-theological thinking that Hobbes regarded as 'vain philosophy'. By contrast, he claimed, 'the Science of Naturall Justice' and his 'Theoremes of Morall doctrine' were straightforwardly derived from the obvious realities of men's natures, passions, wills, behaviour and historical experience.

Leibniz, on the other hand, profoundly admired Plato's *Republic*, his metaphysics and even his mathematics. Leibniz wrote in 1701 that 'the end of monarchy is to make a hero of eminent wisdom and virtue reign'. But even he did not accept Plato's notion of a philosopher king in full. Nor was he thinking of a ruler with 'entire Soveraignty' mounting a desperate rescue operation in a time of political disintegration. Leibniz was envisaging a wise king ruling a well established and stable state, preferably a mixed government rather than an absolute monarchy, and he generally had in mind German rulers whose sovereignty was limited by the framework of the Holy Roman Empire.[3]

His widely influential follower, Christian Wolff, in his short tract *De rege philosophante et philosopho regnante* (1730), argued that an all-powerful monarch who, like Chinese emperors, was also a philosopher could bring great benefits to his subjects and, further, that any king was likely to be a better ruler if he had some philosophical training and competence. But, with his customary moderation or complacency, Wolff remarked that no one could be a philosopher all the time; and for him philosophy was concerned with rational analysis, which might encourage modest improvements. He clearly did not envisage philosophy as a fundamentally radical critique, or expect a philosopher-king to desire, let alone achieve, a dramatic transformation of state and society.[4]

None of these notions of a philosopher king, Plato's, Hobbes's, Leibniz's or Wolff's, was prominent or well developed in eighteenth-century political thinking, though traces can be found of all of them and though other aspects of Plato's thought had considerable influence, especially on Rousseau. It is a quite different concept of a philosopher king that is characteristic of the period. This is best illustrated from the *Encyclopédie*.[5] In the article *Philosopher*, which appeared in 1765,[6] occurs this passage:

> This love of society, so essential to the *philosopher*, demonstrates the truth of the emperor Antoninus's [i.e. Marcus Aurelius's] remark: 'How happy peoples will be when kings are *philosophers*, or when *philosophers* are kings!'
>
> So the *philosopher* is a gentleman (*honnête homme*) whose actions are always guided by reason, and who combines a reflective and judicious mind with sociable habits and qualities. Graft a sovereign on to a *philosopher* of such a stamp, and you will have a perfect sovereign.

This is a significant statement in a number of ways, especially if its context within the whole article is taken into account.

To begin with, the writer avoids attributing the notion of a philosopher king to its original author, Plato, ascribing it instead to Marcus Aurelius, who had been fond of using it but had known very well where it came from. It is not hard to see why this attribution was preferred. A good part of the article is devoted to denying the value of metaphysical speculation and to freeing the word 'philosopher' from the meaning given to it by Plato. The article declares:

> Truth for the *philosopher* is not a mistress who corrupts his imagination and who he believes can be found everywhere; he is content to be able to unravel it when he can perceive it. He certainly does not confuse it with plausibility. He takes what is true as true, what is false as false, what is doubtful as doubtful, and what is merely plausible as plausible.

'He founds his principles on an infinity of individual observations.' Nothing could be more completely opposed to Plato's method, or to the attitudes of the sort of philosopher he imagined as king. It is also of course totally opposed to the method of theologians. As Voltaire said, Plato 'was almost made a father of the Church on account of his trinitarian ideas, which no one has ever understood'.[7] Marcus Aurelius, on the other hand, had been hostile to Christianity and professed a Stoic scepticism about metaphysical reasoning. The article emphasises the difference between the philosopher and the Christian: 'Reason is to the *philosopher* what grace is to the Christian. The Christian's decision to act comes from grace, the *philosopher*'s from reason.' Furthermore, the philosopher is said to 'worship' civil society.

It is not only Plato's metaphysics and Christian theology that are objectionable to the author. So is any form of *esprit de système*, that is, any attempt to work out by deduction from first principles a complete explanation of the universe or of society – something of which Descartes and Hobbes, as well as Plato and Aquinas, had been guilty. Knowledge can be gained only by induction, by observation and experiment, and on this basis is necessarily incomplete. The same message, with insistent repetition of the words *philosophy* and *philosopher*, had dominated D'Alembert's preface (*Discours préliminaire*) to the whole *Encyclopédie*, which appeared in 1751. For D'Alembert the core meaning of 'philosophy' was what we call natural sciences, and of the 'philosopher' was what we call a scientist, or at least a man of scientific bent.

The article *Philosopher* is directed also against a second common meaning of the word, generally identified with stoicism, namely, a person who suffers pain and hardship uncomplainingly, perhaps withdrawing from the world: 'it is easy', declares the author, 'to infer how remote the unfeeling sage of the Stoics is from the perfection of our *philosopher*'. The latter, we are told, enjoys the pleasures of life and of company, and works for the good of society.

This is only one article out of the 72,000 in the *Encyclopédie*, not all of which sang the same tune. But the *Encyclopédie* sold very widely, the article is on a subject of special sensitivity, it attracted notice, and it was presumed by many to be the work of the general editor, Diderot. In fact it was a shortened version made by him of a piece first published in 1743, of which Voltaire said that 'it has been kept to hand by all enquiring persons; it dates from the year 1730'. In other words, this article stood for many decades as a standard definition of the new philosopher. The original was probably the work of César Dumarsais.[8]

This new meaning of *philosopher*, first trumpeted by Bayle in his *Commentaire philosophique* of 1686, had by the mid-eighteenth century been proudly accepted as a title by a group of radical French thinkers, headed by Voltaire and including the chief contributors to the *Encyclopédie*, who were known then and are still known as *les philosophes*. So far is this concept from the traditional meaning of the word that R. J. White could give to his book about them the title *The Anti-Philosophers*,[9] and it has become common in English writing to use the French form *philosophes* to describe them in order to distinguish them from philosophers in general.

By the time the *Encyclopédie* was under way, Voltaire and others had given additional connotations to this new meaning. The classic text here is Voltaire's *English Letters* or *Lettres philosophiques*, first published in English in 1733 and then in French in 1734. A product of his visit to England from 1726 to 1729, this typically – and artfully – unsystematic work contains chapters on the thought of several English philosophers: on Bacon, 'the father of experimental philosophy' and 'the precursor of philosophy'; on Locke, 'who ruined innate ideas', and on Newton, 'the destroyer of Descartes's system'.[10] In addition, the book describes with relish the variety of British religious sects, placing special emphasis on the least orthodox, the Quakers, and praising the British state for tolerating them. Like most of the political writings of the *philosophes*, the *English Letters* was conceived as a critique of the French government, and in particular of the Catholic Church, which since the Revocation of the Edict of Nantes in 1685 had been the only lawful Church in France. Church as well as state authorities possessed and exercised the power to ban such publications and to punish their authors severely. Hence works like the *English Letters* had to be anonymous and, ostensibly or in reality, published outside France. Hence too the *philosophes* tirelessly advocated freedom of thought and writing, religious toleration and, what they regarded as a necessary corollary, state control over the activities of Churches.

It must not be supposed that this new meaning of 'philosopher' supplanted all the others, or that the word was used in precisely the same way by all *philosophes*, or that any *philosophe* used it with complete consistency. The basic meaning of the word remained 'a seeker after truth' and Plato was not actually denied the title. It was very common too in all kinds of discourse to use the word in a loosely stoic sense, of someone putting up with pain and misfortune – though the *philosophes* did their best to remove the Christian accretions of neo-Stoicism. Descartes's system remained fundamental in French education until late in the eighteenth century, and the *philosophes* themselves were distinctly less sceptical about ill-defined secular goals such as 'happiness' and 'utility' than they were about religious concepts. But they certainly succeeded – at least in France – in popularising the new meaning of 'philosopher', thus deliberately subverting the traditional understanding of the word.

French was the international language of the age, and the upper classes in many countries outside France made a point of writing to each other in French; intellectuals everywhere conceded a prominent, if not dominant, role to French culture; and so the works of the principal French writers, such as Montesquieu, Voltaire and Rousseau, were known throughout the western world. But their concepts did not always travel well. In Britain, where the Church authorities had little power and where press freedom and religious toleration were already well developed, the new meaning of 'philosopher' with its full anti-clerical, anti-theological and anti-Establishment connotations never caught on, except, ironically, in a pejorative sense after the outbreak of the French Revolution. But it was normal in English to use the word where we would now use the word 'scientist', to describe someone who tried to find out more about Nature by experiment and observation.[11] In Germany both metaphysics and theology remained highly respectable, though also highly contentious; and in German the word *Philosoph* was rarely used in the new sense.[12]

A further reason for this difference between France and other countries lies in yet another new connotation of the word *philosophe*. It has been discovered that Francophone printers and booksellers described all banned books – all those that were really dangerous to market, and in consequence fetched more per page than respectable volumes – as *livres philosophiques*. In other words, books that were condemned by the authorities because they were heterodox were lumped together with books that were condemned because they were pornographic. Although this terminology does not seem to have extended beyond the book trade, there were certainly works published with *philosophe* in their title that were pornographic as well as anti-clerical, most famously *Thérèse philosophe* (1748). Some of the major *philosophes* contributed to the literature of pornography; and the idea of the *libertin*, which was closely associated with the new meaning of *philosophe*, also conflated the notion of a man of unorthodox opinions with that of a man of loose sexual morality. This aspect of the new meaning did not figure in elevated discussions of *philosophe* kings, but it helps to explain the hostility felt towards the *philosophes* and their attitudes by the more puritanical elements in society, especially outside France.[13]

The remarks about philosopher kings in the *Encyclopédie*'s article *Philosopher*, brief though they are, are none the less telling. In many eighteenth-century writings on monarchy, headed by those of Montesquieu, and including other articles in the *Encyclopédie* like Diderot's

'Autorité politique' and Louis de Jaucourt's group on 'Despotism' and on various types of 'Monarchy', discussion revolves round the need to limit royal power. But in the article *Philosopher*, a *philosophe* king is simply assumed, without argument or regret, to be in a position to give, or deny, his people happiness. This is one of numerous examples of eighteenth-century political thinkers putting their trust in princes – or, at the least, pinning their hopes on them.

No work that could be called a serious theoretical study of the idea of philosophical kingship was written during the eighteenth century, but admiring references to philosopher kings, in the sense of monarchs who are *philosophes*, are scattered through some of the more radical texts of the period. In *La voix du sage et du peuple* (*The voice of the wise man and of the people*) (1750), Voltaire wrote: 'The best thing that can happen to mankind is to have a philosopher-prince.' The Swiss publicist Joseph Lanjuinais began *Le monarque accompli* (*The complete monarch*) (1774) with the assertion that a philosophical monarch, concerned for men's happiness, is the most precious gift that heaven can bestow.

Political thinkers are always to some extent affected by the political practice of their day. But those who in the eighteenth century discussed philosophical kingship – and Enlightened despotism – were influenced to an exceptional degree by the activities and attitudes of contemporary sovereigns.[14] Apart from Britain, Holland, Poland and a few decaying old republics, the states of Europe were governed by rulers who claimed more or less absolute power and who alone – short of a revolutionary upheaval such as few thinkers envisaged before the 1780s – could change the law and carry through reform. As a Saxon reformer wrote in 1762: 'If a prince is not prepared to plan the improvement of his territories himself, I doubt that, as things are, Estates will do much good or change what is bad.'[15] Hence many *philosophes* cherished hopes that their ideas would be endorsed and carried into effect by some sovereign. They also naturally looked to sovereigns for patronage and employment; and most rulers did something to encourage them. Many progressives were state employees before they became known as writers: Pietro Verri served Maria Theresa and Joseph II in Milan, as Joseph von Sonnenfels did in Vienna; in Germany professors like Immanuel Kant and most Protestant clergy, such as Johann Gottfried Herder, had been appointed by the ruler; in France Claude Helvétius was a tax-farmer. Other *philosophes* were given office partly because of their writings. Frederick the Great made

D'Alembert president of his Academy even though he would not reside in Berlin; the physiocrat Turgot became Louis XVI's principal minister from 1774 to 1776; and Cesare Beccaria was appointed to a Chair (of 'cameral sciences') in Milan five years after the publication in 1764 of his *Dei delitti e delle pene* (*Crimes and Punishments*). Even Voltaire became historiographer royal to King Louis XV, and a galaxy of radicals served as secretaries to diplomatic legations or as special envoys: Voltaire again, Hume, Rousseau and Beaumarchais. Moreover, a few monarchs enhanced their claims to the status of *philosophe* by themselves publishing contributions to theoretical discussion.

The influence of practice on theory is highlighted by the fact that so many references to philosopher kings were to particular rulers. In the *English Letters* it was, surprisingly, George II's queen Caroline whom Voltaire called 'an amiable philosopher on the throne'.[16] In 1764 a pamphlet appeared called *The Spirit of the Philosopher Kings, Marcus Aurelius, Julian, Stanislas and Frederick*. The Stanislas referred to was the former king of Poland, now duke of Lorraine, whose 'anodyne' *Oeuvres du philosophe bienfaisant* (*Works of the beneficent philosopher*) had been published in the previous year. Lanjuinais's *Le monarque accompli* of 1774 was a panegyric of Joseph II of Austria, which he followed up in 1776 by another praising Catherine II of Russia.

By far the most important and influential eighteenth-century claimant to the title of *philosophe* king was Frederick II of Prussia. His father and predecessor, Frederick William I (1713–40), though he governed with ferocious efficiency and economy and tolerated more than one Protestant sect, was notorious for his coarse contempt for intellectual and artistic activity, especially French culture and language. He virtually closed the Berlin Academy that his father, Frederick I, with Leibniz's collaboration, had founded in 1701. In educating his son, Frederick William sought by brutal methods to imbue him with his own rigid brand of Calvinism, to make him into a soldier, to suppress his interest in French culture and to stifle his literary and musical tastes. Frederick, though he was even threatened at one point with execution, refused to conform and was eventually conceded a measure of independence. It was a landmark in the history of the notion of the philosopher king when in 1729, at the age of seventeen, he began to sign himself, in French, 'Frederick the philosopher'. He liked to write French poetry, and eagerly ordered and read the works of the *philosophes* as they appeared. In 1736, having failed to establish relations with Voltaire through diplomatic channels, he wrote personally to him, praising his genius and particularly his plays, and asking to be sent all his other works. He enclosed a translation he had made of one of the writings of Wolff, whom Frederick William had exiled but whom Frederick admired. A flowery but brilliant correspondence ensued, the existence of which soon became public knowledge. If they never quoted the precise words of Plato on philosopher kings, 'they continually paraphrased them': Voltaire regularly called Frederick a 'philosophical prince'.[17]

Frederick soon conceived the idea of writing a refutation of Machiavelli's *Prince*. Voltaire commented exhaustively on the prince's draft, was permitted to improve its French and its argument, and then arranged its publication. *Anti-Machiavel* came out in the summer of 1740, with a preface by Voltaire, just after Frederick became king. Though it was anonymous, the identity of the author was easy to guess. The book, innocent of any knowledge of Machiavelli's *Discourses*, denounced his immorality in a rather crude and unoriginal way, but made a great impression as a declaration of Frederick's philosophy of government. A king, he said, should not pursue glory and annexations of territory. He must work for justice and for the happiness, the prosperity and even the liberty of his people as 'the first servant of the state'. While Frederick regards 'Plato's man' as mythical, Marcus Aurelius, 'the crowned philosopher', is his hero.[18]

At the beginning of his reign, living up to his promise, Frederick recalled Wolff to Prussia, arranged a meeting with Voltaire, invited him and other *philosophes* to Berlin, and revived the Academy, filling it with French writers and scientists. He extended toleration to Catholics; he declared that the press was free; he gave asylum to writers threatened by prosecution in France; and he reformed the Prussian legal system to limit both the use of torture in legal proceedings and the number of crimes subject to the death penalty. These last measures later enabled him to assert, with some exaggeration, that he had anticipated the proposals of Beccaria's *Crimes and Punishments*.[19] The accession, in Prussia of all countries, of a monarch who wrote poetry and philosophical tracts, who wished to consort with radical writers and who introduced such progressive measures, caused a sensation. 'With Frederick,' it was commonly said, 'philosophy ascended the throne.'

In 1750 appeared the first of many editions of his *Works of the Philosopher of Sans Souci*, a substantial collection of poems and essays in French. (Sans Souci, 'free from care', was the name of the small but opulent palace he had built for himself at Potsdam.) It is clear that Frederick's use of the word 'philosopher' was somewhat different from the *philosophes*', especially at first. Voltaire soon weaned him from his early admiration for the writings of Wolff, and already in *Anti-Machiavel* he was denouncing Descartes, Leibniz and all creators of metaphysical systems. But for Frederick the core meaning of *philosophe* was always Stoic. He had endured a ghastly upbringing, he saw it as his duty to work unremittingly for the state, he shared the hardships of his soldiers and he often risked his life in battle. He profoundly believed in the play of chance and fully expected to be buffeted by fortune. He was even prepared to describe his philistine father as 'a philosopher on the throne'. Where the king and the *philosophes* found it easiest to agree was on religious questions, because they shared contempt for the Church hierarchy, indifference to theological quarrels and detestation of religious persecution.[20]

Frederick proved far from perfect as a *philosophe* king. The connection between his literary and political activities was in reality slight. Poetry and philosophy, like music, were, as he said, his recreations, his distractions. Voltaire and others found him a capricious friend and host: the king even had Voltaire arbitrarily imprisoned for a few weeks in 1753. Frederick did not in fact allow the publication of many writings critical of his rule. He maintained the brutal discipline of his army and the barracks-like character of his state. He administered his territories – in German, of course – through the machinery established by his father. In the ordinary conduct of government, cameralist principles were much more evident than any English or French influence. Within months of the publication of the *Anti-Machiavel* he showed himself a consummate Machiavellian in seizing Silesia from Maria Theresa of Austria, publicly justifying his actions by arguments he knew perfectly well to be specious. But, if this flagrant breach of treaties and international law blemished his reputation, the fact that he followed it up by showing himself a master general, winning battle after battle and securing the permanence of his conquest, enhanced it.[21] Many, though not all, of the *philosophes* accepted that war was a natural feature of the international system and that it was a necessary part of the duties of a sovereign to fight his corner and expand the boundaries of his state, rather than allow it to be defeated and reduced in size.[22]

In 1770 Frederick published brilliant critiques of two radical works, the *Essai sur les préjugés* (*Essay on prejudices*), which was probably the work of Baron d'Holbach, and *Le système de la nature* (*The System of Nature*), which certainly was. Holbach was one of the principal contributors to the *Encyclopédie*, especially on scientific subjects. He was a complete atheist and a believer in the perfectibility of humanity through education and Enlightenment. These views were too much for Frederick. He argued in his critiques that the mass of the people could not, and ought not to, be given the opportunity of an elite education, and that religion and superstition were indispensable to them. He further maintained that a God of some sort must exist. He thus separated himself from the more extreme *philosophes*. Others thought he carried his religious indifference too far when after the suppression of the Jesuits in 1773 he insisted on retaining them in his dominions. But he continued to commend himself, and to secure good publicity, by publishing in a philosophical vein and by keeping up his correspondence with the older and less radical *philosophes* including, despite a series of open rows, Voltaire.[23]

Frederick's success during a reign of forty-six years gave a shot in the arm to the institution of hereditary monarchy, showing that, as well as kings such as the boorish Frederick William I, the voluptuary Louis XV, the boring Hanoverians in Britain, the idle and dissolute rulers of Portugal and the mad Christian VII of Denmark, it could throw up a multifaceted genius who insisted on governing his state personally and on commanding his armies in the field, and, astonishingly, had the transcendent ability to make a resounding success of both these roles. His example showed too that a monarch might himself be hostile to some of the assumptions of the *ancien régime*, and hence that reform from above was a serious possibility. For more than two decades he was the only serious contender as a *philosophe* king. But in 1759 Charles III became king of Spain, three years later Catherine II usurped the throne of Russia, and in 1764 Stanislas Augustus was elected king of Poland. Then in 1765 Joseph II succeeded as Holy Roman Emperor and co-regent of the Austrian Monarchy while Leopold, his younger brother, the future emperor Leopold II, became grand duke of Tuscany. In 1772 Gustavus III re-established absolute monarchical rule in Sweden. All of these sovereigns of major states, together with many lesser princes, had some claim to the title of *philosophe* kings.

Among this group Catherine II was pre-eminent.[24] As soon as she became empress, she asked D'Alembert to become tutor to her son and heir (though he was too prudent to accept), she began corresponding with Voltaire, and she offered to publish the remaining volumes of the *Encyclopédie*, at that time under the ban of French censorship, if the enterprise would move to Russia. That proposal was not accepted, but in 1765 she bought Diderot's library for more than the asking price, while allowing him to retain the use of it and giving him a handsome pension into the bargain. So far as her policies were concerned, she immediately reduced the power of the Orthodox Church and extended religious toleration. Then in 1767 she published a lengthy instruction (*Nakaz*) which she had given to a legislative commission summoned to review the Russian legal system. This extraordinary document, perhaps not originally composed with a legislative commission in mind, largely consisted of selections she had herself made from the writings of *philosophes*. Of 655 clauses, it has been calculated that 294 derived 'wholly or in substantial part' from Montesquieu's *De l'esprit des lois* (1748), 108 from Beccaria's *Crimes and Punishments* (1764), thirty-five from baron Bielfeld's *Institutions politiques* (1760), twenty-four from J. H. G. von Justi's cameralist textbook, *Die Grundfeste zu der Macht und Glückseeligkeit der Staaten* (*The Basis of the Power and Happiness of States*) (1760–61), twenty from the *Encyclopédie* (completed only in 1765) and even a few, indirectly, from Adam Smith's lectures at Glasgow, long anticipating the publication of *The Wealth of Nations*. Some of the paragraphs are ludicrous:

48. The Chinese are guided by Custom.
49. The Severity of Law tyrannizes in Japan.
50. At one period morals formed the conduct of the Lacedemonians ...
266. The Peasants have generally from 12 to 15 or 20 Children by one Marriage, but rarely does a fourth part of them attain to the Age of Maturity.

Other sections, however, embody serious political discussion. She endorses much of Beccaria's programme of penal reform:

200. In order that Punishment may not appear to be the Violence of one, or many rising up against a Citizen, it ought to be public; conveniently speedy, useful to society, as moderate as the circumstances will allow, proportional to the Crime, and exactly such as is laid down in the Laws.

It is astonishing not only that a sovereign should have been so up-to-date and progressive in her reading, even if she presented it in peculiar ways, but also that she should have been ready to publish this document and to make it available to a commission of more than five hundred persons elected from all the provinces of Russia and almost all walks of life. The text made a huge impression abroad, where it was believed to be a blueprint for a new law code. It pointed the contrast with what most *philosophes* condemned as the confused, heterogeneous and precedent-ridden legal arrangements of countries like France.[25]

In the same year as the *Nakaz* was published, while Catherine and her Court were floating lazily down the Volga, she organised and took part in the translation into Russian of Jean-François Marmontel's *Bélisaire* (1766), a novel describing the work of a good king and advocating toleration. Marmontel expressed a widespread sentiment, at least among *philosophes*, when he wrote:

> A wise man said that peoples would only be happy when philosophers were kings, or kings philosophers. There seemed little likelihood that either would ever occur. But we see in our own day that of all the orders of society the supreme rank is the one where, proportionally, there is the largest number of true friends of wisdom and truth.

The French censorship duly demonstrated its fatuity by banning both the *Nakaz* and *Bélisaire*.

Joseph II[26] first made an impact at the beginning of his reign as Holy Roman Emperor with attempts to reform the imperial courts, but then became better known for his extensive travels 'as a philosopher' throughout his dominions, to Italy (1769, 1775, 1784), to France (1777, 1781), to the Netherlands (1781) and to Russia (1780, 1787) – fact-finding missions during which he avoided pomp and ceremony, made a point of visiting useful buildings like barracks, dockyards, hospitals and prisons as well as Courts, churches and beauty-spots, and met artists, philanthropists and entrepreneurs as well as kings and ministers. He conducted no correspondence with *philosophes*, evaded meeting Voltaire, seems not to have grasped the new meaning of *philosophe* and published nothing which had not originated as an official document. But, on becoming ruler of the Austrian Monarchy in 1780, he launched a frenetic programme of legislation which included granting toleration to the principal Protestant sects, the Orthodox and the Jews and curbing the power and wealth of the Catholic Church, especially of its monasteries. He was duly described as 'a philosopher on the throne'.

Both Catherine and Joseph, like Frederick, troubled some of their admirers by their wars and annexations, especially the first partititon of Poland in 1772. But Voltaire defended even that as giving to some of the backward, aggressively Catholic Poles the benefits of tolerant and Enlightened rule. He and other *philosophes* rejoiced at her victories over the Turks and looked forward to her 're-establishing philosophy in Constantinople'.[27] In the 1780s Joseph obtained the support of the most notorious French publicist of the decade, Simon Linguet, in his campaign to open the Scheldt to revive the economy of the Austrian Netherlands; and some progressive writers saw his war of 1788 with Turkey as a crusade for toleration.[28]

Joseph's brother, Leopold, as grand duke of Tuscany (1765–90), also imposed a vast range of similar reforms from above, but during the course of his reign his approach to government became more and more different from Joseph's. He was determined to maintain neutrality in international affairs; he assisted the publication of a new edition of the French *Encyclopédie* in his dominions; and he enacted an exceptionally progressive criminal law code in 1786. He even wanted to introduce in Tuscany a constitution establishing representative government, and prepared himself to do so by studying the political writings of the past and of his own day, including documents of the American Revolution. But the project was vetoed by Joseph. Just after the latter had died, Leopold, who succeeded him as ruler of the Monarchy, published an extraordinary manifesto, directed at the rebels against Austrian rule in the Netherlands, in which he declared:

> I believe that even a hereditary sovereign is only a delegate and employee of the people ... that in every country there must be a fundamental law or contract between the people and the sovereign which limits his power and authority; that when the sovereign fails to keep it, he forfeits his position ... and people are no longer obliged to obey him ... that the orders of the sovereign do not acquire the force of law and need not be obeyed until after the Estates have consented to them.[29]

As Leopold lived for only two more years, it is impossible to say how far he would have acted upon these principles. But his record inspired some writers to regard him as the best of all the *philosophe* kings.

Leopold was certainly the ruler who came nearest to the ideal imagined by Louis-Sébastien Mercier in his well known Utopia of 1771, *L'an 2440 (The year 2440)*. In Mercier's vision France has ceased to be oppressed by absolutism and has become a smiling land of liberty and prosperity.

> Would you believe it? The revolution came about quite easily, by the heroism of a great man. A philosopher-king, worthy of the throne because he disdained it, more concerned for the happiness of mankind than the appearance of power, concerned for posterity and wary of his own power, offered to restore to the Estates their ancient prerogatives. He sensed that a far-flung kingdom needed to unify its different provinces in order to be governed wisely … In this way, everything lives, everything flourishes.[30]

For the sake of completeness, it should be added that, while in the last decades of the *ancien régime* an exceptional number of monarchs exercised their power personally, in important instances it was in effect delegated to Enlightened or philosophical ministers. In 1762 Voltaire said of Count Firmian, governor of Lombardy under Maria Theresa, 'All that is needed to transform a country is a minister.' Du Tillot in the duchy of Parma was another example. But by far the most notable was the marquis Pombal, the effective ruler of Portugal from 1750 to 1777, who brought about the expulsion of the Jesuits from his country in 1759 and so began the process that led to the suppression of the Order in 1773.[31]

The idea of the Enlightened despot in the eighteenth century[32]

Despite the widespread use during the eighteenth century of the ancient concept of the 'philosopher king', if in perverted forms, modern scholarship has paid little attention to it. In contrast, the notion 'Enlightened despot', an eighteenth-century coinage that was only rarely used at the time, has been freely applied to the period by subsequent writers. So has the closely related concept 'Enlightened absolutism', although in this precise form it has not been traced in any text earlier than 1847.

Let us start with eighteenth-century usage. Just as the new meaning of 'philosophical' was a deliberate perversion of an old term in order to remove from it its metaphysical content, the meanings of 'enlightened' in English and *éclairé* in French were perverted to remove from them their religious content. Before this period one of the commonest meanings of these adjectives was 'illuminated by faith'.

Christ had brought 'a light to lighten the Gentiles'. 'Let your light so shine before men', urged the Book of Common Prayer. A convert was said to have 'seen the light'. In the new meaning the light was understood to come from the advance of secular philosophy, and in many contexts *éclairé* became indistinguishable from *philosophe*.[33]

In the eighteenth century German was the only language to possess an abstract noun which can be directly translated as 'Enlightenment': *Aufklärung*. Paradoxically, this word did not have religious connotations and originally meant 'brightening up' or 'clearing up' rather than 'enlightening'. During the century its meaning gradually moved towards the modern acceptation, though at this time it always denoted a change of attitudes or a process and was never used to describe a period. In French the nearest equivalent noun was, as it still is, *les lumières*, the rays or sources of light, but *philosophie* was commonly employed instead. In German *Aufklärung* and *aufgeklärt* were used in this sense much more frequently than *philosophie* and *philosophisch*. But a *philosophe* king may be regarded as virtually indistinguishable from an Enlightened king, and a *philosophe* despot from an Enlightened despot.

In 1784 Kant, answering the question *What is Enlightenment?* at a time when it was the subject of much debate in Prussia, defined it as 'Man's emergence from his self-incurred immaturity', that is, from his dependence on the views of others, especially in religion. This is not exactly how the *philosophes* would have put it, but they would not have dissented. Kant went on to describe the age as 'an age of Enlightenment, the century of Frederick'. 'Only a ruler who is himself enlightened and has no fear of phantoms, yet who likewise has at hand a well-disciplined and numerous army to guarantee public security, may say what no republic would dare to say: *Argue as much as you like and about whatever you like, but obey!*'[34] For Kant Frederick, even at the fag-end of his reign, is the Enlightened king *par excellence*.

The meanings of the concepts 'despot' and 'despotism', together with 'absolute monarch(y)' and 'absolutism', present far greater difficulties than the meanings of 'Enlightened' and 'Enlightenment'.[35] Despotism in ancient Greece usually meant a master's dominion over his slaves, a fact not forgotten in eighteenth-century writing. But it had also been used by Aristotle as a variant of 'tyranny'. In his celebrated classification of regimes according to the number of persons ruling, monarchy was one-man rule that was responsible and beneficent; while tyranny was its corruption, rule by one man who exploited untrammelled power in his own interests and at his whim to the detriment of his subjects; and despotism was a form of government, especially suited to the East, in which the ruler treated his subjects like slaves. In the seventeenth century despotism was sometimes used more generally, but always with a pejorative sense. This usage was the basis from which most eighteenth-century discussion started. In other words, when 'despotism' was being used in some other way, as it often was, it was in self-conscious divergence from this standard meaning.

However, the terminology had already been complicated by earlier writers. For example, Hobbes insisted that monarchy, despotism and tyranny were all one because the people, when making their contract with their sovereign, had surrendered all power to him without conditions. The supposed differences, said Hobbes, were a matter of mere rhetoric: 'for they that are discontented under *monarchy*, call it *tyranny*'. Further, from the sixteenth century the concepts of 'absolute monarchy', 'sovereignty' and 'arbitrary government' had been brought into play. Many proponents of monarchical rule, and most advocates of sovereignty, thought monarchs were or ought to be absolute, that is to be above most, if not all, the existing laws and to be able to change them on their sole authority. This was the doctrine of Pufendorf and of most Continental theorists of Natural Law and Natural Rights, and also of the cameralists, and commanded wide acceptance in the German and Italian states. Basically, they maintained that men had surrendered all, or almost all, their natural rights to the sovereign when they made their contract with him. Seventeenth- and eighteenth-century French kings too claimed to be absolute, partly on the basis of older traditions of thought. This claim justified their never holding a meeting of the Estates-General between 1614 and 1789 and their overriding in certain cases the remonstrances of the various *parlements*, whose members considered themselves constitutionally entitled to reject royal legislation. However, advocates of absolute monarchy usually claimed that it was quite distinct from 'arbitrary government' or despotism, alleging either that even absolute kings were bound by certain fundamental laws or that they in fact used their power for the good of their state and people, or both. The great French preacher bishop Bossuet, who glorified royal absolutism, in his role as tutor to Louis XIV's heir took care to condemn arbitrary government and would never so much as mention despotism in his presence.

The text of *Anti-Machiavel* conveniently illustrates some of the inconsistencies of absolutist theory and some of the confusions of its terminology. Frederick insists that

> justice ... must be the principal object of a sovereign. It is thus the good of the people he governs that he must prefer to every other interest. It is thus their happiness and felicity that he must augment – or procure it if they do not have it. What becomes then of such ideas as interest, greatness, ambition, and despotism? The sovereign, far from being the absolute master of the people under his dominion, is nothing else but their first servant and must be the instrument of their felicity as they are of his glory.[36]

But he declares it essential for the good of the state and the people that the king should rule personally, without deferring to ministers. He has no time for the view that a monarch ought to be constrained by a constitution, the laws, ministers, parliaments or any intermediary bodies.

> Just as kings can do good when they want to do it, they can do evil whenever they please ... In every country there are honest and dishonest people just as in every family there are handsome persons along with one-eyed, hunchbacks, blind, and cripples ... there are and always will be monsters among princes, unworthy of the character with which they are invested.[37]

He thinks that the only sanction against a bad ruler is that he will acquire a bad reputation. But there is no suggestion that the views of his people should actually be sought, or deferred to, on this or any other issue. In discussing republics he maintains that they all in the long run degenerate into despotisms, while admitting that

> no one will ever persuade a republican ... that monarchy is the best form of government when a king means to do his duty, since he has the will and power to put his good intentions into effect. I agree, they will say to you, but where can this phoenix of princes be found? He would be Plato's man ... Your metaphysical monarchy, if any such existed, would be an earthly paradise; but despotism, as it really is, more or less changes this world into a living hell.[38]

For Frederick, it seems from some of these remarks, despotism is indistinguishable from absolute rule – in another place he talks of the 'absolute despotism in France' created by Richelieu and Mazarin.[39] But he also insists that the king, in order to do his job, must possess what appears like absolute power, and yet that there is a great difference between beneficent monarchy on the one hand and despotism on the other. What makes the difference is purely the character and attitudes of the prince himself.

Soon after the publication of *Anti-Machiavel*, the framework within which discussion of despotism had hitherto taken place was transformed by three developments. First, Montesquieu in *De l'esprit des lois* (1748), as part of his attack on the absolute monarchy of France from the standpoint of a supporter of the *parlements*, deliberately challenged Aristotle's classification of forms of government and defined monarchy and despotism as distinct species. In a monarchy, as he described it, there must be a constitution of sorts, including both a law of succession to the throne and the existence of countervailing forces like the aristocracy and the Church, and/or of intermediary bodies like *parlements* that the ruler was bound to consult about proposed legislation. Unless at least some of these conditions were satisfied, the state was a despotism. On these premisses France was or ought to be a monarchy, but its kings' absolutist theories and practices were in danger of turning it into a despotism. He further argued that despotism was an inherent characteristic of large and of Oriental states, such as Russia. Montesquieu nearly always avoided using the word and concept 'absolute' applied to power and government, refusing to accept that there was a difference between absolute and despotic rule. With these views went his admiration for the English constitution and its balance or 'separation of powers'.

De l'esprit des lois at once became one of those select books that all serious writers had to know and to take into account. Its new classification was rejected by many. Voltaire, for example, a consistent supporter of the French monarchy against the *parlements*, regarded the distinction as laboured (Voltaire, *L'A,B,C*). But the standing of Montesquieu's book led to its being drawn upon even by the absolute rulers themselves. Catherine II's lavish borrowings from it for the *Nakaz* have been mentioned. But, despite her reverence for the book, she was determined to modify its message. She wished Russia to be regarded as European and to qualify as a monarchy rather than a despotism, despite its lack of a law of succession, asserting that she had established adequate intermediary bodies. In the *Nakaz* she twisted Montesquieu's words in order to make this case:

> 9. The Sovereign is absolute, for no other than absolute Powers vested in one Person, can be suitable to the extent of so vast an Empire.

13. What is the Object of absolute Government? Certainly not to deprive the people of their natural Liberty, but to direct their Conduct in such manner that the greatest good may be derived from all their Operations.[40]

When Diderot was at last persuaded to visit her in 1773, he urged her, unsuccessfully, to follow Montesquieu more thoroughly and establish stronger intermediary institutions. Not only Catherine II but also, more improbably, Joseph II admired aspects of Montesquieu's work. In Rome in 1769, he and his brother Leopold were painted together by Pompeo Batoni, with *De l'esprit des lois* on the table beside them. Joseph certainly did not accept Montesquieu's general scheme. But in the special circumstances of the Austrian Monarchy one of Montesquieu's shibboleths, the separation of powers, proved useful to the centralising ruler. In many provinces Maria Theresa had found herself faced with the situation that much executive, some legislative and most judicial power was in the hands of the local nobility in their own right or as members of the local Estates. In this context, to insist upon the separation of justice and administration, which was one of the planks in the empress's reform programme of 1749, was to enhance the power of the monarch and of her courts and administration over against the power of the provincial magnates. Montesquieu could be cited as supporting this separation even though he had specifically commended the exercise of judicial functions by local lords.[41]

The second development in discussions of despotism was that writers began to play with it, to assert for example that the pope was a despot, or the Jesuits despotic, and that interfering bureaucrats or over-mighty nobles were petty despots, against whom the king with his absolute power protected his subjects. From the late 1750s French ministers were being described as despots whose machinations the supposedly absolute king was failing to control.

Thirdly, some writers began to use 'despotism' in a positive sense. The first known example is the formulation of the abbé de Saint-Pierre, according to Voltaire 'half philosopher and half mad', who insisted that 'when power is united to reason, it cannot be too great or too despotic for the greatest utility of society'.[42] This sort of usage was often combined with calling subordinate authorities despotic in a negative sense. Joseph II, for example, liked to condemn lesser officials, such as the agents of landowners, as despots, and also to brand the pope as a despot, but in 1763 he recommended to his mother in a private paper that the provinces should be subjected to despotism for ten years in order to get rid of the absurd old constitution which, he claimed, was frustrating their development. This frank advocacy of 'despotism' was deemed so shocking that the document was suppressed.[43]

Beccaria made rather similar points in *Crimes and Punishments* (1764), despite the fact that his argument started out from Rousseau's *Social Contract*:

> How happy would mankind be, if laws were now given for the first time; now that we see on the thrones of Europe benevolent monarchs, promoters of the peaceful virtues, of the arts and sciences, fathers of their people, crowned citizens; the increase of whose authority augments the happiness of their subjects by removing that intermediate despotism, more cruel because less secure, which suffocates the people's prayers, always sincere and always successful when they can reach the throne. If, I say, these humane princes have allowed the old laws to subsist, this arises from the infinite difficulty of removing from errors the venerated rust of many centuries, which is a motive for enlightened citizens to desire with greater ardour the continual growth of their power.

There is no clearer example of a radical humanitarian thinker of real stature recognising the potentiality of rule by Enlightened monarchs who can make laws, and demanding that their powers be increased to enable them to impose the major changes that are considered to be necessary. While attacking what he chose to describe as intermediate despotism, he was in fact recommending what would now be called Enlightened despotism or absolutism. In an earlier passage he had written: 'the despotism of many can be corrected only by the despotism of one man, and the cruelty of a despot is proportional not to his strength, but to the obstacles he has to contend with'.[44] No wonder his work was excerpted by Catherine II and he was given employment by Maria Theresa and Joseph II. More surprising perhaps is that to some degree these rulers acted on his proposals for drastic reform of the criminal law.

Another positive use of 'despotism', but in a rather different sense, is to be found in certain works of the Physiocrats, Quesnay's *Despotisme de la Chine* (*Chinese despotism*) (1767) and especially Le Mercier de la Rivière's *L'ordre naturel et essentiel des sociétés politiques* (*The natural and necessary order of political societies*) (1767), which was avowedly designed as the political manifesto of the group. They argued that government, society and especially the economy are subject to laws which, like the laws of geometry, are indisputable and self-evident. It is the business of the good ruler to put these laws into effect, or – according to one formulation – to get rid of the existing counter-productive laws and then sit back, do nothing and let the self-evident laws operate. These laws may, by a play upon words, be described, like Euclid's laws, as despotic, and the regime that enacts and sustains them as *despotisme légal*. This concept does not imply, as has sometimes been supposed, that the Physiocrats approved of what is normally des-cribed and condemned as despotism, namely, the arbitrary rule of an individual. Confusingly, they too condemned despotism in this sense, while being strong advocates of absolute monarchy as the best form of government. For, far from acting wilfully or in his own interests, the ruler who enacts Le Mercier's laws will have no discretion; he will be doing the self-evidently right thing, not what he likes but what is natural and essential. Ironically, in the mid-sixties several governments introduced one of the Physiocrats' laws, free trade in grain, thereby causing famine and provoking violent opposition. The experiment had to be abandoned. Furthermore, the concept of 'legal despotism', though initially applauded by Diderot, Catherine II and others, was attacked as absurd and self-contradictory, for example by Rousseau, and soon ceased to be taken seriously.[45]

It was during these years when the concept of despotism was being widened, varied and rehabilitated that the phrases 'enlightened despot' and 'enlightened despotism' were coined. The first unequivocal refer-ence to an 'enlightened despot' which has so far been discovered dates from 1758. It comes from the *Correspondance littéraire*, a manuscript journal compiled in Paris by Friedrich Melchior Grimm, Diderot, Guillaume Raynal and others from 1756 onwards, specifically in order to inform a handful of subscribing monarchs and princes about the writings and doings of the *philosophes* and matters of related interest. On 15 March 1758 Grimm refers to the Danish law of 1665 which gave absolute power to the king: 'It is true that there is no government more perfect than that of a just, vigilant, enlightened, beneficent, despot, who loves the state and his people; but as such princes are rare and there are ten bad or incapable ones to one good, I leave you to judge if the Danish law is a masterpiece of prudence.'

On 1 October 1767 Grimm used the same expression again: 'It has been said that the rule of an ENLIGHTENED DESPOT, active, vigilant, wise and firm, was of all regimes the most desirable and most perfect, and this is a true saying; but it was important not to take it too far. I passionately love such despots.'[46] But this time he said that only one ruler in fifty could be expected to fulfil the role.

During his visit to Russia in 1773 Diderot and Catherine II held lengthy conversations, in preparation for which he wrote what are known as the *Memoranda for Catherine II*. One passage runs:

> All arbitrary government is bad; I do not except the arbitrary government of a good, firm, just, enlightened master ...
>
> A despot, even if he were the best of men, by governing in accordance with his good pleasure, commits a crime ...
>
> One of the greatest misfortunes that could happen to a free nation would be two or three consecutive reigns of a just and enlightened despotism. Three sovereigns in succession like Elizabeth, and the English would have been imperceptibly led towards slavery for an indeterminate period ...
>
> Let us work out the probabilities.
>
> The sovereign can be good and enlightened, but feeble; good and enlightened, but lazy; good, but without enlightenment; enlightened, but wicked.
>
> Out of five cases, the only favourable one is when he is enlightened, good, hard-working and firm, and only then will Your Imperial Majesty be able to hope that the good she has done will last and that her great aims will continue to be pursued.[47]

These remarks of Grimm and Diderot invite many comments. First, none of them was intended to be printed, and all of them were written as part of a private or very restricted dialogue between *philosophes* and rulers. They all accept that an Enlightened despot can exist, indeed that such rulers have existed and do exist. But both writers express qualms about the phenomenon, that such rulers will inevitably be very rare, and in the case of Diderot that they cannot avoid doing harm and storing up trouble for the future even while doing good in the present.

Diderot first put such views into print in the 1774 edition of Raynal's best-selling *Philosophic and Political History of the Commerce and the Establishments of the Europeans in the West and East Indies*. This radical anti-colonialist work contained much material which Raynal had commissioned from other authors, including many passages by Diderot, such as the following:

It has sometimes been said that the best government would be that of a just and enlightened despot. This is a very dubious proposition. It might easily happen that the will of this absolute master would be in contradiction to the will of his subjects. Then, in spite of his justice and his enlightenment, he would be wrong to despoil his subjects of their rights, even to their advantage ...

A first despot, just, steady, and enlightened, is a great calamity; a second despot, just, steady, and enlightened, would be a still greater one; but a third, who should succeed with all these great qualities, would be the most terrible scourge with which a nation could be afflicted.[48]

So, when Diderot finally went public with his concept of the Enlightened despot – he used the abstract form 'enlightened despotism' even more rarely – it was to condemn it. Earlier, his attitude to the progressive rulers of his time had been less hostile. But he was shocked by Louis XV's *coup d'état* of 1771, dismissing the *parlements* and asserting his absolute power, and denounced it as despotism. Then in his unpublished *Pages contre un tyran* (*Pages directed against a tyrant*) of 1771 he turned against Frederick the Great, replying to his attack on Holbach. However, his *Memoranda for Catherine II* make it clear that as late as 1773 he still had high hopes of persuading her to use her power in accordance with his advice. Only when she rebuffed him did he write his critical *Observations on the Nakaz* (1774), and even then he did not publish it.

So the many historians who have denied that the precise concept of 'enlightened despotism' was known in the eighteenth century were mistaken. But these rather off-hand assertions of Grimm and Diderot hardly constitute a developed theory of Enlightened despotism. There exists, however, one major work, admittedly by a second-rank thinker, from the same Milanese background as Beccaria, which makes an elaborate case for what amounts to Enlightened despotism as normally understood, quite explicitly glorifying the despotic element. It is Giuseppe Gorani's *Il vero dispotismo* (*True despotism*) of 1770. Despotism, he says, has been universally condemned as a monstrous form of government. He defines it as the operation of

that will which acts on its own without consulting others, which includes in itself the entire legislative and executive power, which by virtue of the strongest attraction joins and attracts to itself all the vigour and wide-ranging powers of the sovereign, the prince, the government and the whole state, so that the movement of the entire political machine depends on his movement ... Though above the laws, which he can create and destroy at his pleasure, he can through his absolute will arrive at laws as good or better than those existing, which generally and in most countries may be thoroughly bad.

This can yield 'a kind of despotism which ought to result in utility to the public'. Gorani sees rulers like Catherine II and Leopold of Tuscany as undertaking a beneficent 'total reform'. He calls upon 'philosophy, the support of thrones, the preserver of liberty, the joy of nations' to come to the aid of his imagined ruler.[49]

Gorani's work was not especially well known, but it is clear that ideas like these had a wider appeal. Pietro Verri, an economic and political writer and an official of the Milanese government, who had given Beccaria substantial help in writing *Crimes and Punishments*, declared in 1781:

In my opinion, subjects ought never to fear the power of the sovereign when he himself exercises it and doesn't surrender any essential part of it into other hands ... Only intermediate power is to be feared, and I think and feel that the best of all political systems will always be despotism, provided that the sovereign is active and in overall control and doesn't give up any portion of his sovereignty.[50]

Such views also found support from the bitter pen of Linguet, who was notorious for his defence of slavery as a necessary support to a civilised and Enlightened elite. He said that he preferred to all other forms of government,

for the happiness of the people, that is the most numerous and weakest part of a nation, [the form] that we improperly stigmatise with the odious name of despotism, namely, the one in which there are no intermediaries between the prince and his subjects powerful enough to stifle the complaints of the latter and to fetter the influence of the former.[51]

An extraordinary instance of the use of the very words 'Enlightened despotism' is to be found in the writings of Stanislaw Staszic, who in 1787 actually recommended it to his fellow Poles, but in his mind the concept amounted only to an enhancement of royal power, checked by a representative assembly.[52]

It is hardly accidental that most of these resounding defences of

Enlightened or philosophical despotism came from men who, at the time they wrote them, were admirers of Joseph II. He was said to have inaugurated 'the era of Enlightened South Germany'. At the end of 1783 he issued to his officials and published what became known as his 'pastoral letter' in which he declared: 'I have weakened the obstructions resulting from prejudices and old, deep-rooted habits by means of Enlightenment [*Aufklärung*], and combated them with arguments.' He denounced those who put obstacles in the way of his avalanche of legislation, saying that he had enacted it for 'the general best' (*allgemeine Beste*) and for 'the utility and the greatest good of the greatest number'. He had convinced himself that his own inner light was the best guide to Church reform, and so informed the pope. During the 1780s he carried out his earlier threat of subjecting Hungary to ten years of despotic rule. At the beginning of 1789 he told his recalcitrant subjects in the Netherlands: 'I do not need your permission to do good.' This was the apogee of Enlightened despotism in practice.[53]

By the time Joseph II died in February 1790, his troops had been driven out of Belgium and he had been forced to abandon most of the reforms he had introduced in Hungary. A year after Leopold II had succeeded him, a minister who served both of them, Count Karl von Zinzendorf, wrote in his diary: 'What changes in principles and assumptions and decisions since then! Everything used to be directed towards concentration, uniformity; [now] everything is directed towards dispersion, diversity. It used to be all despotic monarchy, now it is all an anarchy of provincial Estates.'[54]

Conclusion

It is not suggested here that the tradition of thought that has been described in this chapter was the only, or even the most important, thread in eighteenth-century political theory. In Britain absolute monarchy, seen as indistinguishable from despotism, had been definitively abolished, and hardly any thinkers saw it as a potentially creative force. One of the few exceptions was Bentham, who was much influenced by Beccaria and in his early work shared his expectations that reform would come from above, through the agency of Enlightened absolute sovereigns.[55] In the surviving republics, in parts of the Holy Roman Empire, in the southern Netherlands and in Hungary, ancient mixed constitutions were stoutly defended. In France, although Voltaire and others had high hopes of strong Enlightened rulers, Montesquieu and Rousseau were the most influential of the many who denounced absolute monarchy. Once the American Revolution had given an example of an alternative way of reform through revolution from below, and still more after the outbreak of the French Revolution, expectations of reform and revolution from above dwindled – at least until the advent of Napoleon, when they emerged in a very different guise. Leopold II presents the extraordinary spectacle of a monarch proposing to use his absolute power to abolish absolutism.

However, this chapter has shown that many *philosophes* and figures of the Continental Enlightenment, down to the 1780s, believed that the only chance, or the best hope, for the acceptance of their ideas was that they would be adopted by like-minded monarchs who would use their power to put them into practice. Especially after the accession of Frederick the Great, they thought that this process was under way. They sometimes deployed a modified version of the traditional concept of the philosopher king, sometimes talked of the absolute power of the Enlightened or philosophical monarch, and occasionally of the Enlightened or philosophical despot. Confusingly, despotism in its ancient meaning of corrupt, wilful tyranny was always condemned, though its emergence was sometimes admitted to be a risk inherent in absolute regime. But a system in which the monarch possessed the full legislative power, under whatever name, was widely regarded as the best form of government and the best hope of securing rational reforms.

Those who took this view were more or less influenced by the political situation of the time. But they were also influenced in varying degrees by general political theories. It is evident that the ideas of philosophical kingship and Enlightened despotism fitted easily into the absolutist branch of the Natural Law tradition represented by Hobbes and Pufendorf. Moreover, thinkers who saw politics as a science and believed that the same or a similar code of laws could and should be adopted in every country – for example, the Physiocrats and the Utilitarians – felt little difficulty in according full legislative power to an Enlightened sovereign. Trust in such a ruler was consistent too with the view of history, most persuasively promoted by Voltaire, that its principal motive forces were ideas and great men. Writers who, on the contrary, emphasised the diversity of peoples and the deeper processes of history – such as Montesquieu, Rousseau and Herder – looked to society as a whole rather than to the individual ruler to bring about beneficent change.

In the late nineteenth and twentieth centuries historians set up the notion of 'Enlightened absolutism' as a more appropriate description of eighteenth-century practice and theory than 'Enlightened despotism'. Those among them who maintained that to apply the notion of 'Enlightened despotism' to the eighteenth century is anachronistic were mistaken. It is the concept 'Enlightened absolutism' which is absent in the eighteenth century. But it is true that many writers of the seventeenth and eighteenth centuries distinguished 'absolute' from 'despotic' monarchy, contending either that the absolute, unlike the despotic, ruler had good intentions, or that in an absolute system, as opposed to a despotic one, there existed some constitutional or legal restraints on him – or that both distinctions were valid. Ironically, an influential school of historians has described the French system of government in the eighteenth century as 'absolutism' while attributing to it the characteristics of Montesquieu's 'monarchy', a concept he had deliberately promoted in order to rebut the claims of absolute monarchy as he saw them. Against this background it is worth looking at the first formulation of the notion of 'Enlightened absolutism', made by Wilhelm Roscher in 1847. He started by denouncing Montesquieu's classification of forms of government and reasserting the merits of Aristotle's. He went on: 'I call … those constitutions truly and completely monarchical … in which a single person, without being responsible in law, possesses, at least for his lifetime, the entire power of the state, or at any rate an overwhelming part of it. For absolute monarchies the king's will is the final earthly reason for everything that happens in the state.' Roscher regarded such governments as the best of all forms, and as characteristic of the modern period. He argued that, broadly speaking, in the sixteenth century absolutism had been confessional and therefore weakened by religious influences; that in the seventeenth century Court absolutism, typified by Louis XIV, had prevailed, and the ruler had been constrained by etiquette and his officials; and that the eighteenth century brought Enlightened absolutism, which left the ruler untrammelled.[56] It is hard to discern a difference between Roscher's notion of Enlightened absolutism and the eighteenth-century idea of Enlightened or philosophic despotism. As Hobbes would certainly have agreed, the problem is semantic. Historians need both to scrutinise eighteenth-century usage closely and to define their own terms with care. But there is no doubt that a concept close to the sort of philosophical kingship that Hobbes had envisaged commanded significant support in the eighteenth century, and that it was quite often described as Enlightened or philosophic despotism.

Notes

This chapter should shortly appear in M. A. Goldie and R. L. Wokler (eds), *Cambridge History of Eighteenth Century Political Thought*. I am most grateful to the editors and to Mr Bill Davies for giving me permission to publish it here.

Professor Simon Dixon, Dr Martina Grečenková, Dr Tim Hochstrasser and Professor Hamish Scott all kindly commented on an earlier text, to its advantage.

1 It is an extraordinary fact that nothing appears to have been published directly on the use of this concept in the eighteenth century. The most useful single work, even though it skirts round this particular issue, is N. O. Keohane, *Philosophy and the State in France: The Renaissance to the Enlightenment* (Princeton, 1980).

2 T. Hobbes, *Leviathan* [1651], ed. R. Tuck (Cambridge, 1991), p. 254.

3 P. Riley (ed.), *The Political Writings of Leibniz* (Cambridge, 1988), quotation from p. 23.

4 Wolff's essay is in his *Horae Subsecivae Marburgensis: Gesammelte Werken, Lateinische Schriften*, vol. XXXIV, ed. J. Ecole, Hildesheim, 1983, pp. 1–3. See for this piece and for the German Natural Law school in general T. J. Hochstrasser, *Natural Law Theories in the Early Enlightenment* (Cambridge, 2000).

5 On the *Encyclopédie* in general see esp. J. Lough, *The Encyclopédie* (London, 1971) and R. Darnton, *The Business of Enlightenment: A Publishing History of the Encyclopédie* (Cambridge, MA, 1979).

6 The article is printed and discussed in H. Dieckmann, *Le Philosophe: Texts and Interpretation* (St Louis, 1948). Cf. Chapter 3, 'Christians and "Philosophes"', pp. 60–3 below.

7 R. Pomeau (ed.), *Oeuvres historiques de Voltaire* (Paris, 1962), p. 1026.

8 On the authorship issue, A. W. Fairbairn, 'Dumarsais and *Le Philosophe*', *Studies on Voltaire and the Eighteenth Century*, LXXXVII (1972): 375–95.

9 R. J. White, *The Anti-Philosophers* (London, 1970).

10 Voltaire, *Lettres philosophiques*, ed. R. Naves (Paris, 1964), pp. 57, 59, 64, 71.

11 Cf. J. Lough, *The Philosophes and Post-Revolutionary France* (Oxford, 1982) and R. Porter, *Enlightenment* (London, 2000) (on Britain as the fount of Enlightenment).

12 See esp. the wide-ranging 'Prologue' to T. C. W. Blanning, *Reform and Revolution in Mainz* (Cambridge, 1974) and H. B. Nisbet, '"Was ist Aufklärung?" The Concept of Enlightenment in C18 Germany', *Journal of European Studies*, vol. XII (1982): 77–95.

13 For this paragraph see R. Darnton, *The Forbidden Best-Sellers of Pre-Revolutionary France* (London, 1996).

14 The most useful work on this interaction is H. M. Scott (ed.), *Enlightened Absolutism* (London, 1990).

15 Quoted in D. Stievermann, 'Politik und Konfession im 18. Jahrhundert', *Zeitschrift für historische Forschung*, 18 (1991): 198.

16 Voltaire, *Lettres philosophiques*, p. 51.

17 C. Mervaud, *Voltaire et Frédéric II: une dramaturgie des lumières* (Oxford, 1985), pp. 37, 545, 546. Mervaud has made a deep study of the background to *Anti-Machiavel*. P. Sonnino has edited it and translated it into English: *Refutation of Machiavelli's Prince: or, Anti-Machiavel* (Athens, OH, 1981). T. Schieder's *Friedrich der Grosse* (Frankfurt, 1983) is a fine biography.

18 Sonnino (ed.), *Anti-Machiavel*, pp. 34, 146.

19 M. Maestro, *Beccaria and the Origins of Penal Reform* (Philadelphia, 1973).

20 C. Besterman, *Voltaire* (London, 1969) gives a lively account of the relationship.

21 See Blanning's essay in Scott (ed.), *Enlightened Absolutism*; E. Spranger, *Der Philosoph von Sanssouci* (Berlin, 1942).

22 A. Lortholary, *Le mirage russe en France au XVIIIe siècle* (Paris, 1951); M. L. Perkins, 'Six French *philosophes* on Human Rights, International Rivalry, and War: Their Message Today', *Studies on Voltaire and the Eighteenth Century*, 260 (Oxford, 1989): 1–158.

23 The two pieces written against Holbach can be found in Frédéric II, *Oeuvres philosophiques* (Tours, 1985).

24 The classic biography of Catherine is by I. de Madariaga (London, 1981). Madariaga's collected essays, *Politics and Culture in Eighteenth-century Russia* (London, 1998) include 'Catherine II and Enlightened Absolutism' and 'Catherine II and the *Philosophes*'. A recent short life is S. M. Dixon, *Catherine the Great* (London, 2001).

25 I have cited Paul Dukes's translation and edition of the *Nakaz* which make up vol. II of his *Russia under Catherine the Great* (2 vols, Newtonville, 1977–78).

26 See D. Beales, *Joseph II. I: In the Shadow of Maria Theresa, 1741–80* (Cambridge, 1987) and Chapter 12, 'Joseph II and Josephism'.

27 Lortholary, *Le mirage russe*, delights in documenting these points.

28 D. G. Levy, *The Ideas and Careers of Simon-Nicolas-Henri Linguet* (London, 1980), ch. 6; Chapter 4, 'Mozart and the Habsburgs'.

29 Printed in A. Wolf (ed.), *Leopold II. und Marie Christine. Ihr Briefwechsel (1781–1792)* (Vienna, 1867), pp. 84–7 (25 Jan. 1790). A. Wandruszka, *Leopold II* (2 vols, Vienna, 1963–65) is the standard biography.

30 Darnton, *Forbidden Best-Sellers*, p. 330.

31 See e.g. H. M. Scott, 'The Rise of the First Minister in Eighteenth-century Europe' in T. C. W. Blanning and D. Cannadine (eds), *History and Biography* (Cambridge, 1966), pp. 21–52; K. Maxwell, *Pombal: Paradox of the Enlightenment* (Cambridge, 1995).

32 The major relevant discussions are: M. Bazzoli, *Il pensiero politico*

dell'assolutismo illuminato (Florence, 1986); K. O. Freiherr von Aretin (ed.), *Der Aufgeklärte Absolutismus* (Cologne, 1974); Scott (ed.), *Enlightened Absolutism*; H. Reinalter and H. Klueting (eds), *Der aufgeklärte Absolutismus im europäischen Vergleich* (Vienna, 2002); L. Krieger, *An Essay on the Theory of Enlightened Despotism* (London, 1975); F. Bluche, 'Sémantique du despotisme éclairé', *Revue historique du droit français et étranger*, 4th series, 56 (1978): 79–87.

33 The best introduction to the Enlightenment is D. Outram, *The Enlightenment* (Cambridge, 1995). The most notable classic studies, widely differing in approach, are E. Cassirer, *The Philosophy of the Enlightenment* (Boston, 1951) and P. Gay, *The Enlightenment: An Interpretation* (2 vols, London, 1967–70).

34 H. Reiss (ed.), *Kant's Political Writings* (Cambridge, 1971), pp. 58–9. See also Nisbet's article cited in n.12 above.

35 As well as the works listed in n.33, R. Koebner, 'Despot and Despotism: Vicissitudes of a Political Term', *Journal of the Warburg and Courtauld Institutes*, XIV (1951): 275–302.

36 Sonnino (ed.), *Anti-Machiavel*, pp. 34–5.

37 Ibid., pp. 32–3.

38 Ibid., p. 73 (retranslated).

39 Ibid., p. 47.

40 Dukes (ed.), *Russia under Catherine the Great*, vol. II, pp. 43–4.

41 Beales, *Joseph II*, vol. I, pp. 259, 271.

42 Keohane, *Philosophy and the State*, pp. 362–76, quotes from pp. 363n., 370.

43 See Chapter 6, 'Joseph II's *Rêveries*', esp. p. 170.

44 C. Beccaria, *An Essay on Crimes and Punishments* (London, 1804), quotations from pp. 16, 111–12.

45 The best account of the Physiocrats remains G. Weulersse, *Le mouvement physiocratique en France* (2 vols, Paris, 1910).

46 Bluche, *Revue Historique* (1978), p. 86.

47 Diderot, *Mémoires pour Catherine II*, ed. P. Vernière (Paris, 1966): 117–18.

48 Raynal, English translation (1784) of 1781 edition, vol. VIII, p. 32. On the role of Diderot in this work see Y. Benot, *Diderot, de l'athéisme à l'anticolonialisme* (Paris, 1981).

49 G. Gorani, *Il vero dispotismo* (2 vols, 'Londra', 1770), vol. I, pp. 6–7; vol. II, p. 97.

50 Quoted in C. Capra, 'Alle origini del moderatismo e del giacobinismo in Lombardia: Pietro Verri e Pietro Custodi', *Studi storici* (1989): 876–7.

51 Quoted in Lortholary, *Le mirage russe*, p. 138.

52 Quoted in J. Lukowski, *The Partitions of Poland* (London, 1999), p. 126.

53 See for the material in this paragraph Chapter 11, 'Was Joseph II an Enlightened Despot?'.

54 I am very grateful to Dr Dorothea Link for communicating to me this entry.

55 See his *Fragment on Government* (1776).

56 Roscher's analysis was originally propounded under the title 'Umrisse zur Naturlehre der drei Staatsformen' in *Allgemeine Zeitschrift für Geschichte*, VII (1847): 79–88, 322–65, 436–73; vol. IX (1848), pp. 285–326, 381–413. It was restated in his *Geschichte der National-Oekonomik in Deutschland* (Munich, 1874).

CHAPTER 3

Christians and '*Philosophes*': The Case of the Austrian Enlightenment

How influential were the great men of the French Enlightenment, the *philosophes*, outside France? Or, how typical were they of the Enlightenment as a whole? These questions have been much discussed, not least by Owen Chadwick.[1] This essay is a small contribution to the debate, from what I think is a fresh standpoint: a consideration of the concept *philosophe*, as understood by the leaders of the French Enlightenment, in relation to the attitudes of some prominent figures associated with the Austrian Enlightenment. Although this standpoint appears so restricted, I think that what is visible from it has wider significance.

I

The concept *philosophe* needs some elucidation. It has been well studied – in English, for example, by Commager, Dieckmann, Lough, Shackleton, Wade, White and Wilson.[2] But for my purposes their work must be brought together and given a particular emphasis.

Unlike the term Enlightenment,[3] the word *philosophe*, used roughly as modern scholars use it, was current in the eighteenth century itself. The great men of the French Enlightenment – or most of them, most of the time – took pride in calling themselves, individually and collectively, *philosophes*. They can with plausibility be described as a party under that name, at least from the early 1750s. Even before that, but especially from the late 1750s, they were attacked as such, notably by their former comrade, Rousseau, and in Palissot's play of 1760, *Les Philosophes*.

One of Palissot's shafts, clearly well aimed, was that they sought to monopolise the concept *philosophe*. In so doing they were try-ing to eradicate its original and accepted meanings. Before the late seventeenth century, *philosophe* had two usual senses, both of them equally applicable to the word 'philosopher' in English and to the corresponding words in other languages: first, the man who seeks wisdom through abstract thought and by reasoning from first principles, perhaps erecting an intellectual system supposed to explain the universe in all its aspects – the metaphysician; secondly, the thinker who withdraws from ordinary affairs, probably in a morose temper, to contemplate with detachment the follies of his fellow men and to suffer with resignation the outrages of fortune – loosely, the Stoic. In 1694 a third meaning was acknowledged by the *Dictionnaire de l'Académie française*: 'a man who, through waywardness of mind, puts himself above the ordinary duties and obligations of civil and Christian life. It is a man who denies himself nothing, who does not restrain himself in any way, and who leads the life of a philosopher.'[4] This definition, of course, pejoratively recognised the use of the word by *esprits forts* like Bayle in anti-Catholic if not anti-Christian connotations. His *Commentaire philosophique* dates from 1686. From this third sense stems the usage of the great *philosophes* themselves. It never became fully established in any language other than French.

The *Encyclopédie* contains the classic statement of the concept *philosophe* in the article under that title in volume XII, published in 1765. This is a late appearance for a document so fundamental to the French Enlightenment. However, the article is in fact Diderot's version – much shortened but essentially faithful – of an essay first printed in a collection called *Nouvelles libertés de penser*, published in 1743. This compilation was the work of radicals and free-thinkers; its component pieces had previously circulated in manuscript; and its publication 'inaugurated ... a period of intense intellectual activity'.[5] Voltaire wrote of the original essay *Le Philosophe* when he in his turn republished it in 1773: it 'has been known for a long time and has been kept to hand by all inquiring persons; it dates from the year 1730'. Its author was probably Dumarsais.[6] So the article in the *Encyclopédie* has a very good claim to have embodied the view of the *philosophe* held by most writers of the French Enlightenment over a period of half a century.

It explicitly rejects both the traditional meanings of *philosophe*. The original essay included a lengthy critique of universalist systems of thought. Although Diderot cut this section severely, he left the essential points: the *philosophe*, though a rationalist, relies on proved observed facts and does not expect to be able to explain everything.

Rather more survives in the *Encyclopédie* article of the critique of Stoicism. For example,

> Our *philosophe* does not imagine that he is in exile in this world; he does not suppose himself to be in enemy country ... He seeks pleasure from the company of others ... he is an *honnête homme* who desires to please and to make himself useful ... it is easy to grasp how far removed the unfeeling sage of the Stoics is from the perfection of our *philosophe*: such a *philosophe* is a man, and their sage was only a phantom. They blushed for humanity, and he glories in it.[7]

By very strong implication, the *philosophe* is represented as anti-Christian. For instance, in Diderot's version: 'Reason is in respect to the *philosophe* what Grace is in respect to the Christian ... Civil society is, so to speak, a divinity on earth for [the *philosophe*]; he worships it.'[8] It seems plain that this rejection of Christianity is integrally related to the rejection both of *esprit de système* and of Stoicism. Roman Catholic theology had come to terms with Cartesianism, the reigning metaphysical system; and the resulting hybrid now dominated the teaching of philosophy in French universities.[9] Similarly, the neo-Stoicism of the late sixteenth and early seventeenth centuries, especially assocated with the writings of Lipsius, had been easily reconciled with Catholicism. The Jesuits themselves became the chief promoters of 'Christian Stoicism', and one of them published in 1637 a volume entitled *Seneca Christianus*.[10] The *philosophe* naturally could not countenance any tendency of thought that subserved *l'infâme*.

However, as the article illustrates, his attitude to *esprit de système* differed from his attitude to Stoicism. Whereas he totally condemned the former he applauded aspects of Stoic thought – or Stoicism understood in a certain sense. Only five historical figures are mentioned in the article, four of them Roman, of whom two were Stoics. Cato the Younger receives praise for having always acted in a manner true to his character, and Marcus Aurelius is quoted with approval for having remarked: 'How happy peoples will be when kings are philosophers, or philosophers kings.'[11] This, of course, must rank as a disingenuous quotation, first since it originally derives from the arch-metaphysician, Plato, and secondly since Marcus Aurelius hardly meant by 'philosopher' what Diderot and his friends understood by *philosophe*. But the citation from Marcus Aurelius is heavy with significance. While the most Christian, servile and respectable authors admired him, and no exception could possibly be taken by minister or censor to the glorification of his name, yet for the *philosophes* he counted as one of themselves, an enemy of superstition and a persecutor of Christianity. This was the guise under which they praised him, and the same applied to Stoicism as a whole. As Peter Gay has argued, the *philosophes* were influenced by Stoicism – but it was by Stoicism conceived as pagan and anti-Christian. Moreover, for their purposes it had also to be separated from its connotation of morose detachment. The true Stoic, the Stoic who was to be admired, played his part in society and politics, trying to give practical effect to his philosophy – like, they claimed, Marcus Aurelius.[12]

Voltaire's article *Philosophe* in the second edition of his *Dictionnaire philosophique* (1765) reinforces the argument. Unlike the article in the *Encyclopédie*, it contains no carefully stated definition. But it does offer a wider variety of examples of *philosophes*, who are chiefly commended for the supposed purity of their morals. Those who receive the greatest praise are Confucius; Bayle and Fontenelle; and, bracketed together, Epictetus, Marcus Aurelius and Julian. Further, one of the less orthodox seventeenth-century neo-Stoics, Charron, qualified for favourable reference on the ground that his life had been threatened by pious persecutors. In addition, 'Julian the *philosophe*' was honoured with a special article in which his hostility to Christianity was excused.[13]

So it formed an essential part of the programme of the *philosophes* to impose their new meaning on the word in place of older meanings. In particular, Stoicism had to be condemned if it was understood as unsocial and quietist or if it was treated as compatible with Christianity, and especially with Roman Catholicism.

II

In trying to assess the influence of the *philosophes* outside France, we can use as an index – though only one index among many – the way in which the concept *philosophe* was employed and Stoicism was regarded. White claimed that the new meaning of *philosophe* had won the day by the middle of the eighteenth century; and Oestreich, the author of notable studies of neo-Stoicism, asserted that by the same period the influence of Lipsius in Germany was 'played out'.[14] These propositions can be tested when studying the attitudes of prominent figures associated with the Austrian Enlightenment.

It is natural to begin with the reign of Maria Theresa (1740–80) and with the royal family, taking first Francis Stephen, her husband, emperor from 1745 to his death in 1765. Born and brought up in Lorraine, he married Maria Theresa in 1736. It was from this event that the prince de Ligne, an exemplar of Enlightened French culture and one of the few men who had standing both with the *philosophes* and at the Court of Vienna, dated the adoption there of French as 'the common language, which greatly contributed to the spread of urbanity'.[15] Ligne exaggerated, of course. French had been much used at Court before the marriage or accession of Maria Theresa. Further, Francis Stephen was an imperfect advertisement for French culture: he shocked the more sophisticated by his tolerance of German comedies; and his spelling in French embarrassed even his wife.[16] But he brought a number of French artists and *savants* to Vienna; and the pre-eminence of the French language there seems to date from the early years of Maria Theresa's reign.[17]

Students of the early Radical Enlightenment seize on Francis Stephen as proof of its influence in bigoted, benighted Austria, since he was initiated as a Freemason by Walpole at Houghton in 1731 and is believed to have practised the craft privately in Vienna even after it had been banned there by his wife.[18] But his surviving writings give no encouragement to such students. He left two sets of instructions for his children, of 1752 and 1765, which urged on them sobriety, modesty and economy, together with regular prayer, communion, confession and self-examination. He also composed two tracts, whose dates are unknown, entitled 'The Hermit in the World' and 'Christian Reflections and Short Prayers'. The burden of these pieces is that the ruler, though enveloped in business, pomp and flattery, must keep his soul secret and entire for the service of God and in preparation for death. They seem to depend on writers of Jansenist tendency like Pascal, Fénelon and Muratori – and on Cicero and Marcus Aurelius. It is evident that the Stoic element is completely assimilated to Catholic Christianity and retains its connotation of withdrawal from the world. If the emperor, with his French background and Masonic affiliations, was aware of the attitudes associated with the new meaning of *philosophe*, he rejected them completely.[19]

During the 1750s he and his wife superintended, with much assistance from ministers and other advisers, an elaborate programme of education designed to fit their heir, the future Joseph II, for the throne. He was two years of age when *Nouvelles libertés de penser* was published, seven when *De l'esprit des lois* came out, and ten when the first volumes of the *Encyclopédie* appeared. But the French Enlightenment had little part in his studies: the only major work by a *philosophe* to figure in them was the *Esprit des lois*, and that very selectively. Further, the Stoics, unless Cicero is counted among them, scarcely appear. On the other hand, Pufendorf dominated Joseph's education in political theory, and the Natural Law school that Pufendorf belonged to owed much to the Stoics.[20] But it is the prince's education in philosophy that is most interesting here. This was entrusted to a Jesuit, Father Frantz. The 'little treatise' he wrote in Latin for his pupil avoided 'the disputations of the schools' and 'all the subtleties that are more ingenious than useful, like categories, universals ...' – the formula comes from the Jansenist popularisation of Descartes, *L'art de penser*. In other words, it claimed to reject, in the Renaissance tradition, Aristotelianism and Scholasticism. But it dealt with logic, deductive reasoning and metaphysics. *Esprit de système* imbued it, and its system was Descartes's, Christianised or Catholicised. Such few later writers as are mentioned are almost all criticised, like Leibniz. In so far as it comes to grips with sceptics, it is with Spinoza, who had died as long ago as 1677.[21] There is no sign of any awareness of the French *philosophes* whether as individuals or as a class of philosophers.

The Jesuits retained their monopoly of theological teaching at the University of Vienna until 1759. It was only in 1735 that they had been instructed to teach Cartesian metaphysics; they had previously been identified with Scholasticism. But Father Frantz was one of their most progressive scholars, concerned not only with the reform of the university curriculum but also with mitigating the rigours of the censorship. Both these processes advanced during the 1750s under the aegis of Gerard van Swieten, the empress's physician. One of his most notable successes was to secure the admission into the Monarchy of the *Esprit des lois*.[22] So Joseph's education took place during a decade of reform. But it was painfully slow reform and, by European standards, from a remote starting-point. To Prince Albert of Saxony, brought up as a Catholic but in a Protestant state, Joseph's education in logic and metaphysics was indistinguishable from 'peripatetic philosophy'.[23]

In 1760 Joseph married Isabella of Parma, whose intelligence and personality were to make a profound impression on him and on the whole Court during her three remaining years of life. Her mother was a French princess, Louis XV's daughter, and their personal ties were with France rather than with Spain, where Isabella had been born. In the late 1750s the duchy of Parma became heavily dependent on France. In 1758 Condillac was summoned from Paris to tutor the heir to the throne; and in the next year its ruler appointed a prime minister of French extraction and reformist views, Du Tillot.[24] Isabella had received an unusually sophisticated education: she not only played the violin well and patronised Gluck's new brand of opera; she also read such books as *La Nouvelle Héloïse*, and herself wrote with some distinction. But her temperament was 'sombre', she yearned for an early death, and her remarkable writings are suffused with religious melancholy. After she died, her *Christian Meditations* were published by Maria Theresa.[25]

One of Isabella's essays was entitled 'The True Philosopher'. 'I have developed the habit', she wrote, 'of considering what affects me personally without any emotion.' But she finds that she does not always succeed. Where her friendships are concerned, she cannot remain indifferent. She – and, she believes, all other self-styled 'philosophers' – are 'philosophers *manqués*'. Nevertheless, she is emphatic that 'The principles that a philosopher sets up for himself … can be summed up as follows: indifference to all the chances of life … and absolute disinterestedness, which makes [him] love what is good by reference only to good itself.'[26] Her idea of a philosopher corresponds exactly to the Stoicism rejected by the *Encyclopédie*.

However, she also wrote a treatise called 'On Fashionable Philosophy'. Unfortunately, only its table of contents seems to survive. From this it appears that she knew a good deal about some other brand of philosophy, presumably that associated with the French *philosophes*, in particular Condillac, but that she rejected it almost wholly:

1 The Principles are varied
2 The Principles are extreme
3 The Principles are false
4 The Principles are dangerous
5 The Attitudes are not consistent
6 The Attitudes are culpable
7 There is, however, some good in them
8 This is what leads them astray
9 This is what gives them their reputation
10 What use ought to be made both of the good and the bad that they contain.[27]

Maria Theresa herself considered French the appropriate language for her family correspondence, promoted the alliance of 1756 with France and employed a number of officials who were influenced by the French Enlightenment. In the early 1750s Voltaire sent her copies of his historical works and in 1752 received from her for the *Siècle de Louis XIV* a watch and a snuff-box. The Diplomatic Revolution no doubt accounts for Voltaire's two uncharacteristic effusions of 1756, a contribution to the *Festschrift* compiled to celebrate the opening of the new Aula of the University of Vienna, and the following 'quatrain' commemorating the empress's visit to Carnuntum:

> Marc-Aurèle autrefois des princes le modèle
> Sur le devoir des Roys écrivoit en ces lieux;
> Et Marie Thérèse fait à nos yeux
> Tout ce qu'écrivoit Marc-Aurèle[28]

Voltaire can hardly have supposed that Maria Theresa resembled his vision of Marcus Aurelius, and this verse is clearly inconsistent with his usual attitude. Equally, Maria Theresa's graciousness towards him at this period was unnatural. It is notorious that she frequently denounced *philosophie* and the *philosophes*, and particularly dreaded the prospect of Joseph's visiting Voltaire during the journey to France planned for 1774 and eventually undertaken in 1777.

The precise terms of her denunciations bear examination. Her first onslaught on *philosophie*, like most of them, refers to Joseph. On 17 November 1768 she wrote about her younger son, Ferdinand:

> He will not have Leopold's great industry, but more charm, and will be fonder of pleasures, if the emperor doesn't turn him, as he puts it, into a philospher. I'm not worried on this score, since I see no attractions in this so-called philosophy, which consists of avoiding close ties and of enjoying nothing, whether theatre, hunting, cards, dancing or conversation.[29]

In May–July 1772 she and Ferdinand exchanged letters about philosophy. She declared:

> All these titles so fashionable at the moment hero, *savant, philosophe,* are simply the inventions of *amour-propre* to cover up weaknesses. Those who are so called do not deserve it; they just want to cut some sort of figure.

Again,

It is better to feel too much than too little. Honest men can be attracted by sentiment alone, but not by philosophy, which is so fashionable at present, and which is only refined *amour-propre* and harshness
towards others. Don't let yourself be carried away … If we accept
worldly things as Christian philosophers, we feel the same in all situa-
tions, in adversity as in prosperity.

And finally she compliments him on quoting the adage 'neither
philosophy nor reason stands when the heart speaks'.[30]

In 1774 she corresponded with her ambassador in Paris, the comte
de Mercy-Argenteau, about Joseph's projected visit to France and
especially his 'idea of returning through Switzerland to see Voltaire,
Tissot, Haller and all these extremists'. Mercy replied:

I think [the project] will not materialise; first because it would take
H.M. too much out of his way, secondly because there will be objections to be made against Voltaire which might dispel the desire to
make his acquaintance. Tissot is a doctor, Haller a poet. Further, I
shall make a point of showing H.M. here a sample from which he will
be able to judge the worth of these modern *savants* and *philosophes*
who, in their private lives, their works and their detestable principles,
set a pattern calculated to overturn society and introduce trouble and
disorder.

The empress answered: 'It is true that even here people can't stop
praising these wretches as great men and superior geniuses, but I
hope you'll succeed in bringing home to the emperor all that is base,
inconsistent and contemptible in their characters and behaviour.'[31]

Later in the same year, she sent her youngest son, Maximilian, a
similar diatribe:

If I saw these self-styled *savants*, these *philosophes*, achieving more
success in their enterprises and more happiness in their private lives, I
should be able to charge myself with bias, pride, prejudices, obstinacy
for not following them. But … no one is weaker, more easily discour-
aged than these *esprits forts*, no one more cringing, more frantic at the
least slight. They are bad fathers, sons, husbands, ministers, generals,
citizens. Why? They lack the essential foundation. All their *philosophie*,
all their maxims derive simply from their *amour-propre*.[32]

These statements of 1774 show that Maria Theresa thought she
knew what the French *philosophes* stood for, and purveyed a crude

critique of their position as she understood it. But she evidently had not grasped the implications of the new meaning of *philosophe*; and her indiscriminate bracketing of Voltaire with Haller and Tissot reveals her ignorance of their work. Her earlier attacks on 'philosophy' seem directed against the sort of unfeeling and misanthropic Stoicism that the *Encyclopédie* itself denounced. But in her mind the chief exemplar of this outlook must surely have been Frederick the Great – together with Joseph II, in so far as he was modelling himself on her great enemy.

It is 'Christian philosophers' she applauds. The use of the phrase in her letter to Ferdinand can be matched in several others. When Joseph's only daughter died in 1770, she wrote: 'He feels this loss very deeply, but as a Christian philosopher.' She spoke in 1772 of Gerard van Swieten dying 'as a philosopher the death of a saint, a great consolation for me'. Seven years later she said her son Maximilian bore his painful illness 'as a philosopher, but Christian'. Most tellingly, when in April 1778 she was praising Joseph for his letters to Frederick about the Bavarian crisis, she announced: 'I love my Cato, my Christian philosopher.'[33] Her ideal remained the neo-Stoic, Catholicised.

III

While Maria Theresa lived, she ensured that the Monarchy was insulated from many aspects of French cultural influence. Contemporary travellers found her regime bigoted, superstitious and intolerant. They were astonished to have their books impounded at the frontier.[34] Even ambassadors had difficulty in bringing in their libraries.[35] The Monarchy's index of prohibited books was longer than the pope's.[36] Wraxall, who spent some months in Vienna in 1778–79, made the severest judgement. He was 'inclined to believe, that fewer persons of extensive reading and information are found [here], proportion observed, than in any of the German Courts' – 'The Austrian youth of rank or condition are in general insupportable … distinguished only by pride, ignorance and illiberality.' He met no learned women at all. 'Natural philosophy has scarcely made greater progress in Vienna, than sound reason and real religion.' He estimated that 3,000 persons were engaged in seeking the philosopher's stone.[37]

Yet, according to one notable scholar, Hans Wagner, the latter part of Maria Theresa's reign marked 'the highpoint of French cultural influence in Austria'.[38] The judgement can be sustained, if at all, only by placing great emphasis on the attitudes of a small circle of wealthy nobles and officials. However, it must be acknowledged that among this group was to be found a remarkable awareness of the latest developments in the French Enlightenment and an extraordinary freedom in discussing them. The empress, while enjoining bigotry on the vast majority of her subjects, would permit a few trusted servants to defy it and would even, within strict limits, listen to advice founded on progressive views.

A special place must be accorded to count (from 1763 prince) Kaunitz, who after a spell as Austrian ambassador in Paris returned to Vienna to direct the Monarchy's foreign policy in 1753, and continued to do so for the next forty or so years. It was not long before he became a force in internal polices too, especially from the foundation of the Staatsrat in 1760.[39] He was known for his admiration of France both as a potential ally and for its culture. He was in touch with Voltaire.[40] From the mid-1760s he became a ruthless promoter of ecclesiastical reforms which he justified by reference to many sources, including the *Encyclopédie*.[41] But in fact he never accepted the *philosophes'* approach to traditional philosophy. Professor Klingenstein, who has studied his early life and work, writes of him:

> Perhaps there was no Enlightened statesman in whom the mathemat-
> ical–deductive method in political thought was so strongly rooted
> as in [Kaunitz]. The statement of political premises *more geometrico*,
> the deductions following logically from them about the possible
> decisions and actions available to the various European states within
> the European state-system, the related bases for making predictions
> about future trends and events – the deployment of this method gave
> Kaunitz that superiority and self-assurance among Maria Theresa's
> ministers which ... brought [her] under his spell.

The thinker to whom he owed most was not Descartes, but nor was it any *philosophe*; it was Wolff, in whose method he had been schooled at Leipzig.[42] He drew upon the work of the great men of the French Enlightenment, but within an alien metaphysical framework. Moreover, contrary to what has often been claimed, he was not a Freemason, and he was some sort of Catholic.[43]

One especially valuable source enables us to observe the French Enlightenment percolating into aristocratic and bureaucratic circles in Vienna after 1761. Count Karl von Zinzendorf arrived there in February of that year prospecting for a career in government service.

Every day he recorded in his diary what he had read and talked about and with whom. He immediately gained an *entrée* into the highest social circles because his brother was already an established official. As early as 16 March 1761 he was discussing Voltaire and the *Encyclopédie* at Princess Esterházy's. In January 1762 he came across in his reading the problem of defining 'philosopher' – though not in a recent work: '[Fontenelle's] *Dialogue between Anacreon and Aristotle* [1683] pleased me very much, when Anacreon says that the name "Philosopher" is nowadays given only to astronomers and physicists, while the Philosopher ought to think only of himself; but since no one would want to be a Philosopher on this condition, people had banished Philosophy as far as possible from themselves.'

In 1763 we find him at the French ambassador's talking about Rousseau and Helvétius, and reading some Hume and the *Contrat social*.[44] In the following year, having obtained a permanent post in the administration, he travelled to Switzerland at government expense and met both Rousseau and Voltaire. He had been recommended to the latter as travelling *en philosophe*.[45] Among his numerous later references to advanced writings two may be singled out. Discussing *L'esprit de l'Encyclopédie* enlivened one of his flirtations in 1771; and at almost the same time he was much impressed by Voltaire's *Questions sur l'Encyclopédie*, the enlarged version of the *Dictionnaire philosophique*.[46]

It is tempting to present this remarkable record as evidence for the unadulterated influence of the *philosophes* in the Vienna of Maria Theresa. But the context makes this impossible, even in so far as Zinzendorf's own thinking is concerned. He arrived in Austria a devout Pietist. But his brother, Kaunitz and the empress herself made it clear that if he wished for a prosperous career in the bureaucracy he must become a Roman Catholic. The issue came to a head in the early months of 1764. On 10 January he wrote that he would convert only in 'ultimate despair', and two days later he thought of fleeing the country. On 1 February he prepared a letter of resignation from his temporary post, heard Count Philipp Sinzendorff and the French ambassador vying with each other in satirising the Christian religion, but – on the recommendation of this same Count Philipp – began reading Bossuet. He found 'both good and bad' in Voltaire on toleration.[47] On 1 March he decided that one of his great misfortunes was never to have taken a course in philosophy, which meant that he lacked 'the philosophical and geometric spirit'. He had been put off the subject, presumably in his Pietist youth, as effacing 'from the heart those tender feelings which the great truths of the Christian religion have implanted there'. He finally made his general confession to Müller, the Jansenist abbot of St Dorothea, on 13 March, and his confession of faith the next day – but on the 15th did not dare acknowledge himself a Catholic before Kaunitz's assembly. On the 23rd he read Isabella's *Christian Meditations*, where he found 'traces of the purest and soundest piety'. He later took vows of celibacy as a member of the Teutonic Order, although throughout his long life he hankered after the religion of his youth.[48]

Hence it is no wonder that, after his visit to Voltaire, he recorded that he could not trust everything the great man had said. And what he especially admired in the *Questions sur l'Encyclopédie* were Voltaire's attack on despotism *and* his defence of the existence of God.[49] It is clear that Zinzendorf saw his deep and broad interest in French Enlightened writing as compatible with strong religious feelings. He must have grasped the implications of the concept *philosophe*, yet rejected them.

The cosmopolitan prince de Ligne – great landowner in Belgium, prince of the Holy Roman Empire, grandee of Spain, etc., etc. – serving in the army of Maria Theresa, visited Voltaire in 1763. They corresponded regularly, and in 1772 the *philosophe* wrote to the prince: 'I prophesy that you will make wholesome *philosophie* known to minds still somewhat removed from it.' This has been assumed to mean that Voltaire expected Ligne to spread the gospel to the *philosophes* in Vienna.[50]

Ligne cut a figure at the Court of Vienna for sixty years, was a friend and general of Joseph II, and won a reputation all over Europe for intelligence, Enlightenment and self-indulgence. It has seemed impossible to associate this master of persiflage with serious, still less religious, opinions.[51] But of all my examples, he showed the clearest understanding of the issues raised by the new usage of *philosophe*. He composed – when seems unfortunately to be unknown – a dialogue between an *esprit fort* and a Capuchin. Both men pride themselves on their philosophy. For the Capuchin it is the crown of his religious development, and is both Stoic and metaphysical. He declares: 'I involve myself in nothing, because I am a philosopher.' He denies to the *esprit fort* the right to call himself a philosopher at all. But the *esprit fort* responds: 'I involve myself in everything, because I am a *philosophe*. I'm always writing; I study everything deeply; I remove from Divinity its thunderbolts, from kings their sceptres, from Europe its Balance of Power, and from the dead their immortality.'[52]

Ligne's correspondence with Voltaire survives only in part, but what remains has considerable interest for the views of both men. Each flatters the other archly and wittily. In particular, Ligne often expresses his indebtedness to Voltaire's *philosophie*.[53] A letter of 10 November 1768 thanks the old man for sending by Gottfried van Swieten, who has just visited him *en philosophe*, 'all your new *gaietés philosophiques* – and thoroughly Christian of course. May the God of Abraham, if you like, or of the Rock, or of Socrates always treat you as favourably as you have treated us.' In his reply of 3 December Voltaire is triumphant over the rapid decay of superstition.[54]

It is never easy to determine what either writer really means. But behind the calculated flippancy some letters of 1772 seem to embody a serious clash of opinions. Ligne writes that he has been demonstrating to his friends that Voltaire has 'never denied the truths of religion', ranks indeed as a Father of the Church, 'only rather more amusing than your comrades'. 'The declamations of Diderot and the arid conversation of D'Alembert, that cold if perhaps able geometer, almost induce in me the desire to become a Capuchin.' Voltaire, he goes on, has a more salutary religious influence. He has 'blasted the seven or eight atheists of the great Frederick'. Ligne then imagines many Classical writers glorying in the role of bishops, praises the Roman Catholic Church for its patronage of the arts, denounces Jansenists, suggests that Voltaire quite likes Jesuits and enlists him to purify the Church: 'I should like good *curés*, Christian magistrates, polite and politic, speaking only from the pulpit (without wishing to set up teachers of transfiguration, transubstantiation etc.) and always preaching morality and good sense on duty to family and to society and on the practice of religion. Unbelievers would have to be ridiculed.'

Voltaire's reply contains his prophecy, already quoted, that Ligne 'will make wholesome *philosophie* known to minds still somewhat removed from it'. But in context the remark seems less than enthusiastic:

> Since, then, you make me realise I'm a prophet, I predict for you that you will continue to be what you already are, one of the most amiable and one of the most respectable men in Europe. I predict that you will introduce taste and style to a nation which up to now has perhaps supposed that its good qualities ought to be a substitute for charms.

I predict for you that you will make wholesome *philosophie* known to minds still somewhat removed from it, and that you will be happy in cultivating it.[55]

It looks as though Ligne has gone rather too far in associating Voltaire with the defence of established religion. Certainly, what the prince has been advocating does not sound much like the *philosophe*'s usual brand of 'wholesome *philosophie*'.

So even these three luminaries of the Austrian Enlightenment, Kaunitz, Zinzendorf and Ligne, wore their *philosophie* with a difference. Kaunitz revelled in traditional, deductive philosophy; Zinzendorf remained at heart a Pietist; and Ligne understood, and felt the force of, Catholic neo-Stoicism.

IV

With the accession of Joseph II as sole ruler of the Monarchy at the end of 1780, the position was transformed. One of his advisers, Gebler, wrote exultantly to Nicolai in Berlin three years later:

For a man who thinks philosophically, no period is more remarkable than that which began in 1781. Such a rapid change in the general attitude – even among the common people, who put many obscurantist members of higher classes to shame – is, so far as I know, unexampled. The ... abolition of the religious brotherhoods, of most so-called devotions and of all monastic sermons has now given the final blow to all superstition ... But freedom of the press, and still more, *freedom of reading* (for, practically speaking, there is almost no book left that is not openly for sale) also contributes greatly.[56]

This was the time of the 'pamphlet flood' in Austria – or of a sudden 'thaw' after a long chill winter.[57] Vienna could now be represented as 'the *philosophes*' homeland'.[58]

It is impossible to deal here with the immense range of writings published during Joseph's sole reign, the decade 1780–90, though a study from the standpoint of this chapter would surely be revealing. But it is instructive to consider two individuals, each in his own way of striking significance: the emperor himself, and one of the humbler supporters of his reforms, I. A. Fessler.

The *philosophes* had claimed Joseph for themselves since the 1760s.

In 1769 Voltaire was assured that he was 'one of us'.[59] When the emperor visited Paris in 1777, Grimm's *Correspondance littéraire* declared: 'Only in this century has *philosophie* persuaded rulers to travel purely for instruction.' The same source recorded Joseph showing respect towards Buffon, attending a demonstration by Lavoisier, listening to D'Alembert and (and less attentively) to Marmontel and La Harpe, asking why Diderot and Raynal were not members of the French Academy, and visiting Tissot and Haller in Switzerland.[60] He met Turgot and studied his state papers.[61] Next year, Le Bret, a prominent populariser of Enlightenment in Germany, remarked 'how benignly the Philosopher on the Viennese throne smiles on the Muses'.[62] The traveller Riesbeck called him 'a philosopher in the true sense of the word' – whatever that meant.[63] In 1781 Joseph won further favourable publicity from the *philosophes* by sitting down to dinner at Spa with Grimm and Raynal.[64] On his death the following famous manifesto was ascribed to him, and accepted very widely as genuine: 'I have made Philosophy the legislator of my Empire.'[65]

Most elaborately, there appeared in 1774 a three-volume work by Lanjuinais entitled *Le Monarque accompli*, 'The Accomplished Monarch, or Prodigies of Benevolence, Knowledge and Wisdom which redound to the Credit ... of Joseph II'.[66] Voltaire docketed his copy of this astonishing production 'Roast Monarch'.[67] After it was banned in France as part of the battle between Turgot and his rivals in 1776, it became well known.[68] In it, Lanjuinais, referring occasionally to some fact about the emperor, and more frequently inventing some myth about him, painted the portrait of an ideal king. This paragon in the guise of Joseph is favourably compared to the most respectable Roman emperors such as Trajan and Marcus Aurelius, and to the most notable kings of France. He is wise, tolerant, humane, 'enlightened' and *philosophe* – *ad nauseam*. Towards the end of the third volume Lanjuinais embarks on a disquisition about philosophy. No one, he asserts, knows better than the emperor how *l'esprit philosophique* differs from *philosophie*. Philosophy is just one branch of knowledge, whereas *l'esprit philosophique* embraces all branches. The basis of *l'esprit philosophique* is 'enlightened metaphysics'. According to Lanjuinais, Joseph has reacted against 'modern peripatetics', finds Voltaire instructive but is very judicious in appraising his, Rousseau's and Montesquieu's works. Surprisingly, the emperor turns out also to be 'pious' and 'Christian', a prince who wants the clergy better educated, an enemy of *libertinage* and a man proof against the blandishments not only of

Greeks and Romans but also of 'contemporary unbelievers, modern blasphemers'.[69]

Lord Acton pronounced, in one of his maddening displays of fantastic erudition, that 'Joseph II borrowed his ideas from the *Monarque accompli'*.[70] But any resemblance between Lanjuinais's paragon and the living emperor, whether before or after the book was published, seems accidental. It is true that his knowledge of Voltaire passed muster with Frederick the Great;[71] that a close friend wrote of his weakness for the ideas of Holbach and Helvétius;[72] and that the French strategist, Guibert, having met him in 1773, claimed that the word *philosophie* was often in his mouth.[73] Moreover, Joseph was violently opposed to many of his mother's policies, and soon after he gained power embarked on the reform programme which Gebler partly described in his letter to Nicolai.

Yet Joseph ostentatiously drove past the gates of Voltaire's estate in 1777, and in 1789 refused to permit the circulation within the Monarchy of a German translation of his works on the ground that 'in this tawdry dress, as always in a translation, the wit is lost, and the bald result becomes all the more harmful to religion and morals'.[74] Unlike Frederick II and Catherine II, he carried on no correspondence with *philosophes*. Writers as a breed excited his scorn.[75] He explicitly denied the influence on him of theoretical approaches. He wrote in 1765: 'I have learned nothing more firmly than to fear intelligence and all its subtleties. I recognise no argument which comes from the ancient Greeks or the modern French.'[76] Zinzendorf thought him 'very well versed in the maxims that are at present being applied [by the government], and very ignorant of any kind of principles'.[77] Although both these remarks referred specifically to financial affairs, they have wider relevance.

As for Guibert's statement that the word *philosophie* was always in Joseph's mouth, if it relates to the new meaning of *philosophie*, it is not borne out by the emperor's surviving writings. He never said he had made philosophy the legislator of his empire – or anything like it.[78] He did employ the word quite often, but in senses that can loosely be called Stoic. 'One must be content', he wrote, 'with the smallest of blessings, that is what we learn from Philosophy, and unfortunately from experience as well.'[79] This, like several other instances, occurs in a discussion of the limitations of women – in one of which he says his 'system ... is close to Epicurus'.[80] But, even when writing to Mercy about his projected visit to France, with the *philosophes* in his mind, he called them *savants* and spoke of himself as being 'pretty philosophical about the chapter of accidents'.[81] He refers at least once to an *encyclopédiste*, but calls Voltaire 'the self-styled *philosophe*'.[82] This is his longest passage of self-conscious philosophy:

The idea of being able to do good and render one's subjects happy is undoubtedly the finest and the only attractive aspect of power, as it is the most powerful spur for any feeling and honest man. But when one knows at the same time that every false step is counter-productive, that evil is so easily and quickly done, and good is of its very nature so difficult and slow and cannot (except slowly) impress itself solidly on a vast state – then this comforting illusion is much weakened, and there rests only the satisfaction that one has inside oneself, which makes one uniquely contented through knowing oneself in good company when one is alone and through seeking, without the least regard to any personal consideration, to do only what the general good of the State and the great number requires.

It is rarely possible to look after the happiness of individuals without spoiling the whole, and it is apparent that under good laws and a good system, founded and regulated in accordance with the spirit and character of the nation as well as the geographical position of the State, each citizen ought to find a way of being happy if he has intelligence and is willing to take the trouble – the sovereign being the upholder of the laws and the shield protecting them against any violence, administering the money entrusted to him by his subjects simply and solely for this purpose.

If there is too much philosophy in all that, if I have gone too far in laying aside the royal mantle, the crown and the sceptre, and shown the sovereign *déshabillé* and in front of his *valet de chambre*, please forgive me for having always held the principles of going back to the primitive source of everything and of trying to see every person and thing in its natural state, plain and unadorned. I don't on that account feel more unhappy. No, every individual, I say to myself, is created to occupy a position in the world for a certain span of years. Well, I am one of those marionettes that Providence, without my being able to choose, ask or seek it, has been pleased to put in the place I occupy so that I can complete my term. She has given me only the intelligence and abilities that she intended, she will offer me only such opportunities and conditions as she pleases for being or appearing to be of some consequence; and when she has had enough, the curtain will fall and the farce will be over for me, as for all those who have preceded me.[83]

This is certainly not *philosophes' philosophie*, but it breathes the spirit of Stoicism.

However, it is not specifically Christian, still less Catholic. In this respect it gives a misleading impression of Joseph's attitude. When he was disputing with his mother about her treatment of Moravian Protestants, he said both that he favoured 'complete freedom of worship' and that he would 'give what I possess if all the Protestants of your states could become Catholic'.[84] One of the principles of his legislation was that much of the proceeds from his suppressions of contemplative monasteries should go to funding more parish clergy. He was not atheist, deist or Protestant, but a Catholic reformer.[85]

As well as the *philosophes*, their opponents had tried to claim his allegiance. He was eulogised in Italy during his visit of 1769 as a 'Christian hero', 'the true Catholic Marcus Aurelius'.[86] In 1781 Belgian propagandists urged him to keep the influence of *philosophie* at bay.[87] Joseph contrived to hold at the same time opinions that were sponsored by both groups and were considered by them mutually incompatible.

Ignatius Fessler was born in Hungary in 1756. He was destined for the Jesuit Order and educated in its schools, but with its suppression in 1773 he became a novice of the Capuchins under the name Innocent. However, the views of his superiors and the discipline they exercised alienated him. He made contact with the Church reformers who looked forward to the accession of Joseph II and who thereafter supported his programme. In the early 1780s he left the cloister for the University of Vienna, published the first two parts of what was intended to be a massive disquisition on the emperor's rights in ecclesiastical matters, *What is the Emperor?*, and was appointed by Joseph to a Chair of Old Testament and Oriental Studies in the University of Lemberg in Austrian Poland. Fessler's views meanwhile fluctuated between atheism, deism and Jansenism. After 1787 he became disillusioned with the emperor's policies, and in 1788 he left the Monarchy. He converted to Lutheranism and henceforth called himself Ignatius Aurelius Fessler. Both before and after his departure from Lemberg he was an active Freemason. While in Prussia he fell in and out of love with the philosophy of Kant, and was much influenced by Herder. He ended his days in 1839, after a spell teaching at a Russian

Orthodox seminary, as the Lutheran bishop of Saratov on the Volga. In 1824 he had published an autobiography, *Dr Fessler's Retrospects on his Seventy-Year Pilgrimage.*[88]

His special interest for this chapter arises from his enthusiasm for the Stoics. His novice-master recommended him to study Seneca's philosophical works with the words: 'Learn from the pagan Christian humility, mortification of the flesh, and resignation.' Fessler revelled in Seneca, in whom he 'discovered a certain mysticism' which he thought could only have derived from divine inspiration. When he read writings of Jansenist spirit like Fleury's *Church History* and Muratori's *True Devotion*, his dedication to the monastic life was shaken. But he was held back from abandoning his profession, and from moral depravity, by the influence of Seneca. Fessler always took with him on his journeys an edition of the Stoic philosopher's works. Further, he wrote, 'As for what is *called* Philosophy, I had enough in Plato, Cicero, Seneca, Bacon of Verulam, Stanley, Malebranche and Brucker. Of what Philosophy *is*, I had as yet no inkling.'[89]

He continued to love Seneca, but his exile and conversion were associated with study of Marcus Aurelius. In 1790 appeared the first three volumes of what Fessler called his 'psychological novel' about the Stoic emperor, which went into three editions and achieved considerable notoriety. As the author acknowledges, anyone who took the work for an attempt at history found it 'bad'. The emperor is represented, for example, as a model of the constitutional monarch. According to Fessler, 'the whole book is written, not with art as its midwife, but with feeling as its inspiration, that is, from a heart steadfast and peaceful in God. If I have written anything good and true, it comes from God, the source of all goodness and truth.' He was at pains to deny that he had desired 'to be counted among those who in our day have arrogated to themselves the titles of Philosophers and Men of Enlightenment'.[90] Through all the changing scenes and attitudes of his bizarre 'pilgrimage', Fessler clung to a view of Stoicism as essentially Christian.

V

So, in the Austrian Monarchy during the Age of Enlightenment, there were few who grasped the significance of the redefinition by Diderot and others of the term *philosophe*; and even those few did not fully accept it. For many, not only of the older generation such as Francis Stephen and Maria Theresa, but also of the younger like Joseph II and Isabella, the word remained for ordinary purposes a synonym for Stoic or Stoical – understood more or less loosely. For the empress, 'Christian philosopher', as used by neo-Stoics, was a natural expression. For her children, 'philosophy' and Catholicism were perfectly compatible. Even to her more advanced ministers like Kaunitz and Zinzendorf, and to the prince de Ligne, the new usage was for differing reasons and in varying degrees unpalatable. Whereas the writings of Seneca helped to inspire Rousseau's ideas on education, and Diderot devoted years of labour to rehabilitating the philosopher's reputation as an Enlightened minister of state,[91] for Fessler he ranked as a forerunner of Christian mysticism, the stern teacher of morality who held him to his monastic obligations.

It would not be difficult to widen the range of evidence in support of the argument of this chapter. Here are a few further examples. In Fessler's homeland, Hungary, Lipsius was twice reprinted in the vernacular after the date when Oestreich considered his influence at an end.[92] Leopold II, younger brother and successor of Joseph II, though patron of the second Italian edition of the *Encyclopédie*, still used the word *philosophe* in the traditional sense, and combined with deep interest in the French Enlightenment dogmatic zeal for the reform of the Roman Catholic Church.[93] In the 1780s the great monastery of Strahov in Prague, spared from dissolution by Joseph because of its proven usefulness, began building a second, 'philosophical' library to match its theological collection. When frescoes were applied to the new building in the 1790s, the incorrigibly Baroque painter, Maulbertsch, was asked to depict, in a scheme that glorified divine revelation, along with other ancient and modern philosophers, the Encyclopaedists.[94]

According to Peter Gay, 'neither Gibbon nor the other *philosophes* could ever grant that philosophical Christians or Stoic Christians were men with a coherent world view'.[95] Historians have been inclined to feel the same. On the one hand, all Josephists have been condemned as heretical by some modern Catholic scholars;[96] on the other, signs of Enlightenment and Jacobinism within the Monarchy have been studied out of their Christian, generally Catholic, context.[97] The combinations of influences acknowledged at any one time by, say, Francis Stephen, Zinzendorf and Fessler seem as mutually irreconcilable as the Catholicism, Classicism, astrology and alchemy that jostled together at the Court of Rudolf II. But the latter *mélange* has recently been studied with sympathy, among others by Robert Evans.[98] It is unhistorical not to accord the same respect to the mentality of the Austrian Enlightenment.

The study of intellectual influences is notoriously treacherous ground. An obvious pitfall, not always avoided, is to assume that in the period roughly from 1740 to 1790 French influence meant Enlightened influence. The vogue of the French language and of French thought at the Court of Maria Theresa, and even under Joseph II, gave as much scope to the ideas of Bossuet, Pascal, Descartes and Fénelon – not to mention Mesmer[99] – as to those of Voltaire and Diderot. Jansenism was primarily a French movement, and the height of its influence in Vienna coincided with the age of Enlightenment.[100] Yet for Voltaire, Jansenists were worse even than Jesuits.[101]

No doubt the Monarchy was peculiar by the standards of Enlightened Europe as a whole. But these considerations apply, at least to some extent, everywhere. Voltaire usually saw himself as embattled against *l'infâme*, and did not always imagine that he was winning. He complained in 1769 that he had not found three *philosophes* to follow him, while 'a madman and an imbecile like St Ignatius' had found a dozen.[102] His full doctrine – like the redefinition of *philosophe* – won few converts. On the other hand, his many ferocious enemies did not include all Roman Catholics, all priests and all Austrians. It was the king of England, where Voltaire thought everyone was a *philosophe*, who talked to Zinzendorf 'of burning Voltaire with his books, and said he would never permit him to come to England'.[103] More typical than the strident and self-conscious French *philosophes* or their rabid opponents were Lutheran *Aufklärer*, Enlightened Italian clergy like Pope Benedict XIV and Muratori, and even the *abbés* who contributed to the *Encyclopédie*.[104] A *curé* of Mouzay, though he read and recommended to others writings critical of Voltaire and Rousseau, paid the two *philosophes* the unique compliment of incorporating funeral eulogies for them in his parish register.[105]

One does not usually expect to find in Bentham's work penetrating insights into ecclesiastical history. But allowing for his prejudices, one may regard the following remarks, published in 1789, as impressive evidence for the interrelationship between religion and Enlightenment with which this chapter has been concerned:

> Happily, the dictates of religion seem to approach nearer and nearer to a coincidence with those of utility every day. But why? Because the

dictates of the moral sanction do so; and those coincide with or are influenced by these. Men of the worst religions, influenced by the voice and practice of the surrounding world, borrow continually a new and a new leaf out of the book of utility: and with these, in order not to break with their religion, they endeavour, sometimes with violence enough, to patch together and adorn the repositories of their faith.[106]

Like Bentham, Peter Gay, while recognising this development, sees it as 'treason of the clerks', 'doing the philosophes' work'.[107] But the Christian, even the Catholic, philosopher, though he could hardly become a full-blown *philosophe*, could adopt, even promote, some elements of French Enlightened thinking, not merely without doing violence to his religion, but under its banner and to its perceived advantage.

Notes

This chapter originally appeared in D. Beales and G. Best (eds), *History, Society and the Churches: Essays in Honour of Owen Chadwick* (Cambridge, 1985). I am grateful for help and references given me by my wife, Professor T. C. W. Blanning, Professor J. A. Crook, Dr J. C. McKeown, Professor H. B. Nisbet, the late Dr S. O'Cathasaigh, the late Professor R. S. Porter, Mr S. P. Salt, Professor Q. R. D. Skinner, Mr R. C. Smail, Professor E. Wangermann and Dr R. L. Wokler. Professor Blanning and Dr Wokler very kindly read and commented on the text, but they are of course not responsible for it. I should also like to acknowledge that this essay benefited from opportunities I had to lecture on a similar theme at the universities of Leeds and Newcastle and at Clare College and Trinity Hall, Cambridge. I was assisted by grants from the British Academy and the Leverhulme Trust.

1 E.g. O. Chadwick. *The Popes and European Revolution* (Oxford, 1981), pp. 406–7 and passim.

2 H. S. Commager, *The Empire of Reason* (London 1978), esp. Appendix, 'The Term "Philosophe"', pp. 236–45; E. Dieckmann, *Le Philosophe: Texts and Interpretation* (St Louis, 1948); J. Lough, 'Who Were the *Philosophes?*', in J. H. Fox, M. H. Waddicor and D. A. Watts (eds), *Studies in Eighteenth-Century French Literature Presented to Robert Niklaus* (Exeter, 1975), pp. 139–50; R. Shackleton, 'When Did the French "Philosophes" Become a Party?', *Bulletin of the John Rylands Library* (hereafter *BJRL*), LX (1978): 181–99; I. O. Wade, '*The Philosophe*' in the French Drama of the Eighteenth Century (Princeton, 1926); R. J. White, *The Anti-Philosophers* (London, 1970), esp. ch. I; A. M. Wilson, *Diderot* (Oxford, 1972), esp. pp. 70–2, 181–2, 210, 221–2, 245–6. The next few paragraphs derive mainly from these works.

3 Cf. O. Chadwick. *The Secularization of the European Mind in the*

Nineteenth Century (Cambridge, 1975), esp. p. 144. *Aufklärung* is of course an eighteenth-century usage.

4 Quoted in Dieckmann, *Le Philosophe*, p. 72: 'un homme, qui, par libertinage d'esprit, se met au dessus des devoirs et des obligations ordinaires de la vie civile et chrétienne. *C'est un homme qui ne se refuse rien, qui ne se contraint sur rien, et qui mène une vie de Philosophe.*' It seems right to give the original French version of quotations whose precise phrasing is important to a study of the *philosophe*, while noting that it is always difficult to decide whether to render the word in English as 'philosopher' or as *philosophe*.

5 Shackleton, *BJRL*, LX (1978): 189. Cf. M. C. Jacob, *The Radical Enlightenment* (London, 1981), p. 217.

6 The quotation from Dieckmann, *Le Philosophe*, p. 7. A. W. Fairbairn, 'Dumarsais and *Le Philosophe*', *Studies on Voltaire and the Eighteenth Century*, LXXXVII (1972): 375–95. I am most grateful to Dr Fairbairn for giving me a copy of this article.

7 Dieckmann, *Le Philosophe*, pp. 44, 60: 'Notre *philosophe* ne se croit pas en exil dans ce monde; il ne croit pas être en pays ennemi ... Il veut trouver du plaisir avec les autres ... c'est un honnête homme qui veut plaire et se rendre utile ... il est aisé de conclure combien le sage insensible des stoïciens est éloigné de la perfection de notre *philosophe*: un tel *philosophe* est homme, et leur sage n'était qu'un fantôme. Ils rougissaient de l'humanité, et il en fait gloire.'

8 Ibid., pp. 32, 46: 'La raison est à l'égard du *philosophe* ce que la grâce est à l'égard du chrétien ... La société civile est, pour ainsi dire, une divinité pour lui sur la terre; il l'encense ...'. The original essay is less categorical in the first passage, more so in the second, and contains lengthy aspersions on superstition, dogma, religion, etc., that Diderot largely omitted.

9 L. W. B. Brockliss, 'Philosophy Teaching in France, 1600–1740', in *History of Universities*, vol. I (1981), pp. 131–68. Cf. O. Chadwick, *From Bossuet to Newman: The Idea of Doctrinal Development* (Cambridge, 1957), p. 55.

10 In English, G. Oestreich, *Neostoicism and the Early Modern State*, ed. B. Oestreich and H. G. Koenigsberger (Cambridge, 1982), esp. pp. 63–4, 99–109; N. O. Keohane, *Philosophy and the State in France* (Princeton, 1980), esp. pp. 129–33; R. J. W. Evans, *The Making of the Habsburg Monarchy, 1550–1700* (Oxford, 1979), esp. p. 113. T. Zielinski, *Cicero im Wandel der Jahrhunderte* (3rd edn, Leipzig, 1912).

11 Dieckmann, *Le Philosophe*, p. 56. The other individuals named in the article are Velleius Paterculus for the information on Cato, and Terence and La Rochefoucauld, also for quotations.

12 P. Gay, *The Enlightenment: An Interpretation* (2 vols, London, 1967–70), esp. vol. I, pp. 50–1, 120–1, 300–4, 320.

On Marcus Aurelius and the Stoics themselves I have found most useful, apart from A. Birley (ed.), the *Meditations, Lives of the Later Caesars* (Harmondsworth, 1976), see esp. p. 135; A. S. L. Farquharson, *Marcus Aurelius, His Life and His World*, ed. D. A. Rees (Oxford, 1951); A. Birley, *Marcus Aurelius*

(London, 1966); and P. A. Brunt, 'Stoicism and the Principate', *Papers of the British School at Rome*, vol. XLIII (1975), pp. 7–35.

13 Voltaire, *Dictionnaire philosophique*, ed. J. Benda (Paris, 1954), esp. pp. 342–7; English translation ed. T. Besterman (Harmondsworth, 1971), esp. pp. 334–8.

14 White, *The Anti-Philosophers*, pp. 6–7; Oestreich, *Neostoicism*, p. 101.

15 Prince de Ligne, *Fragments de l'histoire de ma vie*, ed. F. Leuridant (2 vols, Paris 1927–28), vol. I, p. 264n.

16 A. Wolf, 'Relationen des Grafen von Podewils, Gesandten K. Friedrich's II, von Preussen, über den Wiener Hof in den Jahren 1746, 1747, 1748', *Sitzungsberichte der kaiserlichen Akademie der Wissenschaften*, vol. V (1850), p. 499; H. O. Mikoletzky, 'Kaiser Franz I. Stephan in Briefen', in *Études européennes; Mélanges offerts à Victor Tapié* (Paris, 1973), pp. 270–1.

17 Information about French influence in Vienna is brought together usefully by J. Schmidt, 'Voltaire und Maria Theresia', *Mitteilungen des Vereines für Geschichte der Stadt Wien* [hereafter *MVGSW*], XI (1931): 73–115 – a much broader article than its title suggests. See also H. Wagner, 'Der Höhepunkt des französischen Kultureinflusses in Österreich', *Österreich in Geschichte und Literatur* [hereafter *ÖGL*] V (1961): 507–17. I am grateful to the Librarian of the Austrian Cultural Institute in London for supplying me with a copy of this article.

18 E.g. Jacob, *The Radical Enlightenment*, p. 111.

19 A. Wandruszka, 'Die Religiosität Franz Stephan von Lothringen', *Mitteilungen des österreichischen Staatsarchivs* [hereafter *MÖSA*], XII (1959): 162–73.

20 D. Beales, *Joseph II. I: In the Shadow of Maria Theresa, 1741–80* (Cambridge, 1987), pp. 43–68; R. F. Tuck, *Natural Rights Theories: Their Origins and Development* (Cambridge, 1979), p. 17; Oestreich, *Neostoicism*, esp. pp. 123–4.

21 'Das Lehrbuch der Metaphysik für Kaiser Josef II., verfasst von P. Josef Frantz', ed. T. M. Wehofer (Paderborn, 1895), in supp. Vol. II of *Jahrbuch für Philosophie und spekulative Theologie*, with a valuable commentary. See Beales, *Joseph II*, pp. 46–7.

22 E. Winter, *Der Josefinismus* (2nd edn, Berlin, 1962), p. 41. G. Klingenstein, *Staatsverwaltung und kirchliche Autorität im 18. Jahrhundert* (Vienna, 1970), esp. pp. 165, 176–8. Wehofer's edn of Frantz (see previous note), p. 102.

23 Quoted from Albert's MSS memoirs by A. Ritter von Arneth, *Geschichte Maria Theresias* [hereafter *GMT*], 10 vols, Vienna, 1863–79), vol. VII, p. 532.

24 U. Benassi wrote a long series of excellent articles on 'Guglielmo du Tillot, un ministro reformatore del secolo XVIII' in *Archivio storico per le province parmensi*, new series, vols XV–XVI (1915–16), XIX–XXV (1919–25). The rise of Du Tillot is described in vol. XVI, esp. pp. 193–213, 334–68. More accessibly, F. Venturi, *Settecento riformatore*, vol. II (Turin, 1976), pp. 214–16. On the cultural side, in English, A. Yorke-Long, *Music at Court* (London, 1954), esp. pp. 19–32.

25 J. Hrazky, 'Die Persönlichkeit der Infantin Isabella von Parma', *MÖSA*, XII (1959): 174–239.

26 Ibid., p. 194.

27 Haus-, Hof- und Staatsarchiv [hereafter HHSA], Vienna, Familien-Archiv, Sammelbände 68.

28 Schmidt, *MVGSW*, XI (1931): esp. 91–7; Wagner, *ÖGL*, V (1961): esp. 509–13.

29 Maria Theresa to Maria Beatrix, printed in *Briefe der Kaiserin Maria Theresia an ihre Kinder und Freunde* [hereafter *MTKuF*], ed. A. Ritter von Arneth (4 vols, Vienna, 1881), vol. I, p. 99.

30 Ibid., vol. I, pp. 125, 130, 135 (Maria Theresa to Ferdinand, 22 May, 11 June and 9 July 1772).

31 Maria Theresa to Mercy, 1 Jan. and 3 Feb. 1774; Mercy to Maria Theresa, 19 Jan. 1774. In *Marie-Antoinette: Correspondance secrète entre Marie-Thérèse et le comte de Mercy-Argenteau*, ed. A. von Arneth and M. A. Geffroy (3 vols, 2nd edn, Paris, 1875), vol. II, pp. 89, 101–2, 105.

32 Maria Theresa's instructions for Maximilian, Apr. 1774: *MTKuF*, vol. IV, p. 322. The empress's references to *amour-propre* must be related to the important tradition of writing on this theme discussed in Keohane, *Philosophy and the State*, esp. pp. 184–97, 255, 294–302, 427–32. In this connection she appears to follow Bossuet (or Rousseau) rather than the Jansenists.
On French influence at the Court of Vienna under Maria Theresa and Joseph II, from a rather different standpoint but using some of the same material, see A. D. Hytier, 'Joseph II, la cour de Vienne et les philosophes', *Studies in Voltaire and the Eighteenth Century*, CVI (1973): 225–51.

33 To Maria Beatrix, 23 Jan. 1770 and 12 Apr. 1779; to Countess Enzenberg, 15 June 1772: *MTKuF*, vol. III, pp. 107, 354; vol. IV, p. 506. Cf. also her letter to Ferdinand, 14 Aug. 1779. To Joseph, 21 Apr. 1778, in *Maria Theresia und Joseph II. Ihre Correspondenz*, ed. A. Ritter von Arneth (3 vols), (Vienna, 1867–68), vol. II, p. 214.

34 E.g. *Journal d'un Voyage en Allemagne, fait en 1773, par G. A. H. Guibert* (Paris, 1803), pp. 248, 276–7; [J. Moore], *A View of Society and Manners in France, Switzerland and Germany* (2 vols, London, 1779), vol. II, p. 300; [C. A. Pilati] *Voyages en differens pays de l'Europe en 1774, 1775 & 1776* (2 vols, The Hague, 1777), vol. II, pp. 103–4.

35 *GMT*, vol. VII, pp. 197–8.

36 [Pilati], *Voyages*, vol. I, p. 6. Cf. L. Bodi, *Tauwetter in Wien* (Frankfurt, 1977), esp. pp. 47, 51.

37 N. W. Wraxall, *Memoirs of the Courts of Berlin, Dresden, Warsaw and Vienna, in the Years 1777, 1778 and 1779* (2 vols) (3rd edn, London, 1806), vol. II, pp. 246–7, 249, 257–9, 278–89. I am very grateful to Professor L. Colley for helping me to obtain from Yale the MSS of this work on microfilm, which tends to confirm its value as a record of the years of Wraxall's stay in central Europe, despite the fact that the book was not published until 1799.

38 Wagner, *ÖGL*, V (1961). Cf. E. Wangermann, *The Austrian Achievement, 1700–1800* (London, 1973), pp. 80–8, 130–4.

39 F. Walter, 'Kaunitz' Eintritt in die innere Politik', *Mitteilungen des*

österreichischen Instituts für Geschichtsforschung, XLVI (1932), pp. 37–79; F. A. J. Szabo, *Kaunitz and Enlightened Absolutism, 1753-1780* (Cambridge, 1994).

40 Schmidt, *MVGSW*, XI (1931): 115. See *Voltaire's Correspondence*, ed. T. Besterman (107 vols, Geneva, 1953–65), e.g. vol. CLIII, p. 128, Voltaire to Kaunitz, 25 Nov. 1763.

41 F. Maass, *Der Josephinismus* (5 vols, Vienna, 1951–61), vol. I, esp. pp. 94n., 347.

42 G. Klingenstein, *Der Aufstieg des Hauses Kaunitz* (Göttingen, 1975), esp. pp. 170–1.

43 H. Wagner, 'Die Lombardei und das Freimaurer Patent Josephs II', *MÖSA*, XXXI (1978), p. 143; A. Novotny, *Staatskanzler Kaunitz als geistige Persönlichkeit* (Vienna, 1947), pp. 145–71.

44 The diary is in HHSA, Vienna. There is a volume a year. I give references only where the exact date does not appear in my text. The discussion of Fontenelle is to be found under 18 Jan. 1762, the reference to Rousseau and Helvétius under 17 Jan. 1763. The early years of the diary have been published as *Karl Graf von Zinzendorf. Aus den Jugendtagebüchern, 1747, 1752–63*, ed. M. Breunlich and M. Mader (Vienna, 1997).

45 Zinzendorf's diary, 7–10 Sept. and 3 Oct. 1764. Zinzendorf's entries are reproduced in *Correspondance complète de Jean-Jacques Rousseau*, ed. R. A. Leigh, vol. XXI (Geneva 1974), pp. 328–34. Louis Eugene, prince of Württemberg, to Voltaire, 28 Sept. 1764 (*Voltaire's Corespondence*, ed. Besterman, vol. LVI, p. 54).

46 Zinzendorf's diary, 24 and 31 Dec. 1771, 7 Jan. 1772.

47 Ibid., 27 Feb. 1764.

48 Zinzendorf's religious difficulties are discussed in A. Wolf, *Geschichtliche Bilder aus Oesterreich* (2 vols, Vienna, 1880), esp. vol. II, pp. 265–7, 305–6.

49 Zinzendorf's diary, 3 Oct. 1764, 7 Jan. 1772.

50 E.g. by Schmidt, *MVGSW*, XI (1931): 98. See n.55 below.

51 See, e.g., the introduction by L. Ashton to *Letters and Memoirs of the Prince de Ligne* (London, 1927). Maria Theresa spoke of his *légèreté* (*Marie Antoinette*, ed. Arneth and Geffroy, vol. II, p. 485), Zinzendorf of his lack of *sens commun* (diary, 10 Nov. 1770).

52 *Mémoires et mélanges historiques et littéraires, par le Prince de Ligne* (5 vols, Paris, 1827–28), vol. II, pp. 127–47. Quotation from p. 135.

53 E.g. Ligne to Voltaire, 30 Dec. 1763, 1 June 1766, ?June/July 1774 (*Voltaire's Correspondence*, ed. Besterman, vol. LIII, pp. 213–14; vol. LXI, pp. 122–3; vol. LXXXVIII, pp. 74–5).

54 Ibid., vol. LXX, pp. 177–8. See also Hennin to Voltaire, 2 Oct. 1768 (ibid., pp. 84–5).

55 Ligne to Voltaire, ?Aug./Sept. 1772, and Voltaire to Ligne, 29 Sept. 1772 (ibid., vol. LXXXII, pp. 188–91, and LXXXIII, p. 53). There is a difficulty about the text as well as the date of the Ligne letter, since it is known only in his later printed version; but it makes a very plausible provocation for this reply of Voltaire's.

56 Gebler to Nicolai, 16 Nov. 1763 in *Aus dem josephinischen Wien*, ed. R. M. Werner (Berlin, 1888), p. 12.

57 See Bodi, *Tauwetter in Wien*.

58 [J. Pezzl] *Skizze aus Wien* (Vienna, 1789–90), p. 45. Cf. his *philosophischer Roman* of 1784, *Faustin*.

59 Voltaire to D'Alembert, 28 Oct. 1769 (*Voltaire's Correspondence*, ed. Besterman, vol. LXXIII, p. 142), quoting Grimm.

60 *Correspondance littéraire, philosophique et critique par Grimm, Diderot, Raynal, Meister etc.*, ed. M. Tourneux (16 vols, 1877–82), vol. XI, pp. 468, 471–4, 526, 529.

61 H. Wagner, 'Die Reise Josephs II. nach Frankreich 1977 und die Reformen in Österreich', in *Österreich und Europe. Festgabe für Hugo Hantsch zum 70. Geburtstag* (Graz, 1965), pp. 224–6. This useful article much exaggerates the influence of the visit on Joseph. See my *Joseph II*, pp. 379–80.

62 Le Bret to Bertolà, 7 Jan. 1778. In J. U. Fechner, *Erfahrene und erfundene Landschaft: … Bertolà's Deutschlandbild* (Opladen, 1974), p. 230. On Le Bret, M. L. Pesante, *Stato e religione nella storiografia di Goettingen* (Turin, 1971).

63 C. Riesbeck, *Travels through Germany*, trans. Maty (3 vols, London, 1787), vol. I, pp. 255–6.

64 *Correspondance littéraire*, ed. Tourneux, vol. XIII, p. 6.

65 See Chapter 5, 'The False Joseph II', pp. 117, 121–2, 142–3.

66 J. Lanjuinais, *Le Monarque accompli, ou prodiges de bonté, de savoir, et de sagesse qui font l'éloge de … Joseph II* (3 vols, Lausanne, 1774).

67 *Voltaire's Correspondence*, ed. Besterman, vol. XCIV, p. 165.

68 See E. Faure, *La Disgrâce de Turgot* (Paris, 1961), pp. 505–6.

69 Lanjuinais, *Le Monarque accompli*, esp. vol. III, pp. 250–62, 284–91. Joseph is a *'monarque philosophe'* from vol. I, p. 1. Comparison with Trajan and Marcus Aurelius is reached on vol. I, p. 6.

70 Lord Acton, *Essays on Church and State*, ed. D. Woodruff (London, 1952), p. 355.

71 Frederick the Great to Voltaire, 18. Aug. 1770 (*Voltaire's Correspondence*, ed. Besterman, vol. LXXVI, pp. 112–13).

72 Countess Leopoldine Kaunitz to Princess Eleonore Liechtenstein, 1782, in A. Wolf, *Fürstin Eleonore Liechtenstein* (Vienna, 1875), p. 165.

73 *Journal d'un voyage en Allemagne, fait en 1773, par G. A. H. Guibert*, vol. II, p. 250.

74 Quoted in O. Sashegyi, *Zensur and Geistesfreiheit unter Joseph II* (Budapest, 1958), p. 117.

75 See Chapter 5, 'The False Joseph II', pp. 138–9.

76 Memorandum of 1765 (*MTuJ*, ed. Arneth, vol. III, p. 338).

77 Zinzendorf's diary, 27 Oct. 1773.

78 See Chapter 5, 'The False Joseph II'.

79 Joseph to Lacy, 12 June 1773 (HHSA Familien-Archiv, Sammelbände 72).

80 Joseph to Leopold, 28 July 1768 (*MTuJ*, vol. I, p. 228).

81 *Correspondance secrète du Comte de Mercy-Argenteau avec l'Empereur Joseph II et le Prince de Kaunitz*, ed. A. von Arneth and J. Flammermont (2 vols, Paris, 1889–91), vol. II, p. 446: Joseph to Mercy, 4 April 1774.

82 W. C. Langsam, *Francis the Good: The Education of an Emperor, 1768–1792* (New York, 1949), p. 38. Joseph to his circle of ladies, 16 July 1777 (Czechoslovak state archive, Litomerice – Žitenice section: LRRA – P-16/22-3 [copies]).

83 A. Beer and J. von Fiedler, *Joseph II. und Graf Ludwig Cobenzl: Ihr Briefwechsel* (2 vols, Vienna, 1901), vol. II, pp. 391–2: Joseph to Grand-Duke Paul of Russia and his wife, 24 Feb. 1781.

84 Joseph to Maria Theresa, 20 July 1777 (*MTuJ*, vol. II, p. 152).

85 The best evidence for these statements is to be found in Maass, *Josephinismus*, vol. II; Winter, *Josefinismus*, pp. 100–14; and in H. Schlitter, *Die Reise des Papstes Pius VI. nach Wien* (2 vols, Vienna, 1892–94).

86 HHSA Familien-Akten, Hofreisen I: report from Naples, 8 Apr. 1769.

87 E.g. Delobel, *A S.M.I. Joseph II, père de la patrie* (Mons, [1781]).

88 *Dr Fessler's Rückblicke auf seine siebzigjährige Pilgerschaft* (Breslau, 1824) can be supplemented by the works of P. F. Barton, esp. *Jesuiten, Jansenisten, Josephiner, Eine Fallstudie zur frühen Toleranzzeit: Der Fall Innocentius Fessler*, part I (Vienna, 1978). *Was ist der Kaiser?* was published in Vienna in 1782.

89 *Fessler's Rückblicke*, esp. pp. 35–6, 43–5, 158, 324n.

90 Ibid., pp. 241–4, 487, 489.

91 G. Pire, 'De l'Influence de Sénèque sur les théories pédagogiques de J.-J. Rousseau', *Annales de la Société Jean-Jacques Rousseau*, XXXII (1953–55), pp. 57–92; W. T. Conroy, Jr, 'Diderot's 'Essai sur Sénèque', *Studies in Voltaire and the Eighteenth Century*, CXXXI (1975).

92 Evans, *Making of the Habsburg Monarchy*, p. 113n.

93 A. Wandruszka, *Leopold II* (2 vols, Vienna, 1963–65), esp. vol. I, pp. 219–26, 279–87, vol. II, part IV.

94 K. Garas, *Franz Anton Maulbertsch 1724–1796* (Budapest, 1960), pp. 154–7, 276.

95 Gay, *Enlightenment*, vol. I, p. 320.

96 Explicitly by H. Rieser, *Der Geist des Josephinismus und sein Fortleben* (Vienna, 1963), who divides Joseph's subjects into those who were *Romtreu* and the rest. See e.g. p. 82 for a denial that the Josephists' reforms were Catholic reforms.

97 This seems to be true e.g. of E. Wangermann, *From Joseph II to the Jacobin Trials* (2nd edn, Oxford, 1969), though not of his more recent writing.

98 R. J. W. Evans, *Rudolf II and His World* (Oxford, 1973).

99 R. Darnton, *Mesmerism and the End of the Enlightenment in France* (Cambridge, MA, 1968).

100 See P. Hersche, *Der Spätjansenismus in Österreich* (Vienna, 1977).

101 R. Pomeau, *La religion de Voltaire* (Paris, 1956), esp. pp. 25–7.

102 Voltaire to Frederick the Great, 30 Oct. 1769 (*Voltaire's Correspondence*, ed. Besterman, vol. LXXIII, p. 145).

103 Zinzendorf's diary, 28 Apr. 1768.

104 Cf. T. C. W. Blanning, *Reform and Revolution in Mainz* (Cambridge, 1974), pp. 23–32; Chadwick, *Popes and European Revolution*, esp. pp. 395–402; R. Shackleton, *The 'Encyclopédie' and the Clerks* (Zaharoff lecture, Oxford, 1970). More generally, *The Enlightenment in National Context*, ed. R. Porter and M. Teich (Cambridge, 1981).

105 Pomeau, *Religion de Voltaire*, p. 343 and n.

106 J. Bentham, *An Introduction to the Principles of Morals and Legislation*, ed. W. Harrison (Oxford, 1948), p. 241.

107 Gay, *Enlightenment*, vol. I, p. 22.

CHAPTER 4

Mozart and the Habsburgs

I

Most of the writing about Mozart in relation to his age, much of it impressive, has been the work of musicologists, using the term in a broad sense; but influential contributions have come from play-wrights, novelists, literary critics, Freemasons, cryptographers and various brands of medical men. Relatively little has been heard from historians, though some of their stereotypes have been rather indiscriminately employed by others. Mozart has been variously fitted into the *ancien régime*, the age of Enlightened despotism, the epoch of the French or democratic Revolution and 'the rise of the bourgeois public sphere'. In describing and discussing the relationship between Mozart and the Habsburgs, I hope to contribute to a more subtle understanding of both the composer and his age.

It is notorious that musicians had a low social status in eighteenth-century society. Nearly all of them were either servants of the Church – mostly as organists or singers and very likely schoolteachers too – or servants of some prince, aristocrat or lesser lord. Many musicians doubled as valets. A few, like Dittersdorf, were expected to double as bureaucrats.[1] The great Haydn had to wear the livery of his patron, Prince Nicholas Esterházy; he ranked on a level with the household officials; he could not travel without the prince's permission; it was his duty to play exactly when, where and what his patron wanted; and his compositions were straightforwardly the property of his patron.[2] Similarly, Mozart had to get permission from his employer, the archbishop of Salzburg, to travel and to take part in other lords' concerts. 'This inhuman villain', as Mozart called him, while on a visit to Vienna with his musicians in 1781, refused the composer leave to stay on there, which finally led Mozart to assert his independence and leave the archbishop's service, at the cost of a kick downstairs from a chamberlain.[3]

But there was another side to the story. Music was part of the education of almost every German ruler. Many composed, most

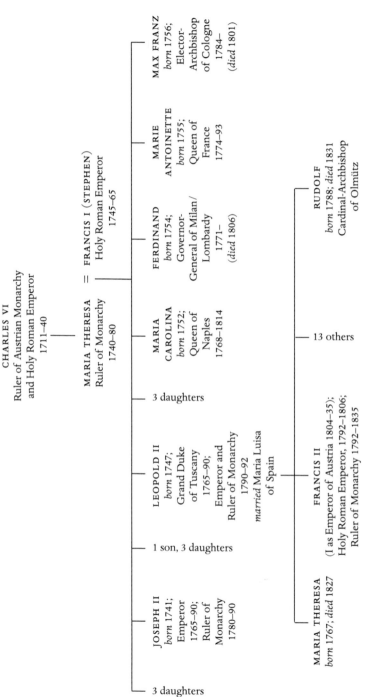

CHARLES VI
Ruler of Austrian Monarchy
and Holy Roman Emperor
1711–40

MARIA THERESA
Ruler of Monarchy
1740–80

= **FRANCIS I (STEPHEN)**
Holy Roman Emperor
1745–65

3 daughters

JOSEPH II
born 1741;
Emperor
1765–90;
Ruler of
Monarchy
1780–90

1 son, 3 daughters

LEOPOLD II
born 1747;
Grand Duke
of Tuscany
1765–90;
Emperor and
Ruler of Monarchy
1790–92
married Maria Luisa
of Spain

3 daughters

**MARIA
CAROLINA**
born 1752;
Queen of
Naples
1768–1814

FERDINAND
born 1754;
Governor-
General of Milan/
Lombardy
1771–
(*died* 1806)

**MARIE
ANTOINETTE**
born 1755;
Queen of
France
1774–93

MAX FRANZ
born 1756;
Elector-
Archbishop
of Cologne
1784–
(*died* 1801)

MARIA THERESA
born 1767; *died* 1827

FRANCIS II
(I as Emperor of Austria 1804–35);
Holy Roman Emperor, 1792–1806;
Ruler of Monarchy 1792–1835

13 others

RUDOLF
born 1788; *died* 1831
Cardinal-Archbishop
of Olmütz

Genealogical Table of the House of Habsburg-Lorraine

could play an instrument or sing. Hence most of them had some appreciation of others' musical skill. The promotion of opera was considered almost indispensable to a significant Court, and the standard of production affected the ruler's prestige. Music, in sum, was a royal, aristocratic and gentlemanly – as well as ladylike – activity.[4] Good professional musicians were prized by rulers and moved with unusual freedom between classes or status-groups. A talented singer, player or librettist would have a better chance of meeting a ruler on something like equal terms than almost any other subject.

Very few people, even among the highest aristocracy and diplomats, even members of royal families, knew as many sovereigns as Mozart did. The sequence began when his father Leopold, himself a famous violinist, touted him and his sister around the Courts of Europe as child prodigies. These tours started in 1762, when Wolfgang Mozart, the future composer, was six. To take first the reception they received from non-Habsburg rulers: in 1764 they were summoned to join the French royal family at their private dinner – truly, as Leopold claimed, 'a most extraordinary honour';[5] and George III of England, having previously heard the family play, recognised them in St James's Park and opened the window of his carriage to salute them.[6] In 1770 Pope Clement XIV made Wolfgang a Knight of the Golden Spur, first class.[7] As well as reigning kings and queens, there was the Dutch Stadtholder, William V, for whose installation the ten-year-old Mozart wrote an extraordinary set of pieces;[8] and in Germany of course there were lesser rulers to the number of 1,003, many of whom Mozart encountered.

The dynasty with whom Mozart had easily the most to do was the Habsburgs – technically, after the death of Charles VI, the House of Habsburg-Lorraine. The relevant members of the family are included in the genealogical table on page 91. Among them, by far the most important in this story, is Joseph II, and the next most important Leopold II. I shall take the others first. To look on the positive side, the Emperor Francis I was so condescending as to go out himself into the anteroom in 1762 to call in the Mozart children and their parents. On that occasion Maria Theresa not only let the child Wolfgang jump on to her lap but also gave him and his sister some fine clothes.[9] She later commissioned from him the serenade *Ascanio in Alba* for the marriage of her third surviving son, the Archduke Ferdinand, in Milan in 1771. Immediately afterwards, Ferdinand proposed taking Mozart into his service.[10] As for her youngest son, Max Franz, who was the same age as Mozart and became elector-archbishop of Cologne in 1784, when only twenty-seven, it was his cast-offs that were presented to Mozart during the visit of 1762, it was his visit to Salzburg in 1775 that provided the occasion for the composition of the serenade *Il rè pastore*, and in 1781, according to Mozart, Max Franz would have employed him if he had by then succeeded to his electorate.[11] Maria Carolina, daughter of Maria Theresa and Queen of Naples, 'always [greeted] them with quite exceptional friendliness' during their visit in 1770.[12] In the next generation it was originally intended that *Don Giovanni* should be the opera with which Prague would celebrate the marriage of Francis's sister, Maria Theresa, in 1787 – surely a strange choice for such an occasion;[13] and the piano version of the six German dances, K.600, was dedicated to her in 1791.[14]

That is the positive side. Now for the negative. When Archduke Ferdinand, having celebrated his marriage to the strains of *Ascanio in Alba*, wrote to his mother Maria Theresa that he would like to take Mozart into his service, she replied with this notorious put-down:

> you ask me about taking the young Salzburger into your service. I do not know why, not believing that you have need of a composer or of useless servants. If however it would give you pleasure, I have no wish to hinder you. What I say is only intended to prevent your burdening yourself with useless people. And never give titles to people of that sort. If they are in your service it degrades that service when these people go about the world like beggars. Besides, he has a large family.

As often, she was behaving like anyone's mother at her worst, but this was a mother with the power of an absolute ruler, who ultimately controlled her son's purse-strings. She was also being monstrously unfair to Mozart, which is difficult to condone even if she had reason to be concerned about Ferdinand's extravagance.[15]

Ferdinand naturally did not take Mozart into his service, and nor in the event did Max Franz. Patronage of Mozart by their numerous sisters is conspicuous by its absence, except in so far as the Queen of Naples may have been helpful as well as gracious. Marie Antoinette, for example, seems to have done nothing for the Mozarts during their stay in Paris in 1778.[16] *Don Giovanni* was not ready in time for the young Maria Theresa's marriage, and she did all she could to prevent it being replaced by *The Marriage of Figaro*, preferring another composer's opera.[17] So far as I can see, hardly any works by Mozart were dedicated to Habsburgs – only the dances to Archduchess Maria

Theresa and the opera *Lucio Silla* in 1772 to Archduke Ferdinand
and his wife. Even the pieces composed for Habsburgs' visits and
weddings are not actually dedicated to them.[18] Yet Mozart dedicated
early sonatas to a daughter of Louis XV of France and *Mitridate,
Rè di Ponto* to the duke of Modena[19] – and, of course (for what
it's worth in this context), Beethoven dedicated many works to his
chief patron, Archduke Rudolf, another son of Leopold II.[20] I cannot
explain this curious shortage of Mozart dedications to members of
the Habsburg family.

II

Now for Joseph II. The play and still more the film *Amadeus* have
done students of Joseph II a great service. Before they appeared,
when I said I was studying him, people would look blank. Thanks
to *Amadeus*, people now know who I am talking about provided that
I call him Mozart's emperor. And the film caught Joseph's physical
appearance marvellously. But it got his character and his approach
to music completely wrong.

There is certainly a down side. The emperor did not leap for
joy when Mozart left the service of the archbishop of Salzburg and
at once offer the composer a post with the sort of salary we think
his genius merited – or commission from him all the operas and
other compositions we should like to have had. Mozart sometimes
complained of his meanness and of his predilection for Antonio
Salieri, his chief opera composer.[21] Joseph's expulsion of his detested
but musical spinster sisters to their convents deprived Mozart of two
possible Habsburg patrons. The emperor's virtual abolition of the
Court as a social entity deprived him of many more.[22] Joseph disliked
opera seria, the grand classical tradition to which *Mitridate, Idomeneo*
and *La clemenza di Tito* belong, and, since after 1776 he personally
directed the principal theatres of Vienna, Mozart wrote no such opera
between his arrival in Vienna and the death of Joseph.[23] The emperor
also, as a Catholic reformer, disapproved of large-scale instrumentally-
supported church music and banned it. Hence, with the exception of
the C minor Mass, designed for a special occasion in Salzburg, Mozart
composed virtually no such music over the same period.[24]

As he is represented in *Amadeus*, the emperor had no opinions of his
own, behaved like the doll of a ministerial ventriloquist, and showed
his lack of appreciation of music and Mozart by his comment on *Die*

Entführung, 'too many notes'.[25] The truth is that, more than almost any other ruler, he regularly received subjects individually on his own, he had emphatic opinions, and he often went against the advice of his ministers, especially in artistic matters. He took a personal interest in every aspect of the government of his vast territories, and that meant almost every aspect of his people's lives. But there were few things he cared more about than the theatre, music and opera. In many of his letters to his brother Leopold in Tuscany, after dealing with family matters and weighty political affairs, he turned to discussing opera performances and libretti. Sometimes he sent on a libretto or a score, as with Salieri's first notable opera, *Armida*, in 1771.[26] In 1782 he kept Count Zinzendorf up late by talking 'endlessly' about music, especially about the piano competition he had arranged in the previous January between Mozart and Clementi.[27] During 1788, when ill and engaged in a desperate campaign against the Turks in the east, he still sent detailed comments and orders about the opera to Count Rosenberg, the minister in charge.[28]

Despite what has been said by reputable writers, Joseph was not, so far as I can discover, a composer.[29] But he was well taught by Georg Christoph Wagenseil, himself a pupil of J. J. Fux, author of the best known eighteenth-century textbook of counterpoint, *Gradus ad Parnassum*. Another of Wagenseil's pupils was one of Beethoven's teachers; and it is possible to construct a genealogical table of music teachers and pupils which links Joseph with most major composers of the period.[30] In the words of Charles Burney, the great musical historian: 'the Emperor [is] perhaps just [musical] enough for a sovereign prince, that is,with sufficient hand, both on the violoncello and harpsichord, to amuse himself; and sufficient judgment to hear, understand, and receive delight from others'.[31]

It happens that we have a record of a dialogue said to have taken place in 1786 between Joseph II and the composer, Dittersdorf, much of which is about Mozart. It was published only in Dittersdorf's old age, more than twenty years after the event – but that is still a good deal fresher than some of the material Mozart scholars have relied on. To me it rings absolutely true.

The emperor had characteristically insisted on dealing personally with a petty request which Dittersdorf had intended to make to a clerk – it was a question of changing the date of a concert. Joseph then started a conversation on music. He asked Dittersdorf about Mozart's compositions. Dittersdorf replied: 'He is unquestionably one of the greatest original geniuses, and I have yet to come across any composers with such an astonishing wealth of ideas. I wish he would not be so prodigal with them. He leaves the listener no time to breathe.' 'In his operas,' said the emperor, 'he has the same fault … and drowns the singers with the accompaniment.' Of course at that time they would insist on using authentic instruments. 'I once made a parallel,' persisted Joseph, 'between Mozart and Haydn. You make one, so that I can see whether you agree with mine.' Dittersdorf knew a trick worth two of that. 'May I ask you a question in return?' he said. 'Of course.' 'How would you draw a parallel between Klopstock and Gellert [two poets of the German literary revival]?' Joseph: 'Hm! That both are great poets. That one has to read Klopstock's poems more than once to appreciate all their beauties, but that Gellert's beauties appear plainly at first glance.' Dittersdorf: 'Y.M. has my answer.' Joseph: 'Mozart would then compare with Klopstock and Haydn with Gellert?' Dittersdorf nods, and the emperor says, 'Now I have a stick to beat Greybig out of his stupidities.' Greybig or Kreibich was Joseph's valet and the leader of the chamber ensemble with which the emperor played every day when in Vienna. Joseph's comment bears out other evidence that Kreibich was unsympathetic to Mozart's music.[32]

This is not the most penetrating criticism, but it is far from contemptible, and it makes the point for me that Joseph maintained his admiration of Mozart in the face of much contemporary opposition, from Count Rosenberg and Count Zinzendorf as well as from Kreibich, and more generally from those who thought Mozart's music too learned and complex, in the emperor's words 'too difficult for the singers'.[33] As Mozart several times mentioned in his letters, Joseph was fond of fugues – an old-fashioned taste which Mozart was happy to indulge.[34] The emperor's encouragement of Mozart's music went back a long way. The opera *La finta semplice* of 1768 owes its existence to a request from Joseph II that the twelve-year-old Mozart should write an opera. The foundation of the National Theatre in 1776 and the German opera company in 1778 were initiatives of the emperor's, detested by the great aristocracy; and without them the *Entführung* would not have been written and performed.[35] In 1782 Joseph recruited a wind-band or *Harmoniemusik*, which included Mozart's clarinettist friend Anton Stadler, and thus set a fashion for such groups in aristocratic houses.[36] Hence Mozart's splendid music for wind ensemble. Only the intervention of the emperor made possible the staging of *The*

Marriage of Figaro as an opera after he had forbidden the performance of the play. He attended rehearsals as well as performances, and he personally decided to allow dances within the opera.[37] The opera *The Impresario* was a direct commission.[38] It was a peremptory order from Joseph that forced the young Maria Theresa to accept *The Marriage of Figaro* at her wedding celebration.[39] Since he exercised control over the minutest details of the operation of the Court theatres, he must have had more to do with *Don Giovanni* and *Cosí fan tutte* than can be proved from surviving documents.

More important still, on 7 December 1787 the emperor appointed Mozart to a salaried post. The traditional view of this action is as follows: the great opera composer and reformer Gluck held the post of *Kammermusikus* or Court composer, at a salary of 2,000 florins, until his death in November 1787, when the mean-spirited emperor replaced him with Mozart at a mere 800 florins.[40] In the first place, supposing that were straightforwardly true, Joseph could perfectly well have appointed somebody else, or paid Mozart even less. But Gluck's payment was a pension, and the job to which Mozart was appointed was a new and superfluous post, virtually without duties. This was a personal despotic decision, communicated orally to Count Rosenberg by the emperor, and given written form by Rosenberg later. It was taken at a time of financial crisis when the emperor's entire musical establishment was being remodelled and the German opera troupe dissolved as an economy measure. The motive is not stated at the time, but when Mozart died and the post became vacant, the following explanation was given in official documents: 'Mozart in fact received the title of Kammer Kompositor with a salary of 800fl. per year from H.M. the late Emperor solely out of consideration that so rare a genius in the world of music should not be obliged to seek abroad for recognition and his daily bread.'[41] That is an extraordinary statement to leap out of a bureaucratic document, surely one of the earliest appearances of the word genius even with reference to Mozart and certainly one of the earliest uses of the word in an official document. It resembles quite closely the arrangement made in 1809 by three noblemen, including Archduke Rudolf, to provide Beethoven an income of 4,000 florins a year, virtually without conditions, to enable him to write the music he wanted to write.[42] Both agreements show that, while subscriptions and the purchase of tickets by the Viennese nobility and public could now provide considerable income, they could not provide enough to maintain a demanding and prestigious composer. Enlightened patronage, without strings attached, was a necessary supplement. In neither case was it sufficient to keep the composer concerned out of debt.[43] But it helped, and in each case it kept him in Vienna.

III

It was once said of an Anglo-Saxon king: 'It is a sign of his competence as a ruler that his reign is singularly devoid of recorded incident.'[44] By that criterion Joseph was the most incompetent of monarchs. His foreign policy, to put it politely, was restless.[45] He stepped up his mother's rate of legislation seven times.[46] The French *philosophes* influenced him less than some well-known false letters have led many historians to suppose.[47] But he was a drastic reformer none the less. He sought to curb the nobles' power and abolished most of the attributes of serfdom. He brought the Catholic Church in all his territories under his direct control, establishing himself as the final authority over nearly every aspect of its work, liturgy and property except the sacramental role of the clergy. The most conspicuous of his measures in this field were the suppression of more than a third of the two thousand or so monasteries in his lands, the removal of most censorship restrictions and the introduction of toleration in varying degrees for the main Protestant sects, for Greek Orthodox and for Jews. In secular affairs he tried to impose a uniform legal and administrative system in all his diverse dominions, which meant destroying the ancient constitutions of Hungary and Belgium.[48] I have examined in the Vatican Archives the excellent reports to Rome of the papal nuncios in Vienna, Garampi and Caprara, who were fascinated and appalled by these changes. Garampi reported on 5 May 1783 that, as part of the emperor's reforms, many officials were being retired and given pensions of a third to a half of their salaries. Such officials were charmingly known as Quiescenti. The Viennese were saying 'that the emperor has [decided] that Jesus Christ ... having given useful service to the House of Austria for many centuries, deserved, in accordance with the guidelines laid down, to have his salary reduced and to be placed among the Quiescenti'.[49]

Many writers on Mozart assume him to have been a radical in politics, at least a sympathiser with Joseph's policies, perhaps more radical still and even a supporter of the French Revolution. Professor Neal Zaslaw, for example, in his invaluable recent book on Mozart's symphonies, declares that the last three of 1788, culminating in the 'Jupiter', were musically revolutionary and contained 'irrational' and 'illogical' elements incompatible with the *ancien régime*, from which he thinks it follows that Mozart must have been a supporter of major changes in politics and religion.[50] It is indisputable that Mozart bridled at the restrictions placed on him by the archbishop of Salzburg, resented the privileges of the nobility and often scoffed at clerical behaviour.[51] But in his hundreds of surviving letters there are extraordinarily few pronouncements which bear directly on contemporary politics or political theory, and historians who believe him to have been politically radical rely on a mere handful of statements. Here is one. When the British fleet relieved Gibraltar in 1782, Mozart expressed his joy to his father, 'for you know I am an arch-Englishman'. Zaslaw writes: 'the Catholic Mozart's pleasure at the defeat of two Catholic countries at the hands of a Protestant country can only be explained by England's position in the eighteenth century as the most Enlightened country in Europe'.[52] But there is no hint in the text that Mozart is thinking of such things, and one might have expected a truly Enlightened person to be on the side of the American colonies. It seems to me that he just liked to follow the fortunes of war, that he had become strongly anti-French during his visit to Paris in 1778 and that he was fascinated by the siege, as is suggested by his setting part of an ode on the subject.[53]

However, Mozart certainly became a Freemason in 1784 and took his membership seriously; and Freemasonry had been condemned by the pope and was considered by many to be subversive of religion and social order. Further, Mozart set a number of Masonic texts, including a particularly utopian hymn of 1791; and notoriously *The Magic Flute* of the same year is full of Masonic symbolism, though commentators differ widely as to its precise message.[54]

I obviously cannot discuss exhaustively the vexed question of Freemasonry. But all students of Mozart and of his relationship with Joseph II have to come to terms with it. This can be done only by setting it in its context of the peculiar thought-world of the 1780s. Many modern writers cannot shake themselves free from the assumption that all Freemasons must have been anti-Catholic, anti-clerical and, still more, anti-monastic, and on the side of progress, freedom of thought and expression, liberty, equality and fraternity, and peace.[55] Some Masons were undoubtedly radical, and many radicals were Masons. But two successive abbots of Melk, who held the office between

1746 and 1785, belonged to a lodge; and, 'following the tradition of the house', their aprons were buried with them in the abbey cloister. Numerous Masons were to be found among the Church dignitaries of Salzburg.[56] In the 1780s it was clearly possible to be both a Mason and a pillar of the Catholic Establishment.[57] This is less surprising than historians have usually implied. They rarely cite the rule, found among the statutes of every regular lodge, which categorically outlawed the discussion of religious and political issues.[58]

Only one passage in Mozart's surviving letters proclaims his devotion to the craft. He was writing to his father, who was 'really ill', early in 1787:

> I am longing to receive some reassuring news from yourself ... [But] I have now made a habit of being prepared in all affairs of life for the worst. As death, when we come to consider it closely, is the true goal of our existence, I have formed during the last few years such close relations with this best and truest friend of mankind, that his image is no longer terrifying to me, but is indeed very soothing and consoling! And I thank my God for graciously granting me the opportunity (you know what I mean) of learning that death is the *key* which unlocks the door to our true happiness. I never lie down at night without reflecting that – young as I am – I may not see another day.[59]

This passage, profoundly Masonic though it may be, lends no support to the belief that Mozart had Enlightened, let alone radical, views. Historians of the Enlightenment agree that the movement rebelled against preoccupation with death and the other world, and encouraged on the contrary attention to what it saw as the possibility of improving Man's life on earth, the possibility in other words of progress.[60] What Mozart is explicitly saying here is that Freemasonry has given him a view of the world irreconcilable with Enlightenment as ordinarily understood. Indeed, it seems to me, though I hesitate to pronounce on such a point, that this is a statement perfectly compatible with a rather old-fashioned Catholic orthodoxy.

Mozart's correspondence contains many discussions of the details of opera libretti, but all of them seem to me to refer not to their content but to their effectiveness on stage and to the composer's musical problems in setting them. We possess only two attempts by Mozart himself to write a dramatic text. Both of them are crude popular comedies, apparently without music, featuring such characters as Kasperl and Wurstl, Herr von Dummkopf and the Salzburg clot.[61]

It is not surprising that writers resort to study of his music, and particularly of the texts he set, for further evidence of his views. But one must be extremely sceptical about any attempts to identify the words of any parts of these texts with Mozart's opinions, and still more about attempts to read into libretti which ostensibly refer to events in other countries at other periods, or to mythology, references to contemporary developments. I acknowledge that this is justified in the case of certain operas by other composers. For instance, Paisiello's opera *Rè Teodoro in Venezia* of 1784, for which Giambattista Casti wrote the libretto, purports to be about King Theodore of Corsica. But Garampi told the papacy that some of its allusions could be understood only if you had heard the stories circulating in Venice and Vienna about the conduct of King Gustavus III of Sweden during his recent tour of central and southern Europe. When, for example, King Theodore sings that his three cherished passions are for 'love, glory and oysters', this is a reference to Gustavus, who while in Venice had both an affair with a hotel-keeper's daughter and a surfeit of oysters. *Rè Teodoro in Venezia* created a new style of comic opera and had a considerable effect on Mozart and Da Ponte.[62]

IV

I am not aware of any comparable examples of such direct allusions concealed in Mozart's works. But he did set four texts in which the emperor is explicitly mentioned. I do not think they have ever been very seriously studied, certainly not from this point of view or as a group. Yet, so far as I know, Joseph is the only living or recent ruler – almost the only living person – who is so honoured. The pieces in which he figures acquire *ipso facto* a special relevance to the events of their time, and they offer some at least circumstantial evidence about Mozart's own situation and attitudes.

The first two of these works form part of Mozart's Masonic music. On 20 April 1785 he entered in his catalogue of his own works *Die Maurerfreude*, 'the Mason's Joy', a cantata for men's chorus and orchestra. It contains the words:

> To see how wisdom and virtue
> turn graciously to the Mason, their disciple,
> and say: Take this crown, beloved,
> from the hands of our eldest son, from Joseph's hands –

that is the feast of rejoicing for the Masons,
This the Mason's triumph …
Joseph the Wise has twined laurels together,
bound the temple of the wise man of the Masons with laurel.

This cantata marks the high point of Masonic influence in Vienna. Ignaz von Born, the effective leader of the movement there, had just been rewarded by the emperor for his discovery of a new metallurgical process.[63] Joseph was never, as his father had been, a Freemason. But, according to the nuncio, Joseph had also just sent a letter to the Bohemian Chancery saying that he was 'very far from being prejudiced against [Freemasons]; that as long as they behave well, and observe certain rules laid down by him, he wishes them to be left undisturbed in the conduct of their Lodges'.[64] Even if there was never such an original, that wording corresponds with other remarks of Joseph's and reflects the position in the middle of 1785. Lodges and Freemasons had greatly increased in number since he had succeeded Maria Theresa in 1780; they had exploited the relaxation of the censorship to the point that they were publishing a periodical whose circulation was not restricted to those who had sworn Masonic oaths of secrecy; a high proportion of Joseph's officials belonged to lodges; and Masons were seen as the most reliable supporters of his programme of reform.[65]

But the position was about to change. The emperor had always had reservations about Freemasons. Like his chief minister, Prince Kaunitz, he thought their goings-on rather silly. He disapproved of their international connections and of their secrecy and came to suspect some of them of disloyalty, corruption and broils.[66] On 11 December 1785 he issued one of his most withering rescripts in which he spoke of the *Gaukelei* or hocus-pocus of Freemasonry, ordered the closure of all but a small number of lodges and a reduction in the total membership, and instructed them to report the names of their members to the government.[67]

The terms of this edict pained the Masons, but it did give legal sanction to an organisation previously of doubtful legality. The remaining Masons still saw themselves as under Joseph's protection. At the beginning of January 1786 Mozart composed music to a three-part chorus with organ for the opening of one of the lodges established under the new system. The text asserted that

Joseph's good will …
has crowned our hope anew.

With united hearts and tongues
let this song of praise be sung to Joseph,
to the father, who has bound us closer together.
To do good is the loveliest of duties;
he has seen us ardently perform it
and crowns us with a loving hand.[68]

It is sometimes suggested that he became henceforth suspicious of Masons as potentially revolutionary, so that for example Mozart became a marked man. This cannot be sustained. Many of Joseph's officials remained Masons. When an informer offered at the end of 1787 to penetrate a revolutionary international conspiracy of Masons based in Frankfurt, Count Cobenzl, Kaunitz's deputy, advised the emperor: 'I do not believe that the spirit of Masonry, though highly fashionable, is solidly enough established to be able to hatch such revolutions ... However, as all kinds of intrigues and cabals do enjoy the favour of Masonry now that great aristocrats and courtiers, ministers and clerks, imbeciles and knaves take a serious part in it,' he thought Joseph might wish to follow up this offer. Joseph refused to have anything to do with it.[69] It was at almost exactly this time that Mozart received his appointment as Court composer.

The remaining two pieces in which the emperor is named concern the Turkish war. Joseph went to war early in 1788 because in 1787 the Turks attacked Russia and because his secret treaty of 1781 with Catherine II of Russia bound him in those circumstances to support her with all his forces.[70]

Much has been made of the unpopularity of this war in Vienna; and among the worthy attitudes commonly ascribed by historians to Freemasons is pacifism or, at least, non-belligerence.[71] But there were signs of a revival of bellicosity in the Monarchy before the Turkish war broke out. Two books published in 1787, *Abdul Erzerum's neue persische Briefe* and *Dya-Na-Sore*, both declared that men were becoming too soft and that only war would bring out the best in them and nurture love of the fatherland. These books were probably both the work of Friedrich von Meyer or Meyern, who was a Mason.[72] The fact that Prince Karl Liechtenstein was a Mason did not stop him, so long as his health permitted, leading his troops against the Turks in the campaign of 1788.[73] Schikaneder, librettist of *The Magic Flute*, who had at least some experience of Masonry, introduced bloodthirsty patriotic songs into his productions during the war, for example into

Die beiden Antone oder der dumme Gärtner, which Mozart saw and enjoyed.[74] Here are two sample lines:

> Now then, German brothers, gird up your courage!
> Pursue the Turks, squirt out their blood [*verspritzet ihr Blut*].[75]

Victory in the war, when it came, was unquestionably popular. Pezzl in his *Skizze von Wien*, Caroline Pichler in her memoirs, the Prussian ambassador and the papal nuncio in their despatches all described the wild enthusiasm of the Viennese at the news of the capture of Belgrade in October 1789.[76]

Here, for once, some of Mozart's works are directly related to specific political events. Altogether there are two war songs, two dances celebrating successful battles, and a piece for mechanical organ or clock in memory of Marshal Laudon, the victor of Belgrade.[77] Both the songs mention the emperor. On 5 March 1788, just after the Austrian declaration of war, Mozart set Gleim's old patriotic song of 1776, 'I would dearly love to be the emperor', which continues:

> I would shake the East,
> The Muslims would tremble,
> Constantinople would be mine.[78]

Much more remarkable, though far less familiar, is Mozart's other patriotic song, *Beim Auszug in das Feld*, dated 11 August 1788, the day after the 'Jupiter' symphony was completed. It was believed lost until the early twentieth century and was not included in collected editions until the most recent. It seems that only one complete copy survives. The author of the words is unknown.[79]

If the true interest of the text is to be grasped, we must not only examine the full eighteen verses, a translation of which I have supplied in the Appendix to this chapter (with the music, pp. 107–10), but also the amazingly elaborate explanatory notes that were appended to them, about which I can say only a little. The first verse talks of the emperor fulfilling his promise and mobilising his armies which are thirsting for victory and glory. Verses 2 and 3 praise his paternal concern for his soldiers' welfare. The next verse stresses the overriding importance for the troops of their confidence that God is on their side. Then in verse 5 the poet changes gear, very clumsily, and talks about the emperor's sympathy with those who suffer unfairly because of the war. Verses 6 to 9 may reasonably be called Masonic, at least in a generalised sense: God cares for all nations including Jews, Turks and heathen; all men are brothers. In verses 9 and 10 the gears are crashed a second time. The emperor, says the author, has extended toleration to both Turk and Jew.[80] He has also been seeking peace between nations. But alas! *one* nation – the Turks – has stood out and thwarted his benevolence. With that the song can return to martial fervour. In verse 14 God does not want brothers to die, but equally certainly he wants to correct injustice. In the last four verses patriotism takes over: the brave troops are fighting for the right and for mankind; God will reward the heroes whose blood is shed; future generations will bless them; their heroism will not have been in vain.

The notes to the song, like other pieces in the periodical from which it comes, are manifestly propagandist, directed at persuading young men of the justice of the emperor's cause. Though it is admitted that some exceptional Turks bear the marks of civilization, 'the true ordinary Turk remains ... an inhuman, ungovernable monster'. An attempt is made to counteract the revulsion against the war produced by food shortage and other economic problems. On 31 July, we are told, bakeries throughout the capital had been stormed by the usually phlegmatic inhabitants. The annotator claims that none of this would have happened if Joseph had not been away from Vienna on campaign. Young men – future conscripts into the army – must be persuaded of the invariable wisdom of the emperor, God's representative on earth.[81]

The song has not fared well at the hands of editors and commentators. When the music was first published in England, as late as 1960, it was headed with a delicious editorial note: 'Written apparently for a youth rally, the song had an enormous number of verses which seem to refer to the Turkish war ... The words have no interest whatever outside their own period and purpose. For the present edition, therefore, the lovely tune has been provided with new English words.' The title given to this improved version was 'The Maiden and the Fawn'.[82] I know of only one recording of the original, in the Philips complete CD series, where the song is oddly located among the arias and where only six verses are sung, chosen so that its message is uncomplicatedly warlike. A recent writer prints only the first eight verses, which minimises the song's bellicosity.[83]

As with nearly all the texts Mozart set, we do not know what he thought of this one. One commentator is confident that he wholeheartedly supported Joseph's war policy. The *Neue Mozart Ausgabe* assures us on the contrary that the setting by 'MOZART THE FREEMASON'

skilfully highlighted the Masonic elements in the song.[84] This is manifest nonsense: the music is the same for every pair of verses, whether
their sense is cosmopolitan or patriotic, humanitarian or heroic.

V

Leopold II becomes a mere tailpiece. He had admired Mozart's performance as a child in Vienna and a boy in Tuscany, and the composer
had had hopes of him as an employer in the early seventies.[85] But
they then had little or no contact until Leopold succeeded Joseph.
The new ruler lived only two years more, and Mozart died three
months before he did. The composer retained under Leopold the
sinecure post and salary given him by Joseph.

The new emperor loved *opera seria*, and so Mozart was able to go
back to that genre in 1791 with *La clemenza di Tito* – though Leopold
seems not to have relished the result.[86] It has become commonplace
to say that, in glorifying Titus's clemency, the opera was setting up
a model of Enlightened absolutism.[87] Or, as Professor Heartz puts it:
'Clemency was a virtue ardently espoused by the Enlightenment, an
age during which Montesquieu, Beccaria, and Voltaire led the fight
against penal torture.'[88] These views seem to me mistaken. Clemency
in individual cases, such as Titus displays, is a virtue of Christian and
even non-Christian rulers through all ages. But there is a fundamental
difference between this essentially arbitrary practice and the general
mitigation of the criminal law on Enlightened principles. Beccaria
disapproved of rulers exercising clemency in special cases. He thought
that the punishment appropriate to a certain crime could and should
be determined by calculating precisely how much pain had to be
inflicted on the criminal to deter him and others from committing
the same offence in future. The ruler has no business to disturb the
arithmetic by merciful caprice.[89] Furthermore, a ruler deserving the
name Enlightened must surely propose reforms. In the opera Titus
takes no political actions other than oscillating between severity and
clemency and granting relief for the victims of Vesuvius.[90]

Mozart was also happy to be able to write instrumental church
music again, possible now because Leopold withdrew some of his
brother's prohibitions.[91] The composer walked in the Corpus Christi
procession at the Piarist Church in Vienna in 1791, when he seems to
have felt awkward carrying a candle. But he had just written his new
motet *Ave verum corpus* for performance at the same Feast in Baden.

Later in the year, he worked to get his son admitted to the Piarists' school.[92] He had obtained the promise of the lucrative organist's post at St Stephen's cathedral in Vienna, which fell vacant too late for him to enjoy it.[93] It looks as though he was destined for a second career as a church musician. Whether Leopold would have come to appreciate his talents better we cannot know.

VI

My essential points about the relationship between Mozart and the Habsburgs are these. Unlike any of the others, Joseph had an enduring admiration for Mozart and gave him a sinecure post in recognition of his genius. This was a matter of musical taste and appreciation, unaffected by political considerations. Mozart was a Freemason, but this by no means implies that he was anti-Catholic, radical or pacifist; and nor would it have troubled Joseph. Mozart's letters tell us almost nothing unequivocal about his political views. If we look at the texts he set in order to discover more about his attitudes, we are on dangerous ground and cannot hope for certainty. But in doing so we should surely pay more than perfunctory attention to the words of the few songs which have a direct bearing on contemporary politics. And it would not be surprising if a song like *Beim Auszug in das Feld* expressed something like Mozart's sentiments, since it mirrors in its confusion the confusions of the age and of Joseph II himself, humanitarian and militaristic, reformist in religion but in his own view an orthodox Catholic – a despot imposing far-reaching changes, some of them Enlightened, apparently even Liberal, by *fiat* from above.[94]

Appendix: When troops are leaving for the front (*Beim Auszug in das Feld*)

Poem anonymous, translated by Derek Beales with much help from Professor H. B. Nisbet

1 True to the emperor's lofty word,
   Joseph called up his armies:
   They flew together, as if on wings,
   Full of thirst for victory and honour.
2 For all are glad to heed the call
   Of a father who loves his children,

Whose care protects them all from harm,
From every threat of danger.

3 Wherever they appeared, they found
Their fill of food and drink;
And do not good will and thanks alone
Often repay a hero's efforts?

4 But more than by all this the breasts
Of men are steeled for the conflict
By the consoling thought that God himself
Accompanies them into battle.

5 For on their hearts was deep impressed
Father Joseph's example:
Where fellow men felt injustice,
They also suffered with them.

6 For human beings everywhere
Are God Almighty's creatures;
Heathen and Turk, Christian and Jew
Are all alike his children.

7 He causes thus his rain to fall
For Jew and Turk and heathen;
For Christians too he clothes the bare fields
And makes them rich and fertile

8 But so it also is his will
That men should never harm each other,
Given that each one seldom thinks
The same way as his brother.

9 Thus Joseph, like a God on earth,
Showed Turks and Jews toleration,
And shielded them from oppression and hurt
And sought peace for every nation.

10 This too the whole world gave to him,
Save *one* that stood out against it:
This one believes itself the only chosen race
And knows no other brothers;

11 And knows no right but its own hand
And no duty but murder,
So that many a lovely land
Has sunk in waste and horror.

12 But it hides behind a mask
And prates of truth and loyalty,
And whispers in other people's ears
As if it were the victim.

First edition of *Beim Auszug in das Feld* (KV 552) from *Wochenblatt für Kinder zur angenehmen und lehrreichen Beschäftigung in ihrer Freystunden*, vol. IV (1788), reproduced by kind permission of the British Library.

13 And hopes by this hypocrisy
To ensnare the hearts of brothers
So that many, stirred up and quarrelsome,
Should even come to its aid.

14 But this our glorious Lord above
Will surely not let happen:
He doesn't want our brothers' death,
He wants to right injustice.

15 All brothers who love humanity and right
Will stand and fight beside us,

For it's to help humanity's cause
That our swords are sharpened.
16 So, brave warriors, fight with courage
For your crowns of honour!
God himself will recompense
Your heroes' blood at his throne!
17 Your descendants will bless you too
With warm and fervent thanks
For every well-aimed blow
That once helped to secure their happiness.
18 For we're recording all your names,
As if in the Book of Life,
So that they can show you their love and gratitude,
Your heroes, let it not be in vain!

Notes

An earlier version of this chapter was given as the Stenton Lecture of the University of Reading for 1992. Further relevant material will be found in two articles which overlap with this piece: 'Court, Government and Society in Mozart's Vienna' in S. Sadie (ed.), *Wolfgang Amadè Mozart* (Oxford, 1996), pp. 1–20, and 'The Impact of Joseph II on Vienna' in M. Csáky and W. Pass (eds), *Europa im Zeitalter Mozarts* (Vienna, 1995), pp. 301–10.

I owe thanks for financial support in my research to the Barbican Arts Centre, the British Academy, the University of Cambridge and Sidney Sussex College, Cambridge; and for other help to the Austrian Art Service, the Cambridge Faculty of Music, Professor T. C. W. Blanning, Professor P. Branscombe, Dr A. Fox, Professor H. B. Nisbet, Dr S. A. Sadie and Professor H. M. Scott.

1 An excellent survey covering these matters is N. Zaslaw (ed.), *The Classical Era* (London, 1989). On Dittersdorf his *Lebensbeschreibung*, ed. E. Schmitz (Regensburg, 1940), esp. pp. 191–2.

2 On Haydn the path-breaking works of H. C. Robbins Landon. The contract made between Prince Nicholas Esterházy and the composer in 1761 is to be found in Landon's *Haydn: Chronicle and Works*, vol. I (London, 1980), pp. 350–2.

3 E. Anderson (ed.), *The Letters of Mozart and His Family* (3rd edn, London, 1985), esp. pp. 716–35.

4 As well as Zaslaw, *The Classical Era*, see A. Yorke-Long, *Music at Court* (London, 1954). The notion propagated by (e.g.) R. Leppert in his *Music and Image* (Cambridge, 1988), chs 6 and 7, that musical studies were considered effeminate in the eighteenth century, may possibly have some application to Britain but is fatuous in relation to Germany and the Austrian Monarchy.

5 Anderson, *Letters*, pp. 34–5.

6 Ibid., p. 46.

7 Ibid., p. 148; O. E. Deutsch (ed.), *Mozart: A Documentary Biography* (2nd edn, London, 1966), pp. 123–5.

8 Anderson, *Letters*, pp. 59, 64; Deutsch, *Mozart*, pp. 49, 53. On the pieces N. Zaslaw, *Mozart's Symphonies* (Oxford, 1991), pp. 48–64.

9 Anderson, *Letters*, pp. 6, 8.

10 Ibid., pp. 186n., 193; Deutsch, *Mozart*, pp. 135–7; G. Barblan and A. Della Corte, *Mozart in Italia: I viaggi e le lettere* (Milan, 1956), pp. 150–60, 185–6.

11 Anderson, *Letters*, pp. 8, 253 and n., 794–5; Deutsch, *Mozart*, pp. 151–2.

12 Anderson, *Letters*, p. 142.

13 Ibid., p. 911; Deutsch, *Mozart*, p. 300.

14 L. von Köchel, *Chronologisch-thematisches Verzeichnis sämtlicher Tonwerke W. A. Mozarts* (7th edn, Wiesbaden, 1965), p. 687. It is not made clear whether this is actually Mozart's dedication or the publisher's.

15 Deutsch, *Mozart*, p. 138; Barblan and Della Corte, *Mozart in Italia*, pp. 186–7 and Pl. XXXI (p. 168).

16 See for unsuccessful efforts to involve Marie Antoinette, Anderson, *Letters*, pp. 439, 537 and n.; Deutsch, *Mozart*, p. 171. Antonia Fraser has recently pointed out that the queen was pregnant at the time and unable to help Mozart: *Marie Antoinette* (London, 2000), p. 151.

17 For the young Maria Theresa, Anderson, *Letters*, p. 911; Deutsch, *Mozart*, pp. 300–1.

18 See n.14 above for K.600. For *Lucio Silla*, Deutsch, *Mozart*, p. 143; Barblan and Della Corte, *Mozart in Italia*, pp. 165–73 and Pl. XXXII (p. 169).

19 Deutsch, *Mozart*, pp. 29, 129.

20 *Thayer's Life of Beethoven*, ed. E. Forbes (Princeton, 1970), e.g. pp. 475, 660, 745, 879.

21 E.g. Anderson, *Letters*, pp. 782, 814–15.

22 I deal with the question of the Court in my paper in Sadie, *Wolfgang Amadè Mozart*. Cf. V. Braunbehrens, *Mozart in Vienna* (Oxford, 1991), pp. 42–3.

23 D. Heartz, *Mozart's Operas*, ed. T. Bauman (Oxford, 1990), passim.

24 The most thorough account of Joseph's legislation on church music is O. Biba, 'Die Wiener Kirchenmusik um 1783', *Beiträge zur Musikgeschichte des 18. Jahrhunderts* [*Jahrbuch für österreichische Kulturgeschichte*, I, 2] (Eisenstadt, 1971), pp. 7–79. Useful discussions in English are R. G. Pauly, 'The Reforms of Church Music under Joseph II', *Musical Quarterly*, 43 (1957): 372–82 and B. C. Macintyre, *The Viennese Concerted Mass of the Early Classic Period* (Ann Arbor, 1986), esp. p. 46, references on p. 691. I am very grateful to Professor Linda Colley for giving me a copy of Macintyre's book. The C minor Mass poses many problems, on which see, e.g., H. C. Robbins Landon, *Mozart: The Golden Years, 1781–1791* (London, 1989), pp. 91–5.

25 The first known mention of this comment dates from 1798. Hence its authenticity is doubtful, though the fuller version sounds plausible if 'our

ears' is understood to refer to the Viennese: 'Too beautiful for our ears, my dear Mozart, and monstrous many notes!' Cf. T. Bauman, *Die Entführung aus dem Serail* (Cambridge, 1987), p. 89.

26 D. Beales, *Joseph II. I: In the Shadow of Maria Theresa, 1741–80* (Cambridge, 1987), (esp. ch. 10. Joseph II to Leopold, 3 June and 4 July 1771, Haus-, Hof- und Staatsacrchiv, Vienna [hereafter HHSA], Familien-Archiv, Sammelbände 7, not printed in *Maria Theresia und Joseph II. Ihre Correspondenz*, ed. A. Ritter von Arneth (Vienna, 1867–68).

27 Deutsch, *Mozart*, p. 207.

28 For this correspondence and for Joseph's preoccupation with theatrical issues see R. Payer von Thurn, *Joseph II. als Theaterdirektor* (Vienna, 1920).

29 I am assured, on the authority of Dr O. Mazal, that the National Library in Vienna, which possesses many of the exercises Joseph wrote during his education, has no musical compositions of his.

30 See W. Kirkendale, *Fuge und Fugato in der Kammermusik des Rokoko und der Klassik* (Tutzing, 1966), pp. 62–3, 81.

31 Beales, *Joseph II*, p. 316.

32 Dittersdorf, *Lebensbeschreibung*, pp. 208–09, 212–13. On Kreibich and Joseph, see Deutsch, *Mozart*, pp. 369–70; Beales, *Joseph II*, pp. 316 and nn., 319.

33 Deutsch, *Mozart*, pp. 314, 315. This statement of Joseph's was not, as V. Braunbehrens says in his generally reliable *Mozart in Vienna*, p. 165, 'rumoured'. It appears in the emperor's letter of 16 May 1788 to Count Rosenberg (Deutsch, *Mozart*, p. 315).

34 E.g. Anderson, *Letters*, pp. 718, 843. Of course, Gottfried Van Swieten's concerts of the music of Bach and Handel revived the interest of Mozart and others in earlier contrapuntal music during the 1780s.

35 Beales, *Joseph II*, pp. 230–6, 316; Heartz, *Mozart's Operas*, ch. IV.

36 Landon, *Mozart*, p. 33; H.-J. Irmen, *Mozart Mitglied geheimer Gesellschaften* (Neustadt, 1988), p. 245 and n.

37 Heartz, *Mozart's Operas*, pp. 133–8, and Landon, *Mozart*, pp. 155–62 and 243, discuss and largely vindicate the librettist, Lorenzo da Ponte's, account in his *Memoirs*, ed. A. Livingston (New York, 1967), pp. 149–51, 159–61.

38 Deutsch, *Mozart*, pp. 261–3.

39 Anderson, *Letters*, p. 911.

40 One example is K. Thomson, *The Masonic Thread in Mozart* (London, 1977), p. 124.

41 Deutsch, *Mozart*, pp. 305–7, 430, 445. See for fresh interpretation of this gesture Irmen, *Mozart Mitglied geheimer Gesellschaften*, pp. 246–9. Robbins Landon's description of Joseph's motives as 'negative' (*1791: Mozart's Last Year* [London, 1988, p. 41]) strikes me as curious.

42 *Thayer's Life of Beethoven*, pp. 453–9.

43 Mozart's debts are notorious, but it is impossible to calculate them precisely. Cf. J. Moore, 'Mozart in the Market-Place', *Journal of the Royal Musical Association*, 114 (1989): 18–42. Dr C. R. Wilson kindly supplied me

with a copy of this article. For a re-evaluation of Viennese concert life see M. S. Morrow, *Concert Life in Haydn's Vienna: Aspects of a Developing Musical and Social Institution* (Stuyvesant, NY, 1989). The situation in Britain was of course much more favourable to the performer.

44 It was said of King Edgar. See F. M. Sterton, *Anglo-Saxon England* (2nd edn, Oxford, 1947), p. 363.

45 I have tried to show that it was less aggressive and exapansionist than has often been maintained in my *Joseph II* and in my article, 'Die auswärtige Politik der Monarchie vor und nach 1780. Kontinuität und Zäsur', in R. G. Plaschka and G. Klingenstein (eds), *Österreich im Europa der Aufklärung* (2 vols, Vienna, 1985), vol. I, pp. 567–74.

46 P. G. M. Dickson, *Finance and Government under Maria Theresia* (2 vols, Oxford, 1987), vol. I, pp. 318–19.

47 See Chapter 5, 'The False Joseph II'.

48 See Chapter 11, 'Was Joseph II an Enlightened Despot?'. The main authority remains P. von Mitrofanov, *Joseph II* (2 vols, Vienna, 1910).

49 Archivio segreto vaticano: Nunziatura di Vienna [hereafter ASVNV] 182, Garampi's despatch, 5 May 1783. Garampi was nuncio until the middle of 1785, Caprara thereafter. Their despatches were addressed to a succession of papal secretaries of state. I should like to thank Mgr C. Burns for his generous guidance in the Vatican Archives.

50 Zaslaw, *Mozart's Symphonies*, ch. 13. A. Arblaster, *Viva la Libertà: Politics in Opera* (London, 1992) asserts that historians of opera are too inclined to treat the genre as apolitical. This is simply not true for Mozart. See W. Weber, 'The Myth of Mozart, the Revolutionary', *Musical Quarterly*, 78 (1994): 34–47, in which he argues that musical historians get Mozart wrong because they are out of touch with recent scholarship on the French Revolution. Professor Weber kindly sent me a copy of this article.

51 Anderson, *Letters*, e.g., pp. 734–5, 757–8, 779.

52 Ibid., p. 828; Zaslaw, *Mozart's Symphonies*, pp. 526–7.

53 Anderson, *Letters*, pp. 558, 833.

54 The utopian hymn is KV 619. For a judicious discussion of Free-masonry in *The Magic Flute* see P. Branscombe, *Die Zauberflöte* (Cambridge, 1991), esp. ch. 2.

55 For enthusiastic appraisals see Thomson, *Masonic Thread*; P. A. Autexier, *Les oeuvres témoins de Mozart* (Paris, 1982); and H. Reinalter's numerous and repetitive works. Irmen's *Mozart Mitglied geheimer Gesellschaften* has brought to light much new material, the significance of which has yet to be evaluated.

56 *Österreich zur Zeit Kaiser Josephs II* (catalogue of the Melk bicentenary exhibition, 1980), p. 592. H. Dopsch and H. Spatzenegger (eds), *Geschichte Salzburgs*, vol. II, part 1 (Salzburg, 1988), p. 409.

57 See the impressive article by F. Wehrl, 'Der "Neue Geist". Eine Unter-suchung der Geistesrichtungen des Klerus in Wien von 1750–1790', *Mitteilun-gen des österreichischen Staatsarchivs* [hereafter *MÖSA*], 20 (1967): 36–114. He

concludes on p. 107: 'If a cleric attended a Lodge, that must ... not be taken as evidence that his orthodoxy was dubious, still less that he was irreligious.'

58 Even L. Abafi, *Geschichte der Freimaurerei in Österreich-Ungarn* (5 vols, Budapest, 1890–99), e.g. vol. IV, pp. 73, 138, acknowledges this, although it does not stop him writing as though all lodges were politically radical. For relevant extracts from the *Journal für Freymaurer* and other documents, see E. Lessing et al. (eds), *Die Übungslogen der gerechten und vollkommenen Loge ZUR WAHREN EINTRACHT im Orient zu Wien 1782–1785* (Vienna, 1984).

59 Anderson, *Letters*, p. 907.

60 R. Porter, *The Enlightenment* (London, 1990) is a strident example.

61 Branscombe, *Zauberflöte*, p. 6.

62 ASV, Nunziatura di Vienna 184, 3 Jan. 1785. Some students of Casti have been aware that the opera lampoons Gustavus III, e.g. L. Pistorelli in *Rivista musicale italiana*, vol. II (1895), pp. 37–45 (who actually cites on p. 41 a passage quoted by Garampi in which the king takes pride in his clothes) and G. Muresu, *Le occasioni di un libertino* (Florence, 1973), pp. 132–47. But I am not aware that any modern writer has understood the rather elaborate references to oysters (it is suggested to Teodoro that he raise money by granting an oyster monopoly, which the king refuses to do, saying he needs them all for his own table). Nor has the following quatrain, said by Garampi to mock Gustavus for travelling incognito and rejecting etiquette, been picked out:

> I Ceremonial, sorella mia,
> Pei gran Principi è vér che sono inezie.
> Ma per li Ré miei pari,
> Indispensabil sono, e necessari.

This might be thought to have struck as much at Joseph as at Gustavus.

The text of the libretto in *Opere Varie di Giambattista Casti* (6 vols, Paris, 1821), vol. VI, pp. 59–132, contains all the points mentioned by Garampi. The text published in London in 1787 for a King's Theatre performance, with an English translation, lacks most of them.

On the influence of this opera on Mozart, see Heartz, *Mozart's Operas*, pp. 127–8 and nn.

63 Deutsch, *Mozart*, pp. 245, 247–8; Irmen, *Mozart Mitglied geheimer Gesellschaften*, pp. 153–7. *Die Maurerfreude* is KV 471.

64 ASVV, 184, dispaccio straordinario of 24 Apr. 1785. Section G: 'Liberi Muratori'. Cf. Irmen, *Mozart Mitglied geheimer Gesellschaften*, pp. 147–52.

65 This is a constant theme of the nuncios' despatches, as of modern writings such as H. Reinalter (ed.), *Joseph II. und die Freimaurerei* (Vienna, 1987).

66 See Beales, *Joseph II*, pp. 477, 486; H. Wagner, 'Die Lombardei und das Freimaurer Patent Joseph II', *MÖSA*, XXXI (1978): 143.

67 Reinalter, *Joseph II. und die Freimaurerei*, reproduces Joseph's rescript and the main pamphlets it provoked. See Irmen, *Mozart Mitglied geheimer Gesellschaften*, pp. 168–79.

68 KV 483. Irmen, *Mozart Mitglied geheimer Gesellschaften*, pp. 180–2.

69 Philip Cobenzl to Joseph, late Nov./Dec. 1787, HHSA, Staatskanzlei, Vorträge 144, with the emperor's reply and the memorandum from the informer, Ponte Leon. Cobenzl had himself been involved with the Illuminati.

70 The story of the Turkish war is garbled by many writers. For a reliable account of its origins see K. A. Roider, Jr, *Austria's Eastern Question, 1700–1790* (Princeton, 1982), pp. 160–2, 174–5.

71 E.g. Mitrofanov, *Joseph II*, vol. I, pp. 211–22; Irmen, *Mozart Mitglied geheimer Gesellschaften*, pp. 250–4, 259–63; Thomson, *Masonic Thread*, chs 14 and 15.

72 On Meyer(n) see P. Horwath, 'The Altar of the Fatherland: William Friedrich von Meyern's Utopian Novel *Dya-Na-Sore*', *Austrian Studies*, I (1991): 43–58; L. Bodi, *Tauwetter in Wien* (Frankfurt-am-Main, 1977), pp. 313–17, 320–1. It has been generally supposed that Johann Pezzl, another Mason, wrote the *Neue persische Briefe* (see G. Gugitz, 'Johann Pezzl', *Jahrbuch der Grillparzer-Gesellschaft*, xvi [1906]: 195–7), but the book has been attributed to Meyern in J. Kunisch, 'Das "Puppenwerk"der stehenden Heere: Ein Beitrag zur Neueinschätzung von Soldatenstand und Krieg in der Spätaufklärung', *Zeitschrift für historische Forschung* (1990): 49–83. Professor E. Wangermann kindly gave me the reference to this important article.

73 Irmen, *Mozart Mitglied geheimer Gesellschaften*, p. 252.

74 For a cool appraisal of Schikaneder's involvement with Freemasonry, usually greatly exaggerated, see Branscombe, *Die Zauberflöte*, pp. 43–4. See also S. Hock, 'Österreichische Türkenlieder (1788–1790)', *Euphorion*, XI (1904): 93–4; Anderson, *Letters*, p. 940.

75 Hock, *Euphorion* (1904): 101.

76 J. Pezzl, *Skizze von Wien* (2 vols, Vienna, 1789–90), vol. I, pp. 813–20; Caroline Pichler, *Denkwürdigkeiten aus meinem Leben*, ed. G. Gugitz (2 vols, Vienna, 1914), vol. I, pp. 97–8; Jacobi to Hertzberg, 17 Oct. 1789 (Zentrales Staatsarchiv, Merseburg, Rep. 96 154H); Caprara in ASVNV, 200, 15 Oct. 1789.

77 The songs are KV 539, 552; the dances *Die Belagerung Belgrads* (or *La Bataille*) (23 Jan. 1788), KV 535, and *Der Sieg vom Helden Coburg* (Dec. 1789), KV 587; the mechanical organ piece (probably) KV 594 (late 1790).

78 I discuss this song briefly in my two Mozart conference papers (see the opening para. to these notes). Cf. Irmen, *Mozart Mitglied geheimer Gesellschaften*, p. 253; Deutsch, *Mozart*, p. 311.

79 The song was originally published in the fourth volume of a (now very rare) periodical (to which Mozart subscribed) entitled *Wochenblatt für Kinder zur angenehmen und lehrreichen Beschäftigung in ihren Freystunden*, vol. IV. See Deutsch, *Mozart*, pp. 285–6, 326. The words were reprinted with related material in E. Mandyczewski, 'Kostbarkeiten aus dem Archiv der k.k. Gesellschaft der Musikfreunde in Wien', *Der Merker*, IV (May 1913): 324–30.

80 In the original annotations to the song, it is stated that Joseph has accorded rights of citizenship in his states to both Turks and Jews, and indeed has given them one *Begünstigung* ('favour') after another. The writer sounds

uneasy at this benevolence, and also apprehensive that many young men may not sympathise with it. They are urged to obey Joseph in this as in his foreign policy, since to be intolerant towards any fellow citizens is to sin against both God and emperor. Mandyczewski, *Merker* (May 1913): 329. Joseph's favours to Muslims seem to have been missed by historians, and I know of only two: (i) permission to bury their dead in a special cemetery (I. De Luca, *Politische Codex* [6 vols, Vienna, 1789], vol. II, p. 223) and (ii), after war broke out, an order that resident Turks should not be molested.

81 This paragraph derives from Mandyczewski (see n.79).

82 Curwen edn, London, 1960, ed. Jack Werner, words by Margaret Lyell.

83 Irmen, *Mozart Mitglied geheimer Gesellschaften*, p. 261.

84 *Neue Mozart Ausgabe* (20 vols, 1955–91), vol. III, 8, pp. 56–7.

85 Anderson, *Letters*, pp. 2, 125, 222, 224–6; Barblan and Della Corte, *Mozart in Italia*, pp. 87–8, 187–90, 231.

86 J. A. Rice, *La Clemenza di Tito* (Cambridge, 1991) on this opera. On Mozart and *opera seria* in general, Heartz, *Mozart's Operas*, is fundamental. See also Landon, *Mozart's Last Year*.

87 A. Wandruszka, 'Die "Clementia Austriaca" und der aufgeklärte Absolutismus: Zu politischen und ideellen Hintergrund von "La Clemenza di Tito"', *Österreichische Musikzeitschrift*, XXXI (1976): 186–93, is followed, e.g., by Rice, *Clemenza di Tito*, p. 14.

88 Heartz, *Mozart's Operas*, p. 272.

89 C. Beccaria, *Dei delitti e delle pene*, ch. XLVI, in *Edizione nazionale delle opere di Cesare Beccaria*, ed. L. Firpo (Milan, 1984), vol. I, pp. 127–8.

90 I have discussed these issues rather more fully in my article in Sadie, *Wolfgang Amadè Mozart*.

91 Rice in Zaslaw, *The Classical Era*, pp. 159–61.

92 Anderson, *Letters*, pp. 957, 969, 971; Deutsch, *Mozart*, pp. 397, 409.

93 Anderson, *Letters*, pp. 949–50; Deutsch, *Mozart*, p. 395.

94 Cf. Chapter 3, 'Christians and *Philosophes*'.

CHAPTER 5

The False Joseph II

I

'Since I have ascended the throne, and wear the first diadem in the world, I have made philosophy the legislator of my empire.' Of all the sayings attributed to the Emperor Joseph II, this is easily the most hackneyed. It figures in many surveys of eighteenth-century history, whether old like W. O. Hassall's and A. H. Johnson's or newer like those by Stuart Andrews, Maurice Ashley, R. W. Harris and E. N. Williams; in what used to rank as the best biography of Joseph in German, by Viktor Bibl; in the most extended and best-known Life in English, Saul K. Padover's *The Revolutionary Emperor*; in Hans Magenschab's more recent *Joseph II: Revolutionär von Gottes Gnaden*; in Herbert H. Rowen's collection of documents, *From Absolutism to Revolution*; in Albert Sorel's *Europe and the French Revolution*; in Victor-L. Tapié's *The Rise and Fall of the Habsburg Monarchy*; and in Walter W. Davis's *Joseph II: An Imperial Reformer for the Austrian Netherlands*.[1] The remark is the first sentence of a letter which the emperor is supposed to have written to Cardinal Herzan, his minister in Rome, in October 1781, and which goes on:

> In consequence of its logic, Austria will assume another form, the authority of the Ulemas will be restricted, and the rights of majesty will be restored to their primitive extent. It is necessary I should remove certain things out of the domain of religion which never did belong to it.
>
> As I myself detest superstition and the Sadducean doctrines, I will free my people of them; with this view, I will dismiss the monks, I will suppress their monasteries, and will subject them to the bishops of their diocese.
>
> In Rome they will declare this an infringement of the rights of God: I know they will cry aloud, 'the greatness of Israel is fallen'; they will complain, that I take away from the people their tribunes, and that I draw a line of separation between dogma and philosophy; but

they will be still more enraged when I undertake all this without the approbation of the servant of the servants of God.

To these things we owe the degradation of the human mind. A servant of the altar will never admit that the state is putting him into his proper place, when it leaves him no other occupation than the gospel, and when by laws it prevents the children of Levi from carrying on a monopoly with the human understanding.

The principles of monachism, from Pachomius up to our time, have been directly opposed to the light of reason; respect for their founders ultimately became adoration itself, so that we beheld again the Israelites going up to Bethel, in order to adore golden calves.

These false conceptions of religion were transmitted to the common people; they no longer knew God, and expected every thing from the saints.

The rights of the bishops, which I will re-establish, must assist in reforming the ideas of the people; instead of the monk, I will have the priest to preach, not the romances of the canonized, but the holy gospel and morality.

I shall take care that the edifice, which I have erected for posterity, be durable. The general seminaries are nurseries for my priests; whence, on going out into the world, they will take with them a purified mind, and communicate it to the people by wise instruction.

Thus, after the lapse of centuries, we shall have Christians; thus, when I shall have executed my plan, the people of my empire will better know the duties they owe to God, to the country, and to their fellow-creatures; thus shall we yet be blessed by our posterity, for having delivered them from the overgrown power of Rome; for having brought back the priests within the limits of their duties; and for having subjected their future life to the Lord, and their present life to the country alone.[2]

As well as in some of the books already cited, phrases from this letter, other than the first sentence, are represented in Ernst Benedikt's German biography, long the chief rival to Bibl's.[3]

Another batch of familiar quotations derives from a letter said to have been written by Joseph to the archbishop of Salzburg in February 1781:

Mon Prince, — I have conducted the affairs of the German Empire alone, since the death of my father, and also for a long time the department of war. In the former, I have been assisted by a vast number of the laws of the empire, and the vice-chancellor Colloredo; the latter is superintended by my Lascy, one of the most able generals of the age; his great talents guarantee to me the good condition of my armies, and the security of my empire.

But the internal administration of my states requires immediate reform. — An empire which I govern must be swayed according to my own principles; prejudice, fanaticism, partiality, and slavery of the mind must cease, and each of my subjects be re-instated in the enjoyment of his native liberties.

Monachism has considerably increased in Austria; the number of ecclesiastical establishments and of monasteries has risen to an extravagant height. The government till now, according to the rules of these people, had little or no right over their persons, and they are the most dangerous and useless subjects in every state, as they endeavour to exclude themselves from the observance of all civil laws, and on all occasions have recourse to the Pontifex Maximus in Rome.

My minister of state, Baron von Kres[s]el, the enlightened Van Swieten, the prelate Rautenstrauch, and several other men of approved talents, will be nominated for the Aulic commission, which I have appointed for the suppression of the unnecessary monasteries and convents; and from their zeal for the good cause, and their attachment to the crown, I can expect all the good services which they will thereby render to the country.

When I shall have torn away the veil from monachism, when I shall have removed from the chains[4] of my universities Andromache's[5] web of the Ascetic doctrine, and when I shall have converted the monk of mere show into a useful citizen, then perhaps some of the party zealots will reason differently of my reforms.

I have a difficult task before me; — I have to reduce the host of monks, I have to transform Fakirs into men: those, before whose shorn head the common people fall down on their knees in veneration, and who have acquired a greater influence over the heart of the citizen, than any thing capable of making an impression on the human mind. Adieu![6]

These statements are reproduced in whole or in part by Benedikt, Bibl, Davis, Magenschab and Padover; by Sorel, who however alters the date of the letter and patriotically translates the addressee to the humbler diocese of Strasbourg; and by Leo Gershoy, in *From Despotism to Revolution*.[7]

Historians have also relished a letter allegedly written by the emperor to Gottfried Van Swieten, who was in charge of the censorship, in December 1787, part of which runs:

> Fanaticism shall in future be known in my states only by the contempt I have for it; nobody shall any longer be exposed to hardships on account of his creed; no man shall be compelled in future to profess the religion of the state, if it be contrary to his persuasion, and if he have other ideas of the right way of insuring blessedness.
>
> In future my Empire shall not be the scene of abominable intolerance. Fortunately no sacrifices like those of Calas and Sirven have ever disgraced any reign in this country ...
>
> Tolerance is an effect of that beneficent increase of knowledge which now enlightens Europe, and which is owing to philosophy and the efforts of great men; it is a convincing proof of the improvement of the human mind, which has boldly reopened a road through the dominions of superstition, which was trodden centuries ago by Zoroaster and Confucius, and which, fortunately for mankind, has now become the highway of monarchs.[8]

Andrews, Bibl, Harris, Magenschab, Padover and Rowen all quote this letter, as do T. C. W. Blanning in *Joseph II and Enlightened Despotism* and Perry Anderson in *Lineages of the Absolutist State*.[9]

Extracts from a fourth reputed letter of Joseph's, dated July 1773, this time to Aranda, the Spanish ambassador in Paris, are printed in Andrews's *Enlightened Absolutism*, and in Bibl's, Magenschab's and Padover's biographies. Gershoy quotes its first phrase, which indicates its content: 'Clement XIV has acquired eternal glory by suppressing the Jesuits.'[10]

Rowen represents Joseph by three letters altogether, the two already cited and a third, dated October 1787, to an unnamed correspondent. Williams gives its central passage:

> Since my accession to the throne, I have ever been anxious to conquer the prejudices against my station, and have taken pains to gain the confidence of my people; I have several times since given proof, that the welfare of my subjects is my passion; that to satisfy it, I shun neither labour, nor trouble, nor even vexations, and reflect well on the means which are likely to promote my views; and yet in my reforms, I everywhere find opposition from people, of whom I least expected it.[11]

A. J. P. Taylor, in his widely used *The Habsburg Monarchy*, quotes

Joseph II as writing: 'I am Emperor of the German *Reich*; therefore all the other states which I possess are provinces of it.'[12]

All these letters, together with others which are less well known, were first published in a small volume called *Neu gesammelte Briefe von Joseph dem II. Kaiser der Deutschen*, which appeared in 1790, the year of the emperor's death, with the manifestly false imprint 'Constantinople, printed in the private Court press'.[13] The collection was proved to be largely, if not entirely, spurious over a century ago.

Sebastian Brunner, in his *Die theologische Dienerschaft am Hofe Joseph II*, published in 1868, tells how, while working on the genuine correspondence of Cardinal Herzan in the archives at Vienna, he became suspicious of documents deriving from the Constantinople collection.[14] He consulted Alfred Ritter von Arneth, the vice-director of the Haus-, Hof- und Staatsarchiv. Arneth had already begun publishing volumes of the emperor's correspondence from the archives in his charge. Moreover, he had recently helped to expose as spurious a set of letters of Marie Antoinette which had been forged by a French official, Feuillet de Conches, and published with considerable *éclat* in 1864.[15] Arneth, says Brunner, collated half a dozen of the Constantinople letters with undoubted originals, and 'brilliantly revealed the falsity of the former from internal evidence, often including absurd nonsense'. The letter quoted first in the present chapter, which Joseph is supposed to have written to Herzan, is not to be found, according to Brunner, in the surviving correspondence of either man and is nowhere referred to in it; the style of the document, in Arneth's opinion, is quite different from the emperor's; further, given Herzan's character and position, and the fact that he usually dealt with Kaunitz rather than directly with Joseph, 'such a bombastic [*pathetisch*] letter (Joseph always wrote *very much to the point and never declaimed*) was quite superfluous'. Brunner had also discovered that a number of books of prayers attributed to the emperor were complete fabrications. Having exhausted the ordinary German vocabulary of fraudulence, he denounced this widespread *Interpolation* and *Humbug*. In particular, he pointed out that the letters to Herzan and the archbishop of Salzburg had been quoted in nearly all works published about Joseph II since his death. 'We can now', he concluded, 'put an end to this unhistorical deception for all future authors who possess conscience, honour and love of truth.'

Subsequent historians who have been aware of the problem have accepted the view that the entire Constantinople collection is spurious.[16] Dahlmann-Waitz simply writes it off as *unecht*.[17] A large number, perhaps a majority, of scholars who have worked in the field since Brunner's day have avoided citing any of the Constantinople letters. Paul von Mitrofanov, the Russian author of what is universally regarded as the best account of the emperor's work, went further and declared that every letter attributed to Joseph and published during his lifetime was bogus.[18]

Unfortunately, it will be evident from what has already been said that Brunner was over-optimistic in believing that he would 'put an end to this unhistorical deception'. Very few writers cite his work on the Constantinople collection.[19] There appears to be only one more recent discussion of the matter, in an unsigned article in *Historisch-politische Blätter für das katholische Deutschland* for 1904, which adds little to Brunner's.[20] The original edition of *Neu gesammelte Briefe* is a rare book, difficult of access;[21] the later versions are not much easier to obtain; and there is no account readily available of their contents. Some of the pieces in the collection have been so widely cited that any historian who relies at all on secondary work is likely to be deceived into accepting them. Even some exceptionally scrupulous scholars who have based themselves almost entirely on archival material have fallen for the odd phrase from one of the Constantinople letters. H. Marczali succumbed in *Magyarország története II. József Korában*, as did M. C. Goodwin in *The Papal Conflict with Josephinism*, H. Gnau in *Die Zensur unter Joseph II*, and even F. Maass in *Der Josephinismus*.[22]

After the Second World War, indeed, especially in Anglophone countries, the false letters were given a new lease of life, mainly through the influence of Padover. His biography of the emperor was generally acknowledged to be the best available, at least in English, and most other writers on the period recommended and used it. Some of them, admittedly, warned their readers that it was not wholly reliable.[23] The original reviewer in the *English Historical Review*, after a cool appraisal of the book, wrote: 'With the bibliography we enter another world.'[24] It has been remarked that there are only two footnotes in the whole volume, both referring to letters of Lafayette in an American collection.[25] Edward Crankshaw, in his well-known biography of Maria Theresa, pointed out that Padover caricatured the attitudes and activities of the empress.[26] As for the second edition, which the publishers claimed had been 'completely revised in the light of recent research', a critic has observed that the only differences from the first edition are some unimportant omissions and the addition to the bibliography of one book, R. R. Palmer's *The Age of the Democratic Revolution*.[27] But it has not been noticed that something like a quarter of Padover's numerous quotations derive from the *Neu gesammelte Briefe*. Of forty-nine letters in the original Constantinople edition, he quotes twenty-six, many of them at some length.[28]

The Revolutionary Emperor was republished in a German translation in 1969, but not even German reviewers showed awareness of the deception. Professor Max Braubach himself, the distinguished biographer of Prince Eugene and of Joseph's brother, Max Franz, elector-archbishop of Cologne, obviously felt something was wrong, but questioned in his review only one specific piece of evidence, a letter in which the emperor spoke of the Edict of Nantes when he must have meant its Revocation. This is an easy slip to make, and one which Maria Theresa herself made in a well-known letter.[29] But Braubach's comments show plainly that he had not appreciated that this remark, like so many others quoted in the book, originated in the Constantinople collection.[30]

There is evidently justification for recalling the attention of historians to the work of Brunner, and to the fact that many of the best-known statements credited to the emperor have been pronounced spurious. The most important consideration arising, of course, is how far our view of Joseph has been distorted by reliance on this material. In order to make it possible to answer that question, some lesser problems must be tackled. Brunner did not attempt to show that every single letter in the *Neu gesammelte Briefe* was false, and no one since his day has carried his argument much further. It is necessary to ask whether any of the Constantinople correspondence is genuine. The background also needs investigation, especially to determine whether there were in fact any authentic letters of the emperor available in his lifetime and whether any of the faked pieces antedated 1790. It would obviously be of great interest to identify their author and to uncover his motives in fabricating the collection. None of these questions is easy to settle, but the present article represents an attempt at deciding them. It aims, in addition, to show that the *Neu gesammelte Briefe* is worthy of study not only for its influence on the historiography of Enlightened despotism but also as a tract of the Austrian Enlightenment in its own right.

II

Bibliographically, the story of the Constantinople letters is somewhat peculiar. The title-page of the original edition gives no clue to the name of the editor or author, no date, and an obviously fictitious place, of publication. However, there is no doubt that it appeared in 1790,[31] and most authorities agree that it was published at Klagenfurt.[32] The authorship will be discussed below.[33] In 1821 Brockhaus of Leipzig brought out *Briefe von Joseph dem Zweiten ... (Bis jetzt ungedruckt)*, which contained the same letters in very slightly improved spelling and punctuation, but without the original footnote descriptions of the addressees, introduced by a preface asserting the importance and authenticity of the collection.[34] In the following year a new edition came out, also from Brockhaus, with a character sketch of the emperor as well as the 1821 preface. This last was now augmented by the republication in the form of a gross footnote of an article from the *Literarische Wochenblatt* of 1820, which had served as a trailer for the 1821 edition.[35] The version of 1822 claimed to be the second edition. Each of these printings included the same forty-nine letters, all in German. Then in 1846 F. Schuselka edited, again with Brockhaus, a 'third' edition under the title *Briefe Josephs des Zweiten*. He suppressed the preface and character sketch of the previous Leipzig editions, supplied a good deal of new explanatory matter, and incorporated in the canon five more letters, all of which derived from sources other than the Constantinople collection and were genuine.[36]

An English translation was made of the 1821 edition for the *Pamphleteer* of 1822, which omitted five of the six letters to Count Pálffy, described as 'Chancellor of the Kingdom of Hungaria'. This is the text from which Padover derived almost all his quotations from the Constantinople collection, and which it has therefore seemed convenient to use in the present chapter. A French translation of the 'second' edition appeared in 1822, with one of the letters to Pálffy missing and another shortened.[37] Portions of sixteen of the letters were published in a review article in the *North American Review* of 1830, translated afresh.[38]

The total number of addressees, if the correspondents who are described as 'a lady' or '***' are each treated as distinct, is thirty-five. Pálffy appears most often, with six letters; Maria Theresa next, with five. Others to whom more than one letter is addressed are: Kaunitz (3), Choiseul (2), Van Swieten (2) and Kollowrat, 'Grand Chancellor of Bohemia, and First Chancellor of Austria' (2). The letters average about 350 words in length. Most of them illustrate some episode in Joseph's life or some facet of his supposititious views and personality. The letters will be found listed by date, addressee and principal subject in the Appendix to this article.

Brunner proved the letter to Herzan spurious, but he did not indicate which other pieces Arneth had helped him to expose, though he did specifically mention the letter to the archbishop of Salzburg as false. If there remained any doubt about this document, it could easily be resolved as follows. First, the emperor would hardly have written a letter to the archbishop in February 1781, without reference to the fact that the latter was on a visit to Vienna.[39] But in any case, on the evidence of Joseph's letter-books, the first communication he sent to the archbishop after Maria Theresa's death was dated 28 March 1784, and began by saying that the archbishop would be very surprised to hear from him at all.[40] The two men were hardly on the intimate terms which alone could explain the forthrightness of the letter. As for its contents, the sections in which the emperor praises a list of subordinates are utterly uncharacteristic. He complained incessantly of the inadequacies of his servants, except for Kaunitz.[41] In general, his objections to monasticism were less fundamental than appears in this document.[42]

The writer of the article in the *Historisch-politische Blätter* made one substantial new point about the Constantinople collection, that the forms of address, the dating practice and the concluding formulae found in it were different from those used habitually by Joseph. He certainly did begin letters to Catherine II, as the article states, with 'Madame ma Soeur' and not with plain 'Madame'; he usually gave full dates, not just the month; and he ended his letters formally.[43] But the fault here might be casual editing, not outright fabrication.

Another general ground for doubting the authenticity of the collection is that all the letters are in German and there is no suggestion that they have had to be translated. Indeed, in the 1821 preface it is claimed: 'they have been printed, exactly as transcribed, with many faults of style and spelling; very possibly, so that knowledgeable collators would find in that very fact a proof of their genuineness'.[44] But in fact the emperor's authentic correspondence with many of the addressees was invariably or usually in French, as with his family, most foreigners, Kaunitz and noble ladies; and he wrote to the pope in Italian or Latin.[45]

More telling still, none of the Constantinople pieces is to be found in its chronological place in the emperor's letter-books, which are preserved for the years 1781 to 1789 inclusive in the Haus-, Hof- und Staatsarchiv in Vienna.[46] Negative evidence is less than conclusive, and there were certain classes of communication normally excluded from this compilation: most Habsburg family correspondence, notes scribbled on papers submitted to the emperor, and some administrative documents.[47] But most of the letters for these years which appeared in *Neu gesammelte Briefe* ought, if genuine, to be present in the letter-books; and it is especially improbable that such important pronouncements as those supposed to have been made in the letters to foreigners like the pope, the count of Provence, Frederick William II, Montmorin and 'Charles, Prince of Nassau, General in the Russian Service', not to mention those to the principal officials of the Monarchy, should be absent.

Many individual letters from the collection, in addition to the two exposed by Brunner, can be proved spurious by comparing them with other letters of Joseph's which are of undoubted authenticity. This argument disposes of at least the following fifteen letters: the four to Maria Theresa from the year 1778, the three to Kaunitz, and the single pieces to each of Marie Antoinette, Frederick the Great, Marie Christine, Catherine II, Pius VI, 'Ferdinand, Count of Trautmannsdorf', 'Francis Charles, Baron von Kressel' and Marshal Lacy.[48]

All six letters to Pálffy are dated 'Vienna, July 1786', and become questionable when it is realised that during the whole of that month Joseph was on manoeuvres in Bohemia.[49]

Special difficulties are raised by the letter of January 1770 to Choiseul, in which the Society of Jesus is denounced. The piece begins:

> I thank you for your confidence. If I were regent, you might boast of my support. With respect to the Jesuits, and your plan for their suppression, you have my perfect approbation.
>
> You must not reckon much on my mother; attachment to this order has become hereditary in the family of the house of Habsburg. Clement XIV himself has proofs of it. However, Kaunitz is your friend; he can effect everything with the Empress. With regard to their suppression, he is of your and the Marquis Pombal's party; and he is a man who leaves nothing half done.[50]

This letter is cited in Pastor's *History of the Popes*, although the author shows himself aware in a footnote that the authenticity of a letter of the same month between the same correspondents has been questioned in the *Historisch-politische Blätter*.[51] Maass, too, quotes the phrase: 'Cependant Kaunitz est votre ami; il peut tout auprès de l'impératrice.' He states that a Jesuit scholar has communicated the passage to him, having discovered a copy of it in the Jesuit manuscripts of the Biblioteca Vittorio Emanuele at Rome.[52] This is evidently Pastor's source also. Both authors give the date 15 January 1770, which is more specific than the Constantinople version.

An examination of the document from the Biblioteca Vittorio Emanuele shows it to be derived from the Constantinople collection. The text is identical with that of the French translation published in 1822, except for a tell-tale Italianate spelling, 'accadémiciens'. Accompanying it is the other letter from the *Neu gesammelte Briefe* which denounces the Jesuits, that to Aranda of July 1773, again adorned with a more precise date, the 31st of the month. It becomes plain what sort of a scholar has copied these pieces when one reads his prefatory note:

> The Emperor Joseph II was secretly consumed, throughout his life, with the craving to win public reputation as a prince and a great warrior ... His rule was disastrous not only for the ample states of Austria, but for Europe as a whole, since all the misfortunes which have afflicted it for so many years take their origin from his reign, produced by the crazy examples he was first to give, of debasing sovereign authority, ruining Religion, despoiling the Church and the nobility.

All this because he 'set about wooing the *philosophes* and professing their doctrines'.[53]

The archival evidence from Rome, then, works against, rather than for, the authenticity of the letter to Choiseul. So does the fact that Joseph had pronounced himself neutral on the question of suppressing the Jesuits in 1769, and that Choiseul wrote to the French ambassador in Rome on 23 January 1770 reporting that Maria Theresa had acquiesced in it.[54] The document relied on by Pastor and Maass may confidently be declared false.

New problems are raised by the letter quoted by A. J. P. Taylor: 'I am Emperor of the German *Reich*; therefore all the other states which I possess are provinces of it.' Joseph had been 'Holy Roman Emperor of the German Nation' for fifteen years before he became sole ruler of the Austrian Monarchy. He knew perfectly well that his position as emperor had nothing to do with his sovereignty over the lands of the Monarchy. He had been elected emperor; he inherited the Monarchy. He considered his role as emperor as a liability because it gave him almost no power. It is impossible to imagine Joseph writing in the terms of this letter.[55]

So far, a minimum of nineteen of the Constantinople letters have been shown to be unquestionably spurious by means of documentary criticism and comparison.[56] All the remainder have been put in more or less serious doubt. If it were thought worthwhile, further work of this kind could doubtless dispose of the others.[57]

Here, another approach will now be taken: consideration of the sentiments of the letters in relation to undoubtedly authentic expressions of opinion. This method is less conclusive, but more instructive. For example, it is well known that the emperor disliked almost all members of his family, except Marie Antoinette, his brother, Max Franz, and perhaps his brother Leopold.[58] The friendly letters in the *Neu gesammelte Briefe* to his sister, Maria Anna, and his sister-in-law, Maria Beatrix, are therefore highly uncharacteristic;[59] and the letter to the count of Provence, in which Joseph dilates on the virtues of his brothers and sisters, is preposterous.[60]

Disquisitions on foreign affairs occur in the letters to Frederick William II, Montmorin and Nassau.[61] These contain passages in themselves most implausible, like the following: 'The time has arrived when I come forward as the champion of humanity, and take upon me to compensate Europe for the hardships she has suffered from these barbarians [the Turks], and when I hope to succeed in ridding the world of a race of barbarians, that have so long been a scourge to her.'[62] Anyway, in his authentic correspondence the emperor had expressed great doubts about entering the war at all, and, within two months of the alleged date of the quotation, was talking of the desperate need to make peace with the Turks.[63]

One of the most striking letters from the Constantinople collection is that of December 1787 to Van Swieten on toleration, quoted above.[64] By comparison with other pronouncements of Joseph's on this subject, it is too idealistic and general to be credited: he usually employed chiefly utilitarian arguments, and the scope of his toleration was not unlimited.[65] Further, he was not inclined to draw on the history of France or to identify himself with the French Enlightenment; and the references to Zoroaster and Confucius, unparalleled in his authentic correspondence, suggest a desire on the part of the falsifier to associate him with Freemasonry, to which in fact he was unsympathetic.[66]

In another letter, the first of the two to Van Swieten, he is made to compare himself with the principal Enlightened rulers of his day, on these lines:

> I do not know how some monarchs can occupy their minds with such trifles, as to acquire literary accomplishments; to seek a sort of greatness in making verses, in drawing a plan for a theatre, which is to be placed beside the works of Palladio ...
>
> The Margrave of Brandenburg has become the head of a sect of kings, who occupy themselves in writing memoirs, poems, and treatises. The Empress of Russia imitated him, studied Voltaire, and wrote dramas and verses to Vanhal; then some odes to her Alcides. Stanislaus Lesczinsky wrote letters of pacification; and, lastly, the King of Sweden letters of friendship...
>
> You see how I think on these matters. The illustrious Greeks and Romans are not unknown to me; I know the history of the German empire, and that of my states in particular; but my time never allowed me to make epigrams, or to write Vaudevilles. I read for instruction; I travelled for the enlargement of my views; and when I patronise men of letters, I do them more service than if I were sitting down with one of them to compose unmeaning sonnets.[67]

There are elements of justice in the attitude here attributed to Joseph. He did laugh at the pretensions of Catherine II and Gustavus III.[68] He did, as other passages in the letter insinuate, regard the French Academy as the puppet of Frederick the Great.[69] But he was proud of his taste in operatic libretti and music, painting and architecture, his promotion of the German theatre, and his theological expertise.[70] The following sentences from his famous memorandum on the state of the Monarchy, of 1765, show that he was critical of Voltaire, but from a standpoint which cannot be reconciled with the tone of the two letters to Van Swieten:

> It seems to me that I am a good Capuchin father discussing principles with Voltaire. The latter would reduce him to silence, but the Capuchin would nonetheless be right. In fact, from all that I have seen and heard, I have learned nothing more firmly than to fear intelligence [*esprit*] and all its subtleties. I recognise no argument which comes from the ancient Greeks or the modern French.[71]

A group of the letters presents Joseph as strongly anti-aristocratic. He violently condemns duelling in a letter of August 1771 to 'General

****', and in writing to 'the Landgravine of Fürstenberg', Kollowrat, 'Madam****' and 'a Lady' he shows himself unwilling to employ or maintain nobles in administrative posts except on grounds of sheer ability. The most eloquent of these pieces runs:

> I do not conceive that a monarch is bound to give any one of his subjects an appointment, merely because he is by birth a nobleman ...
>
> I know your son, and I know the qualifications requisite for an officer. From this knowledge I am convinced that your son has not the character of a military man, and that he is too much occupied with his birth, for me to expect from him such services, as might one day be the boast of his country.
>
> What I pity you for, Madame, is this, that your son is fit neither for an officer, a statesman, nor for a priest. In short, he is nothing but a nobleman, and this he is from the bottom of his heart.
>
> Thank your good fortune, which, while it denied your son all talents, put him in possession of considerable estates, which sufficiently indemnify him, and, at the same time, render my services very superfluous.[72]

This letter is unique among the original Constantinople collection for the apparently flippant footnote attached to the mysterious formula 'Madam ****': 'Where do you really think this lady is? Read Fontenelle's dialogue on the plurality of worlds, I wager you will find her in the moon.'[73] Such a remark might be enough in itself to make one doubt the authenticity of the piece. Further, there exist in the letter-books many of the emperor's replies to requests from titled ladies for preferment for their male and female relatives. These documents are almost uniformly polite and often accommodating, and never advance general anti-aristocratic arguments.[74] As for duelling, Joseph seems to have been against it, but the letter from the *Neu gesammelte Briefe*, with its Voltairian references to ancient Rome, Tamerlane and Bajazet, is highly implausible.[75]

III

Probably the reader now feels that the whole Constantinople collection had better be written off without further ado. But there is more to be said – especially because there are at any rate seven items in the *Neu gesammelte Briefe* which have claims to genuineness. Of the six letters to Pálffy, although they are given an impossible date, five make up (with minor changes) a German memorandum of Joseph's from the appropriate year,[76] and the other is identical with a paragraph from an extended instruction issued by the emperor, also in German, on 30 December 1785:

> The privileges and liberties of a nobility or a nation, in all countries and republics of the world, consist not in the right of contributing nothing to the public burdens; on the contrary, they bear more than any other class, as in England and Holland; but those privileges consist solely in this, that they may impose on themselves the burdens required by the state and the common advantage, and by their consent take the lead in the increase of the taxes. The liberty of persons is carefully to be distinguished from that of possessions; in respect of which the proprietors represent not the nobleman, but simply the cultivator or the grazier, and in cities the citizen and consumer, in the highway and on the passage, the traveller merely and the passenger; in which cases, for the sake of preserving the free competition that alone makes the system useful, they must be put on an equal footing, according to their possessions, with all other citizens and inhabitants.[77]

The Constantinople collection also contains a letter from Joseph to 'the Magistrates of the Royal City of Ofen, in Hungaria' [i.e. Buda], dated June 1784, which runs as follows:

> I thank the magistrates and the citizens for the honour they intend me by erecting a statue to me in one of their principal public places. That, for the expediency of affairs, and for the more easy survey of the boards of administration of the empire, I have concentrated them in Ofen, and thus have procured to the city some advantages, this indeed does not deserve such an honour.
>
> When, however, I shall have succeeded in making the whole of Hungary understand what the real relations between the king and the subject are; when I shall have removed all ecclesiastical and civil abuses; when I shall have awakened the inhabitants to activity and industry; when I shall have caused commerce to flourish, and shall have provided the country from one end to the other with roads and navigable canals, as I hope will be the case; if the nation will then erect a monument to me, I may then, perhaps, have deserved it, and will acknowledge the honour with gratitude.[78]

This seems to be a somewhat garbled reminiscence of the following genuine letter in German:

When prejudices are eradicated, and true love of country, and ideas for the general good of the whole Monarchy take hold; when everyone cheerfully does his fair share to serve the needs of the state, to work for its security and success; when enlightenment through improved studies and simplification in clerical training is achieved; when, by the reconciliation of true concepts of religion with civil laws, a more effective system of justice is established; when wealth is attained, through increased population and improved agriculture, through recognition of the true interests of the lord in relation to his serf, and of the serf in relation to his lord, through industry, the manufacture and distribution of goods, and the general circulation[79] of all products throughout the Monarchy – as I confidently hope will come to pass: it is then that I shall deserve a statue, but not now, when the town of Ofen has merely, through my happening to move the administration there in the interests of more thorough supervision, been enabled to secure better prices for its wine and higher rents for its houses.[80]

It is noticeable that the spurious version, as well as being less concrete, omits the characteristic final jibe.

Evidently the falsifier was particularly interested in Hungarian affairs, and had some knowledge of them. When not dealing with Hungarian questions, the collection is nearly always out of character. But it has to be admitted that there are moments of verisimilitude. The phrase 'the positiveness of my principles' has a genuine ring.[81] The most instructive case is that of the letter of October 1787, quoted on page 120 above. After the passage already reproduced, it goes on:

As a monarch, I do not deserve the distrust of my subjects; as the Regent of a great empire, I must have the whole extent of my state before my eyes, and embrace the whole in one view; I cannot always listen to the voices of single provinces, which consider only their own narrow sphere.

Private advantage is a chimera, and while on the one hand I lose it in order to make a sacrifice to my country, I may on the other hand share in the common welfare. — But how few think of this!

If I were unacquainted with the duties of my station – if I were not morally convinced, that I am destined by Providence to wear my diadem, together with all the load of obligations which it imposes on me – melancholy, discontent, and the wish not to exist, would fill my bosom. But I know my heart; I am internally convinced of the honesty of my intentions, and hope that when I am no more, posterity will examine, and judge more equitably, more justly, and more impartially, all that I have done for my people.[82]

There are a number of instances in Joseph's genuine writings when he condemns provincial particularism and rivalries, though not in these precise terms;[83] and the similarity is remarkable between the personal credo enunciated above and the following authentic passage in a letter to Grand-Duke Paul of Russia and his wife, of 24 February 1781:

> The idea of being able to do good and render one's subjects happy is undoubtedly the finest and the only flattering aspect of power; as it is the most powerful spur for any sensible and honest man. But when one knows at the same time that every false step is counter-productive, that evil is so easily and rapidly done, and good is of its very nature so difficult and slow, and cannot (except slowly) impress itself solidly on a vast state, then this comforting illusion much weakens, and there rests only the satisfaction that one has inside oneself, which makes one incomparably happy in knowing oneself in good company when one is alone and in seeking – every personal consideration apart – to do only what the general good of the State and the great number requires.
>
> One can rarely occupy oneself with individuals' happiness without spoiling the ensemble, and it seems that under good laws and a good system, founded and governed on the basis of the spirit and character of the nation as well as the geographical position of the State, each citizen ought to find a way of being happy if he has intelligence and is willing to take the trouble – the sovereign preserving order ...
>
> If there is too much philosophy in that ... and I have shown the sovereign *déshabillé* and in front of his *valet de chambre*, please pardon me the principles I have always held of going back to the primitive source of everything ... I am one of those marionettes that Providence, without my willing or choosing it, has been pleased to put in the place I occupy ... and when she has had enough, the curtain will fall and the farce will be over for me.[84]

This is a rather forced statement, written to people Joseph despised but whose good-will he desperately wanted, and couched in terms likely to please the grand duke's mother, Catherine II.[85] It is unusual in the degree of pessimism expressed about the possibilities of doing good, and almost uncharacteristic in its acknowledgement of variations between nations and states – a concession Joseph rarely extended to provinces within the Monarchy. But the letter proves that, *pace* Brunner, the emperor sometimes philosophised, declaimed, was bombastic and unspecific; and the presumably false piece, cited previously, catches the tone from time to time. However, even in this striking case of similarity, the appeal in the Constantinople letter to the verdict of posterity sounds spurious. Further, the divergence between the melancholy pessimism of the authentic document and the spirit of the false letters as a whole, which breathe the conviction that great changes may easily be carried through with the expectation of general applause, is arresting.

The *Neu gesammelte Briefe*, then, contain genuine elements, but not many. Brunner was right in his implication that the letters as a whole are too general. Overall, they exaggerate Joseph's intellectualism, his inclination to philosophise, his readiness both to deal in abstractions and to make literary and historical references. They also make him appear more liberal, tolerant, anti-aristocratic, anti-clerical, and much more free-thinking, than he actually was.

IV

Contrary to the assertion of Mitrofanov, there were many genuine letters of Joseph II in print by the time of his death. For example, in 1782 the *Wiener Zeitung* carried, on the orders of the emperor, a correspondence with the pope.[86] Exchanges of letters with, among others, Kaunitz, the elector of Trier and the balloonist Blanchard had been published.[87] A great many well-publicised official documents, like the celebrated 'pastoral letter' to all functionaries of the empire, were partly or wholly of Joseph's own composition.[88] Twelve out of the fifteen parts of Geisler's *Skiz[z]en aus dem Karakter und Handlungen Josephs des Zweiten* had appeared by the end of 1789.[89] A contemporary reviewer in the *Allgemeine deutsche Bibliothek* unkindly called it 'the Geislerian mish-mash', in which truth and falsehood were inextricably confused.[90] But in fact it contained many authentic pieces, including Hungarian documents used in the Constantinople collection.[91] There was of course also some spurious material in print before the emperor's death, for instance, a letter published by the papacy, according to Leopold of Tuscany and others, to give a wrong impression of Joseph's attitude in his disputes with Rome at the beginning of his sole reign.[92] However, the falsifier of the *Neu gesammelte Briefe* evidently preferred to start afresh.

Immediately after the emperor's death, other spurious material was produced about him, including the prayer-books which troubled Brunner, at least two *Testaments politiques* and an *Epistola posthuma Josephi II Rom. condam. Imperat. ad summum Rom. Pontificem* about Christian reunion.[93] But these fabrications seem to have no connection with the Constantinople letters.

That compilation, as its false imprint indicates, was in some degree clandestine. Presumably it was not submitted to the censor. It does not appear in the extensive booksellers' advertisements in the *Wiener Zeitung* of 1790. But letters from the collection can be traced emerging into daylight in the successive commemorative publications of 1790. Professor Meusel's punctual *Ueber Kaiser Joseph den Zweiten*, with a preface dated 27 February, seven days after the emperor's death, is innocent of any of the *Neu gesammelte Briefe*.[94] So is Johann Pezzl's *Charakteristik Josephs II*, first announced in the *Wiener Zeitung* of 17 March as due to appear 'at latest in 3 or 4 weeks'.[95] A *Leben und Geschichte* from Amsterdam, whose first volumes were advertised on 7 April, is equally free of the taint, as is a *Vita e Fasti* from Lugano and Caracciolo's *La Vie de Joseph II* from Paris.[96] But on 8 May was announced *Anekdoten und Charakterzüge von Kaiser Joseph II nebst eine Skizze seines Lebens*, which prints several of the Constantinople letters – though not those which later became the most popular, to Herzan, the archbishop of Salzburg and Van Swieten – while acknowledging that the authenticity of the letter to the pope which appears in the collection has been challenged.[97] The *Lebensbeschreibung Kaiser Josephs II bis an seinen Tod*, advertised on 4 September, expressly refers to the *Neu gesammelte Briefe*, and prints many of them.[98] Another compilation of 1790 heavily dependent on the false letters is L. Hübner's *Lebensgeschichte Josephs des Zweyten*.[99] By the end of the year, the Constantinople collection had displaced the substantial number of authentic letters which had been reproduced in earlier works. Even the appearance of large quantities of genuine material, published by the Belgian revolutionaries to blacken Austrian rule and on behalf of counts D'Alton and Trauttmansdorff in reply, made little impact.[100] Only in the 1860s, with the work of historians such as Meynert, Wolf, Arneth and Brunner, scrupulously based on surviving documents, did serious study of Joseph's reign begin.[101]

V

Plainly, most of the *Neu gesammelte Briefe* were the original composition of a skilful author. Those few who have considered the question[102]
concur in identifying him as Franz Rudolph von Grossing – to use
the style he himself adopted.[103] His real name was Franz Matthäus
Grossinger. He was born at Comorn in Hungary in 1752. He was saved
from being or becoming a Jesuit by the suppression of the Society.
After a spell as a private tutor, he was given in 1777 an unestablished
post in the imperial bureaucracy at Vienna. He later claimed that he
had seen much of Maria Theresa, that she had treated him like a
mother, and that he had played an important role in the first years
of Joseph's reign, especially in Hungarian affairs and over toleration.
However, in 1782 he lost his government post, and was sentenced to
eight days in irons for *Schmähschriftverfassung*, writing lampoons. In the
following year he was convicted of *Dukatenbeschneidung*, coin-clipping,
and exiled for life from the *Erbländer*. He preferred to go to Germany
rather than back to Hungary. He now set himself up as a writer,
journalist and confidence trickster. He wrote books about toleration,
Hungarian law, the history of the popes and Church–state relations.
He ran a *Damenjournal* and various other periodicals for women, and
a *Staatenjournal* (1787–88), claimed to be the first German periodical
of political discussion, a rival to Linguet's *Annales*.[104] He advertised a
Rosenorden, a semi-secret society presided over by an imaginary lady,
Frau von Rosenwald, whose secretary he alleged himself to be – thus
obtaining perhaps 3,000 subscriptions. He was always getting himself
involved in personal disputes. Nicolai and he pursued a vendetta in
the pages of their journals. Grossing was put under house-arrest in
Magdeburg for publishing without the permission of the local censor, who was another of his enemies, Professor Forster. He dabbled
in Prussian intrigues in Hungary during the later years of Joseph's
reign.[105] At last, after being harried from city to city, he eloped in
1788 with the wife of Count Bissing of Rottenberg, who called on
the emperor to intervene. This Joseph gleefully did. Grossing was
captured, brought to Vienna, and there imprisoned.[106]

Leopold II was told in a police report of 17 March 1790, a few
weeks after his accession:

> This Grossing, immediately after he had been brought here, pledged
> himself to make important revelations for the states of the Monarchy
> with regard to the Prussian Court. He was most graciously given

permission to unburden himself about this in writing, and these vast and sometimes not entirely unimportant treatises were from time to time submitted to His Majesty …

As well as the above-mentioned political revelations, this secret prisoner also prepared with restless energy many treatises, which were always submitted to the monarch of blessed memory, partly on account of their useful contents, and partly with a view to reminding His Majesty of the existence of this prisoner and to further his release. But His Majesty was at no time inclined to this, and made his attitude emphatically understood; and so to this hour the man remains in captivity.[107]

On 8 August 1790 Count Pergen, the chief of policy, wrote to Leopold describing the range of Grossing's literary activities in prison. The list he gave was long, but he acknowledged it was not exhaustive; and he did not mention any compilation of Joseph's letters. Moreover, he remarked that the late emperor had given permission for the publication of one, and one only, of these writings, a translation from Latin of a work on Hungary by Tubero. But he said that the work had not appeared, because Grossing remained in prison.[108] So, if Franz Rudolph wrote the Constantinople collection, he composed it while in captivity and arranged for its printing surreptitiously.

These facts were presumably not known to the writers who credited him with authorship or editing of the false letters. But they had what, as interpreted, was a weighty piece of evidence in their favour. Franz Gräffer, a bibliophile and journalist, who published a large number of anecdotal works about Viennese life, especially its literary aspects, under Joseph II and his immediate successors, included in his *Wiener-Dosenstücke* of 1846 a couple of pages on the story of the Constantinople collection. These are the crucial passages:

In 1819 Jos. v. Grossing, who lived on a pension in Graz, sent me the manuscript, requesting that I include these letters in the *Conversations-blatt* that I had started at that time. I at once realised that these *Briefe* were none other than copies of those *Briefe Joseph's* which had already appeared at Klagenfurt in the late 'eighties, supplied only with the names of the addressees. To lose no time, since Grossing was manifestly already awaiting the payment, I at once took the requisite steps with the manuscript; and, since it was not thought suitable, I immediately returned it to Grossing. A short time afterwards, the letters appeared from Brockhaus … Grossing himself had sent the manuscript to Leipzig, and received the payment of 100 thalers through Ferstl's bookshop in Graz. So far as the *Charakteristik* of Joseph, which prefaces the letters, is concerned, one cannot doubt for a moment that it is *not* by Grossing. He was certainly a man of talent, but too *arrierirt* [reactionary]; perhaps Schneller wrote it. Grossing had had a post in Joseph's *Cabinett*, but was dismissed on a number of excellent grounds and pensioned off, in effect 'by grace'. He lived at Graz, where he died in 1830. He understood a multitude of languages, and was engaged in preparing a polyglot dictionary.[109]

It has been generally assumed that, when Gräffer wrote 'Jos. v. Grossing', this was a simple error for 'Franz Rudolph von Grossing'. On this basis it could be believed that the *Neu gesammelte Briefe* were founded on information or documents to which the latter had had access in his official capacity. But even historians who have recognised the spuriousness of the collection have adhered to this identification of its author. Moreover, this paragraph from *Wiener-Dosenstücke* has been almost universally accepted as authority for the statement that Franz Rudolph lived and wrote on until 1830.[110]

However, he did have a brother Joseph. To separate them is now a difficult undertaking, especially as nearly all the *Grossingakten*, the file which the exasperated Vienna government found it necessary to keep on their activities, has apparently been lost.[111] Fortunately, R. Gragger in his *Preussen, Weimar und die ungarische Königskrone*, made good use of the material in the file and reproduced much of it.

Joseph Grossing[112] never held an administrative post under Maria Theresa or her son. He did, however, have a scarcely less lively career than his brother. He too, after the suppression of the Jesuits, to which he may also have belonged, tried to make a living by writing, but based in Vienna and with special reference to Hungarian topics. In 1785 he came to the government's and the emperor's notice as the author of pamphlets in support of the opposition in Hungary, using documents from the government offices improperly communicated to him by one Bisztriczey. The emperor took a lenient line, for characteristically cynical reasons. He dismissed Bisztriczey with a reduced pension, but refused to ban the publication of the documents. Experience had taught him, he said, 'to entrust [to the departments] only those of my thoughts which I consider to be suitable for [?display on] the town gates'. Joseph II handed Joseph Grossing over to Pergen to be dealt with, and it seems that Pergen took him on as a police informer and government pamphleteer.[113] At latest by the end of 1788, he was being paid to write on behalf of the regime.[114] In October 1789 he asked for a rise, but the emperor rejected the request contemptuously: 'Nothing will come out of all these *Schrieblereyen* [*sic*], and the fellows are not worth the trouble of paying a *groschen* for them.'[115] In 1790, after Joseph II's death, he published anonymously the most influential of his writings in support of the government, *Irrthümer in den Begriffen der meisten Ungarn von der Staatsverfassung ihres Vaterlandes, und von den Rechten ihrer Könige.*[116] This work seems to form part of the campaign waged under the more or less direct auspices of Leopold II to state the case of the central administration against the Hungarian opposition's appeal to the old constitution of their country.[117]

It is in fact natural to assume that Gräffer meant Joseph Grossing when he said it. Gräffer writes as though he knew the man. No doubt he accepted the inclusion in Joseph's career of events which actually belonged to Franz Rudolph's, a confusion which the preface to the 1821 edition of the letters fostered and which presumably Joseph was happy to encourage.[118] Gräffer was a child in the reign of Joseph II, and could not have known about the earlier part of the brothers' careers at first hand.

If the passage in the *Wiener-Dosenstücke* refers to Joseph and not to Franz Rudolph, then there appears to be no other evidence for the survival of the latter into the nineteenth century. Whereas Joseph is still listed in the 1801 supplement of Meusel's *Das gelehrte Teutschland*, Franz Rudolph drops out after the fifth edition of 1796.[119] A letter recently cited by B. K. Király in *Hungary in the Late Eighteenth Century*, as written by 'Grossinger' to the Emperor Francis in December 1792, turns out to be signed 'Joseph Grossing', although Király places the writer in Joseph II's Cabinet.[120] A recent Hungarian biographical dictionary, relying on a newspaper report of 1789 that Franz Rudolph was in that year imprisoned for life in the fortress of Kufstein, has presumed that he died there soon afterwards; and this seems likely.[121]

There appears to be no obstacle in the way of believing that it was Joseph Grossing who sent Gräffer and Brockhaus the manuscript of the letters in or after 1819. If so, he is the only person who can be connected by good evidence with a manuscript of the Constantinople collection. This is far from conclusive as to his authorship. He might, after all, have copied out the 1790 text. But there is a strong *prima facie* case that he was himself the falsifier.

Whoever invented the false letters presumably intended to display the emperor in a particular light. The impression of Joseph II created by the collection, that he was more libertarian, progressive and philosophical than in reality, must have been given either to blacken him in the eyes of conservatives or to tint him red for the admiration of radicals. The latter seems much more likely. The natural interpretation is that the author wished to associate the great name of the emperor with attitudes which at the end of his reign were losing support within the government.

The author's full coverage of the Hungarian schemes of the emperor suggests an impatience with Hungarian constitutionalism and obscurantism which both Grossings were voicing in the years 1789–90. This element in the *Neu gesammelte Briefe* would make it conceivable that the collection was itself part of Leopold's propaganda campaign against the Hungarian rebels, but for the fact that it was published so early in his reign. It seems more probable that it was composed in the last months of Joseph's life, possibly under the aegis of Pergen, who was evidently trying, in the face of discouragement from the emperor, to appeal to public opinion on his behalf.[122] This conjecture would be supported by the absence from the collection of any letter dated after January 1789, and by the omission of any reference to Joseph's recantation of most of his reforms late in 1789 and early in 1790. It is tempting to attach significance to the fact that neither Leopold nor Pergen figures among Joseph's alleged correspondents.

Especially if Joseph Grossing was the author, however, it would be unwise to assume that he was pursuing a clear aim in writing the letters. An official described him as 'this man whom one cannot trust because of his ambiguous [*zweideutig*] character'.[123] One example of apparent flippancy in the *Neu gesammelte Briefe* has already been mentioned.[124] Here is another, from the preface to the 1821 edition: 'whoever would have wanted to fabricate many of these letters, would have had to be another Joseph II'.[125]

VI

Historians have in certain respects neglected the Constantinople collection. A small number have taken an interest in its authenticity.[126] One scholar, in an unpublished thesis, has done much to show the influence of the false letters on the early historiography of Joseph II.[127] But, though they obviously formed an important aspect of the reactions to the emperor's death, they were not mentioned in the standard survey of the subject by F. Engel-Jánosi.[128] It would be worth enquiring how much they contributed to buttress the interpretations of the Liberal historians and publicists of nineteenth-century Austria-Hungary, who often claimed Joseph as an unimpeachable forerunner of their anti-clericalism and reformism.[129] Schuselka's edition of the letters, issued two years before the 1848 revolution, was a tract for the times as well as a bibliographical curiosity.[130]

Moreover, the Constantinople collection deserves notice in relation to wider historical developments. A great deal of attention has recently been given to the large pamphlet literature of Joseph's reign and especially to the more radical writings of the period that ended with the stemming of the *Broschürenflut* by the repression of the mid-1790s. Another unpublished thesis, for example, has discussed publications of a political character from Joseph's reign.[131] Several historians, notably K. Benda, P. P. Bernard, L. Bodi, A. Körner, D. Silagi, F. Valjavec and E. Wangermann, have uncovered with great skill the personalities and story of the 'Jacobin' movement in the monarchy.[132] Wangermann in *The Austrian Achievement, 1700–1800* has painted a glowing picture of Radical Enlightenment in the Vienna of Joseph and Leopold, culminating in the glories of *The Magic Flute*.[133] Silagi has described Leopold's Hungarian publicists and collaborators.[134] But none of these authors includes any treatment of the false letters. They have been relegated to the category of mere forgeries, to be discussed, if at all, only in works on historiography. Yet, with the possible exception of the libretto of *The Magic Flute*, there is no publication from the period which has had a greater influence on the views of historians about the age; and it has had so wide an impact because it was so swiftly and generally accepted at the time. Evidently, a great number of publicists credited the picture it presented of Joseph II, and this fact shows that, because of the skill and plausibility of the author, the tenor of the letters chimed in with what many contemporaries believed or hoped about the age they lived in. The lively style of the pieces no doubt helped; it sometimes almost deserves the adjectives 'Swiftian' and 'Byronic' which Padover, under the impression that Joseph was their author, applied to them.[135] While it is important that historians should treat the collection, with the few exceptions mentioned above, as spurious, it is also important that scholars should recognise its value as one of the most influential and effective pieces of radical propaganda from the Austrian Enlightenment.

VII

It will already have emerged how the Constantinople letters misrepresent the views of Joseph II. But almost no historian has confined himself to them, and few writers have used many of them. On the other hand, the fact that they have never been thoroughly exposed has made it possible for them to exert a widespread hidden influence. Anyone who has relied on Padover's and Magenschab's books has necessarily taken a large dose from the collection.[136] And it is noticeable that even a single isolated quotation from it commonly crowns an argument. Maass's use of the letter to Choiseul, for instance, dovetails perfectly into the author's main thesis that Kaunitz was the principal architect of early Josephism.[137] Sister Goodwin relied on a fragment from the spurious letter to the pope to clinch her argument about Joseph's attitude to monasticism.[138] The importance of the phrase 'I have made philosophy the legislator of my Empire' is patent in all the numerous works which employ it.

Because of the continuing direct and indirect influence of Padover's biography, despite the appearance of excellent correctives such as Blanning's *Joseph II*,[139] English readers in particular still need to exorcise the spirit of the Constantinople collection. Publishers continue to reprint without alteration books such as Stephen J. Lee, *Aspects of European History, 1494–1789* and E. N. Williams's *The Ancient Regime in Europe*, which quote heavily from the false letters. Even in German, Magenschab's biography of 1979, still in print, is largely based on them. The following main adjustments will be necessary to correct the record. Joseph II, it must be understood, did not say that he had made philosophy the legislator of his empire, and was sceptical of many of the general propositions of Enlightened wisdom, especially those associated with French thinkers. He often showed himself anti-noble in theory and in principle, and he certainly wished to reduce the privileges of the aristocracy in his territories; but he did not surround himself with commoners and he seems to have been perfectly ready in practice to employ nobles. He was tolerant of some sects to a certain degree, but by no means of all sects, or of any without restriction: he expressed the hope that all his subjects might be Catholics,[140] and was disturbed when more than a small proportion of them revealed Protestant tendencies. He was strongly anti-papal, and wished to exercise a wide-ranging control over the Church in his dominions; but he did not propose to appropriate religious funds to secular uses, or decide to suppress all monasteries. He could be witty or at least sardonic, but unfortunately he was not 'Swiftian' or 'Byronic'. Even before his recantation, he was decidedly more pessimistic about the potentialities of reform than the false letters make him appear.

All these points, of course, need elaboration, for which there is not the scope here. For a full account of the emperor's aims and attitudes it would be necessary to consider many areas unrepresented or barely mentioned in the *Neu gesammelte Briefe*: the affairs of Italy and the Austrian Netherlands for instance, military matters, foreign policy questions and so on. But it is hoped that this chapter may persuade historians not only of the value of enquiring into the false letters, but also of the need to look again at the true Joseph II.

Appendix: The Constantinople Collection

No.	Date	Addressee	Subject	Page*
1	Apr. '64	Elector of Mainz	Coronation as King of the Romans	
2	Aug. '65	'Prince of Batthian'	Death of father	29
3	Oct. '71	Maria Beatrix	Her marriage to his brother	
4	Aug. '71	General ****	Duelling	138
5	Jan. '70	Choiseul	Suppression of Jesuits	41
6	July '73	Aranda	do.	42
7	June '75	Maria Theresa	Visit to Venice	
8	May '74	Marie Antoinette	Accession of her husband	74
9	July '78	Frederick II	Outbreak of war	102
10	14 Aug. '78	Maria Theresa	War of Bavarian Succession	
11	18 Aug. '78	do.	do.	
12	1 Oct. '78	do.	do.	
13	Oct. '78	do.	do.	
14	May '79	***	Peace of Teschen	109
15	Dec. '80	Choiseul	Plans on accession	125–6, 158
16	Dec. '80	Catherine II	Accession	
17	Jan. '81	Maria Christina	Her appointment in Belgium	227
18	Feb. '81	Archbishop of Salzburg	Plans on accession	159
19	Oct. '81	Cardinal Herzan	Religious policy	158
20	Dec. '80	Van Swieten	Monarchs and literature	194–5
21	June '82	'Landgravine of Fürstenberg'	Patronage	129
22	Oct. '82	Maria Anna	His friendship for her	125
23	Feb. '83	Kollowrat	Career open to the talents	128
24	29 Apr. '84	Max Franz	Max's accession in Cologne	

No.	Date	Addressee	Subject	Page*
25	June '84	Magistrates of Ofen	Erection of a statue to Joseph	216
26	July '84	Pius VI	Religious funds	162
27	Oct. '84	Kollowrat	Customs duties	204
28	Jan. '85	*** ('A Hungarian Magnat')	Imposition of German	216, 220
29	Mar. '85	Gebler	Taxation	198, 207–8
30	Feb. '86	Count of Provence	His joy in his family	
31	July '86	Pálffy	Hungarian county reform	
32	do.	do.	Hungarian legal reform[†]	
33	do.	do.	Hungarian administrative reform[†]	
34	do.	do.	Rights of nobility[†]	219
35	do.	do.	Separation of powers[†]	
36	do.	do.	The Vice-Gespan[†**]	
37	May '87	Kaunitz	His travels in Russia	
38	June '87	do.	do.	
39	4 Aug. '87	'Madam ***'	Appointment of nobles	
40	Sep. '87	'Trautmannsdorf'	Spread of revolution	
41	Oct. 87	***	Desire to do good	
42	Dec. '87	'a Lady'	Appointment of nobles	
43	Dec. '87	Van Swieten	Toleration	147
44	Jan. '88	Frederick William II	War with Turkey	269
45	28 Feb. '88	Kressel	Religious policies	
46	Feb. '88	Lascy	Turkish war	
47	9 Feb. '88	Kaunitz	Turkish war	270
48	6 July '88	Montmorin	do.	272
49	Jan. '89	'Charles, Prince of Nassau'	do.	275–6

*   Page references are to the second edition of Padover, *Revolutionary Emperor* (London, 1967).
†   Omitted from the translation in *The Pamphleteer*.
** Omitted from the French edition of the *Letters*.

Notes

This chapter first appeared in the *Historical Journal*, XVIII, 3 (1975). I have to some extent brought it up to date by reference to more recent publications; and I have included discussion of the quotation used by A. J. P. Taylor, the falsity of which I did not feel sure about when I wrote the article. I should like to thank the following archivists and librarians who took special trouble on my behalf: the late Gräfin Dr Anna Coreth of the Haus-, Hof- und Staatsarchiv in Vienna, Dr Dennis Rhodes of the British Library, Dr Oskar Sashegyi of the Hungarian State Archives in Budapest, and the Director of the Biblioteca Nazionale Centrale in Rome.

  1 W. O. Hassall, *The Balance of Power* (2nd edn, London, 1898), p. 358;

A. H. Johnson, *The Age of the Enlightened Despot* (London, 1909), p. 227; Stuart Andrews, *Eighteenth-Century Europe* (London, 1965), p. 141; Maurice Ashley, *A History of Europe, 1648–1815* (Englewood Cliffs, 1973), p. 113; R. W. Harris, *Absolutism and Enlightenment* (2nd edn, London, 1967), pp. 221–2; E. N. Williams, *The Ancient Regime in Europe* (London, 1970), p. 424; Viktor Bibl, *Kaiser Josef II.* (Vienna and Leipzig, 1943), pp. 140–1; H. Magenschab, *Joseph II. Revolutionär von Gottes Gnaden* (Vienna, 1979); Saul K. Padover, *The Revolutionary Emperor* (2nd edn, London, 1967), p. 158; Herbert H. Rowen, *From Absolutism to Revolution* (New York, 1963), p. 174; Albert Sorel, *L'Europe et la Révolution française* (3rd edn, Paris, 1912), vol. I, p. 120 [trans. and ed. Alfred Cobban and J. W. Hunt as *Europe and the French Revolution* (London 1969), where the quotation falls on p. 149]; Victor-L. Tapié, *The Rise and Fall of the Habsburg Monarchy* (London, 1971), p. 241; Walter W. Davis, *Joseph II: An Imperial Reformer for the Austrian Netherlands* (The Hague, 1974), p. 203.

2 I have throughout reproduced the original English version of the *Neu gesammelte Briefe* (see p. 124) from *Letters of Joseph II* (London, 1821–22) [*The Pamphleteer*, XI (1822): 79–96, 273–96], hereafter cited as *Letters*, though with the spelling modernised and corrected. Where there is divergence of any importance from the original German, the fact is mentioned in the Notes. The letter to Herzan is from *Letters*, pp. 274–5. I have thought it right to reproduce the first two letters cited *in extenso*. They are especially significant as confessions of faith; they were of particular importance to Brunner (see p. 121); they have been very frequently quoted, but usually in snippets; and it seems desirable to put before the reader at least two complete texts.

3 Ernst Benedikt, *Kaiser Joseph II.* (Vienna, 1936), p. 128. Large tracts of the letter are printed by Davis, Padover and Rowen.

4 This is a mistake for 'Chairs' (*Lehrstühle*), which Padover (*Revolutionary Emperor*, p. 159) has perpetuated. The French edition ignores the problematic phrase, the American translates 'lecture-rooms' (see p. 124 and *North American Review*, XXXI [1830]: 10).

5 All four German editions (see p. 124) read 'Andromache'. The French edition omits it, the American amends to 'Arachne' (*North American Review*, loc. cit.).

6 *Letters*, pp. 95–6.

7 Benedikt, *Kaiser Joseph II.*, pp. 128; Bibl, *Kaiser Josef II.*, p. 187; Davis, *Joseph II*, p. 203; Magenschab, *Josef II.*, p. 187; Padover, *Revolutionary Emperor*, p. 159; Sorel, *Europe and the French Revolution*, p. 150; Leo Gershoy, *From Despotism to Revolution* (New York and London, 1944), p. 267.

8 *Letters*, p. 290.

9 Andrews, *Eighteenth-Century Europe*, p. 150; Bibl, *Kaiser Josef II.*, p. 179; Harris, *Absolutism and Enlightenment*, pp. 222–31; Magenschab, *Josef II.*, p. 187; Padover, *Revolutionary Emperor*, p.147; Rowen, *From Absolutism to Revolution*, pp. 176–7; T. C. W. Blanning, *Joseph II and Enlightened Despotism* (London, 1970), p. 64; Perry Anderson, *Lineages of the Absolutist State* (London, 1974), p. 234n.

10 S. M. Andrews, *Enlightened Absolutism* (London, 1967), p. 133; Bibl,

Kaiser Josef II., pp. 83–4 (see n.57 below); Magenschab, *Josef II.*, p. 291; Padover, *Revolutionary Emperor*, p. 42; Gershoy, *From Despotism to Revolution*, p. 266; *Letters*, pp. 289–90.

11 Rowen, *From Absolutism to Revolution*, pp. 175–6; Williams, *Ancient Regime*, p. 425; *Letters*, pp. 288–9.

12 A. J. P. Taylor, *The Habsburg Monarchy* (London, 1948), p. 20.

13 No date of publication or name of editor is given.

14 For this whole paragraph see S. Brunner, *Die theologische Dienerschaft am Hofe Joseph II.* (Vienna, 1868), pp. 7–8, 515–31 (the quotations come respectively from pp. 518, 8 and 517). J. Schleicher, *Sebastian Brunner. Ein Lebensbild* (Würzburg and Vienna, 1888), though four of its chapters describe its quarrelsome hero's *Conflicte* with various temporal and spiritual authorities, does not mention his attacks on other historians of Joseph's reign. Alfred Ritter von Arneth, *Aus meinem Leben* (2 vols, Vienna, 1891–92), does not mention Brunner or the *Neu gesammelte Briefe*. But he thinks it *würdiger*, even perhaps *edler*, not to indulge in polemic (vol. II, p. 248). What I later discovered about Joseph's opinion of Herzan strengthens the case (see D. Beales, *Joseph II. I: In the Shadow of Maria Theresa, 1741–1780* [Cambridge, 1987], p. 481 and n.).

15 Arneth, *Aus meinem Leben*, vol. II, pp. 247–56; H. von Sybel, 'Briefwechsel der Königin Maria Antoinette', *Historische Zeitschrift*, XIII (1865): 164–78 and XIV (1865): 319–50; *Maria Theresia und Marie Antoinette. Ihr Briefwechesel* (Paris and Vienna, 1865) and *Marie Antoinette, Joseph II. und Leopold II. Ihr Briefwechsel* [hereafter *MAJL*], ed. A. R. von Arneth (Leipzig and Vienna, 1866).

16 Cf., as well as the works cited in nn.17, 18 and 20, A. Fournier, *Historische Studien und Skizzen* (Prague and Leipzig, 1885), vol. I, p. 132n.

17 *Quellenkunde der deutschen Geschichte*, ed. H. Haering (9th edn, Leipzig, 1931), p. 730.

18 P. von Mitrofanov, *Joseph II. Seine politische und kulturelle Tätigkeit* (Vienna and Leipzig, 1910), vol. I, p. 5.

19 The article cited in the next n. relies heavily on Brunner's work.

20 'Eine gefälschte Briefsammlung des Kaisers Joseph II', *Historisch-politische Blätter für das katholische Deutschland*, ed. F. Binder and G. Jochner, CXXXIII (1904): 786–95.

21 The University Library at Vienna possesses the editions of 1790, 1821 and 1822, but the British Library, the Bodleian Library and the Cambridge University Library have none of them. Only Schuselka's edition of 1846 is reasonably easy to find.

22 H. Marczali, *Magyarország története II. József Korában* (Budapest, 1885–88), vol. II, p. 4 and n. [the letter of 1780 to Choiseul]; M. C. Goodwin, *The Papal Conflict with Josephinism* (New York, 1938), pp. 49–50 [the letter of 1784 to the pope]; H. Gnau, *Die Zensur unter Joseph II.* (Leipzig, 1911), p. 293 [the letter to Herzan]; F. Maass, *Der Josephinismus: Quellen zu seiner Geschichte in Österreich, 1760–1790* (Vienna, 1951), vol. I, p. 97n. [the letter of 1770 to Choiseul]. See, pp. 126–7, 142.

23 E.g. Paul P. Bernard, *Joseph II* (New York, 1968), p. 149 – but, on Pado-

ver's authority, he credits (p. 47) the letter of 1770 to Choiseul (see p. 142); C. A. Macartney, *The Habsburg Empire, 1790–1918* (London, 1968), p. 843.

24 C.S.B.B. in *English Historical Review*, LI (1936): 177–8.

25 Peter Fuchs in *Historische Zeitschrift*, CCIX (1969): 158.

26 Edward Crankshaw, *Maria Theresa* (London, 1969), p. 343. Cf. Bernard, *Joseph II*, pp. 145–6.

27 Fuchs, *Historische Zeitschrift*, CCIX (1969): 157.

28 See list in Appendix.

29 *Maria Theresia und Joseph II. Ihre Correspondenz* [hereafter *MTuJ*], ed. A. Ritter von Arneth (3 vols, Vienna, 1867–68), vol. II, p. 157 (Maria Theresa to Joseph, ?July 1777).

30 Max Braubach, *Historisches Jahrbuch*, XC (1970): 412n.

31 The evidence produced on p. 135, seems to clinch the case, though W. Heinsius, *Allgemeines Bücher-Lexikon*, vol. I (Leipzig, 1812), col. 421, has the publication date 1791.

32 The true place of publication is stated by M. Holzmann and H. Bohatta, *Deutsches Anonyme-Lexikon* (7 vols, 1902–28), vol. VI, p. 111, to be Copenhagen. But Heinsius, *Allgemeines Bücher-Lexikon*, op. cit., E. Weller, *Die falschen und fingirten Druckorte* (Leipzig, 1864) and C. von Wurzbach, *Biographisches Lexikon des Kaiserthums Oesterreich* (60 vols, Vienna, 1856–91), vol. V, p. 376 agree with Gräffer (see p. 137) that Klagenfurt is the answer.

33 See pp. 136–40.

34 *Briefe von Joseph dem Zweiten, als charakteristische Beiträge zur Lebens- und Staatsgeschichte dieses unvergesslichen Selbstherrschers. (Bis jetzt ungedruckt.)* (Leipzig, 1821) [hereafter *Briefe* (1821)].

35 Ibid., pp. ix–xviii.

36 F. Schuselka (ed.), *Briefe Josephs des Zweiten. Dritte Auflage. Zeitgemäss eingeleitet und erklärt* (Leipzig, 1846).

37 See n.2 above for the English translation. The French is: *Lettres inédites de Joseph II ... traduit de l'allemand par M.V.* (Paris, 1822).

38 *North American Review*, XXXL (1830): 1–26. There is also a Dutch edition, *Brieven van Joseph II; naar het Hoogduitsch* (The Hague, 1821), which I have not seen. See *Alphabetische Naamlijst van Boeken, ... 1790 ... 1832* (The Hague and Amsterdam, 1835), p. 86.

39 See O. E. Deutsch, *Mozart; A Documentary Biography* (2nd edn, London, 1966), p. 193.

40 Haus-, Hof- und Staatsarchiv, Vienna [hereafter HHSA]; Protocollum separatum aller Hand Billets ... 1784, no. 149. See n.45 below.

41 Here is just one example. From the same month as the supposed letter to the archbishop; 'Vous avez connu le détraquement de la machine, et vous avez connu les chefs et les aides avec lesquels je me trouve, vous jugerez le reste' (Joseph to Leopold of Tuscany, 12 Feb. 1781; *Joseph II. und Leopold von Toscana. Ihr Briefwechsel von 1781 bis 1790* [hereafter *JuL*], ed. A. Ritter von Arneth [Vienna, 1872], vol. I, pp. 8–9). No doubt, if Joseph had written to the

archbishop, he would have exempted the latter's father, 'the vice-chancellor, Colloredo', from his criticisms, but he would hardly have gone out of his way to praise all the others mentioned.

42 See Maass, *Der Josephinismus*, esp. vol. III, pp. 311–20.

43 The comparison with genuine letters to Catherine II can be made from *Joseph II. und Katharina von Russland. Ihr Briefwechsel* [hereafter *JuK*], ed. A. Ritter von Arneth (Vienna, 1869). *Historisch-politische Blätter*, CXXX (1904): 794.

44 *Briefe* (1821), p. iii.

45 Maass, *Der Josephinismus*, vol. II, contains many of the letters to the pope. Arneth's various editions of correspondence, A. Beer's edition of some correspondence with Kaunitz (*Joseph II., Leopold II. und Kaunitz: Ihr Briefwechsel* [Vienna, 1873]) and of course the letter-books in the HHSA illustrate the varying use of languages.

46 There is a volume a year of what may be described as ordinary *Handbillets*, running to something like 1,000 a year; then there are, for the early years of the reign, three volumes of *Handbillets* relating to the work of the *Staatsrat*, each covering two years, gradually dwindling in scale until the separate compilation ceased at the end of 1786.

47 I have not fathomed the precise criteria, if indeed there are such, which governed the inclusion of documents in these compilations. Hungarian matter seems to appear relatively rarely.

48 The letters to Maria Theresa conflict with those in *MTuJ*, vols II–III; those to Kaunitz with material printed in Beer, *Joseph II. Leopold II. und Kaunitz*, pp. 259–68 and in *Correspondances intimes de l'Empereur Joseph II avec … Cobenzl et … Kaunitz*, ed. S. Brunner (Mainz, 1871), pp. 71–2; the letter to Marie Antoinette with authentic correspondence in *MAJL*; the letter to Frederick the Great with documents in *Politische Correspondenz Friedrich's des Grossen*, vols XL–XLII (Leipzig, 1928–31); the letter to Marie Christine with H. Schlitter, *Die Regierung Josefs II. in den österreichischen Niederlanden* (Vienna, 1900), esp. pp. 11, 147; the letter to Catherine II with the correspondence in *JuK*; the letter to Pius VI with material in Maass, *Der Josephinismus*, vol. II; the letter to Trauttmansdorff with correspondence in *Geheime Correspondenz Josefs II. mit … Trauttmansdorf. 1787–1789*, ed. H. Schlitter (Vienna, 1902); the letter to Kressel with documents in Maass, *Der Josephinismus*, vol. III; the letter to Lacy with what is said in E. Kotasek, *Feldmarschall Graf Lacy* (Vienna, 1956), p. 173.

49 Cf. Beer, *Joseph II. Leopold II. und Kaunitz*, pp. 231–4.

50 *Letters*, pp. 83–4.

51 L. Freiherr von Pastor, *History of the Popes* (40 vols, London, 1951), vol. XXXVIII, p. 257 and n. 5.

52 Maass, *Der Josephinismus*, vol. I, p. 97n.

53 Biblioteca Nazionale Centrale Vittorio Emanuele II, Rome, MS. Ges. 1389 [formerly 3518].

54 Pastor, *History of the Popes*, vol. XXXVIII, pp. 14–23, 256–62; cf. Frédéric Masson, *Le Cardinal de Bernis depuis son Ministère, 1758–1794* (Paris, 1884),

p. 218. See Chapter 8, 'Maria Theresa, Joseph II and the suppression of the Jesuits'.

55 See Chapter 7, 'Love and the Empire'.

56 The letters discussed by Brunner, and the letter to Choiseul, together with the fifteen listed in Chapter 7, 'Love and the Empire'.

57 Early candidates for attack would be the letter to the elector of Mainz, that to Aranda (see Bibl, *Kaiser Josef II.*, pp. 83–4, where grounds are given for thinking it 'eine gute Fälschung'!) and those to Maria Beatrix and Max Franz (this last is hard, but not impossible, to reconcile with the letter from Joseph to Leopold on 22 Apr. 1784 [*JuL*, vol. I, p. 208]).

58 Adam Wandruszka, *Leopold II.* (2 vols, Vienna and Munich, 1964–65) has shown how much his subject hated Joseph, and what a divided family Maria Theresa's was (see esp. vol. I, pp. 332–55). Joseph, however, appears not to have suspected the depth of his brother's feeling against him, and to have confided in him to some degree.

59 *Letters*, pp. 277, 82–3.

60 Ibid., pp. 283–4.

61 Ibid., pp. 290–1, 294–6.

62 Ibid., pp. 294–5.

63 Joseph to Leopold, 30 Aug. 1787 (*JuL*, vol. II, 115); Joseph to Kaunitz, 26 Aug. 1788 (Beer, *Joseph II., Leopold II. und Kaunitz*, p. 309).

64 *Letters*, pp. 289–90.

65 The most convenient discussion is Charles H. O'Brien, 'Ideas of Religious Toleration at the Time of Joseph II', *Trans. Amer. Phil. Soc.*, new series, vol. 59, part 7 (1969).

66 Cf. Paul P. Bernard, *Jesuits and Jacobins* (Urbana, 1971), esp. p. 121; Ernst Wangermann, *From Joseph II to the Jacobin Trials* (2nd edn, Oxford, 1969), p. 36. Discussions of *The Magic Flute* abound, and their conclusions are legion; but they are informative on Masonry, and are mostly in no doubt that Sarastro is part of the Masonic element in the opera (e.g. J. Chailley, *The Magic Flute, Masonic Opera* [London, 1972], passim).

67 *Letters*, pp. 275–6.

68 E.g. Joseph to Leopold, 13 June 1782; 4 Feb. 1783; 20 Oct. 1783 (*JuL*, vol. I, pp. 125, 153, 177).

69 Cf. Ronald Grimsley, *Jean D'Alembert* (Oxford, 1963), p. 87; and letters to D'Alembert declining to supply his portrait to the Academy (25 March 1783, HHSA, letter-book for 1783; no. 272: 'Si quelques arrangements et ordonnances que j'ai faites m'ont rappellé, Mr, à votre souvenir, croyés moi, que pour être bien sûr de ne pas avoir la peine de décrocher un jour mon portrait, il vaudra mieux attendre leur reussite, et leurs effets, qui sont la seule pierre de touche des plus belles paroles'), and to Mercy commenting on this reply (31 Mar. 1783; HHSA, letter-book for 1783, no. 288: 'Il me paroit que la composition de cette Academie et son Sécrétaire perpetuel, l'ame damnée du Roi de Prusse meritoient cette response.').

70 The interest in libretti and music emerges in the correspondence in the letter-books. Painting and architecture are mentioned perhaps less often, but still quite frequently. On the theatre, see R. Payer von Thurn, *Joseph II. als Theaterdirektor* (Vienna, 1920). On his pride in theological learning see the famous letter to the elector of Trier, 25 Sept. 1781: 'mes Quesnels, mon Busembaum et même l'orthodoxe Febronius sont restés dans ma Bibliothèque' (HHSA, letter-book for 1781). (This letter was published first in 1782 (see below, n.87), then in 1834 (D. G. Mohnike, 'Briefwechsel zwischen Kaiser Joseph dem Zweiten und Clemens Wenzel, Churfürsten von Trier', *Zeitschrift für die Historische Theologie*, IV [1834]: 241–90), and appears in Schuselka's 1846 edition of the Constantinople letters (see p. 124 and n.36).

71 *MTuJ*, vol. III, p. 338.

72 *Letters*, pp. 286–7.

73 *Neu gesammelte Briefe*, p. 121n. Dr R. L. Wokler helped me with this reference.

74 It is true that, where preferments for men are concerned, the emperor commonly says that the matter must be dealt with through the usual channels.

75 *Letters*, p. 83; Carl Freiherr von Hock, *Der österreichische Staatsrath* (Vienna, 1879), p. 312.

76 Marczali, *Magyarország története II. József*, vol. I, pp. 433–40. The five letters appear in the following order in the original: 31, 36, 33, 35, 32 (see Appendix).

77 Mitrofanov, *Joseph II.*, p. 421, has the same passage garbled, presumably through translation into and out of Russian, and dated 10 Feb. 1786: Hock, *Der österreichische Staatsrath*, p. 183. This translation comes from the *North American Review*, vol. XXXI (1830): 12–13, in the absence of a version in the *Pamphleteer* collection.

78 *Letters*, pp. 279–80.

79 I have adopted the emendation of Herder (*Briefe sur Beförderung der Humanität* 'Gespräch nach dem Tode des Kaiser Josephs II', in B. Suphan [ed.], *Herders Sämmtliche Werke* [Berlin, 1881], vol. XVII, p. 63). Both Marczali's transcription (*Magyarország története II. József*, vol. II, p. 419n.) and A. F. Geisler, *Ski[z]en aus dem Karakter und Handlungen Josephs des Zweiten* (Halle, 1783–91), vol. III, 8te Sammlung, p. 214, read *Limitation*.

80 Geisler's and Herder's versions punctuate differently from Marczali's, and I have tried to translate the original.

81 *Letters*, p. 282.

82 Ibid., pp. 288–9.

83 E.g. E. Hubert, *Le voyage de l'Empereur Joseph II dans les Pays Bas, … . 1781* (Brussels, 1899), pp. 404–5.

84 *Joseph II. und Graf Ludwig Cobenzl: Ihr Briefwechsel* (*Fontes rerum austriacarum*, ed. A. Beer and J. von Fiedler, vols 53–4) (Vienna, 1901), vol. I, pp. 391–2.

85 See many letters in *JuL*, vol. I, about their visit to Vienna and Florence in 1782.

86 Maass, *Der Josephinismus*, vol. III, pp. 87–8, 322–3 and 323n.

87 An exchange with Kaunitz was published at the beginning of the reign in the *Wiener Zeitung* (see Geisler, *Skizzen*, vol. I , 2te Sammlung, p. 24); one of the editions of the Trier correspondence is *Correspondance entre l'Empereur et l'Electeur de Treves, évêque d'Ausbourg* (Avignon, 1782); *Anekdoten und Charakterzüge von Kaiser Joseph II*, (Vienna and Leipzig, 1790), p. 117.

88 Cf. Joseph to Leopold, 30 Oct. 1783 (HHSA, Familien-Akten, Sammelbände, Karton 8, not in Arneth).

89 See n.79.

90 *Allgemeine deutsche Bibliothek*, CVII (1791): 501–14, review article on seven books or pamphlets, by Lk. (none other than Meusel [see G. Parthey, *Die Mitarbeiter an Friedrich Nicolai's Allgemeiner Deutscher Bibliothek* (Berlin, 1842), pp. 62–3]). The quotation comes from p. 510.

91 Geisler, *Skizzen*, vol. IV, 10te Sammlung, pp. 91–103; vol. III, 8te Sammlung, p. 214. See n.77 above.

92 Leopold to Joseph, 10 Feb. 1782 (HHSA, Familien-Akten, Sammelbände, Karton 8), not published by Arneth; Maass, *Der Josephinismus*, vol. II , pp. 322–3.

93 The last named has no place of publication but is dated 1790. Its author is said to be Sam. Csernansky (G. Petrik, *Bibliographia Hungariae*, 1712–1860, vol. II [Budapest, 1890], tome I, p. 292). I am excluding from consideration works which are avowedly inventive like *Josephi II. condam inper. litterae de coelis missae* (1790). One *Testament politique* claims to have been 'traduit de l'allemand par M. Linguet' (Brussels, 1790). The other is alleged to have been published in Vienna in 1791 (2 vols).

94 Leipzig, 1790.

95 Vienna, 1790.

96 *Leben und Geschichte Kaiser Joseph des Zweiten* (5 vols, Amsterdam, 1790–91). *Vita e Fasti Giuseppe II* (?3 vols, Lugano, 1790). *La Vie de Joseph II* (Paris, 1790).

97 Vienna and Leipzig, 1790. See esp. p. 101n.

98 Frankfurt and Leipzig, 1790. See esp. p. 4.

99 2 vols, Salzburg, 1790.

100 E.g. *Recueil de lettres originales de l'Empereur Joseph II, au General d'Alton* (Brussels, 1790); *Recueil de Lettres de ... Albert et Marie Christine, au comte Trauttmansdorff* (Brussels, 1790); *Mémoires pour servir à la justification de feue Son Excellence le Général Comte D'Alton* (n.d. ?1790); *Fragmens pour servir à l'histoire des événemens qui se sont passés aux Pays-Bas ...*(Amsterdam, 1792). The review article by Meusel in *Allgemeine deutsche Bibliothek*, CVII (1791): 507, cast doubt on the authenticity of the *Neu gesammelte Briefe*, mentioned in one of the works under review.

101 Many of Arneth's editions have already been cited, and one of Brunner's works. H. Meynert, *Kaiser Joseph II.* (Vienna, 1862), and Adam Wolf, *Marie Christine, Erzherzogin von Oesterreich* (2 vols, Vienna, 1863), are among the earliest works on the period based on documentary material.

102 E.g. Fournier, *Historische Studien*, vol. I, p. 132n. And see n.108.

103 Much of this paragraph is based on Friedrich Wadzeck, *Leben und Schicksale des berüchtigen Franz Rudolph von Grossing, eigentlich Franz Matthäus Grossinger genannt, nebst der Geschichte und Bekanntmachung der Geheimnisse des Rosen-Ordens* (Berlin, Frankfurt and Leipzig, 1789), which publishes a number of authentic documents. The emperor's letter-books provide some additional information, as does R. Gragger (ed.), *Preussen, Weimar und die ungarische Königskrone* (Berlin and Leipzig, 1923), pp. 22–37 and the related end-notes.

104 *Staatenjournal*, I (Nuremberg, 1787): 3.

105 Gragger (ed.), *Preussen, Weimar und die ungarische Königskrone*, pp. 24, 33–7 and nn.

106 Handbillet to Pergen, Lugos, 7 Oct. 1788 (HHSA, letter-book for 1788): 'Sobald als er in Wien ankommt, ist er in den geheime Arrest abzugehen, und … die weitere Untersuchung vorzunehmen.' Gragger (ed.), *Preussen, Weimar und die ungarische Königskrone*, p. 29.

107 Ibid., pp. 32–3.

108 Ibid., p. 33.

109 Franz Gräffer, *Wiener-Dosenstücke*, Erster Theil (Vienna, 1846), pp. 36–7. I have not pursued the question of the authorship of the *Charakteristik*.

110 Even Gragger (*Preussen, Weimar und die ungarische Königskrone*, p. 29) and Fritz Valjavec (*Die Entstehung der politischen Strömungen in Deutschland, 1770–1815* [Munich, 1951], p. 122), who has studied the writings of F. R. Grossing in detail, still adhere to this view.

111 The documents appear to have been removed to Budapest after the First World War, but the Hungarian State Archives have only what seems to be a portion of the original file, containing merely a copy of *Irrthümer in den Begriffen der meisten Ungarn*.

112 Gragger, *Preussen, Weimar und die ungarische Königskrone*, esp. pp. 81–4, 147–9.

113 Oskar Sashegyi, *Zensur und Geistesfreiheit unter Joseph II.* (Budapest, 1958), pp. 133–5. Professor John Reddick helped me with this passage.

114 This must be the significance of the passage quoted by Mitrofanov, *Joseph II.*, p. 825n., though he thinks it refers to F.R.

115 Gragger, *Preussen, Weimar und die ungarische Königskrone*, p. 148.

116 'Gedruckt im Römischen Reiche, 1790'. On the authorship, see ibid., p. 81.

117 In the remnant of the Grossingakten in the Hungarian State Archives (see n.107), Staatsrat Izdenczy noted of the *Irrthümer* that it appeared to be the work of Joseph Grossing, who 'gab sich in der Folge bei S.M. selbst als der Verfasser'. Denis Silagi, *Ungarn und der geheime Mitarbeiterkreis Kaiser Leopolds II.* (Munich, 1961), seems to have missed this book and the Grossing brothers.

118 At the end of the preface (*Briefe* [1821], p. xii) appears this statement over the name F. A. Brockhaus: 'Die Verlagshandlung fügt diesem Vorworth

noch hinzu, dass ihr diese Briefsammlung von einem in Auslande lebenden Deutschen, der in früherer Zeit an Joseph II. attachirt war, zur öffentlichen Bekanntmachung ist überlassen und ihr die Aechtheit derselben auf das Bestimmteste ist zugesichert worden.' Brockhaus's catalogue (Heinrich Brockhaus [ed.], *F. A. Brockhaus in Leipzig. Vollständiges Verzeichniss* ... [Leipzig, 1872], p. 159), describes F. R. Grossing as *Herausgeber* of the *Briefe*.

119 J. G. Meusel, *Das gelehrte Teutschland* (5th edn, Lemgo, 1796), vol. II, pp. 681–3; vol. IX (suppl., Lemgo, 1801), p. 466.

120 Béla K. Király, *Hungary in the Late Eighteenth Century* (New York and London, 1969), p. 156 and n. The original letter is in HHSA, Kaiser Franz Akten, Fasc. 151 [formerly 154], K.I.

121 Dr O. Sashegyi kindly informed me that the entry in *Magyar Életrajzi Lexikon, I* (Budapest, 1967), p. 624, was based on the statement in *Hadi történetek* (Vienna, 1789), vol. I, p. 442 that F. R. Grossing was condemned to life imprisonment and sent to Kufstein. Meusel (*Das gelehrte Teutschland*, vol. II, p. 68), says that since 1788 he has been in the Bergschloss zu Grätz. Gragger's documents, however, show that he was imprisoned in Vienna at least until 1790.

122 Gragger, *Preussen, Weimar und die ungarische Königskrone*, pp. 148–9. Cf. Wangermann, *From Joseph II to the Jacobin Trials*, esp. pp. 10–11, 86.

123 In what remains of the Grossingakten (Hungarian State Archives).

124 See p. 130.

125 *Briefe* (1821), p. iii.

126 See above, p. 122.

127 Johanna Schmid, 'Der Wandel des Bildes Josephs II. in der österreichische Historiographie von den Zeitgenossen bis zum Ende der Monarchie' (PhD thesis, 1972, Nationalbibliothek, Vienna). She has not, however, concentrated on the question, and has not fully appreciated the influence of the *Neu gesammelte Briefe*, of which she believes the 1821 edition to be truly the first.

128 F. Engel-Jánosi, 'Josephs II. Tod im Urteil der Zeitgenossen', *Mitteilungen des österreichischen Instituts für Geschichtsforschung*, XLIV (1930): 324–46.

129 Cf. H. Schlitter's preface to the German translation of Mitrofanov (*Joseph II.*, p. 5).

130 On Schuselka see Robert A. Kann, *The Multinational Empire* (New York, 1970), pp. 63–8 and end-notes, pp. 363–5.

131 H. Winkler, 'Die Reformen Josephs II. im Urteil der Broschüren' (PhD thesis, 1971, Nationalbibliothek, Vienna).

132 K. Benda (ed.), *A magyar Jakobinusok iratai* (3 vols, Budapest, 1952–57); Bernard, *Jesuits and Jacobins*; Körner (ed.), *Die Wiener Jakobiner*; D. Silagi, *Jakobiner in der Habsburger-Monarchie* (Vienna, 1962); Valjavec, *Die Entstehung der politischen Strömungen in Deutschland*; Wangermann, *From Joseph II to the Jacobin Trials*.

133 E. Wangermann, *The Austrian Achievement, 1700–1800* (London, 1973).

134 Silagi, *Ungarn und die geheime Mitarbeiterkreis Kaiser Leopolds II.*

135 Padover, *Revolutionary Emperor*, pp. 42, 109.

136 A notable instance of reliance on Padover resulting in gross error is the entry for Joseph II in G. M. D. Howat and A. J. P. Taylor (eds), *A Dictionary of World History* (London, 1973), p. 780.

137 See above, pp. 126–7.

138 Goodwin, *Papal Conflict with Josephinism*, pp. 49–50.

139 Cambridge, 1994. Cf. Williams, *Ancient Regime* and Stephen J. Lee, *Aspects of European History, 1494–1789* (2nd edn, 1984), where chapters on Joseph II are full of false letters.

140 To Maria Theresa, 20 July 1777 (*MTuJ*, vol. II, p. 152).

PART TWO

Joseph II and Reform

CHAPTER 6

Joseph II's *Rêveries*

Historiography

In the seventh volume of his magisterial *Geschichte Maria Theresias*, which appeared in 1876, Alfred Ritter von Arneth, head of the Haus-, Hof- und Staatsarchiv in Vienna, devoted four pages to summarising a paper entitled *Rêveries* which he affirmed that the future Joseph II had composed in 1761. Arneth asserted the importance of this document as evidence of the crown prince's youthful views, but stressed that most of them were utterly impractical and could therefore have no influence.[1] He had included in his edition of the correspondence between Maria Theresa and Joseph, published in 1867, the latter's two other earliest surviving memoranda, that of 3 April 1761 and the long and famous *Memorandum* of late 1765 on the state of the Monarchy.[2] But Arneth never published the text of the *Rêveries*.

Several subsequent historians, mainly biographers of the emperor, have referred to the document. But in every case except one, which will be discussed below, they obviously depend on Arneth's précis. The full account in Bibl's *Joseph II* is almost word for word the same as Arneth's. Two biographers, Fejtö and Bernard, have confused and conflated it with the memorandum of 3 April 1761.[3]

The exception is the Hungarian historian, Henrik Marczali. At the beginning of the second volume of his great *Magyarország története II. József Korában*, originally published in 1884, he summarised the *Rêveries*, quoting a few lines from it which had not figured in Arneth's book. In a footnote he thanked Arneth for having, in his capacity as archivist, supplied these extracts. But he added: 'This document is not yet in print, and moreover is not available for publication.' He ascribed it to 'the nineteen-year-old Joseph', that is to 1760–61.[4] Then in the second edition of this volume (1888), although the body of the work remained unaltered, he was able to include on pp. v–xiv a nearly complete text of the *Rêveries*, for which he again thanked Arneth. He stressed that the document was of great political as well as biographical importance. 'The transcription', he wrote, 'is absolutely faithful except that I have omitted a few lines in which the lion's claws show themselves too savagely.'[5]

So far as I know, no later writer has made use of Marczali's text or attempted to fill its lacunae. The only historian apart from Arneth and Marczali whose writings show that he had actually seen the original document is Carl Freiherr von Hock, who states in his *Der österreich-ische Staatsrath* that he had come across it in the secret archives.[6]

History of the document itself

In the Haus-, Hof- und Staatsarchiv it is not to be found among the correspondence between Maria Theresa and Joseph. Nor is it catalogued with the latter's memoranda from the period of his co-regency with his mother (1765–80).[7] But, through the great kindness of the late Dr Christiane Thomas, I was able to obtain and study a copy of the surviving original in the Kaiser Franz Akten (neu 212).

Although Marczali's transcription (or was it Arneth's?) proves to be largely accurate, it is not perfect; and of course the passages omit-ted, 'in which the lion's claws show themselves too savagely', are of unique interest. In any case, Marczali's book is by no means readily accessible in either of its editions. A new and complete text of the *Rêveries* is printed in the Appendix below, translated into English from the original French.

I shall first discuss its history and try to date it. Then I shall go on to draw attention to its great significance not only as evidence of Joseph II's youthful views but also of his long-term plans, and not just for the biographer of the emperor but for the historian of the Monarchy and of Enlightened despotism or absolutism.

I must begin by considering the note which Arneth attached to the document in the archive. He wrote it underneath the usual archivist's brief description of the piece, which is in another hand and reads romantically: 'Reveries of an unknown person about the means of maintaining the power of the state and increasing it.'[8] Arneth's words are as follows:

> In the archive of the *Staatsrat* (Council of State) a second copy of this memorandum is to be found with the heading: 'H.M. the Emperor's first memorandum on the political system'. Maria Theresa sent it to Kaunitz (?) with the following autograph letter: 'this is the second part

of the Emperor's report, much of which Kaunitz has followed; the French piece was given to me six or more years ago; it shows the way of thinking that keeps on coming back.'[9] It cannot be doubted that these are the *rêveries* to which Joseph himself refers in his memorandum, published in the third volume of the correspondence of Maria Theresa, which therefore probably constitutes the 'second memorandum' [referred to by the empress].[10]

Arneth was clearly right that the 'Unbekannte' was Joseph. The copy I have used is in a secretarial hand, and was evidently written from dictation. But it contains one autograph correction, and the doodle above the title is characteristically Joseph's. In any case, its style and content stamp it as his.

Arneth must again have been right in thinking that it was to this document that the emperor was referring when he wrote in his *Memorandum* of 1765: 'I have abandoned my *rêveries*.'[11] This remark confirms the obvious inference that the document had been submitted to Maria Theresa.

The rest of Arneth's note is more difficult to accept. To begin with, the letter from Maria Theresa which he reproduced can hardly have been addressed to Kaunitz, who is referred to in the third person. Arneth himself made in his *Geschichte Maria Theresias* the much better suggestion that the addressee might have been Count Blümegen, from 1771 the head of the Austro-Bohemian Chancellery.[12]

As for Arneth's (and Maria Theresa's) chronology, it can at once be established that less than five years, not 'six or more', separate the *Rêveries* and the Memorandum. Joseph must have written the latter before the end of 1765, because he speaks of that as the current year.[13] In the former he talks of the Council of State not only as a going concern, but as a body with whose proceedings he is completely familiar. Yet it first met on 26 January 1761,[14] and he did not join it until some months later.[15] If the empress's use of the phrase 'six years or more' is dismissed as a careless chronological lapse, there remains another hurdle to be surmounted before Arneth's identification of the documents she was sending with her letter can be upheld. Both the *Rêveries* and the *Memorandum* of 1765 were written in French.[16] She would not therefore have differentiated them by calling one of them 'the French piece'.

Among Joseph's memoranda two stand out as good candidates for identification as 'the second part of the emperor's report'. Both were written in German. The first is the document he submitted to his mother at the end of November 1771, in which he made sweeping recommendations for administrative and other reforms following his tour of famine-stricken Bohemia, and which he himself called 'the second part of my Prague report'.[17] The other possible document is the 'second plan' in his 'Note' of 27 April 1773 advocating the total or partial supersession of the Council of State by a Cabinet.[18] This 'Note' amounted to a criticism and refutation of an immense memorandum of Kaunitz's dated 15 April.[19] It is perhaps a more likely candidate than the Bohemian report because of words used by Kaunitz when commenting on it to Maria Theresa on 1 May. He wrote that the views he had expressed were 'largely drawn from the various writings of His Imperial Majesty and only ... put into another order'.[20] Maria Theresa may well have been echoing this statement in the letter Arneth quoted.[21] In either case, 'the French piece' must have been the radical *Memorandum* of 1765, and Maria Theresa's chronology is more or less vindicated.

What grounds are there, other than chronological, for this assertion that the empress must have been referring to the *Memorandum* of 1765 rather than to the *Rêveries*? So far as their contents are concerned, either is plausible. But, first, Joseph's remark in the *Rêveries* about his basic aim, 'the humbling of the nobles', that 'even the Council of State should know nothing of it', seems to make it impossible that his mother would have shown the document to her ministers. Secondly, when Joseph's brother, Grand Duke Leopold of Tuscany, came to Vienna in 1778, as Professor Adam Wandruszka revealed from his coded memoranda,

> the empress gave me a document written by the emperor when he
> first married, containing his ideas at that date on the government
> of the state and its system. This is confused and unsystematic, but
> includes very strong and violent principles of arbitrary despotism,
> involving the removal of all privileges of the Estates, even those that
> have been guaranteed by promises and oaths.[22]

This statement must surely refer to the *Rêveries*, and strongly suggests that Maria Theresa had been horrified by the content of the document and had kept it secret. If she actually surrendered it to Leopold in 1778, that would account for its preservation among the Kaiser Franz Akten. Significantly, it is filed with the two political testaments of Maria Theresa, which were also for royal consumption only.

Although it seems impertinent to question a statement made by Arneth about the archives he controlled, this naturally makes one wonder whether there could ever have been a copy of the *Rêveries* in the files of the Council of State. These were destroyed by Russian soldiers in 1945, but there is no mention of such a document in the indexes, which survive.[23] Further, Hock, an official of the Council of State as well as its historian, is careful to say that he found the *Rêveries* elsewhere.[24] At least it can hardly have been possible for the ministers of Maria Theresa and Joseph to read the *Rêveries* in the archive of the Council of State or anywhere else.

The document seems to have retained a horrifying aspect even in the 1880s. Marczali took upon himself the responsibility for the omissions made in the text which he was eventually able to publish. But it appears likely that Arneth had been reluctant to allow it to be printed in the first place and that, when he permitted it, he had asked Marczali for the excisions. All later historians of the Monarchy have reason to be immensely grateful for Arneth's pioneering work on a colossal scale as archivist and writer. But, whether on his own initiative or because of pressure from above, he did not always live up to his own best standards. For example, he wrote in the preface to his edition of the correspondence between Maria Theresa and Joseph:

> In this collection are included all writings of whatever nature which were exchanged between Joseph II and his mother at this time, except in so far as they count as wholly unimportant. From the writings of Joseph to Leopold, likewise, only those of slight interest are left out. Omissions of particular passages have almost never occurred, since here the same discretion did not have to be observed as in the case of the correspondence between Maria Theresa and Marie Antoinette.[25]

However, Professor Wandruszka found and used large numbers of letters of great interest between Joseph and Leopold which Arneth had not published; and there are more which were not relevant to Wandruszka's biography of Leopold.[26] Arneth frequently omits a few lines without giving the slightest hint that he has done so.[27] In complete contradiction to his words just quoted, he had precisely the same problem here as with the letters between Maria Theresa and Marie Antoinette, namely that some of them were explicit about sexual matters; and he solved it in exactly the same way, by cutting the letters.[28] Moreover, it is difficult to escape the conclusion that he printed as few documents as possible which might tend to discredit the Monarchy's bureaucracy[29] or to reflect badly on its policy in the late nineteenth century.

These were the passages garbled by Marczali:

(a) [I should wish] to humble and impoverish the grandees, since I don't think it very useful that there should be little kings and great subjects who live comfortably without caring what becomes of the state. I believe as [a principle].
(b) [It is the lords] I am attacking.
(c) As for the humbling of the nobles, which I think the most useful and necessary, it is something one hardly dares speak about to oneself. But we must have it in view in all our actions. [Even the Council of State should know nothing of it.][30]

The world must not know that Joseph secretly planned to attack, humble and impoverish the nobility.

The background and dating of the *Rêveries*

It is desirable to date such a striking document as accurately as possible. Maria Theresa's statement to Leopold that it was written when Joseph 'first married' (see above) throws it impossibly far back into 1760. Marczali's assertion that it was composed by 'the nineteen-year-old Joseph' (see above) is similarly untenable. We have seen already that, given the knowledge it shows of the Council of State, the latter part of 1761 is the earliest conceivable period for its origin.[31] At first sight this seems an acceptable date. The crown prince's discussion of the defects of the administration fits quite well with the debates in the Council of State and outside on the remodelling of the system introduced on the advice of Haugwitz in 1749. These disputes culminated in the dismantling of the Directorium in publicis et cameralibus and its replacement by the Austro-Bohemian Chancellery, together with the establishment of a new financial administration, at the end of 1761 and the beginning of 1762.[32] Troubles in Transylvania, to which Joseph refers, had been considered by the Council of State during 1761, as had the position of Hungary and the problems raised by the tax immunity of the Hungarian nobility, including the question whether and with what proposals to call the Diet.[33]

Certain of Joseph's remarks in the *Rêveries*, however, force consideration of a later date for its composition than 1761. First, he speaks approvingly of 'the Council of War [*Hofkriegsrat*] as it is at present

... As for military matters, generals, worthy and capable men, who have given unmistakable proofs of competence, must understand them better than we.' He could hardly have used these words of the Council of War under the veteran Count Harrach, nor spoken of him as one of the two satisfactory heads of departments. These passages must have been written after the appointment of marshal Count Daun as president of the Council of War on 30 January 1762 and the simultaneous removal of many civilian councillors to make room for generals.[34] Secondly, Joseph also mentions favourably the chancellor and vice-chancellor of Hungary. During 1761 and 1762 the Council of State repeatedly heard complaints from its members about the unwillingness of the chancellor, Count Pálffy, to carry out the Court's plans. It caused Maria Theresa great annoyance that he objected to the discussion of Hungarian affairs by this new Council. He was replaced by Count Esterházy in November 1762.[35] The date of the *Rêveries* must therefore be at least as late as this. Thirdly, the way in which Joseph deals with the financial position in the *Rêveries* compels the conclusion that he was writing in time of peace, or at least when peace was assured. But the Treaty of Hubertusburg ending the Seven Years' War was not signed until 15 February 1763, and the outcome of the negotiations had been uncertain until just beforehand.[36] If these arguments are accepted, then the *Rêveries* cannot have been written before 1763.

Working backwards from 1765, equally good grounds can be found for concluding that it cannot have been written later than 1763. Joseph speaks of 'the first Diet' in Hungary. It seems unnatural to use that phrase if the decision had been taken to summon the assembly. The question appears to have been settled before the end of 1763.[37] Again, his words about the possible necessity for bloodshed in Transylvania are difficult to relate to any period after the massacre of Mádéfalva on 7 January 1764, while they fit easily into the previous year, when the Vienna government was debating whether to follow the hard line advocated by Buccow, the provincial governor. The decision to give him firm support was taken on 11 October 1763.[38]

Within 1763, what Joseph says about finance makes it possible to pin down still further the date of the document. Still working backwards, we know that on 24 September 1763 Joseph's father, the Emperor Francis I, was put in charge of operations to reduce the debt and the interest rate paid on it.[39] The crown prince could hardly have made his detailed proposals in this field, with an air of discovery, after his father had taken up the question. Further, according to the autobiography of Count Ludwig von Zinzendorf, president of the Hofrechenkammer (Audit Office), a patent for a 'Schulden-Steuer' (debt tax) or 'Klassen-Steuer' (class, i.e. graduated, tax) was drafted on 19 June 1763, on the basis of a pamphlet just published in Paris, entitled *Les richesses de l'état* (The wealth of the state).[40] The fact that there is no allusion to this recommendation in the *Rêveries*, and that Joseph does not refer to the pamphlet, suggests that he was writing during the first half of the year 1763.

Zinzendorf mentions the preparation of the *Staats-Inventarium*, intended to give for the first time accurate information about the revenue and expenditure of the Monarchy. He ascribes its compilation to the four months following 30 August 1762, but in fact it took much longer. The text of the *Rêveries* does not make it possible to tell whether Joseph had before him the results of the *Inventarium*. However, the existence of some deficit had been accepted since 1761. Zinzendorf further speaks, with reference to 1763, of 'various conferences between the Austro-Bohemian Chancellery and the financial departments'.[41] The agenda of the Council of State on 8 March 1763 included the item 'Reduction of the interest rate on Estates bills from 5% to 4%'. On 15 April the Council discussed 'Council of War, Treasury, control of the Bank, Audit Office (economy measures)'. On 8 April Transylvanian problems, involving 'unrest', had been considered.[42]

I conclude, then, that the *Rêveries* dates from the spring or summer of 1763. This suggestion can be squared even with Maria Theresa's chronology if she may be supposed to have meant the period of Joseph's first marriage, which ended with his wife's death on 27 November 1763, rather than the moment when he contracted the union.

The significance of the *Rêveries* for the history of the Austrian Monarchy

Modern historians are likely to agree with Maria Theresa and Leopold in the eighteenth century, and Arneth and Marczali in the nineteenth, that the most striking sections of the *Rêveries* are those in which Joseph talks of humbling and impoverishing the great nobility, and of getting the constitutions of the provinces suspended. It is hard to think of contemporary parallels, even among radical writers, for such sweeping denunciations of the aristocracy. The egalitarianism of the passage beginning 'What geniuses' is startling. Joseph's contempt for local privileges can more easily be matched: at least in the case of Hungary, many of the members of the Council of State wrote almost as strongly.[43]

But Joseph's statements about 'limited despotism' – by which he seems to mean unlimited despotism for a period of ten years – are altogether exceptional. In the mouth of an heir apparent to the Monarchy, these sentiments were revolutionary. Incidentally, they were far removed from what his education had sought to inculcate.

When he wrote in the *Memorandum* of 1765 that he was abandoning his *Rêveries*, it was evidently to these parts of the earlier document that he was referring, since he repeated many of its other points. For example, he again demanded greater administrative centralisation, he renewed his attack on the waste of time and money by government departments, and he launched another tirade against the quality and motivation of officials. In the later *Memorandum* he showed himself more critical of the Council of State than before. But the only opinion to be found in the *Rêveries* which he directly contradicted in the *Memorandum* of 1765 – though without actually acknowledging error or admitting he had changed his mind – was his original condemnation of Kaunitz's management of his departments. Maria Theresa's campaign to bring her son, now co-regent, and the state chancellor together was obviously yielding results.[44]

So far as his proposed attack on the aristocracy and the provincial constitutions was concerned, Joseph just left these subjects virtually unmentioned in the memorandum. It looks as though he suppressed or deferred his aims in these fields, rather than permanently 'abandoned' them. His later views on Hungary are indistinguishable from his attitude in the *Rêveries*: he always insisted that the nobles must surrender their tax exemption if the country was to be treated favourably in the matter of tariffs; and he refused to be crowned king, since he did not intend to be bound by oaths to the constitution which were an inescapable part of the coronation.[45] His treatment of Belgium, at least after 1785, suggests that he never in his heart gave up his youthful plans. He told the Estates of Brabant in 1789: 'I do not need your consent to do good.'[46] His tax legislation embodied strong assertions of egalitarianism.[47]

On many lesser points too he remained of the same opinion all his life. His remarks on the bureaucracy in the *Rêveries* and in the

Memorandum of 1765 correspond closely with the exhortations of the 'pastoral letter' of 1783.[48] His frequent later suggestions for the improvement of the Council of State – for converting it from a think-tank to an executive Cabinet of responsible ministers – are consistent with what he wrote in the *Rêveries*.[49] He always took the same line about extravagance at Court.[50] His concern to reduce the state debt led to his surrendering the fortune he inherited from his father, in order to make possible a lowering of the interest rate paid by the government.[51]

Admittedly, there is no trace in the *Rêveries* of the interest in ecclesiastical reform which characterised his later activity. Nor is there anything about territorial aggrandisement, which he is generally supposed to have ardently desired.[52] The position of the serfs is scarcely mentioned, and the introduction of the canton system and of military conscription are present only by implication – but these were issues that he had dealt with in his memorandum of 3 April 1761.[53]

The *Rêveries*, then, embodies not just youthful ideals soon to be abandoned in the light of experience, but rather some of the prince's long-term aims, including perhaps those which he cherished most fervently. It may be that the more general of these aims should be regarded by historians as (in Arneth's words) 'utterly impractical', even though Joseph himself did not come to accept this view, if ever, until the last days of his life. But while parts of the document raise fundamental issues which could only have been settled over a long period, other sections have reference to the specific and immediate problems of 1763. These passages read like a 'Votum' (written opinion) by a member of the Council of State. Indeed, Joseph refers in one place to 'the other *votants*'. The *Rêveries* resemble from this point of view the memoranda he wrote during the co-regency. He seems never to have written the long and careful 'Vota' expected of other members.[54] But from time to time he composed an extended piece that he submitted privately to his mother, which corresponded in many ways to a 'Votum'.

There is a historiographical problem here. Biographers have generally neglected the more bureaucratic of his writings. Other historians, especially of the administration, have often taken little or no account of his more personal and private utterances. But in the case of an absolute monarchy the distinction cannot be maintained. It was through private family conversations, of which his letters reveal something, through the letters themselves, and through papers like the *Rêveries*, rather than through regular official channels, that Joseph exerted influence.

Students of the financial and administrative changes of 1763–65 ought to be able to make use of the *Rêveries*. If my dating of the document is correct, it contains one of the earliest demands made by a member of the Council of State for a new round of administrative reform, anticipating by a year Haugwitz's *Vortrag* of 15 March 1764 with which Friedrich Walter began his account of the process.[55] Joseph's *démarche* may well help to explain why Maria Theresa commissioned this paper. It is true that no more was heard of the crown prince's criticism of Kaunitz's management of Italy and the Netherlands. Presumably, no one else dared make that point. But the debates of 1764–65 turned on other issues that had been raised by Joseph in the *Rêveries*: the need to unite rather to separate, especially by bringing the three financial departments together and by subordinating the Council of Trade (*Commercienrat*) to the resulting complex. Maria Theresa's final decision of 26 August 1765 represented a move in the direction of her son's views. It was characteristic of her reactions to his memoranda that, while rejecting the fundamental changes that they proposed, she headed him off by giving him some satisfaction on points of detail.

Comparison with Frederick the Great's *Rêveries politiques*

Historians have given Joseph's *Rêveries* virtually no attention. They have shown tremendous interest, on the other hand, in a piece of writing with a similar title, the *Rêveries politiques* which Frederick the Great of Prussia appended to his political testament of 1752. Comparison between the two is instructive.

In his *Rêveries politiques* Frederick set out various possible annexations which Prussia might hope to make in the future, peacefully for preference, but if necessary by war and, if convenient, by breaking treaties. When these passages were discovered in the archives in the late nineteenth century, the German government would not permit their publication, since their cynicism would have shocked liberals – and others too – and their revelation of Frederick's schemes would have cast doubt on the mythology of national unification. After the First World War the ban was lifted, and the *Rêveries politiques* was printed in 1920. A debate ensued on the morality of Frederick's attitudes and the significance of the views he had expressed in the document. The argument turned to some extent on the meaning of the title. Were these far-reaching *rêveries* to be understood as fantasies, speculations, pipedreams, or as realistic future plans which Frederick seriously hoped to implement?

He had begun his discussion by contrasting the 'solid', which he had already treated, with the 'chimerical', on which he was about to embark. But soon he was talking of 'the spacious field of chimerical projects, which can sometimes become real if one does not lose sight of them, and if successive generations, marching towards the same goal, are sufficiently skilled to hide their designs deeply from the curious and penetrating eyes of the European Powers'. Before long, still under the heading *Rêveries*, he was proposing means of acquiring the territories concerned, and producing a detailed plan for the conquest of Saxony. While he recognised that elements of the future were unpredictable, he believed that rational calculation could prepare for most eventualities.

In these *Rêveries politiques* Frederick was manifestly discussing serious possibilities and, in some cases at least, matured plans. This interpretation gains force from the fact that in the eighteenth century the word *rêveries* came to mean 'reflections', 'meditations', 'musings' as well as 'fantasies' or 'pipedreams'. Joseph cannot possibly have known of these thoughts of his great rival. But the same considerations apply to both sets of *Rêveries*. Indeed, the two documents illuminate each other. They were not wild, 'impractical' imaginings; they were considered, though secret, plans for a future which their authors hoped would not be distant.[56]

Frederick, of course, was writing for posterity as a king of twelve years' standing, with great achievements behind him. Joseph was evidently looking to his own reign after his mother's death, but he had to submit his ideas to her as the effective ruler of the Monarchy at the moment. He was still very inexperienced. But it reflects the permanent and fundamental difference in the approach of the two men that Frederick's secret talk should be of aggrandisement through war, and Joseph's of reform through despotism. It is entirely fitting that what embarrassed the Monarchy's historians in the late nineteenth century in Joseph's *Rêveries* was not any designs he harboured against other Powers, but rather the savagery of his enmity to the aristocracy.

The contrast between the two rulers' *Rêveries* raises fundamental questions for the historiography of Enlightened despotism or absolutism. It is clearly impossible to pursue them here. But one point must be made in conclusion. Some historians have presented Enlightened absolutism as a necessary response to the society typified by 'the second serfdom'.[57] Collaboration with the aristocracy was certainly the programme of Catherine II as well as of Frederick. But, if the forces of history required it of Joseph also, he was unaware of the fact, and he defied them.

Appendix: *Rêveries* (translated from the original French)[58]

Note: I have divided the originally continuous text into paragraphs. As in many of Joseph's writings, the cascade of his ideas sometimes overwhelms his grammar and punctuation. In some cases I have made additions [in square brackets] in the interests of clarity, but I have tried so far as possible to preserve the flavour of the original.

Rêveries

Two first principles by which our actions must be governed, which are [, first,] the absolute power to be in a position to do all possible good to the state and [, secondly,] the means to maintain this state without foreign aid. To attain these two aims, I should propose

1) to humble and impoverish the grandees, for I do not believe it is very beneficial that there should be little kings and great subjects who live at their ease, not caring what becomes of the state. I believe it to be fundamental that every man, as a subject, owes to the state, which maintains him, protects him and secures him his rights, such services as the state, whose spokesman is the sovereign, considers him capable of – and not what suits his convenience or pleasures. For on that basis individuals are no longer being suited to jobs, but jobs are having to be made in order to suit individuals. This smacks of despotism, but without an absolute power (as I've already said) to be in a position to do all the good which one is prevented from doing by the rules, statutes and oaths which the provinces believe to be their *palladium*, and which, sanely considered, turn only to their disadvantage, it is not possible for a state to be happy or for a sovereign to be able to do great things. I believe it to be fundamental that, in order to direct the great machine, a single head, even though mediocre, is worth more than ten able men who have to agree among themselves in all their operations. God keep me from wanting to break sworn oaths, but I believe we must work to convert the provinces and make them

see how useful the limited despotism, which I propose, would be to them. To this end I should aim to make an agreement with the provinces, asking them [to yield to me] for ten years full power to do everything, without consulting them, for their own good. This will cost a lot of trouble to secure, but I think that now is the favourable moment; and experience of it will make them see its utility. Many individuals will not be at all happy with it, but the main body of the nation should be preferred to this portion.

As soon as I have obtained that, it is the nobles I shall attack. I shall impose on them a double tax on their demesnes[59] together with the taxes which have already been proposed in [the discussions about] the financial system. I approve all of them, because they fall equally on the noble and the subject, and relief can always be given to the subject by reducing the Contribution.[60] As the price of this relief subjects would have to put up with providing quarters for troops, since I believe that they ought to stay outside barracks, not only for the advantage of the military, and because its consumption will bring profit back to the landlord, but also in order to inspire in the whole nation a military spirit.

Since I shall greatly reduce the revenues of the lords, I must by no means ask or expect to have a brilliant Court. But what use is that anyway? Internal strength, good laws, firm administration of justice, well-ordered finances, an impressive army, flourishing industries, respect for the sovereign, will better distinguish one of the great Courts of Europe than festivities, gala days, rich clothes, diamonds, gilded halls, gold plate, sledge races etc. In consequence, since the one cannot be had without the other, I shall not ask of my subjects this lavish lifestyle: no great dinners, no expensive clothes made abroad, at most embroidery done here.

By reducing the wealth of the grandees and the pay [of officials], which I shall be proposing later, you would have people showing greater keenness to serve. Everyone would want to serve, and would work hard in consequence. Young men who know that for their whole life they will be rich enough not to need to serve the state don't apply themselves to anything, spend large sums rashly, run up debts, which, since they are never settled, ruin the poor man and the artisan who pay taxes, while these [young men] are of no use whatever. But if people knew that the only way to live in comfortable circumstances would be to rise by hard work in the service [of the state], and that only genuine merit [would count], regardless of recommendations, family, or even merit of one's ancestors – for nothing is more just than to reward a father who has served the state well so long as this reward does not burden the state with worthless subjects who have nothing of their fathers but his name! Personal merit is everything. If this rule is strictly observed, what geniuses will not emerge, who are now lost in obscurity either through laziness or because they are oppressed by nobles! Everyone will work hard, knowing this, and setting himself from his birth the aim of winning the opportunity to live in comfort, which he can achieve only through being in the pay of his sovereign.

With me there would be few people employed, but they would be very carefully chosen. After a year's probation their pay would rise every five years. Having become unfit to serve, they would revert to their first salary level. But none who were lazy, negligent, incapable would have anything to hope for. Faults arising from bad faith would be punished with maximum severity, with no account taken of birth, since I don't know by what right a man who possesses old parchments can be a rascal with impunity, while another who behaves in the same way and lacks these scraps of paper would now be hanged.

To get a gentleman to serve the state, even very feebly, you have to pay him lavishly in gold; to get a chief to be willing to lend his name to an office without doing any work, to sit down for three hours three times a week, to set his secretaries writing, costs ten or twelve thousand florins [a year]. If he had no need of rich clothes, if his wife and daughters had no need of diamonds, and he didn't require six horses, he would be quite happy with 4,000. So that a councillor shall set his clerks writing, go to the Prater,[61] to the German comedy and some taverns, he must be paid 6,000 or at least 4,000. If the chief were properly regulated, the others would automatically be reduced in number – for who is it that does the work at the moment? it is the poorest officials, who have only 4 or 500 florins. Since the state pays [the chiefs] more highly, they consider themselves entitled to do as they please.

Under my plan, which would at the same time greatly diminish the quantity of writings [produced by officials], and would greatly simplify the machine, removing the inefficient without regard to rank, and the lazy, I can certainly reckon the cost of all the departments as halved. I believe that, to control such a machine, one head with power of decision, but informed by a council like the Council of State, is enough. The method which I have in mind to propose is in my opinion the only one: instead of separating things, we must unite them.

In my opinion there are only two departments in the whole Monarchy which are well organised, that is the Council of War as it is at present, and the Supreme Council of Justice. I would exempt these two in their running from any connection with the Council of State. As for justice, after having chosen competent subjects, the sovereign should rely on them. As for military matters, generals, worthy and capable men, who have given unmistakable proofs of competence, must understand them better than we.

So far as the provinces [i.e. Austria and Bohemia] are concerned, I think one Chancellery is enough, if it has the will. If it hasn't, it should be changed. In financial matters I must confess that the farrago of long words that one doesn't understand, but whose effects have yielded no good, do not convince me that our arrangements are well constituted. I think that the regiment of number-crunchers, whose infallibility is unproven but in whom one must piously believe, should be much reduced by creating a department of finance in which the three others would be absorbed. One chief, one head, but a good one, and with full power, would improve matters more than all this complicated scheme, which is based entirely on arguments culled from libraries that are proved worthless by the facts. I am not much of an expert in financial affairs, but few words and plenty of results will always attract me. With four departments I would run the machine (I understand here all the provinces except Hungary).[62] As for Italy and the Netherlands, which in my opinion cannot be governed by a single head who has other work, by a minister too busy to be able to do more than brush the surface [of their affairs] once a month, and the sovereign knows less about them than about the government of France. For the political business of these provinces, I think that a [separate] Chancellery would not be *de trop*.

As for foreign affairs, I think that, so long as there is a Conference made up as it is, it is preferable, particularly for the sake of secrecy, to give freedom of action to an able head whose integrity can be relied on.[63]

As for Hungary, the [separate] Chancellery should continue, but its papers, as with Italy and the Netherlands, should come to the Council of State. I would judge that, before we can reasonably expect anything more from this country, we must work to make it happy. To achieve this, we must reform their internal system, enable them to sell their products, promote trade. Above all, we must work to increase population and to educate youth, and to convert the reasonable old men by proving to them that it is for their good that we are working. We must be especially careful to create no suspicion that we want to infringe their privileges, although in private we feel no respect for them at all. But we must never allow this to appear except when we are sure of achieving the result we aim at.

It is said that Hungarian trade would be prejudicial to the Austrian provinces. But if Hungary contributed [taxes] as they do, of which I don't despair in the long run, it would be another Peru discovered. But in order to achieve that, we must ask absolutely nothing by way of increased taxes at the first diet, because the small amount that we should obtain would prevent us making internal arrangements, since feelings would have been roused; and while gaining one million, we should lose the chance of enjoying six or seven in a few years' time.

The great nobility ought to be kept quiet either by honours or by fear. The lesser nobles should be supported against the great, and won over by appointing them to all types of offices, which the sovereign ought to keep within her control. The serfs should be upheld against the tyrannous domination of the nobles; if they had the opportunity to sell their produce, my aims would be readily achieved.

As for Transylvania, I think that we must first examine whether what is being asked of them is founded on justice. Is it? [If so,] we must get our way without any other kind of enquiry. I must state my opinion that, if the matter had been put on a different footing from the start, both here and there, it would have been concluded. But as that is not the case, we must now force the issue, since I don't know anything more harmful, and more dangerous in its consequences for all our plans, than to reveal to subjects that, if they don't like something which the sovereign asks, even though it is just, they can stop it. I certainly regret all violence and bloodshed, but this is of too great importance for future generations for us not to decide to insist on it, since it is just, whatever it costs. If we adopt this firm resolution, and leave no hope that we will make any adjustments behind the scenes, I believe that the thing will be easier than is envisaged.

2) The method that I am going to propose to restore the state at this moment will strike hard at the most useless appurtenances of the state, which are the people who live off their capital. I should declare that, since the state is in no position to continue to incur debt after debt, that from this moment we would not pay any inter-

est above 3 per cent, with no exception for any bank or debtor. At the same time we would declare that those who don't want to leave their capital with us at 3 per cent must announce the fact within a certain time, that a list would be made of them and that repayments of both capital and interest would be made in the course of time at the rate of 3 millions a year, starting with the smallest. In this way free will would be exercised, and promises most precisely kept. For, if those who have their capital at 6 per cent decide to leave it in at 3, they cannot complain. Those who don't wish to do so will have their capital repaid with interest after some years, according to when the dividend of 3 millions of amortisation per annum falls to them. The consequence is clear. Either they leave their money in at 3 per cent, as I expect, since it will have been ordered at the same time that no private person may take interest at a higher rate than 3 per cent, on pain of forfeiting the protection of the courts, and that all subjects are expressly forbidden to put their money anywhere except in our provinces. Thereby, as well as the benefit that leaps to the eye, that instead of 5 millions interest per year we shall pay no more than 9 if everyone leaves his money in, if not, we shall pay still less interest but we will give 3 millions a year in amortisation, and in at most 70 years the debts would be paid off even if no one left his money in. In this way we are covered, we keep our word to the letter, we have fewer debts every year and yet our credit is maintained. Private persons will employ their money in trade and agriculture to enjoy a better return on their money.

Having introduced the double tax on demesnes, the halving of [the bill for] salaries and pensions by their reduction and by employing a smaller number of people – which in order to achieve a just equality would extend to restricting the pleasures of the sovereign – and [by cutting] the pay of ministers abroad, having also done what the other *votants* have proposed to make up the deficit – except the Interest and Property Tax, which is no longer applicable – that would yield altogether nearly 10 millions: we have calculated 15 millions of interest payments, by my method we would need only 9 and the amortisation fund of 3, which would grow in proportion as the debts diminish. All the new taxes would diminish every year in proportion to the debts. What a consolation to the people! Thus I would retain 3 millions of savings and 10 for additional expenditure, that is 13.

Of these, I assign two to the military, as it is only allocated 14 millions, one for fortifications: these 17 millions would be entirely under the control of the Council of War. 3 I assign to trade, establishment of manufactures, for roads, canals, to render the country prosperous by the sale of its merchandise etc. These 3 would be controlled by a Council of Commerce, composed of the most enlightened people of my state, who would nevertheless be under the direction of the head of the finances. One million I assign to relieve Contributions in case of fire and storm in some province. Another to recompense those who serve me well, and to add to the pay (which would be small) of those who distinguish themselves by their zeal. These two millions would be controlled by the [Austro-Bohemian] Chancellery. I am then left with 5 millions in the bank. These I regard as a sacrosanct fund, which could not be touched except in time of war. It is money extracted harshly from my subjects, it should therefore be used only for their defence. A man respected by the public for his probity would be its treasurer and would be accountable only to the sovereign, whom the Council of State represents. 10 years of peace, 50 millions in the bank. Although I believe that war can be waged more cheaply, this would in any case pay for a first campaign. If it is successful – as we may trust it would be if the military is kept on a good footing and freedom of action is given to the Council of War, which ought to recognise able subjects (but, again, no favouritism, only personal merit) – we shall be [operating] in enemy country, which greatly reduces the expense. If not, we have provinces who have had their rustical Contribution[64] reduced and been enriched by trade, and our credit has been maintained.

By these means the Monarchy would be in the most brilliant condition. Some individuals, and particularly the grandees, would suffer. But for serious illnesses one has to take an emetic, and I think these means still the easiest way of attaining the great aim of relieving the Monarchy for the present and sustaining it for the future. I cannot believe that in following these principles and intentions we can be failing in our duty to God or to men. But these are only crude ideas, and [describe] only the principles that we ought to have before our eyes in all our actions. This is the favourable moment. Everyone is expecting to be charged double, wild doubts are beginning to be expressed about our credit. No one will complain – or very few – about these taxes which I propose, since people see their purpose and [have reason to] hope that they will not be permanent.

As for the humbling of the nobles, which I think the most useful and necessary, it is something one hardly dares speak about to oneself.

But we must have it in view in all our actions. Even the Council of State should know nothing of it. But the sovereign's decisions should follow from it.

As I am adding to the [purview of the] Council of State Italy, the Netherlands and Hungary, it needs two more members. This Council ought to meet every day from 9 until midday in the antechamber. As a result paperwork will be cut, minuting made easier and decisions speeded up. I shall leave trifling matters to the relevant departments. The [royal] decision should not be written on the submission itself but on a separate sheet, so that one can add or delete whatever one wants. Ordinary judicial and military affairs should not be matters for [the Council of State]; [but] the [Austro-Bohemian] Chancellery together with the general finance department and the Hungarian Chancellery should report to it. The success of the operation depends on the choice of personnel: although it is difficult, I think one could find 4 or 5 men [to head] these departments. For the justice and war departments they are already provided. For finance I know no one better than Count Choteck, who should be given a free hand. For the Austro-Bohemian Chancellery M. de Hatzfeld, whom I believe to be a man of integrity. For the Netherlands and Italy either Cobenzl or Firmian with a council subordinate to the Council of State. For Hungary the chancellor and the vice-chancellor seem to me capable. For trade M. Senzendorff will, I believe, serve well under M. de Choteck.[65] In this way the [number of] councils and departments will be reduced, many fewer officials will be needed and, if mistakes are committed, it will be clear who is responsible. Foreign affairs under a chief with no other duties would be dealt with more quickly, and we should then get more benefit from this great mind.[66]

If we reward good [officials], remove the incompetent and punish the bad, I believe that, according to this plan for the present and for the future, the state would be [rendered] flourishing and formidable. But, the decision once taken, it must be upheld through thick and thin in all its elements. For, if one is dropped, the whole scheme becomes unjust.

Notes

This chapter first appeared in the *Mitteilungen des österreichischen Staats-archivs* [hereafter *MÖSA*], 33 (1980): 142–60. I have modified the text to make it more accessible to an Anglophone historical audience, most importantly by translating the *Rêveries* and foreign-language quotations into English. I have also added some footnote references to recent work.

I should like to thank for their help the British Academy and the Leverhulme Trust; Professor T. C. W. Blanning, Professor P. G. M. Dickson, Dr G. Gömöri, Mr T. D. Jones, the late Dr Christiane Thomas, Dr R. L. Wokler and Mr T. S. Wyatt; and my wife and children. Dr Thomas was unstinting in assisting me in the archives and as editor of the *Mitteilungen*.

1 *Geschichte Maria Theresias* [hereafter *GMT*], ed. A. Ritter von Arneth, vol. VII (Vienna, 1876), pp. 65–9.

2 *Maria Theresia und Joseph II. Ihre Correspondenz* [hereafter *MTuJ*], ed. A. Ritter von Arneth, vol. I (Vienna, 1867), pp. 1–12; vol. III (1868), pp. 335–61.

3 S. K. Padover, *The Revolutionary Emperor* (2nd edn, London, 1967), p. 20; V. Bibl, *Kaiser Josef II.* (Vienna, 1943), pp. 29–32; F. Fejtö, *Un Habsbourg révolutionnaire. Joseph II.* (Paris, 1953), p. 79; P. P. Bernard, *Joseph II* (New York, 1968), pp. 20–1. Of works written since the publication of this article, H. Magenschab, *Josef II.* (Vienna, 1979), based largely on the false *Letters of Joseph II* first published in 1790 [see Chapter 5, 'The False Joseph II'], ignores the *Rêveries*; the more scholarly work by K. Gutkas, *Kaiser Joseph II.* (Vienna, 1989), p. 44, although its bibliography contains the present article, makes no use of it.

4 H. Marczali, *Magyarország története II. József Korában*, vol. II (Budapest, 1884), pp. 1–3, p. 2, n.1.

5 Ibid. (2nd edn, 1888), p. iv: 'A közlés teljesen hű, csak néhány sort hagytam el, hol nagyon is élesen mutatja körmét as oroszlán.'

6 C. von Hock and H. I. Bidermann, *Der österreichische Staatsrath* (Vienna, 1879), p. 23, n.1. According to Bidermann (p. iii), Hock wrote the first 130 pages.

7 Haus-, Hof- und Staatsarchiv [hereafter HHSA], Habsburgisch-lothringisches Familien-Archiv, Sammelbände 4, contains nearly all the correspondence between Maria Theresa and Joseph. Most of his memoranda are in Sammelbände 5, 87 and 88.

8 I think this is right, but there has been some correction made which renders the title difficult to read.

9 I have used the version of this quotation given by Arneth himself in *GMT*, vol. VII, p. 194.

10 Part of this statement was reproduced, inaccurately, by Marczali, *Magyarország története II. József Korában* (2nd edn), vol. II, p. xv.

11 *MTuJ*, vol. III, p. 360; *GMT*, vol. VII, p. 194; D. Beales, *Joseph II, I: In the Shadow of Maria Theresa, 1741–1780* (Cambridge, 1987), p. 106 and, for an analysis of the memorandum of 1765, pp. 164–76.

12 *GMT*, vol. VII, p. 199. On Blümegen's position see Beales, *Joseph II*, pp. 207, 343.

13 *MTuJ*, vol. III, p. 338.

14 *GMT*, vol. VII, p. 18.

15 Arneth says this happened in May (ibid., p. 32). Later dates have been

given by historians who were able to use the now destroyed records of the Council, e.g. K. Schünemann, 'Die Wirtschaftspolitik Josephs II, in der Zeit seiner Mitregentschaft', *Mitteilungen des Instituts für österreichische Geschichtsforschung* [hereafter MIÖG], 47 (1933): 19, says 1762. But G. Ember, 'Der österreichische Staatsrat und die ungarische Verfassung, 1761–1768', *Acta historica*, 6 (1959): 137, reproduces a brief 'Votum' of Joseph's from the summer of 1761. Cf. Beales, *Joseph II*, p. 97 and n.15.

16 The original dictated text of the *Memorandum* of 1765, with Joseph's autograph corrections, is in Sammelbände 87 and is in French. Arneth's version (see n.2) is reliable.

17 *MTuJ*, vol. I, p. 352 (27 Nov. 1771). This document is printed in Rudolf Khevenhüller and H. Schlitter, *Aus der Zeit Maria Theresias. Tagebuch des Fürsten Johann Khevenhüller-Metsch, 1770–1773* (Vienna, 1925), pp. 373–98.

18 Printed in *Die österreichische Zentralverwaltung*, 2nd part (1749–1848), vol. III, *Vom Sturz des Directorium in publicis et cameralibus [1760–1] bis zum Ausgang der Regierung Maria Theresias. Aktenstücke*, ed. F. Walter (Vienna, 1934), pp. 60–9.

19 Ibid., pp. 73–4. Joseph to Leopold, 22 Apr. 1773: *MTuJ*, vol. II, pp. 6–7.

20 Quoted in *Die österreichische Zentralverwaltung*, ed. Walter, 2nd part, vol. I/I (1938), p. 454, n.3.

21 Maria Theresa also later wrote to Joseph (undated, but Arneth, *MTuJ*, vol. II, p. 32, suggests on 12 March 1774) that Kaunitz's opinion on Joseph's 'great work' 'corresponds in almost every respect with yours'. The 'great work' seems to be the document of 27 Apr. 1773. This letter suggests that the empress consistently took the line that the minister was really saying the same thing as her son, and that the letter quoted by Arneth about the 'second part of the emperor's report' might date from as late as 1774 (see pp. 158–9 above).

22 A. Wandruszka, *Leopold II.*, vol. I (Vienna, 1963), p. 438.

23 Dr Christiane Thomas was kind enough to check the indexes for me. Cf. A. Coreth, 'Das Schicksal des k.k. Kabinettsarchivs seit 1945', *MÖSA*, 11 (1958): 515.

24 Hock and Bidermann, *Staatsrath*, p. 23, n.1.

25 *MTuJ*, vol. I, pp. xiii–xiv.

26 Wandruszka, *Leopold II.*, vol. I, pp. 414, 421 etc. Perhaps the most glaring omissions are the letters of 30 May, 3 June and 19 Sept. 1771, and portions of those of 25 Sept. and 'Nov. 1771' (*MTuJ*, vol. I, pp. 347–9), all revealing the intensity of Joseph's feelings about the situation in Bohemia and Maria Theresa's unwillingness to let him act on them. But there are countless cases. See the next n.

27 An interesting instance is the letter of 'Nov. 1771' just cited, from which Arneth omits without any indication the words after 'commencées': 'O poor Monarchy, how you are treated!' The MSS are in Sammelbände 7. See Beales, *Joseph II*, p. 209.

28 For the correspondence with Marie Antoinette see Paul Christoph [i.e.

David Pollack], *Maria Theresia und Marie Antoinette. Ihr geheimer Briefwechsel* (2nd edn,Vienna, 1980). See Beales, *Joseph II*, esp. pp. 10, 374–5.

29 Why else omit a portion of a letter in which Joseph complains that the State Chancellery does not know that the Bug flows into the Vistula and not the Dniester (*MTuJ*, vol. II, pp. 17–18, Sept. 1773; Sammelbände 7)?

30 The words in square brackets were *not* omitted by Marczali, but I have included them here in order to show the importance of the omissions in obfuscating Joseph's meaning.

31 See p. 160.

32 F. Walter, 'Kaunitz' Eintritt in die innere Politik', *MIÖG*, 46 (1932): pp. 71–2.

33 Ember, *Acta historica* (1959), prints extracts from 'Vota' on these questions, destroyed in 1945 (see n. 15 above).

34 *GMT*, vol. VII, pp. 28–9, 499, nn.30 and 31.

35 Ember, *Acta historica* (1959): 138, 341–3; *Die österreichische Zentralverwaltung*, ed. Walter, p. 30; *GMT*, vol. VII, pp. 107, 511, n.159.

36 Ibid., vol. VI, chs 16 and 17.

37 Ibid., vol. VII, p. 512, n.162: Erizzo's report of 1 October 1763.

38 G. A. Schuller, *Samuel von Brukenthal*, vol. I (Munich, 1967), pp. 126–48.

39 A. Beer, 'Die Finanzverwaltung Oesterreichs, 1749–1816', *MIÖG*, vol. XV (1894): 245, n.2.

40 G. von Pettenegg (ed.), *Ludwig und Karl Grafen und Herren von Zinzendorf... Ihre Selbstbiographien* (Vienna, 1879), p. 19; Rudolf Khevenhüller and H. Schlitter, *Aus der Zeit Maria Theresias, 1764–1767* (Vienna, 1917), p. 569. I am most grateful to Miss A. M. Whitelegge for enabling me to see the five editions of this pamphlet (some of them entitled *La richesse de l'état*, some lacking the article) in the Goldsmiths' Library, University of London, and to the late Professor D. C. Coleman for suggesting that I go there. Cf. G. Weulersse, *Le mouvement physiocratique en France (de 1756 à 1770)* (2 vols, Paris, 1910), vol. I, pp. 83–91; vol. II, pp. 348–51.

41 Pettenegg, *Zinzendorf*, pp. 90–1; H. L. Mikoletzky, 'Johann Matthias Puechberg und die Anfänge der Hofrechenkammer', *Jahrbuch des Vereins für Geschichte der Stadt Wien*, vol. 17/18 (1961–62): 136–7, 141–4.

42 Khevenhüller and Schlitter, *Aus der Zeit Maria Theresias, 1764–1767*, pp. 566–7. Since I wrote this article, a masterly account of these financial discussions has appeared in P. G. M. Dickson, *Finance and Government under Maria Theresia, 1740–1780* (2 vols, Oxford, 1987), esp. vol. II, ch. 2. I originally plumped for April 1763 as the likeliest date for the composition of the *Rêveries*, but I now think his suggestion of 'summer' (vol. I, p. 447) more likely – perhaps June.

43 See Ember, *Acta historica* (1959): 130–7.

44 Beales, *Joseph II*, pp. 43–68, 140–9. Dickson, *Finance and Government*, vol. I, pp. 253–6, 447–8, provides a most useful discussion and summary of Joseph's reform proposals during his mother's reign.

45 See above, pp. 162–3; T. C. W. Blanning, *Joseph II* (London, 1994), esp. pp. 112–16.

46 W. W. Davis, *Joseph II: An Imperial Reformer for the Austrian Netherlands* (The Hague, 1974). See Chapter 10, 'Was Joseph II an Enlightened Despot?'.

47 E.g. Joseph to Count Pálffy, 30 Dec. 1785, quoted above, p. 131.

48 The document was published in many languages and was sent to all departments. It is extensively quoted and much discussed in W. Heindl, *Gehorsame Rebellen: Bürokratie und Beamte in Österreich* (Vienna, 1991). See also P. G. M. Dickson, 'Monarchy and Bureaucracy in Late Eighteenth-Century Austria', *English Historical Review* (1995): 323–67, together with his *Finance and Government*.

49 Much documentation in Walter (ed.), *Zentralverwaltung. Aktenstücke*.

50 Cf. H. Wagner, 'Royal Graces and Legal Claims: The Pension Payments of Maria Theresa and Their Withdrawal by Joseph II', in J. Held and S. B. Winters (eds), *Intellectual and Social Developments in the Habsburg Empire from Maria Theresa to World War I* (London, 1975), pp. 6–29. See D. Beales, 'Court, Government and Society in Mozart's Vienna', in S. Sadie (ed.), *Wolfgang Amadé Mozart: Essays on His Life and Music* (Oxford, 1996), pp. 3–20.

51 Cf. my *Joseph II*, pp. 161–4; Dickson, *Finance and Government*, vol. II, ch. 2.

52 E.g. C. A. Macartney, *The Habsburg Empire, 1790–1918* (London, 1968); Padover, *Revolutionary Emperor*, p. 32.

53 *MTuJ*, vol. I, pp. 1–12. See my *Joseph II*, esp. ch. 11.

54 Ember in *Acta historica* (1959): passim, prints occasional brief sentences of Joseph's appended to lengthy 'Vota' by other members of the Council of State. It is possible that, when Joseph refers in the *Rêveries* to 'the other *votants*', he is thinking also of officials from the administrative departments (cf. Zinzendorf's remarks quoted above, p. 164).

55 See F. Walter, 'Der letzte große Versuch einer Verwaltungsreform unter Maria Theresia', *MIÖG* 47 (1933): 427–69 for this whole paragraph.

56 E. Bosbach, *Die Rêveries politiques in Friedrichs des Großen Politischen Testament von 1752* (Cologne, 1960) prints the text, summarises the writing on the subject and contributes a convincing analysis of her own, which I have followed. Quotations from p. 137. There are later examples of Joseph using *rêveries* in the sense of 'probable dispositions for an immediate future', e.g. Joseph to his mother, 27 Apr. 1778 (*MTuJ*, vol. II, p. 226).

57 Cf. A. Soboul, 'Sur le système du despotisme éclairé', in *Les Lumières en Europe centrale et en Europe orientale: Actes du Troisième Colloque de Mátrafüred* (Budapest, 1977), pp. 19–29; P. Anderson, *Lineages of the Absolutist State* (London, 1974). Cf. the more recent discussion by J. V. H. Melton in H. M. Scott (ed.), *The European Nobilities in the Seventeenth and Eighteenth Centuries* (2 vols, Harlow, 1995), vol. II, pp. 127–43.

58 I published the French text at the end of my article in *MÖSA* (1980). There seems no point in reproducing here my footnotes about the problems

of transcribing the French text. The few notes that follow are designed to explicate the English text.

59 That part of lords' estates which was farmed by established peasants (known as 'rustical' land) paid tax at roughly twice the rate of the demesnes, directly farmed by the lord. It was proposed to double the tax on the demesnes.

60 The Contribution was the main source of royal revenue after Haugwitz's reforms of 1748–49. See Dickson, *Finance and Government*, esp. vol. I and the previous note.

61 When Joseph was writing, this was still a royal park.

62 At this point in the original a new sentence is started with 'As for the finances', but I have omitted these words because they make no sense, since they are followed immediately by the passage on Italy and the Netherlands.

63 The French here is 'une tête d'esprit sur l'honnêteté de laquelle on peut se reposer', which I infer means Kaunitz. The Conference dated back to the sixteenth century, though its role and composition had been frequently modified since. See Dickson, *Finance and Government*, vol. I, pp. 331–2.

64 See n.59 above.

65 The ministers mentioned must be: Count Rudolf Chotek, Austro-Bohemian chancellor since 1762; Count Karl Hatzfeld, a financial minister since 1761; Count Charles Cobenzl, minister in the Austrian Netherlands since 1753; Count Karl Firmian, minister plenipotentiary in Lombardy since 1759; and Count Ludwig Zinzendorf, president of the Hofrechenkammer since 1762.

66 This time the wording is 'et cette grande tête seroit plus ménagée'. See n.63 above.

CHAPTER 7

Love and the Empire: Maria Theresa and Her Co-regents

Aussi je ne suis pas de ces amants vulgaires;
J'accommode ma flamme au bien de mes affaires;
Et sous quelque climat que me jette le sort,
Par maxime d'État je me fais cet effort.

Jason in Corneille, *Médée* (1635)

I

A scriptwriter would scarcely dare to invent a relationship so stormy as that between Empress Maria Theresa and her son, Emperor Joseph II. Maria Theresa played in turns the shattered widow, the besotted mother, the martyred parent and the callous autocrat. She was now open-hearted, now paranoid, at once loving and suffocating, overwhelmingly charming and insufferably overbearing. Joseph would sometimes cower before Big Mother's awesome force of personality. At other times he screamed like an adolescent for attention, special treatment and independence.

The disputes between mother and son took on a peculiar bitterness because of their unique official relationship. From 1740 to 1780 Maria Theresa ruled in her own right, under a wide variety of titles, the vast agglomeration of territories that constituted the Austrian Monarchy. But she made first her husband, Francis Stephen, and then after his death in 1765 her son, Joseph II, her co-regent. It is sometimes stated, for example in the old *Cambridge Modern History*,[1] that she and her husband, and then she and her son, were co-regents together. This is quite wrong. Maria Theresa was never herself co-regent. She remained the absolute sovereign. To complicate matters further, Francis Stephen was from 1745, and Joseph II from 1765, Holy Roman Emperor. In other words, they were sovereigns – though by no means absolute – over a huge Empire which included roughly a third of the Monarchy but was governed on a totally different basis by a separate, rival bureaucracy.² These arrangements inevitably produced tensions, which when Joseph was involved became explosive.

On the first occasion when Joseph actually threatened to resign as co-regent, in 1769, the empress wrote to him:

> You would not force me to procure a change in a solemn agreement so dear to my heart, which was the work of my love on 21 November 1740 and renewed on 19 September 1765, the most cruel day of my life. [She has selected an odd pair of dates but is clearly referring to the grants of co-regency to her husband and son.] Only the hope of finding in you a son worthy of such a father, and of being able to be useful to you, has sustained me so far and will sustain me in future, for I don't want to last a minute unless I'm assured of your love.³

She frequently asserted that she remained on the throne only for Joseph's sake, out of love for him. Almost as frequently, she expressed boundless admiration for his talents and achievements. Yet, as early as 1766, she told him he should cease to 'relish all these *bons mots*, these witty remarks which only result in wounding and ridiculing others, alienating all honest men'. His heart, she said, was not yet bad – but it soon would be.⁴ This is just one of many devastating rebukes preserved in their surviving correspondence. Whether she said as much or more to his face we do not know. She certainly criticised him uninhibitedly behind his back. In 1771 she was writing anguished letters to a confidante, the Marquise d'Herzelles, who had been governess to Joseph's little daughter, now dead, and whom he had asked to become his companion, perhaps even to marry him. 'We never see each other except at dinner ... His temper gets worse every day ... Please burn this letter ... I just try to avoid public scandal.' In another letter to the marquise she wrote: 'I can find solace only in death itself, hoping for God's mercy ... I try to do penance and look to his salvation ... [He has declared] that he needs neither doctor nor confessor ... He avoids me ... I'm the only person in [his] way and so I'm an obstruction and a burden ... Abdication alone can remedy matters.'⁵ She was, of course, induced not to abdicate.

Joseph displayed an equally wide range of feelings towards his mother. As late as July 1778, in the early days of the War of the Bavarian Succession, he wrote to her:

> This very minute ... your precious letter has arrived ... If I wanted to reply to it, I couldn't ... It has brought tears to my eyes ... My

admiration for its sublime manner of thinking is as great as my gratitude. How happy I am to have such a mother and such a sovereign ... I
see again the great, the incomparable Maria Theresa.

[But he could also tell her:] If Y.M. would only experiment with
allowing business which Nature has made masculine in character to be
transacted by men, Y.M. would notice the same difference as I would
if girls and women had been supplied to me as soldiers, foresters,
hunters etc ... Only a *man* versed in affairs can get at the essence of
the thing and single out those points on which judgement is most vital
in coming to decisions.[6]

He frequently bemoaned his unique ill-fortune in being co-regent.
There can properly, he said, be only one ruling voice in a monarchy.
'None of my predecessors, my contemporaries, my colleagues as
heirs presumptive [*sic*] are employed, why must I be? Let her leave
me to my imperial business, my books and gentlemanly amusements.'
Enforced association with her half-baked policies is not only destroying
his hopes, it is also sullying his reputation.[7] As we shall see, he made
repeated threats or offers to resign the co-regency. But he was, of
course, always induced to withdraw them.

Among the other *dramatis personae* the most important was Prince
Kaunitz, the state chancellor (prime minister in all but name) who
brought to the disputes his own competing brands of cunning, para-
noia and emotional blackmail. The most fundamental and revealing of
the numerous rows between mother and son was that of December
1773, the only occasion when all three principals actually put their
resignations on the table at one and the same time. Joseph had been
presenting a series of memoranda which could only be read as demands that he should be made the effective ruler – as he put it in
one of them, 'dictator'.[8] He had just wrested the government of the
newly annexed province of Galicia from the control of Kaunitz; he
was badgering the reluctant chancellor to demand more territory in
the East; they were at loggerheads about the disposal of the lands of
the suppressed Society of Jesus.[9] When Kaunitz sent in his resignation,
Maria Theresa capped it by offering to abdicate. Joseph refused the
opportunity, imploring his mother to stay on, but asking instead to
be relieved of the co-regency. She then gave him the full treatment:
'You used to love the state; you kept yourself for it alone; what has
happened to this proper ambition? ... So give your help to a mother
who for thirty years has had no object in life but you, who lives on

desolate, and will die if she sees all the care and trouble of her love set at naught.' Joseph caved in and wrote to Kaunitz begging him to continue in office. Though minor concessions were made to Joseph, the upshot was that Maria Theresa and Kaunitz continued to lay down the main lines of the Monarchy's policy and to stave off the radical reforms demanded by the emperor.[10]

Clearly the empress and the chancellor had helped each other to manoeuvre Joseph into a weak position. They had the advantage that he had just contrived to offend his best friend in the inner circle of the administration, Marshal Lacy, who had obtained leave to travel abroad, ostensibly for the sake of his health.[11] Lacy was the obvious candidate with whom Joseph might have hoped to replace Kaunitz. Maria Theresa, as during previous confrontations, mentioned as a possible substitute Prince Starhemberg. As usual, the proposal brought Joseph round since, for whatever reasons, he could not abide Starhemberg.[12] But even if Lacy had been available, the bureaucracy was so stuffed with Kaunitz's protégés that any other chancellor would have found himself short of loyal subordinates. Maria Theresa commanded affection and devotion such as Joseph could never match. She generally succeeded in charming even his friends away from him. Both the Marquise d'Herzelles and Marshal Lacy, when it came to the crunch, took her side.[13]

The empress had genuinely considered abdication immediately after her husband's death.[14] But later, although she often found her role as sovereign irksome or worse, her threats of abdication were difficult to take at face value. She evidently believed, as her courtiers wanted her to, that her recovery from smallpox in 1767 was a sign that God wished her to remain in control.[15] She liked to be advised, talked to, comforted, reassured. But, when it was necessary, she took command of herself and others. 'She is capable of anything,' wrote one of her closest associates.[16] Joseph, by contrast, was always claiming that he knew exactly what should be done for the good of the Monarchy, that he was utterly consistent and would never deviate from the policies he had espoused. But in the last analysis he wanted his mother in her place as sovereign – available to be blamed and to spare him the ultimate responsibility that he hardly dared assume. This was the psychological bedrock for the relationship, which goes far to explain the balance of forces at the centre of affairs during the period of Joseph's co-regency.[17]

II

It is the extraordinary clash of characters and wills that has naturally fascinated most historians. But, to grasp the situation properly, one must also understand the constitutional and political basis of the co-regency. I know of just one article on the subject, by Fritz Reinöhl, and that concentrates on Francis's appointment in 1740 rather than on Joseph's in 1765.[18] It is certainly necessary to start from this original grant, and I owe much to Reinöhl's discussion, but I shall have more to say than he does about the case of Joseph II.

Looking at what has been written on the period overall, there seems to be an unfilled gulf between biographical works and studies of administration. The former tend to rely on private letters, to see matters in personal terms, and to be relatively uninterested in public policy and administration. The latter concentrate on the papers and workings of officialdom, and treat the royal direction of affairs as impersonal and monolithic. Ferdinand Maass in his formidable volumes of documents and commentary on Josephism very rarely cites a letter of Joseph's from the period of the co-regency, and is so little acquainted with his attitudes and correspondence that one of the letters he does cite is spurious. Friedrich Walter in his massive volumes of text and documents on the central administration under Maria Theresa barely mentions the co-regency and discounts Joseph's private letters and memoranda.[19] Since Maass ignores the sources which contain the relevant evidence, he naturally cannot be relied on when he maintains that Maria Theresa was the mother of Josephism, Kaunitz its father – and Joseph nowhere.[20] Many of the judgements made in other respected books about the balance of power or influence between the two rulers are founded on even less adequate research. For this reason little weight can be given to Sorel's assertion that Joseph always in the end got his way about foreign policy, to Macartney's statement that his influence on domestic policy was marginal, or to Pastor's that his mother excluded him from 'educational and ecclesiastico-policial affairs'.[21]

The co-regency was most obviously a device to resolve, in the particular circumstances of the Austrian Monarchy, the special problems that, in many countries at many periods, have been deemed to arise when the throne descends to a woman. Here it seems useful to turn for a moment to English history, which furnishes an instructive range of possible responses to such a situation. When Henry I died in 1135 some people were prepared to accept his daughter Matilda as ruler, while others supported the claims of her cousin, King Stephen. The result was civil war. In 1554 Henry VIII's daughter Mary, having been accepted as queen regnant, married Philip of Spain. He was declared and crowned king but was denied 'the regal power', and his status in England disappeared altogether when Mary died childless. Her successor, Elizabeth, by spinning out indefinitely a series of negotiations for her marriage, made it unnecessary to decide what status her husband should have. In 1689, after James II had fled the country, his daughter Mary was recognised as heiress, but she and her husband, William of Orange, were crowned as joint sovereigns and he was accorded the regal power, to be retained even after her death. When Anne succeeded him in 1702, unchallenged, her husband George, prince of Denmark and duke of Cumberland, was denied the title of king and fobbed off with various lesser posts. In 1837 Victoria came to the throne as unquestioned queen regnant, but when she married Albert in 1840 she could not secure any rank or precedence for him and did not dare to make him prince consort until 1857. Another pattern has prevailed during the present queen's reign. It is significant that in each of these cases a different, special arrangement had to be made. Precedent was never followed.

Two considerations that were of importance in most of these English instances were significant in the Austrian case as well. First, until the nineteenth century it was thought almost essential for the monarch to be able to lead troops in war, and impossible for a woman to do so – hence a military role was envisaged for a queen regnant's husband, which ensured him some participation in affairs. Secondly, the attempt to resolve the problem of female succession in one state nearly always raised issues in reference to another state. It had to be taken into account in 1554 that Mary Tudor's husband was destined to become King of Spain and ruler of the Netherlands, and in 1689 that William of Orange was stadholder of the United Provinces. Conversely, a woman could not succeed to the throne of Hanover, and so Victoria's accession to the throne in the United Kingdom broke the personal union between Britain and that country that had existed since 1714.

On 20 October 1740 Maria Theresa succeeded her father, Charles VI, as the ruler of the Austrian Monarchy. Her right to succeed had been solemnly accepted in advance by the constituted authorities of all the provinces concerned and by almost all foreign powers. It is notorious that her position was almost immediately challenged by

Frederick the Great and other foreign rulers. What is less well known is that her accession posed serious domestic problems for the officials of the Austrian Monarchy. She was already married to Francis Stephen, who was titular duke of Lorraine and actual grand duke of Tuscany, but these were independent principalities. Within the Monarchy he possessed virtually no lands and standing. In documents prepared at the time of the marriage in 1736 it had been stated that he would 'take part in the government of the Hereditary Lands'.[22] Charles VI had used him as a councillor in Vienna, as his viceroy in Hungary and as generalissimo against the Turks, and may well have intended or expected him rather than Maria Theresa to be his effective successor, especially as she had not been initiated into official business. She placed great trust in her husband, wanted to give him precedence immediately after herself and felt the need of his assistance in governing her lands. No doubt she was conscious that she was likely to be often pregnant – she had already given birth to three daughters in four years of marriage and was expecting another child. She was also aware, though regretful, that she could not personally lead her armies in the field. On the other hand, she made it absolutely clear at her accession that she intended to exercise her rights as sovereign and to rule the Monarchy personally.[23]

Against this background the co-regency can be seen as a formal method of meeting all these potentially conflicting desires of Maria Theresa's. The documents which declared Francis co-regent asserted her complete and indefeasible rights of sovereignty over the whole Monarchy but stated that 'on account of her sex' she needed his help in governing it. She appointed him co-regent at least for her lifetime, with 'the joint enjoyment, administration and rule' (*Mitgenuß, Mitverwaltung und Mitregierung*) of all her lands. What this would actually mean in practice was not spelled out. If she died first, leaving an heir under the age of eighteen, Francis was to be regent. Even if the heir was or became eighteen, she expressed the intention of making arrangements for Francis to remain co-regent.

It was not only Maria Theresa's potentially contradictory personal wishes that her officials found hard to accommodate. It was difficult too to reconcile the grant of co-regency with the constitutional position as set out by her father and his ministers during their long campaign to obtain approval for her succession. In commending the family agreement known as the Pragmatic Sanction to the provinces of the Monarchy and to foreign powers, they had laid great stress on the inseparability of all the lands of the Monarchy and the indivisibility of her sovereignty. The first point, it was agreed, made it impossible to give Francis a portion of the Monarchy to govern in his own right. Nothing had been said in the Pragmatic Sanction of a co-regent. Maria Theresa's advisers were emphatic that she would risk invalidating the whole basis of her title under the Pragmatic Sanction if she gave up an iota of her sovereignty. Hence she rested the grant of co-regency on her sovereign authority, and as part of the process her husband formally acknowledged that, in making it, she had surrendered none of that authority. It was also felt necessary for her sister Maria Anna to promise, in case she succeeded to the throne, to confirm Francis as co-regent, and for Charles VI's widow, Empress Elisabeth Christine, to renounce any claim to be regent.

In most provinces the grant of co-regency, dated 21 November 1740, was simply promulgated and provoked no opposition. But the Hungarian Diet made serious difficulties, asserting that by their constitution the sovereignty of Hungary could not be shared. The government maintained that this was not going to happen, that the grant was itself an exercise of undivided sovereignty, that any sovereign ruler had the right to associate anyone he or she liked in the work of ruling, that her sovereignty remained unimpaired and that she could rescind the grant at any time. But it took more than a year to get agreement to the grant of co-regency in Hungary, and then it was made on the authority of the Diet with the queen's concurrence rather than, as elsewhere, on her sole authority. Further, Francis had to accept certain restrictions applicable only in Hungary: for example, he was debarred from exercising those aspects of sovereignty which were reserved in the constitution to the monarch personally, and he was not to continue as regent after Maria Theresa's heir came of age.[24]

This was the public story, which could just about be reconciled with Maria Theresa's description of the grant as 'the work of her love'. Privately, however, she and her ministers had deep political motives in seeking to make Francis Stephen co-regent. As Bartenstein, who had been chief minister in 1740, put it in 1765: 'Francis I ... was named co-regent in order to ease his path towards securing the imperial crown.'[25]

The title of Holy Roman Emperor had been held by all Maria Theresa's predecessors as rulers of the Austrian Monarchy since 1438. It was the only one of her father's dignities to which she could not succeed – because the constitution of the Empire explicitly debarred females from the throne. The loss of this crown was seen in Vienna as extremely damaging to the dynasty and the Monarchy, for reasons that will be discussed later.[26] If Francis could be made emperor, the position would be virtually restored. But in order to recommend him to the electors, it was necessary under the imperial constitution that he should himself rank as a significant ruler within the Empire and be in a position to defend it from Turkish attack. Hence it was important that he should be given a role in the government of Hungary even though it did not form part of the Empire. Within the Empire he was duke of Teschen and count of Falkenstein in his own right, but these were trivial possessions. He was the sovereign of the grand duchy of Tuscany but, if this was part of the Empire at all, it was certainly not part of the German section of it.[27] It was hoped that, if he was made co-regent of the entire Monarchy, he would be accepted as having acquired sufficient standing within the German Empire to be a plausible candidate for the throne, especially as he could then be said to possess the power and strength, through his joint direction of the armed forces of the Monarchy, particularly in Hungary, to protect the Empire from the Turks.[28]

The co-regency, then, was a device which reconciled a highly complex series of aims, personal and political. Previous instances of joint rule can be found in other countries, not only in England but also, for example, in the later Roman Empire, when commonly two or more men were co-emperors or co-regents, and in Russia, where as a youth Peter the Great shared the throne with his half-brother. Probably more significant for eighteenth-century Austria is the currency of the term co-regent in the Holy Roman Empire – though with widely varying meanings. In Hamburg the Bürgerschaft, a body with hundreds of members, counted as *Mitregenten* with the Senate. Another example from the Empire came much closer to the Austrian case. In 1685 Duke Rudolf August of Brunswick-Wolfenbüttel made his brother Anton Ulrich co-regent, partly in order to further a claim to the electorate of Hanover.[29] In none of these instances, however, was a female ruler involved. Whatever its other failings, the Monarchy's bureaucracy, in consultation with the Empire's, showed itself in the affair of the co-regency to be capable of brilliantly resourceful innovation.

The grant of the co-regency was related to another expedient designed to assist the election of Francis as emperor. It was clear that as a woman Maria Theresa could not cast her vote as elector of Bohemia in imperial elections. On 3 November 1740, therefore, she had formally transferred this vote to her husband. This manoeuvre attracted much wider attention than the grant of co-regency, and some contemporary commentators thought the grant was primarily designed to give greater credibility to the transfer of the electoral vote. Perhaps for this reason, M. A. Thomson wrote in the *New Cambridge Modern History* of Francis having been 'appointed co-regent of Bohemia' for this purpose.[30] But, as I have shown, the grant of co-regency covered all the provinces of the Monarchy and had a much wider significance for imperial affairs than merely to validate the Bohemian electoral vote.

In the event the imperial authorities refused to accept the transfer of the vote to Francis and it was suspended for the next election. This was one of many reasons why Francis was not elected emperor to succeed Charles VI in 1742. Instead the elector of Bavaria was chosen and became Charles VII. But he enjoyed the honour for only three years, and Francis was elected to succeed him in 1745.

At this moment the device of the co-regency seemed to have achieved wonderful success. But it is in fact very difficult to tell how important it was in comparison with other factors. With regard to Francis's election as emperor in 1745, what surely mattered most was that Maria Theresa and her armies put up a reasonably good showing in the War of the Austrian Succession, that she had just made peace with Frederick the Great and had received the promise that his vote as elector of Brandenburg would be cast for her husband. Once achieved, Francis's position as emperor would surely have required Maria Theresa in prudence to consult him on all matters of foreign policy that involved the Empire in any way. It is especially difficult to appraise the significance of his co-regency in purely domestic affairs. Indeed, beyond a certain point it cannot be done. There are virtually no surviving letters between him and his wife on political questions. There is little sign that the co-regency was ever an issue between them. It was sometimes suggested that his influence rivalled his wife's. 'We have two masters,' wrote the great chamberlain Khevenhüller, 'the emperor and the empress. Both want to rule.'[31] It was more common to regard him as a virtual nonentity, bored and perhaps embarrassed by his position. Yet he played – and seems to have enjoyed playing – important roles both in military and financial affairs. That he was given these particular tasks, however, depended not on his position as co-regent but on Maria Theresa's belief, better justified in the second case than in the first, that he had special competence in these fields.

In general his influence must have depended at least as much on the fact that he was her adored husband as on the fact that he was her co-regent. The most important point about the co-regency seems to be this: it gave him a legal status throughout the Monarchy which Maria Theresa could draw on whenever she wanted or needed to. For example, she laid down in 1746 that during her current pregnancy he should sign the orders to the Hungarian government in his capacity as co-regent, though she was to be sent copies of them. Thereafter the practice continued when she was not pregnant.[32] No doubt the same thing happened with orders for other provinces. If he was going to be used in this way, it would seem an inescapable corollary that he should take a regular part in the sovereign's decision-making.[33]

III

The circumstances in which Joseph was nominated co-regent on 17 September 1765 bore little resemblance to those of November 1740. The Monarchy had emerged from the Seven Years' War exhausted and financially weakened but with its military standing much enhanced. Maria Theresa was now an enormously experienced and respected ruler, long past the age of child-bearing. Joseph was already emperor. I suppose it was just an extraordinary slip of the pen that made Macartney write: 'Joseph was crowned emperor on his father's death, and therewith the rights and duties connected with the Empire passed to him, formally ceded to him on his coronation by the empress-dowager.'[34] This statement is inaccurate in every respect. Joseph had been elected and crowned King of the Romans in 1764, which meant that he automatically succeeded his father as emperor without further coronation. And if he owed his election largely to the military and diplomatic activities of his parents, none of his rights and powers as emperor depended in the slightest degree on any form of renunciation by his mother. But the question arises: since the main reason for making Francis co-regent had been to assist his election as emperor, why was the title given to Joseph, who had become emperor before he became co-regent?

The written record of Maria Theresa's and her officials' thinking about making Joseph co-regent is obviously incomplete, but still revealing. She implored Kaunitz to arrange the appointment, and clearly considered it of vital importance. She still doubted her capacity to govern on her own, a doubt intensified by personal considerations not operative in 1740. It had been one of the reasons for establishing the Staatsrat or Council of State in 1760 that she no longer felt capable of playing so large a part as previously in remodelling the government of the Monarchy. She thought she had not long to live. She intended to remain in seclusion. She was inclined to abdicate. Both she and her advisers saw the revival of the co-regency as a way of enabling her – and persuading her – to continue as ruler, at least for a time.

But policy considerations also mattered greatly. The main issues we know to have been raised concerned Hungary, the army and the Empire. The problem with Hungary was to avoid following the precedent of 1740–41, when the Diet had imposed limitations on the co-regent's powers – limitations which it was even more important to avoid in the case of Joseph, who would in the normal course succeed his mother as ruler of Hungary. In any case, the Diet of 1764 had proved especially recalcitrant, and the government had no wish to call another. It was decided that, since Joseph was her unchallengeable heir, there was no need to ask for Hungarian approval to associate him with her rule. He was simply declared co-regent of Hungary.[35]

The question of the army is obscure but intriguing. The Sardinian ambassador, Count Canale, wrote to his government:

> I am convinced that this princess, who has privately recognised the virtuous qualities and the solid judgement of her son, the emperor … will not delay in having him declared co-regent, a step useful for the internal constitution of the different provinces and absolutely necessary for external relations, since [otherwise], for example, the Austrian armies could no longer be reckoned imperial or enjoy the prerogatives which belong to them in that capacity.[36]

I have discovered no other statement to this effect, but Canale was a very senior diplomat who had a special relationship with Maria Theresa.[37] It is certainly true that Austrian statesmen used to list among the advantages of the imperial crown to the Habsburg dynasty the opportunities for recruitment of soldiers within the Empire. Imperial troops were also accorded some rights of passage through imperial territory – a very important consideration when Vienna ruled much of Belgium, south-west Germany and northern Italy, but did not control the lands between these outlying provinces and the central core. The Monarchy's army badly needed to be able to exploit these imperial rights.[38]

As in the case of Francis, the relationship between Empire and Monarchy, viewed more generally, was the main problem discussed in connection with Joseph's nomination as co-regent. Even though Joseph was already emperor, the position was stated to be similar to that of 1740. It was argued that, to ward off criticism and to ensure that he was respected in the Empire, he needed to be given territorial standing within it. He possessed even less land there over which he could be considered effectively sovereign than his father had had in 1740. Joseph had just most solemnly surrendered his rights over Tuscany to his brother Leopold, which meant that in his own right he was sovereign only over Falkenstein and Teschen. To meet this difficulty it was seriously debated, as in the case of Francis, whether he might be given a substantial portion of the Monarchy as his own. But, as in 1740, this proposal was abandoned because it would have breached the Pragmatic Sanction. It was pointed out that any such scheme would also have split up the Monarchy's army. So the only admissible means of providing Joseph with the necessary standing in the Empire was to make him co-regent.[39]

Running through all the memoranda can be discerned more serious anxieties. In a paper by the young Bartenstein, who was an imperial official, the hope is expressed that, if Joseph is co-regent, 'he will pay attention only to those counsels which are directed towards the advantage of the lands of the Monarchy and the interest of the dynasty that is bound up with them'.[40] This is surely the rub. The emperor may have had little power over his so-called subjects. But he was the senior crowned head of Europe, in principle he conducted his own foreign policy and had his own Court, and he had his own bureaucracy in Vienna rivalling Kaunitz's. He presided over a judicial system for the Empire which could easily be managed to the disadvantage as well as the advantage of the Monarchy. He possessed a variety of powers and rights over such matters as posts, tolls, coinage and publications, also potentially damaging or beneficial to the Monarchy. In special circumstances an imperial army could be called into existence, which he had the right to command. Perhaps most important of all, the emperor could exercise great influence over Church appointments in the Empire, which included three electorate-archbishoprics and a dozen or so prince-bishoprics. Clearly, immense harm could be done to the Monarchy by a wilful emperor operating independently.[41] The co-regency for Joseph was evidently intended to restrict his freedom of action as emperor and to harness his policies, powers, rights and

prestige in that capacity to the service of the Monarchy – while denying him any power within the Monarchy in his own right.

In case the officials' concern with the Empire should be written off
as mere antiquarianism, here are three instances of problems arising
during his co-regency which led or might have led to a serious clash
between imperial and Austrian interests. Joseph in his early years
as emperor sought to assert his imperial rights, particularly some
much-contested claims in Italy. Over many years, but especially in
1766, reams of paper were consumed in Vienna, France, Italy and
the Empire about the affair of San Remo. Joseph wished to assert
imperial suzerainty over this territory, which the republic of Genoa,
being in possession, denied. Genoa was backed by France. France was
the principal ally of the Monarchy, and the Austro-French alliance
ranked as Kaunitz's greatest coup and pride. From Maria Theresa's
standpoint Joseph's ardour had to be cooled, but it was all she could
do to persuade him not to enforce the favourable decision he had
secured from the imperial courts, after one of the bitterest disputes of
her reign – the one in which she castigated him for his *bons mots*.[42]

Secondly, with regard to the question of the Bavarian succession,
it has seldom been grasped – though Freiherr von Aretin has stressed
it – that two claims and policies competed with each other in Vienna:
one on behalf of the emperor and the Empire, the other on behalf of
the Monarchy and the dynasty. The imperial claim was that most of
the Bavarian lands would revert to imperial control when Elector Max
Joseph, the last of his line, died; they should therefore be seized and
occupied pending their reassignment. There was talk of the emperor
gaining revenue as a result. Kaunitz pointed out that this would
work to the disadvantage of the Monarchy, but Joseph succeeded
in committing the officials of the Monarchy as well as those of the
Empire to this policy from 1772 until 1777.[43] On the other side was
Kaunitz's policy, clearly set out as far back as 1764, to make dynastic
claims on Bavaria for the Habsburgs, regardless of imperial rights
and constitution. When the chancellor in 1777 proposed as a variant
to negotiate with the elector of Bavaria's nearest heir, the Elector
Palatine, in order to gain territory for the Monarchy by treaty, Joseph
accepted this policy and dropped his imperial claims. At the end of
1777 Max Joseph died. Much of Joseph's embarrassment, difficulties
and unpopularity in the crisis and war that followed arose from the
fact that, though emperor, he was pursuing a policy of aggrandisement on behalf of the Monarchy, as co-regent and commander of

his mother's armies. He not unnaturally felt bitter when, having laid aside his imperial pretensions, he found himself disowned by his mother, who made peace proposals behind his back, as she claimed, out of motherly love.[44]

A peculiar switch of roles took place in the affair of Cologne in 1778–80. The archbishop-elector of that diocese was ageing and needed a coadjutor. The emperor was normally expected to take a keen interest in these elections, but Joseph had become disillusioned with imperial matters. It was Maria Theresa who took the initiative and provided the necessary money to obtain this splendid position for her youngest son, Max Franz, both to give him a position worthy of his rank and to increase Vienna's influence in the Rhineland. The emperor refused to take an active part in the negotiations. Instead he went to Russia to promote what he considered a more useful scheme, an alliance between the Monarchy and Catherine II. In this case it proved possible to pursue the two policies simultaneously, and both succeeded. But the incident shows how high the stakes could still be in imperial affairs, and how easily the policies of the emperor and the ruler of the Monarchy could conflict with each other.[45]

Joseph's position as emperor, then, mattered greatly in the establishment of his co-regency, and subsequently. But of course he also had a role in domestic policy-making. He had already, for four years before his father's death, belonged to the new central agency of the Monarchy, the Staatsrat. During this time he had written at least two highly critical disquisitions on his mother's policy.[46] On the face of it, the co-regency would enhance his influence. The younger Bartenstein in his memorandum of 1765 had addressed himself to this delicate problem. If, he said, Maria Theresa and her co-regent differed in opinion, then she could always ask the view of the Staatsrat; its members had been carefully chosen in the past and could be selected with equal care in the future; no one could blame her for accepting the Council's majority view even if it went against her son's. So the Staatsrat could be seen as a means of nullifying the domestic opportunities ostensibly given to Joseph by the co-regency.[47]

I have tried in my *Joseph II* to appraise the balance of forces between Maria Theresa, Joseph and Kaunitz during the period 1765–80. Here I shall merely try to isolate the significance of the device of the co-regency. When he was given the title, Joseph made a declaration in much the same form as his father had done:

We, Joseph the Second, by God's grace elected Roman Emperor, per-
petual enlarger of the Empire, King in Germany, heir to the kingdoms
of Hungary, Bohemia, Dalmatia, Croatia, Slavonia, etc., Archduke
of Austria etc., most gratefully accept the transfer thus signified to
us of the joint administration and joint rule of the aforesaid united
hereditary kingdoms and lands, and likewise we shall always direct
our whole care and all our most strenuous efforts ... to fulfil so far as
possible the great expectation of Her Royal and Imperial Apostolic
Majesty our most beloved lady mother that her hard task of ruling will
thereby be eased.

We further bind ourselves in the strongest possible manner by
means of the present ceremonial renunciations ... to everything which
is included and stated in the above-mentioned document about the
undiminished force of the Pragmatic Sanction, and especially about
the express reservation of the sole and single inherent and continuing
sovereignty over the hereditary kingdoms and lands to our dearest
lady mother's Imperial and Royal Apostolic Majesty, against which ...
the co-regency ... cannot weigh in the slightest, and to derogate from
which is utterly remote from our intentions.[48]

It would be difficult to spell things out more clearly. It was his duty
to assist her in every way she wanted. The wording suggests that he
is to put the interests of the Monarchy before those of the Empire.
But he had no rights whatever against her.

He had raised objections to the arrangement, which had been
overruled. But he continued to strain at the leash. Unlike his father
he expected one day to become the ruler of the Monarchy, and unlike
his father he had well-developed theories of sovereignty. When his
mother suggested that he might take the responsibility of signing
certain documents as co-regent, he told her:

In the nature of the case, my opinion, my way of thinking cannot and
ought not to appear anywhere save at the feet of my august mother. I
am nothing, and in affairs [of state] not even a thinking being, except
in so far as I have to carry out her orders and reveal to her all I know.
If under the vain title of co-regent there is any idea of implying
something else, I hereby declare, with the sincerity I profess and the
firmness I glory in, that I shall never be brought to consent to it, and
that nothing will shake me, since I am firm in this principle, on which
my present tranquillity and happiness as well as my future reputation
and fame depend. Signatures are so contrary to monarchical laws, of

which the essence is one head ... that I see no alternative but to excuse myself and to refuse absolutely to sign.[49]

Maria Theresa seems to have conceded the point. Many more disputes were to arise about this kind of thing but, so far as I know, Joseph adhered to his position and refused to sign as co-regent without her express authority. His aim was either to persuade her to adopt as her own the policies he favoured, or to await the opportunity to carry them through when he himself had the authority.

It is extraordinary how servile Maria Theresa expected her emperor-son to be. He had to secure her approval of the arrangements for his daughter's education.[50] He had to exert continuous pressure to be allowed to travel.[51] She repeatedly made him postpone journeys, particularly the visit he wanted to make to Bohemia during the famine of 1771. An ostensible reason she gave was that she needed his help in Vienna – as co-regent.[52] She allowed him virtually no say in the affairs of Hungary and the Southern Netherlands.[53] In most matters he had to struggle to achieve influence. One of the weapons she used in this running battle was the terms of the co-regency. But it is not easy to say whether they were more or less important in keeping Joseph subordinate than her position as sovereign mother or head of the family.

He used to tell people, especially foreigners, that he was only one of his mother's ministers. His department was the army, which she claimed to have given over to him completely. Although this assignment in a sense restricted him by limiting his activity elsewhere, in another sense it strengthened his position. His mother attached enormous importance to the army, and she gradually came round to approving some of the radical changes he and Lacy proposed. From about 1770 the canton system of recruitment, based on a form of conscription, was brought into force in many provinces of the Monarchy.[54] But he was never in fact given a free hand. Maria Theresa had to be persuaded of the need for any major measure and many minor ones, and constantly interfered, for example in promotions.

Joseph succeeded in exerting very considerable if uneven influence on many aspects of policy. He could not have done so if he had not been kept informed. No doubt the fact that he was co-regent helped to ensure that. But many other factors were at work. His influence over foreign policy owed much to his being emperor. His influence in domestic affairs owed much to his being a member of the Staatsrat, which he had originally joined long before he became co-regent. In family matters he had to be consulted as his mother's heir and, perhaps more importantly, because his father had left his huge fortune, on which the family largely depended, to him and not to Maria Theresa. It seems to have been his position as emperor that gave him the power to impose a drastic reform of Court etiquette in and after 1765.[55] In certain aspects of administration he succeeded in carrying some of his views by travelling to the spot concerned and returning to Vienna well informed. By going to the Banat in 1768, for example, he was able to play an important role in the reform of its corrupt government.[56] It is not clear in any of these cases that the co-regency contributed much to give him his influence.

After showing initial enthusiasm for imperial affairs he became exasperated by the endless obstruction he encountered in making the simplest changes. Since one of the chief purposes of naming him co-regent had been to wean him from over-enthusiastic imperial activity, it is tempting to concede that the grant succeeded in this respect at least. But the title had been intended to secure him higher standing in the Empire, which by 1780 he no longer cared about. Despite all the attendant frustrations, he evidently found more satisfaction in what he was allowed to do as co-regent, especially after the great dispute of 1773 led to his being put in charge of running the Staatsrat. When in 1787 he decided to compile a record of his achievements as ruler, he ordered the departments to go back to 1765 – even for Hungary.[57] As well as by being co-regent, he had been able to influence policy as emperor, heir, minister for the army and member of the Staatsrat, by travel and through the private access to his mother that he, unlike ministers, could always obtain. By threats of resignation he secured notable concessions, usually involving administrative reorganisation and some new appointments. Although the dice were loaded in favour of his mother, who had both the greater power and the stronger character, he had this degree of leverage over her, that she could not bear to think of his abandoning her and telling the world that they could not work together publicly. Hence his role was decidedly greater at the end of his co-regency than at the beginning. But it was still a subordinate role.

There was one case of a remarkable reversal of positions, when he obstructed a revolutionary scheme of hers, her plan to abolish peasants' forced labour in 1776.[58] Otherwise, she contrived by piece-meal concession to avoid fundamental change. While she lived, the constitutions of Hungary and Belgium would not be threatened, few monasteries would be dissolved, religious toleration would not be permitted, the censorship would remain bigoted, and there would be no further drastic reform of taxation and administration. Though Joseph thrashed about to some purpose in the net of the co-regency, he could not escape from it while Maria Theresa lived.

IV

As Joseph used to tell her, the co-regency was a unique and most peculiar device. It conferred a portentous title,[59] but it can hardly be said to have been an office or an employment. With it came no salary, no funds, no land, no personnel, no officials, no specified rights and duties – only precedence, which Joseph already possessed anyway. Potentially it granted immense power and imposed huge duties – or at least made it lawful for the co-regent to exercise power and fulfil duties if the sovereign wanted him to.

However much Maria Theresa and her ministers tried to conceal the fact, the co-regency had significantly different functions for Francis and for Joseph. True, in both instances it was designed to relieve Maria Theresa of some of the awesome burden she carried by removing any legal difficulties about her delegating powers. In both cases it was designed to reconcile the conflicting interests of Empire and Monarchy in favour of the latter, during this unique period when the emperor was not identical with the head of the Monarchy. Both grants were intended to supply a royal commander to her armies. But the emphasis in 1740 was quite different from that in 1765. The original grant to Francis Stephen was constructive, even creative – to build up his position within the Monarchy in order to make possible his election as emperor. The emphasis in 1765 was restrictive – to prevent Joseph from behaving like a rogue elephant within the Monarchy or as emperor. It chained him to the bureaucracy of the Monarchy and curbed what freedom he had in the Empire.

It had one striking attribute that will have emerged from this chapter. It clearly belonged to a type of absolute monarchy in which the personal character, attitudes and emotions of the ruler were unashamedly an aspect of his or her public behaviour. Maria Theresa was well aware that her personal inclinations must sometimes give way to reasons of state, as she avowed, for example, when it came to suppressing the Jesuits in her lands.[60] But in general her very strong feelings were engaged in the furtherance of her policies. She obviously felt no compunction and no hypocrisy in writing to her son: 'You used to love the state ... So give your help to a mother who for thirty years has had no object in life but you.' She found it natural to conflate 'the work of her love' and the pursuit by devious means of the imperial crown.[61] She saw no conflict between aiming at more rational, economical and utilitarian government on the one hand, and capriciously awarding lavish pensions and grants of land on the other.

One element in Joseph's aversion to the co-regency was revulsion against his mother's emotional blackmail. Another was impatience at her inconsistencies. A third was contempt for 'vain titles' and for sovereignties, like the Empire's, that could not be effectively exercised. The concept of co-regency, clever as it was, went with the Court absolutism that in Roscher's famous classification was associated with the seventeenth century. Joseph's brand of absolutism or despotism was Enlightened, glorifying an impersonal state and firmly rooted in the eighteenth century.[62]

There was an ironic epilogue. Late in 1789 and early in 1790 revolution in Belgium, discontent in other provinces, fear of a grand alliance to destroy the Monarchy, together with a terminal illness, forced Joseph to rescind many of his measures. 'I am unfortunate,' he said, 'in everything I undertake.' On 6 February 1790 he wrote to his brother Leopold in Florence that he knew he was dying, and begged him to come to Vienna 'out of friendship for me and out of duty, what you owe to the states that will belong to you, and to our fathers' patrimony, and that of your children'. Two days later he wrote again:

> I forgot to tell you that I have had everything prepared in the Staatskanzlei so that, as soon as you arrive here, I can despatch the necessary declarations that proclaim you my co-regent, exactly as the empress nominated me as hers. In this way you will from the start have full right to give all orders, and your signature will have equal effect with mine both outside and inside [the Monarchy].[63]

Joseph had at last brought himself to follow his mother's example and make an appeal to his brother, linking the claims of personal friendship with those of public duty. In his reply Leopold temporised. But he wrote to his sister Marie Christine recalling the 'fine results' of the co-regency under Maria Theresa. He would never, he said, take any part in the business of the Monarchy, whether as co-regent or not, so long as Joseph lived.[64] So ended the history of the co-regency in Austria.[65]

Notes

This chapter originated as a paper to the Anglo-Austrian Historical Symposium of 1983, 'From the Siege of Vienna to Joseph II (1683–1790)', organised by Professor Ragnhild Hatton at the Institute of Historical Research. It was published in R. Oresko, G. C. Gibbs and H. M. Scott (eds), *Royal and Republican Sovereignty in Early Modern Europe: Essays in Memory of Ragnhild Hatton* (Cambridge, 1997). Although some of what I say here I had already said in my *Joseph II. I: In the Shadow of Maria Theresa, 1741–1780* (Cambridge, 1987), this article deploys new material and puts the co-regency in a new light. Professor T. C. W. Blanning and my wife have helped me to improve my text. Since this article was written, Blanning has published his authoritative *Joseph II* (London, 1994). For the co-regency see esp. pp. 49–51.

1 E. Hubert, 'Joseph II', in *Cambridge Modern History*, vol. VI (Cambridge, 1909), p. 627.

2 See on the Empire Beales, *Joseph II*, ch. 5 and the books cited there on p. 116, together with J. G. Gagliardo, *Reich and Nation: The Holy Roman Empire as Idea and Reality, 1763–1806* (London, 1980).

3 Maria Theresa to Joseph (Jan. 1769): *Maria Theresia und Joseph II. Ihre Correspondenz* [hereafter *MTuJ*], ed. A. Ritter von Arneth (3 vols, Vienna, 1867–68), vol. I, pp. 234–5.

4 Maria Theresa to Joseph, 14 Sept. 1766; ibid., p. 203.

5 Maria Theresa to Marquise d'Herzelles, 10 Jan. and 1 Mar. (1771): Kervyn de Lettenhove (ed.), 'Letters inédites de Marie-Thérèse et de Joseph II', *Mémoires ... Académie Royale ... de Belgique*, 8°, vol. 20 (1868), pp. 22–7.

6 Joseph to Maria Theresa, 12 July 1778 (*MTuJ*, vol. II, pp. 334–5); Joseph's memo of April 1772: F. Walter (ed.), *Die österreichische Zentralverwaltung*, 2nd part (1749–1848), vol. III, *Vom Sturz des Directorium in publicis et cameralibus [1760–1] bis zum Ausgang der Regierung Maria Theresias. Aktenstücke*, ed. F. Walter (Vienna, 1934) (i.e. *Veröffentlichungen der Kommission für neuere Geschichte Österreichs* [hereafter *VKNGÖ*], vol. XXXIX, p. 52.

7 Joseph to Maria Theresa, 9 Dec. 1773 (*MTuJ*, vol. II, pp. 26–7); Joseph to Grand Duke Leopold of Tuscany (April 1773), ibid., p. 5.

8 The most transparent is summarised in K. Schünemann, 'Die Wirtschaftspolitik Josephs II. in der Zeit seiner Mitregentschaft', *Mitteilungen des österreichischen Instituts für Geschichtsforschung* [hereafter *MÖIG*], 47 (1933): 41–3.

9 The easiest approach to these questions is through the letters of 1772, in *MTuJ*, vol. II, pp. 1, 6, 8, 16–17, 20.

10 Ibid., pp. 21–9 and notes for the main documents.

11 The correspondence between Joseph, Maria Theresa and Lacy is fairly

fully given in *Geschichte Maria Theresias* [hereafter *GMT*], ed. A. R. von Arneth, vol. IX, ch. 16, but he too readily discounts the story of a row between Joseph and Lacy.

12 Maria Theresa to Lacy, 20 Dec. (1773): *GMT*, vol. IX, p. 630.

13 Cf. for the relationship over the whole period 1769–73, Beales, *Joseph II*, ch. 7, esp. pp. 198–226.

14 See Maria Theresa to Kaunitz, 28 Aug. 1765: A. Beer (ed.), *Joseph II., Leopold II. und Kaunitz* (Vienna, 1873), pp. 432–3.

15 For example, Maria Theresa to Archduke Ferdinand, 1 Oct. (1771): *Briefe der Kaiserin Maria Theresia an ihre Kinder und Freunde* [hereafter *MTKuF*], ed. A. R. von Arneth (4 vols, Vienna, 1881), vol. I, p. 71; Khevenhüller-Metsch's diary for 27 Feb. 1771: Count Khevenhüller-Metsch and H. Schlitter (eds), *Aus der Zeit Maria Theresias. Tagebuch des Fürsten Johann Josef Khevenhüller-Metsch* [hereafter *K-M*], vol. VII (Vienna, 1925), pp. 62–3. Cf. Leopold's views in 1778 (Beales, *Joseph II*, p. 490).

16 Quoted in Beales, *Joseph II*, p. 418.

17 Much of the last four volumes of *GMT* depends on the correspondence of Maria Theresa and Joseph, most of which Arneth published in *MTuJ*. But in both works Arneth errs on the side of charity towards Maria Theresa.

18 F. Reinöhl, 'Die Übertragung der Mitregentschaft durch Maria Theresia an Grossherzog Franz Stephan und Kaiser Joseph II', *MÖIG*, Supplement XI (1929), pp. 650–61.

19 F. Maass, *Der Josephinismus* (5 vols, Vienna, 1951–61), esp. vols I–III. Walter's main work was the two volumes on the reign of Maria Theresa in the series *Die österreichische Zentralverwaltung* (see n. 6 above). The interpretative volume appeared in 1938 as vol. XXXII of *VKNGÖ*.

20 F. Maass, 'Vorbereitung und Anfänge des Josephinismus im amtlichen Schriftwechsel des Staatskanzlers ... mit Firmian, 1763 bis 1770', *Mitteilungen des österreichischen Staatsarchivs* [hereafter *MÖSA*], I (1948): 297n.

21 A. Sorel, *La question d'Orient au dix-huitième siècle* (Paris, 1889), p. 126; C. A. Macartney, *Maria Theresa and the House of Austria* (London, 1969), p. 108; L. von Pastor, *History of the Popes*, Engl. trans. (40 vols) (London, 1938–53), vol. XXXIX, p. 430.

22 Reinöhl, *MÖIG* (1929): 651 and n. The word 'Erblande' is used, which in some interpretations referred only to the central provinces but, after the Pragmatic Sanction had been accepted, was often used by the government to include Hungary.

23 For this and the next two paragraphs see ibid.; *GMT*, vol. I, pp. 92, 171; H. L. Mikoletzky, *Kaiser Franz I. Stephan und der Ursprung des Habsburgisch-lothringischen Familienvermögens* (Vienna, 1961); F. Hennings, *Und sitzet zur linken Hand* (Vienna, 1961), pp. 187–213.

24 Reinöhl, *MÖIG* (1929): 650–7; *GMT*, vol. I, pp. 172–4 and 287–306.

25 *K-M*, vol. VI, p. 384.

26 See p. 191. The great authority is K. O. Freiherr von Aretin, *Heiliges Römisches Reich* (2 vols, Wiesbaden, 1967), esp. the early part of vol. I. The

best single document that lists the advantages supposed to accrue to the Habsburgs from the imperial title is printed in H. Voltelini, 'Ein Denkschrift des Grafen Johann Anton Pergen über die Bedeutung der römischen Kaiserkrone für das Haus Österreich', in *Gesamtdeutsche Vergangenheit. Festgabe für H. Ritter von Srbik zum 60. Geburtstag* (Munich, 1938), pp. 152–68.

27 The Germanness of the Empire, and the use of the phrase 'German Empire' are vexed questions. See J.-F. Noel, 'Traditions universalistes et aspects nationaux dans la notion du Saint-Empire Romain Germanique du XVIII siècle', *Revue d'histoire diplomatique*, 82 (1968): 193–212.

28 Reinöhl, *MÖIG* (1929): 652–4 and notes. Old Bartenstein recapitulated some of the arguments in 1765 (*K-M*, vol. VI, pp. 583–5).

29 On Peter, V. Klyuchevsky, *Peter the Great* (London, 1965), p. 6. I am grateful to Dr J. E. B. Shepard for help with both this and the classical examples. On the German cases, J. Whaley, *Religious Toleration and Social Change in Hamburg, 1529–1819* (Cambridge, 1985), pp. 19–20; G. Gerkens, *Das fürstliche Lustschloß Salzdahlum und sein Erbauer Herzog Anton Ulrich von Braunschweig-Wolfenbüttel* (Brunswick, 1974), pp. 32–7. I owe my knowledge of the Brunswick case to Dr T. Biskup.

30 M. A. Thomson, 'The War of the Austrian Succession', in J. O. Lindsay (ed.), *New Cambridge Modern History*, vol. VII (Cambridge, 1957), p. 421. On the Bohemian vote Reinöhl, *MÖIG* (1929): 650–1; *Selecta juris publici novissima*, 2. Theil (Frankfurt, 1741), pp. 329–42, and 3. Theil (1741), pp. 213–52; *J. S. Pütter's … historisch-politisches Handbuch von den besonderen Teutschen Staaten* (Göttingen, 1758), 1. Theil, p. 124. Pütter repeats the point in other works.

31 *K-M*, vol. IV, p. 141.

32 Koller's memo of 1765 in ibid., vol. VI, p. 389.

33 On the working of Francis's co-regency the best account is Hennings, *Und sitzet zur linken Hand*, esp. pp. 285–344; on finance, Mikoletzky, *Kaiser Franz I. Stephan*.

34 Macartney, *Maria Theresa*, p. 106.

35 For this and the next paragraph, Maria Theresa to Kaunitz, 28 Aug. 1765: Beer, *Joseph II., Leopold II. and Kaunitz*, pp. 432–3; Reinöhl, *MÖIG* (1929); documents in *K-M*, vol. VI, pp. 381–95.

36 Canale, 16 Sept. 1765; Ada Ruata, *Luigi Malabaila di Canale: riflessioni della cultura illuministica in un diplomatico piemontese* (Turin, 1968), pp. 160–1. I am grateful to Professor J. Black for calling my attention to this book.

37 This emerges especially strongly from D. Perrero, *La diplomazia piemontese nel primo smembramento della Polonia* (Turin, 1894).

38 Cf. Gagliardo, *Reich and Nation*, p. 37. See the Pergen memorandum in *Gesamtdeutsche Vergangenheit*, pp. 160–1 and 167. (See n.26 above.)

39 All this emerges in the documents in *K-M*, vol. VI, pp. 381–5.

40 Ibid., p. 387.

41 Many of these points are made in Pergen's memorandum (see n.26 above). Cf. P. Mechtler, 'Der Kampf zwischen Reichspost und Hofpost', *MÖIG*, 53 (1939): 411–22; U. Eisenhardt, *Die Kaiserliche Aufsicht über Buchdruck,*

Buchhandel und Presse im Heiligen Römischen Reich Deutscher Nation (1496–1806) (Karlsruhe, 1970). See M. S. Anderson, *The War of the Austrian Succession, 1740–1748* (London, 1995), esp. pp. 152–3. Professor H. M. Scott generously gave me a copy of this book.

42 *MTuJ*, vol. I, pp. 191, 193–5, 194–6, nn.200–1. This affair has not been adequately studied. I am very grateful to Professor H. M. Scott for letting me see his notes on relevant material in the archives of the French Foreign Office.

43 *GMT*, vol. X, pp. 286–93; K. O. Freiherr von Aretin, 'Kurfürst Karl Theodor und das bayerische Tauschprojekt', *Zeitschrift für bayerische Landesgeschichte*, XXV (1962): 747–8.

44 Kaunitz's memorandum of 1764 is printed in *K-M*, vol. VI, pp. 342–4. For the rest of my remarks I can only refer to Arneth and Aretin and standard works on the Bavarian war, e.g. H. W. V. Temperley, *Frederick the Great and Kaiser Joseph* (London, 1915), while acknowledging that it is very rare to find any sympathy for Joseph's position. Indeed, Joseph is usually made to bear the entire blame for what was essentially Kaunitz's policy. See Beales, *Joseph II*, pp. 386–427.

45 It is impossible to give full references to these two complex matters. *GMT*, vol. X, pp. 668–712, provides most of the raw material. See also Aretin, *Heiliges Römisches Reich*, vol. I, pp. 128–36; A. Beer, *Die Orientalische Politik Oesterreichs seit 1774* (Prague, 1883), esp. pp. 30–45; Beales, *Joseph II*, pp. 427–38.

46 *MTuJ*, vol. I, pp. 1–12 (3 Apr. 1761); see Chapter 6, 'Joseph II's *Rêveries*'.

47 *K-M*, vol. VI, p. 388.

48 Ibid., pp. 394–5.

49 Joseph to Maria Theresa, 19 Jan. 1769; *MTuJ*, vol. I, pp. 233–4. See also F. A. J. Szabo, *Kaunitz and Enlightened Absolutism, 1753–1780* (Cambridge 1994), p. 105.

50 Joseph's memo of 24 Feb. 1766 in Haus-, Hof- und Staatsarchiv, Vienna [hereafter HHSA], Familien-Akten [hereafter FA], Sammelbände 55.

51 There are three versions in HHSA FA Hofreisen I, fasc. 4, of a lengthy plea by Joseph, evidently of 1768, for permission to embark on a programme of travel within the Monarchy. Disputes about particular journeys continually recur in the published correspondence.

52 Several of the more anguished letters about Bohemia were omitted by Arneth from *MTuJ* but are preserved in HHSA FA Sammelbände 7. Cf. Beales, *Joseph II*, chs 8, 11 and 12.

53 See, e.g., letters in *MTuJ*, vol. II, on recruiting in Hungary etc. in the summer of 1778, and Maria Theresa to Joseph, July 1780 in *MTKuF*, vol. I, p. 3, on Belgium.

54 Arneth's chapter in *GMT*, vol. IX, provides a basis for study of Joseph's and Lacy's military achievement. See also C. Duffy, *The Army of Maria Theresa* (London, 1977), esp. pp. 206–13. The subject badly needs further study.

55 *K-M*, vol. VI, pp. 231–2. Beales, *Joseph II*, pp. 156–61. E. Wangermann,

'Maria Theresa: A Reforming Monarchy', in A. G. Dickens (ed.), *The Courts of Europe: Politics, Patronage and Royalty*, 1400–1800 (London, 1977), pp. 283–303, in his determination to undervalue Joseph's reforms, actually attributes the simplification of Court ceremonial to Maria Theresa in the 1750s! Cf. E. Kovacs, 'Kirchliches Zeremoniell am Wiener Hof des 18. Jahrhunderts im Wandel von Mentalität und Gesellschaft', *MÖSA*, XXXII (1979): 109–42.

56 Beales, *Joseph II*, chs 8, 11 and 12.

57 The documents concerning the Hungarian government are in Hungarian National Archives, Budapest: Kabinettsarchiv: Ungarische Einrichtungen 1765–1788 – I, fasc. 6; but the request applied to all domestic departments.

58 The main letters, omitted by Arneth, are substantially reproduced in F. Fejtö, *Un habsbourg révolutionnaire* (Paris, 1953), pp. 139–41. See Beales, *Joseph II*, pp. 354–8.

59 Casual observation suggests that the title of co-regent was not much used in formal documents. But I have seen a contemporary plaque using the form 'nec non corregens'.

60 Cf. Maass, *Josephinismus*, vol. II, pp. 29–31.

61 See above, p. 184.

62 Wilhelm Roscher seems to have invented the term 'Enlightened absolutism'. His highly intelligent discussion of absolutism in the early modern period first appeared as 'Umrisse zur Naturlehre der drei Staatsformen. Erster Abschnitt: Monarchie' in *Allegemeine Zeitschrift für Geschichte*, 7 (1847): 79–88, 322–65, 436–73.

63 Joseph to Grand Duke Leopold of Tuscany, 21 Jan., 6 and 8 Feb. 1790: *Joseph II. und Leopold von Toscana. Ihr Briefwechsel von 1781 bis 1790*, ed. A. Ritter von Arneth (2 vols, Vienna, 1872), vol. II, pp. 312, 316 and 318.

64 A. Wandruszka, *Leopold II.* (2 vols, Vienna, 1964–65), pp. 222–5.

65 Despite the tensions that the co-regency caused in Vienna, other states showed signs of copying the device. In Russia an attempt was made in 1773 to force Catherine II to associate her son Paul with her as co-regent. (See R. E. McGrew, *Paul I of Russia, 1754–1801* [Oxford, 1992], pp. 81–2. Professor S. M. Dixon generously gave me a copy of this book.) This plan failed, but it appears that in Hesse-Cassel during the 1830 revolution the elector was actually induced to take his son as co-regent. (See *Louis Spohr's Reminiscences* [London, 1865], pp. 175–6.)

CHAPTER 8

Maria Theresa, Joseph II and the Suppression of the Jesuits

By the end of 1767 France, Spain, Portugal and Naples had ordered the expulsion of all Jesuits from their lands. In January 1769 France, Spain and Naples formally requested Pope Clement XIII to suppress the whole Society.[1] The Austrian Monarchy under Maria Theresa refused to join in these *démarches*, either then or later. In the spring of 1768 her son and co-regent, the Emperor Joseph II, described the situation and the Monarchy's agreed policy to his brother, Grand Duke Leopold of Tuscany, as follows:

> Now that the times are more enlightened, the Court of Rome no longer has so much weight in European politics. Some wise and prudent popes, however, have contrived to preserve some influence by not committing themselves to unreasonable positions. But the present pope [Clement XIII] ... seems determined to ruin everything by trying to maintain, at whatever cost, the old abusive authority which everybody has rejected. To preserve a religious Order proscribed by four Great Powers, which is now impossible, Rome, instead of secularising it as they desire, has been behaving in such a way as to challenge them to break away completely and so deprive herself of the little influence she still has there – the liberties of the Gallican Church, which it seems Spain wishes to copy, marking the first step ...
>
> In these circumstances all the Powers, to avoid a crisis, are virtually agreed that they should wait until this pope dies, which is not likely to be long delayed ... The abolition of the Jesuit Order, which the Powers who have expelled them have so much at heart that they have even tried to get us to make common cause with them at the court of Rome, will assuredly be a *sine qua non* at the election of a new pope.
>
> So far as we are concerned, we have not been ready to involve ourselves either for or against, having insufficient reason to desire their destruction, but not regarding their existence as so necessary that we must protect them.

The empress repeatedly declared to diplomats and others that she was unimpressed by the actions of the other Powers, that the Jesuits in her lands were certainly not guilty of the alleged crimes which had been held to justify their expulsion from other countries, and that she regarded them as a thoroughly useful and respectable Order. But her official standpoint remained neutrality.[2]

By the end of 1769, however, after the election of a new pope, Clement XIV, known to be favourable to suppression, she had added a rider to her policy: if the pope decided that it was for the good of the Church that the Society should be suppressed, she would acquiesce. This modification was the furthest she would go towards satisfying the other Catholic Powers. She had made the change as a concession to Choiseul, the minister of her ally, France, during the negotiations for the marriage of her daughter, Marie Antoinette, to the future king Louis XVI. In secret instructions given to Marie Antoinette when she left for France early in 1770, the empress wrote:

> I have one more point to make, concerning the Jesuits. Do not talk about them at all, either for or against them. You may cite me and say that I have asked you to speak neither good nor evil of them: that you know that I esteem them, that in my lands they have done much good, that I should be sorry to lose them, but that if the court of Rome believes it must abolish this Order, I shall put no obstacle in the way; moreover, that I always used to speak of them with respect, but that even in private I did not like people to talk about these unhappy affairs.[3]

In 1773, when the pope concluded that he must suppress the Society, Maria Theresa made no effort to save it. When shown the pope's bull in draft in March, all she stipulated was that the property of the Jesuits should pass to the state rather than, as he had envisaged, to the Church. After the promulgation of the bull, she asked the pope whether he would permit her, contrary to its terms, to appoint ex-Jesuits to serve in parishes that lacked priests. The pope said it was her affair, and a large number of ex-Jesuits found employment in this and other spheres.[4]

According to some historians, her acquiescence in the suppression sealed the doom of the Order. The motives of her policy have naturally been closely, even passionately, scrutinised, as have the influences that shaped it. I shall confine myself mainly to domestic considerations, and in particular to the views and actions of the empress, of Joseph II and of Prince Kaunitz, who as chancellor of state was effectively her chief minister.[5]

I

Easily the most familiar pieces of evidence in the case are the following two passages from supposed letters of Joseph II:

> *Joseph to Choiseul, January 1770*: If I were sovereign, you could count on my support, and you have my approval as regards the Jesuits and the plan to suppress them.
>
> On my mother do not rely so much … But Kaunitz is your friend; he can achieve everything with the empress …
>
> Choiseul! I know [the Jesuits] as well as anyone does: … their efforts to spread darkness over the earth, and to rule and embroil Europe from Cape Finisterre to the North Sea.

> *Joseph to Aranda, Spanish ambassador in Paris, July 1773*: Clement XIV has acquired eternal glory by suppressing the Jesuits … Before they were known in Germany, religion was a doctrine that brought happiness to peoples; but they have made it inspire fear … [Their] principal objects were to acquire glory, to extend their power and to spread darkness over the rest of the world. Their intolerance caused Germany to suffer the horrors of a thirty years war. Their principles cost the Henrys of France their lives and thrones; they were the originators of the loathsome [revocation of the] Edict of Nantes. The powerful influence which they had over the princes of the house of Habsburg is only too well known … To their wise direction were entrusted the education of youth, literature, patronage, the distribution of the principal offices of state, the ear of kings and the heart of queens. We know too well what use they made of their power, what plans they carried out and what fetters they imposed upon the nations … If I was inclined to hate anyone, [it would be the Jesuits,] who persecuted a Fénelon and promoted the bull *In coena Domini* which brought Rome into contempt.

Each of these incendiary letters has been quoted, often at even greater length, by many historians, not only by authors such as S. K. Padover in *The Revolutionary Emperor* and H. Magenschab in *Josef II. Revolutionär von Gottes Gnaden* but also by some of the most distinguished students of the period in works that are accepted as authoritative. The first was quoted both by Ludwig von Pastor in his *History of the Popes* and by Ferdinand Maass in *Der Josephinismus*.[6]

Yet these documents are pure invention. A moment's thought might have led scholars to question whether the emperor would be likely to have written in such wild and imprudent terms to ministers of foreign Powers, especially since no other correspondence is known to have passed between them. In fact, these documents come from a collection of *Letters of Joseph II*, published anonymously in the year of his death with the manifestly false imprint of Constantinople, most of which have been recognised as spurious for more than a century.[7]

Even among historians who are aware of this forgery or have avoided quoting from it, some have accepted the picture it paints of the attitudes of Maria Theresa, Joseph and Kaunitz. Viktor Bibl, for example, in his *Kaiser Josef II.* of 1943, quotes the entire diatribe of the second letter, announces that it is spurious and then declares it to be 'a happy deception' that Joseph might well have written after all. The great Alfred von Arneth, who, using only genuine material from the archives, first put the study of Maria Theresa's reign on a scholarly basis, none the less wrote: 'We possess some statements of the empress's which clearly show that, far from being an enemy of the Jesuits, she cherished a strong predilection for them. It is evident, on the other hand, that Joseph shared the pretty general prejudice against them, while Kaunitz unquestionably ranked with their emphatic opponents.' Among contemporary historians P. P. Bernard, in his *Jesuits and Jacobins* of 1971, has described Kaunitz as 'perhaps the most implacable enemy of the Jesuits in Austria'. Karl Gutkas wrote in his *Kaiser Joseph II.* of 1989 that by 1769 'Joseph was already working hard, together with prince Kaunitz, to bring about the suppression of the Jesuit Order and to influence the empress to take the same line'.[8]

The genuine evidence reveals a different and much more complicated picture. I shall quote extensively from it, in the hope of drowning the echo of the false letters.

II

A second distortion arises from the widespread assumption that from the 1750s onwards the Jesuit issue must have preoccupied the rulers of the Monarchy as much as it did the rulers of France, Spain, Portugal and Naples. This assumption receives powerful support from the great Jesuit historians, Duhr and Maass, who understandably regard the fate of the Society as of overriding importance. But the fact was – as emerges from the way in which Joseph II spoke of the matter in my first quotation – that in Vienna the concentration of other Powers on the Jesuit question seemed obsessive, and certainly not appropriate to the Austrian context.

In Maria Theresa's political testaments of 1750 and 1756 she sketched out plans to reform the Church which have come to be regarded as foreshadowing the whole policy known as Josephism. Her thoughts on the regular clergy occur in this famous passage:

> No monastic house observes the limitations of its statutes, and many idlers are allowed in. All of this will require a great remedy, which I intend to apply in time and after due consideration. I except, however, from such measures the kingdom of Hungary, where much still remains to be done for religion, in which task I shall require the clergy there to cooperate, but not work with them alone, but concert chiefly with laymen on the principles to be followed ... taking careful pains to support and develop what is useful to the public, and not what profits the private advantage of the clergy, monks and nuns in any province.[9]

She makes no reference at all to Jesuits.

The first discussion of the Society by the Council of State took place early in 1765, on the question whether to promulgate a bull of Pope Clement XIII in which he vindicated it against the assaults of so many Catholic rulers. The Council proved to be deeply divided. Some members regarded the Jesuits as pernicious because of their oath of absolute obedience to the pope and their controversial moral teaching. Others praised them for their usefulness and good conduct. It was decided not to publish the bull in the Monarchy but to shelve the general issue.[10]

Later in the same year Joseph II wrote his famous *Memorandum* to his mother 'on the defects of the present system and the most effectual means of remedying them'. He claimed that monasteries were too thriving for the good of the state. 'I should ordain, whatever the pope and all the monks in the universe might say, that none of my subjects could embrace any ecclesiastical condition before the age ... of twenty-five completed years.' And, 'I should have all existing foundations examined by an impartial commission. In the places where the intentions of the founder were being disregarded, I should reform them and employ them for pious purposes which would be at the same time useful to the state, such as the education of children.' He also discusses education at some length, arguing for example that it would be better if the colleges of Vienna were moved to provincial towns, where students would encounter fewer distractions. Many of these colleges were run by Jesuits, but neither in this context nor anywhere else in the document does he refer to the Society. Yet he was writing at the height of the furore over the expulsion of the Jesuits from France.[11]

In February 1766, at the empress's request, Kaunitz wrote a long reply to Joseph's *Memorandum*. It is largely devoted to education, but it contains an extraordinary passage on monks. The chancellor goes out of his way to refute what he calls 'the arguments that the most enlightened statesman and the greatest enemy of the monks might advance against the administration of the regular orders'. Many monks, he says, would be unemployable outside their houses and so would become a burden on the state. And

> if monks live at public expense, they also render services, and that is so true that, unless it was decided to reduce the obligation to attend worship, it would scarcely be possible to do without their help or ministry. It is true that there could be fewer monks if there were more secular priests. But it is not less true that the cost of priests is much higher than that of monks, for it is clear that three monks can live in a community on what it would be necessary to pay one priest living on his own.

In any case, it is the right of an individual adult, if this is his considered intention, to take monastic vows and remove himself from society at large. Kaunitz condemns the mendicant Orders but does not mention the Jesuits.[12] It is impossible, after reading this document, to retain the common view that he was the sworn enemy of monasticism, at least in 1766.

Two years later, however, in his capacity as minister in charge of the duchy of Milan, he persuaded Maria Theresa to approve guidelines for reform of the Church there which asserted her right to act without papal approval in all but strictly spiritual matters. In the next year the government of the duchy began to dissolve monasteries. But no attempt was made to suppress any Jesuit houses, and the grounds on which monasteries were abolished were that they were small, corrupt or useless. 'Usefulness' meant contributing to the cure of souls, the care of the sick or the education of the young.[13] By these criteria the Jesuits, as parish priests, preachers, confessors and teachers, were safe.

Kaunitz was by now advocating a general reform of religious Orders and a substantial reduction in the number of monks and nuns. With the support of the emperor, he succeeded in 1770 in persuading Maria Theresa to raise the age of profession to twenty-four, without papal approval. During the discussions no special reference was made to Jesuits.[14]

In 1769 Count Pergen had been given general oversight of the Oriental Academy which its head, the Jesuit Father Frantz, had mismanaged. Pergen soon became active in discussions about the reform of education more generally, and in 1770 produced a memorandum to the empress urging, among other radical changes, that regular clergy should at once be totally excluded from any part in education whatever. He maintained that their influence was irredeemably pernicious. This proposal, if adopted, would of course have struck at the Jesuits more than any other Order, since they dominated the universities and colleges of the Monarchy. For once, the empress, the emperor and Kaunitz had no difficulty in agreeing that the exclusion of regulars from education was simply unworkable. There were not enough secular clergy to go round. While admitting that monks had inherent drawbacks as educators of lay men, Joseph and the chancellor put their trust in measures to transform clerical education, under which clergy would be trained, according to a curriculum approved by the government, as servants of the state rather than of the Church.[15]

In all these documents Jesuits figure very rarely, except as an undifferentiated part of the whole body of regulars. It is the monasteries as a whole that the government is concerned to take in hand. This contrast with the emphasis of other rulers on the position of the Jesuits must reflect the peculiar ecclesiastical situation in the Monarchy. In many of its provinces the Church owned an exceptionally high proportion of the land, perhaps a third; the ratio of regulars to seculars was extremely high – two to one in Upper and Lower Austria; and numerous monasteries of the old Orders, Benedictine, Augustinian, Premonstratensian, many of them very wealthy indeed, not to mention the Dominicans, Franciscans and Piarists, rivalled the Jesuits as providers of colleges and schools, parish priests, professors and teachers. Virtually none of this was true of France, Spain, Portugal and Naples. The monastic presence in the Monarchy was so strong that, short of drastic social engineering, the government had no choice but to rely on monks both as pastors and teachers. And among the regulars the Jesuits were notable as pastors and stood out as the most successful scholars and educators – in other words, as exceptionally useful. If suppression of the Society meant that its members would cease to perform these functions, then the measure would gravely damage the Monarchy.[16]

III

Despite all this, its rulers were far from uncritical of the Jesuits. To take first Maria Theresa herself, it is true that she told Pope Clement XIII in March 1768 that she would never forsake the Jesuits in her own lands if they behaved as they ought towards God, herself and the people. She made similar promises to others. As we have seen, she insisted on acknowledging the Jesuits' merits. On 16 October 1773, after the promulgation of the bull of suppression, she confided to Countess Enzenberg: 'As regards the Jesuits I am distressed and in despair. I have loved and esteemed them and have seen in them nothing that did not tend towards moral and spiritual improvement. But I've surrendered control over this matter to a commission which has as its head Kressel the state councillor – and [contains] others like him.' And she said much the same to her son Ferdinand.[17]

Yet, long before Joseph became co-regent, and even before Kaunitz was active on the domestic front, she had already done much to curb the power and influence of the Jesuits in educational, religious and cultural affairs. Their power within the Monarchy had been immense, probably greater than anywhere else in Europe. Before 1749 they monopolised the direction of Austrian universities, occupied all Chairs of philosophy and theology, were in charge of most aspects of censorship and supplied all the confessors of members of the royal family. In some ways Maria Theresa had even enhanced their position, by establishing in 1746 the college that became known as the *Theresianum*, where the training of young nobles and government servants was entrusted to them. They were also given charge of the Oriental Academy, founded in 1753 to train future diplomats. But from this time onwards the Society's power was gradually weakened until, just before the suppression, they had few Chairs and royal confessorships left to them, and no representatives on the censorship commission.[18]

In imposing or permitting these changes, Maria Theresa had been subject to numerous influences. Both the secular clergy and other regulars resented the Jesuits' dominance. Hence archbishop Migazzi, appointed to Vienna in 1757, initially worked to displace them as censors; and Augustinian, Benedictine and Dominican theologians coveted their Chairs. The Society's continued promotion of the bull *Unigenitus*, which condemned propositions derived from the Bible and others commonly regarded as orthodox, was seen by many Catholics as gratuitously partisan and divisive. The Jesuits had unwisely tried to ban some of the writings of the moderate Catholic reformer, Lodovico Antonio Muratori, which were widely admired in the Monarchy, not least by the future emperor and the archbishop. As a modern historian, Rudolf Reinhardt, has written:

> The present-day solidarity shown by many Orders with the Jesuits
> suppressed in 1773 is not entirely comprehensible. They ought to
> be grateful to Maria Theresa who tried, long before the suppression
> of the Jesuits, to curb the Society's claims to dominance; other con-
> gregations could now disseminate their piety and theology with the
> necessary vigour. It is always dangerous when one Order believes that
> it alone can quiet the conscience of the ruler.

Maria Theresa put her physician, Gerard Van Swieten, in charge of reforming not only medical training but university education more generally, and in 1759 made him chairman of the censorship commission. Garampi, when papal nuncio in 1781, describing the origins of Joseph II's policies, attributed to Van Swieten the first introduction of what he called Jansenism into the Monarchy.[19]

It is instructive to quote examples of the arguments used by Van Swieten in persuading Maria Theresa to reduce the power of the Jesuits in the censorship. He described to her how they had obtained one 'privilege' after another from her predecessors, and invented a few more, so that they claimed the sole right to authorise the reprinting of any book by a Jesuit author or the reproduction of any picture that they had first published. 'I am in a position to prove conclusively that the true aim of the Society was to make money, and that the religious motive was only a pretext to take advantage of the piety of Your Majesty and her ancestors.' They presumed to give to a particular printer the monopoly of publishing their books, and spent large sums to drive competing printers out of business.

> This is not all; the Society goes even further ... The same Father

Provincial Hermann gives permission to a bookseller of Augsburg to print the four Gospels and the Acts of the Apostles in Greek, but only for the first edition. At its widest, their privilege speaks only of books produced by Jesuits. They must be very impudent to count the Holy Scriptures among their writings.

They treat their own permission to publish as superior to the government's.

Perhaps the Society would claim that nothing but good comes from their stall. However, *The History of the people of God etc.*, written by a Jesuit, has been branded at Paris by the hand of the executioner, has been condemned at Rome and has a place in the catalogue of works prohibited by the Vienna censorship. I omit many others that the censorship has this year examined by order of the archbishop, which contained a detestable morality and seditious maxims injurious to sovereigns.

After the establishment of the censorship commission by Maria Theresa in 1751, they arrogated to themselves the right to appoint and change their representative censor at will. 'Should it be left to the Society', Van Swieten asked the empress, 'to exercise this despotism of appointing a censor without saying a word to the commission?' He succeeded in many of his battles with the Jesuit censors, making possible for example the sale of Montesquieu's *De l'esprit des lois* from 1752. In summary, he felt able to write to Maria Theresa on 3 November 1758: '*The intention of Your Majesty is to limit the exorbitant power that the Society has everywhere appropriated to itself.*' She did not demur.[20]

When in 1767 he felt himself under attack from her as well as from cardinal Migazzi, he asked to be allowed to resign from the commission. She replied that there were no others 'who can continue in the same principles so wisely adopted and continued against all opposition, and I hope you would not refuse my request that you should continue to train as many others as possible who can follow in your footsteps, however imperfectly. My tranquillity depends on it'.[21] This passage compares interestingly with her letter to Countess Enzenberg six years later. The empress's emotional outpourings to her faithful servants, though doubtless heartfelt at the time, are not individually a sufficient guide to her feelings, let alone to her policies. But the support that she gave to Van Swieten leaves no doubt that she saw many actions of the Jesuits as working against moral and spiritual improvement.

Her attitude to Jesuit professors reinforces the point. The emperor wrote in 1768: 'The Jesuits have been deprived of a Chair of Theology to which they had had a prescriptive right, because their moral teaching has been found unsuitable.' In January 1774 she declared: 'No one was so determined as I, when the Society was suppressed, to take away all Chairs of Theology from them immediately.' In this case she had actually stiffened the recommendations of Kressel's commission.[22]

Similar issues were involved in the displacement of Jesuit royal confessors. The first non-Jesuit, Gürtler, was assigned to Joseph's first wife Isabella in 1760. He was soon given other royal charges and accompanied one of them, Archduchess Maria Carolina, when she went to Naples as queen in 1768.[23] But the most interesting case is that of Maria Theresa herself.

Until 1767 the empress's confessor for more than thirty years had been the Jesuit, Father Kampmiller. On 18 July 1767, when she was still recovering from smallpox, Lord Stormont, the British ambassador in Vienna, reported that her Jesuit confessor had been dismissed and that Joseph himself had given Kampmiller the news. Stormont went on to say that the significance of this event was uncertain but that Maria Theresa had never cared much for Jesuits, and that they will have 'still less [credit] in a future reign'. On 22 July the Spanish ambassador in Vienna, Count Mahony, wrote to his Court:

> It is certain that the empress during her illness made her confession to the Prelate of St Dorothea, Müller; she has greater confidence in him than in her own confessor Kampmiller, the Jesuit, who is very old and somewhat deaf. When the latter was in the antechamber, in order to hear the empress's confession during her illness, Her Majesty let him know that in her critical condition she needed a confessor who would not leave her side and could sit up with her all night. Hence she had chosen the Prelate of St Dorothea, who is young enough and strong. The old Jesuit confessor remains still at Court without doing his job but also without being dismissed from it. The empress does not like Jesuits, but tolerates them.[24]

The *Nouvelles ecclésiastiques*, the organ of the Jansenists, in its issue of 19 August 1767, while announcing with satisfaction the retirement of Kampmiller, made the point that he had long wished to give up his post. It is pleasant to find this Jansenist journal corroborated by the Jesuit, Bernhard Duhr, who in his *History of the Jesuits* cites evidence that Kampmiller had always found the task burdensome.[25]

Prince Khevenhüller, a high Court official, whose detailed diary is a uniquely valuable source for Maria Theresa's reign, unfortunately made no mention of this change in 1767, but on 31 August 1773, after the receipt of the papal bull suppressing the Society, he recorded:

> Our Cardinal-Archbishop, who has been by no means a special friend of the Society, has done all he could and has made powerful representations not only to the empress but also to the pope; and in his memoranda, which he has shown me, he has urged that this useful Order should be preserved as a congregation. I also learn from reliable sources that the Council of State, and particularly their spokesman in this important matter, Freiherr von Kressel, supported the Cardinal's opinion in his recommendation. But it was found possible to suborn the empress through the secret correspondence of the king of Spain and the insistent arguments of the Provost of St Dorothea.
>
> The latter has for some years and especially since her last attack of smallpox succeeded in hardening her fundamentally tender conscience in such a way that – although she still made her confession to Father Kampmiller (who had been her confessor since childhood) – she never failed to consult the Provost in all the most important matters and used to hold private conferences with him on the 18th of each month, her day of retreat, about cases of conscience ... This reverend gentleman was always a sworn enemy of the Jesuits – allegedly out of personal pique, because they wouldn't accept him into their Order; and, since he attacked their doctrines of probabilism and mental reservation at every opportunity, he was suspected of being a secret Jansenist.

So not only was Müller's appointment as her effective confessor in itself a blow to Jesuit influence, but it comes to seem of crucial importance if he played a major role in the empress's decision to accept the bull of suppression. However, Khevenhüller was wrong in thinking that the pope was ready in 1773 to accept a Jesuit congregation.[26]

Peter Hersche, author of the fullest discussion of late Jansenism in Austria, is inclined to give credence to a letter written by a son of Prince Khevenhüller, dated 19 July 1767, which claims that there was a more substantive and highly pertinent reason for Kampmiller's dismissal than his diffidence, age and infirmity. The young Khevenhüller passes on an anecdote he has learned from a recent letter, which he swears is true:

> H.M. Theresa confided to Father Kampmiller her confessor, whom you know, on condition that he under no circumstances repeated it, saying among other things 'About you Jesuits there's a great storm blowing up in Spain', and mentioning some details and the expectation that they would be expelled from Spain ... The Father wrote to the General [of the Order], the General sent the original letter to the Spanish Provincial. Father Kampmiller wrote another letter or two to the General; [since they were] on this subject, the General sent them straight on to the Provincial in Spain; when the Jesuits were expelled and their papers were examined, five letters were found from Kampmiller, which the king of Spain sent to our empress. At this she was so angry that she summoned Kampmiller, berated him and removed him from his post, and has taken the prelate of St Dorothea as her confessor.

This tale bears a striking affinity to the long-discredited story that Maria Theresa abandoned the Jesuits to their fate because her Jesuit confessor had in 1772 passed on to his General details of negotiations about the partition of Poland, which he had learned from her general confession. An incident such as young Khevenhüller describes might easily be the grain of truth from which the greater myth sprang. But, on the other hand, there is no supporting evidence for it whatever, even from the contemporary report of the Spanish ambassador; and the relegation of Kampmiller is explained entirely satisfactorily by his age and infirmity coupled with his desire to resign. He was seventy-four in 1767. Further, he was very far from being disgraced. He retained the title and the emoluments of a confessor, and some of the functions. Maria Theresa continued to value him and to pay him, and in 1771 she attended his fiftieth anniversary Mass, on which occasion she presented to his house an altar cushion and a vestment she herself had worked.[27]

In any case, what needs explaining is not the removal of Kampmiller but his replacement by Müller. Clearly, the empress had come to know and trust the latter already. But the change was made during her illness, while Joseph himself was keeping her company day and night,[28] so that he may well have had more to do with it than merely conveying the news to Kampmiller. It may also have been a factor that the king of Spain had just let the empress know of his new determination to destroy the Jesuits, which gave the issue fresh diplomatic significance and made it embarrassing to have a confessor wholly committed to the Society. Her crucial decision to remain neutral over the suppression, from which all the later decisions flowed, must have been made in 1767.

So, despite some of her utterances, she was not a great friend of the Jesuits as an Order. She herself stated the case in a letter of January 1774 to Kressel's commission, from which I have already quoted a sentence:

> I have been not been well disposed towards the Society for many years. I removed both the education and spiritual guidance of myself and my children from it. No one was so determined as I, when the Society was suppressed, to take away from them all theological Chairs immediately ... After all this I cannot be regarded as prejudiced in their favour or too mild towards them, especially as I never allowed myself to act or permit anything against my convictions.[29]

This statement no more reflects her whole mind than do her laments for the passing of the Order. But it does reflect her essential position *as a ruler*.

IV

If Maria Theresa was hardly a firm friend to the Jesuits, Joseph II was only a lukewarm enemy. He once described all regulars as 'by their nature the scourge of all Catholic provinces, and the most implacable leeches of the poor labourer and artisan'. But he never said anything like that about the Jesuits, though he did criticise them, among other clergy, for their neglect of charitable and pastoral duties in Prague in 1771. His attitude in my first quotation, that the whole issue of suppression is something of a joke, surfaces in some of his other utterances. For example, in 1769 he cruelly teased the General of the Jesuits about their imminent suppression; he scoffed at the methodical way in which they required penitents to list their sins; and, when writing from his annual camp to the elector of Trier in 1781 in defence of his early Church reforms, he expressed regret that he had left his Busenbaum at home – referring to a notorious Jesuit treatise long ago banned in the Monarchy. But he had been largely educated by Jesuits and he did not criticise the teaching he had received. In 1776 he paid for an expensive funeral for one of his old tutors, Father Franz. He retained his Jesuit confessor, Höller, until he died in 1770. Many of the tutors he appointed for his nephew, the future Francis II, were ex-Jesuits. The most revealing of his remarks about the Society is what he said, travelling incognito in Italy early in 1769, to Count Papini, whom he met casually as they waited to change horses:

> The [count] asked him about the Jesuits of Germany. The emperor replied that they behave very well there; they are learned and zealous – adding other praises – and concluding that what has happened to them elsewhere wouldn't happen in Germany. Hearing these praises, the count supposed that this was a young man educated at the *Theresianum*, who spoke out of loyalty. 'No,' the emperor replied, 'I was educated at home and I said that out of simple regard for the truth.'

In 1780 Catherine II of Russia was equally surprised by the warmth of his praise for the Society.[30]

To set against the spurious evidence of the false letters, there is genuine evidence from the year 1784 that the emperor was so sympathetic to the Jesuits that he had tried to stop his mother suppressing them! The Danish Protestant minister, Freemason and traveller, Münter, recorded in his diary and in a letter an interview with provost Felbiger, the Catholic educational reformer who was in charge of extending and improving elementary education in the Monarchy. Felbiger told him: 'The emperor was very much against the suppression of the Jesuits. Because he was going off on his travels, he left some sealed instructions in his bureau, to be read [if the issue came to a head]. They were not read, and he made a frightful fuss when he returned.'[31] It is highly significant that Joseph's regard for ex-Jesuits made this seem a plausible story in the mid-eighties. But it is not true. The emperor had indeed left some instructions behind about the action to be taken if the bull of suppression arrived, which were not acted on until he returned. But they were not directed against the suppression as such. That he took as already a *fait accompli*. They were concerned with the disposal of the Jesuits and their lands after the suppression.

This document did, however, contain very favourable remarks about the Society. Joseph began by saying:

> The education of youth, at least of the most important part of it, in religion as well as in other subjects, has been until now almost entirely entrusted in these lands to the Fathers of the Society. Neither among the secular clergy nor in the other regular Orders will it be possible to

find immediately, especially in the bigger towns, a sufficient number of qualified persons to fill the places of the Jesuits, with comparable success, in *Gymnasien*, academies and Universities, and to occupy the many endowed teaching posts.

So it must be considered what provision should be made in education, especially in the noble academies and foundations, in the *Theresianum*, in the colleges at Olmütz, Prague, Tyrnau and all other academies and *Gymnasien*, and whether it would not be desirable – indeed, for the good of religion and the state, necessary – that even after the suppression of the Society the teachers of this Order should remain in their existing posts, and on what basis one could keep them on at least until [other] able persons can be trained to fill the teaching posts in future and match the existing provision.

It will take long application and preparation to educate teachers for this [sort of] instruction, to which the whole institution of the Society was especially devoted.[32]

Clearly, the emperor admired the intellectual and pedagogic achievements of the Order. He evidently minded less about their alleged theological errors than his mother did. But he had supported her loosening of the censorship, and indeed wished to carry it further. After the death of Father Höller, he made his parish priest his confessor.[33] He wanted a drastic reform of monasticism, even if he would not have attacked the Jesuits first. He desired to reform education, which the suppression of the Society made necessary, and the windfall of its lands and revenues more feasible. But there is no evidence in his numerous surviving papers that he tried to persuade his mother to suppress it, or even to join the other Powers in asking the pope to do so. When he wrote early in 1768 that the Order was doomed, he presumably believed it, and was prepared to wait.

V

I have already discussed some of the more important of Kaunitz's interventions. Franz Szabo in his *Kaunitz and Enlightened Absolutism* has highlighted the chancellor's recognition of Jesuits' intellectual attainments, and emphasised that he refrained from pressing Maria Theresa to promote their suppression. In a particularly important case of January 1768, Szabo points out, Kaunitz omitted from his final version of proposals for Church reform a recommendation that

Maria Theresa should support the other Catholic Powers in urging the pope to suppress the Order. This point might be turned round: he had, after all, put the passage into his draft in the first place. After the suppression he showed himself more hostile to employing ex-Jesuits than the empress, and especially to accepting the pope's rulings on the issue. But it is clear that he was less unfriendly to the Jesuits than to other monastic Orders.[34]

VI

In one sense, Maria Theresa's acceptance of the suppression seems a striking testimony to the primacy of foreign policy. Suppression was certainly not a priority of domestic policy for herself, for Joseph or for Kaunitz. Had it not been for the pressure on the pope of the rulers of Portugal, Spain, France and Naples, it would not have happened and the Monarchy under Maria Theresa would never have contemplated it. The other Powers had expelled and expropriated the Jesuits on their own authority, without papal approval, but even they had to accept that the pope alone could definitively suppress an international Order that owed him total obedience. Maria Theresa, Joseph II and Kaunitz, with their determination to assert state sovereignty, still conceded that the pope had the right to dissolve this Order. Since the pope was also a foreign sovereign, the issue was unavoidably a matter for diplomacy.

It is much less clear that foreign policy had primacy in another sense. It does not seem that for the Monarchy considerations of foreign policy, as opposed to domestic considerations, were decisive in determining its attitude to the suppression. Despite the sympathy with Jesuits shown in some of her remarks, Maria Theresa – not in opposition to Joseph and Kaunitz but, with different emphases, in agreement with them – wanted a general reform of monasticism; they all deplored the Society's allegiance to the pope as incompatible with state sovereignty; and they all wished to break its control over the universities, censorship and, at least in the long run, secondary education. For the state to claim to reform or dissolve the Jesuits would be especially controversial because of their papal connection. If the pope himself did the deed, that problem disappeared; and his action would make it more difficult for him to obstruct the suppression of other monasteries and Orders by the state.

The assertion that Maria Theresa could have saved the Order by taking a firm stand in its favour is at least questionable. As we have seen, the emperor thought in the spring of 1768 that suppression was inevitable even if the Monarchy remained neutral, because the other Powers would ensure the election of a pope who would carry it out. In 1773 itself Maria Theresa could not even have tried to block it without abandoning her often stated policy: she had declared that she would not stand in the way if the pope decided to go ahead. She had made the essential decisions in 1767–69 – when, it must be said, she was at her most radical in ecclesiastical policy under the influence of Kaunitz, Van Swieten and Joseph. The question then arises: could she at that stage have halted the process by announcing that she would never accept the suppression of the Jesuits, even if it was ordered by the pope? She could only have adopted this position, risking diplomatic isolation, if she had thought the preservation of the Order the most important interest of the Monarchy or of the Church. This she plainly did not believe – and who can blame her?

Finally, it must be underlined that she did not herself suppress the Society in the Monarchy. It was the pope who did that. Further, in other Catholic countries the Jesuits were not only deprived of position and property, but also expelled. She, on the contrary, secured them, in addition to pensions, the opportunity in some cases to continue their careers, and in other cases to take up new ones. The Jesuit Court preacher retained his position until he died during the reign of Joseph II. Father Hohenwart eventually became archbishop of Vienna. Many of the writers active under Joseph, radical as well as conservative, were ex-Jesuits. As Kressel's commission pointed out to her, they were much better treated than the soldiers who, out of loyalty to her, served and died in her armies.[35]

Notes

This chapter was originally written for a conference on the suppression of the Jesuits, organized by Dr R. Oresko in 1991. This it its first publication.

1 The best account of the process in English is O. Chadwick, *The Popes and European Revolution* (Oxford, 1981), ch. 5, to which I am indebted throughout this chapter.

2 *Geschichte Maria Thersias* [hereafter *GMT*], ed. A. Ritter von Arneth (10 vols, Vienna, 1863–79), vol. IX, pp. 35–40, 90–1, 550–1; B. Duhr, *Jesuiten-Fabeln* (4th edn, Freiburg-im-Breisgau, 1904), pp. 55–6 and nn.

3 *GMT*, vol. IX, pp. 91–2, 564–5; Duhr, *Jesuiten-Fabeln*, pp. 57–60; *Marie-Antoinette. Correspondance secrète entre Marie-Thérèse et le Cte de Mercy-Argenteau*, eds A. Ritter von Arneth and M. A. Geffroy (3 vols, 2nd edn, Paris, 1874–75),

vol. I, pp. 5–6. See also L. von Pastor, *History of the Popes* (40 vols, London, 1938–53), vol. XXXVIII, esp. pp. 257–60.

4 *GMT*, vol. IX, pp. 93–123; Pastor, *History of the Popes*, vol. XXXVIII, pp. 341–7; F. Maass, *Der Josephinismus* (5 vols, Vienna, 1951–61), esp. vol. II, pp. 24–31,with the accompanying documents. On the employment of ex-Jesuits H. Haberzettl, *Die Stellung der Exjesuiten in Politik und Kulturleben Österreichs zu Ende des 18. Jahrhunderts* (Vienna, 1973).

5 As well as by Maass in *Der Josephinismus*, the view that Maria Theresa's policy doomed the Jesuits is propounded by B. Duhr, e.g. in *Geschichte der Jesuiten in den Ländern deutscher Zunge* (4 vols, Munich, 1907–28), vol. IV. Both these works contain immensely valuable material.

For an interesting recent study of Maria Theresa's attitude see R. de Maio, 'Maria Teresa e i Gesuiti', *Rivista storica italiana*, XCIV (1982): 435–54; for the emperor my *Joseph II. I: In the Shadow of Maria Theresa, 1741–1780* (Cambridge, 1987), esp. pp. 455–64; for Kaunitz F. A. J. Szabo, *Kaunitz and Enlightened Absolutism, 1753–1780* (Cambridge, 1994), esp. pp. 241–7.

6 S. K. Padover, *The Revolutionary Emperor* (2nd edn, London, 1967), pp. 41–2; H. Magenschab, *Josef II. Revolutionär von Gottes Gnaden* (Vienna, 1979), pp. 150–1; Pastor, *History of the Popes*, vol. XXXVIII, p. 257 and n.; Maass, *Der Josephinismus*, vol. I, p. 97n.

7 For the *Letters of Joseph II* see Chapter 5, 'The False Joseph II'.

8 V. Bibl, *Kaiser Josef II.* (Vienna, 1943), pp. 83–4; *GMT*, vol. IX, p. 90; P. P. Bernard, *Jesuits and Jacobins* (London, 1971), p. 14n.; K. Gutkas, *Kaiser Joseph II.* (Vienna, 1989), p. 152.

In Walter Oppenheim's *Europe and the Enlightened Despots* of 1990 we are told that 'the expulsion [!] of the Jesuits' from Austria showed the growing power of Joseph as co-regent.

9 Beales, *Joseph II*, p. 53.

10 C. von Hock, *Der österreichische Staatsrath* (Vienna, 1879), p. 48.

11 Beales, *Joseph II*, pp. 164, 167–8.

12 Ibid., pp. 175, 446–7.

13 Maass, *Der Josephinismus*, vol. I, pp. 95–6, 288–90, vol. II, passim; C. Capra in D. Sella and C. Capra, *Il ducato di Milano dal 1535 al 1796* (Turin, 1984), pp. 398–401, 497.

14 Maass, *Josephinismus*, vol. II, ch. I and pp. 144–59; Maass, 'Die Stellungnahme des Fürsten Kaunitz zur staatlichen Festsetzung der Altersgrenze für die Ablegung der Ordensgelübde in Österreich im Jahre 1770/1', *Mitteilungen des östrreichischen Instituts für Geschichtsforschung*, LVIII (1950): 656–67.

15 Beales, *Joseph II*, pp. 456–8; P. P. Bernard, *From the Enlightenment to the Police State: The Public Life of Johann Anton Pergen* (Urbana, 1991), pp. 70–90.

16 Cf. G. Winner, *Die Klosteraufhebungen in Niederösterreich und Wien* (Vienna, 1967); P. G. M. Dickson, 'Joseph II's Reshaping of the Austrian Church', *Historical Journal*, XXXVI (1993): 89–114.

17 Maass, *Josephinismus*, vol. I, p. 253; Duhr, *Jesuiten-Fabeln*, pp. 56, n.2, 65–6; *GMT*, IX, p. 568.

18 The best modern account of these developments, which I have used for this whole section, is G. Klingenstein, *Staatsverwaltung und kirchliche Autorität im 18. Jahrhundert* (Vienna, 1970).

19 R. Reinhardt, *Die Beziehungen von Hochstift und Diözese Konstanz zu Habsburg-Österreich in der Neuzeit* (Wiesbaden, 1966), p. 14; Garampi to Mgr Doria in Paris, 21 May 1781 (Archivio segreto vaticano, Nunziatura di Vienna 180). On Van Swieten, E. Lesky and A. Wandruszka (eds), *Gerard Van Swieten und seine Zeit* (Vienna, 1973); and see next n.

20 All these quotations come from A. Fournier, 'Gerard Van Swieten als Censor', in *Historische Studien und Skizzen* (Prague, 1885), pp. 113–19, 79–80 and 80n.

21 Ibid., p. 93n.

22 Beales, *Joseph II*, p. 180; *GMT*, vol. IX, p. 119.

23 P. Hersche, *Der Spätjansenismus in Österreich* (Vienna, 1977), esp. pp. 138–41.

24 Beales, *Joseph II*, pp. 449–50; Duhr, *Jesuiten-Fabeln*, pp. 54–5.

25 *Nouvelles ecclésiastiques*, 1767, p. 135; Duhr, *Geschichte*, vol. IV, p. 439.

26 R. Khevenhüller-Metsch and H. Schlitter (eds), *Aus der Zeit Maria Theresias. Tagebuch des Fürsten Khevenhüller-Metsch, kaiserlichen Obersthofmeisters, 1742–1776* (8 vols, Vienna, 1907–72), vol. VII, pp. 181–2. Cf. the accounts in works listed in n.4 above.

27 Hersche, *Der Spätjansenismus*, p. 138. I have now read the copy of Count Khevenhüller's letter to Count Diesbach in Haus-, Hof- und Staatsarchiv, Vienna, Nachlaß Schlitter, Karton 5 (supplied to Schlitter from the Fribourg archives, with notes, by Hyrvoix de Landosle). The account I gave of it in *Joseph II*, p. 450, rested on a misreading of Hersche: Kampmiller was not supposed to have revealed material from a confession, only information confided to him in strict confidence.

For Kampmiller's continued favour with Maria Theresa, see Duhr, *Geschichte*, p. 439.

28 Beales, *Joseph II*, p. 450.

29 *GMT*, vol. IX, pp. 118–19.

30 Beales, *Joseph II*, pp. 44, 46, 64, 205, 258, 318, 461–2. On the banning of Busenbaum, Klingenstein, *Staatsverwaltung und kirchliche Autorität*, pp. 106–7.

31 E. Rosenstrauch-Königsberg, *Freimaurer, Illuminat, Weltbürger* (Berlin, 1984), pp. 90, 165–6.

32 Khevenhüller-Metsch and Schlitter (eds), *Aus der Zeit Maria Theresias*, vol. VII, pp. 53–6.

33 Beales, *Joseph II*, pp. 205–7.

34 Szabo, *Kaunitz*, pp. 241–7; *GMT*, vol. IX, p. 122.

35 Duhr, *Geschichte*, vol. IV, p. 469; Haberzettl, *Die Stellung der Exjesuiten*, passim; *GMT*, vol. IX, p. 118.

CHAPTER 9

Joseph II and the Monasteries of Austria and Hungary

Everyone who visits rural Austria for the first time is struck by the number and size of the working monasteries that dominate its landscape. Among them are the vast Augustinian house of St Florian near Linz, Cistercian Wilhering with its exuberant rococo decoration, and the monumental Benedictine abbey of Melk towering above the Danube valley. In the cities of Salzburg and Vienna, too, ancient Benedictine abbeys, St Peter's and the Schottenstift, remain a formidable presence. Most of these institutions appear to date from the late seventeenth and early eighteenth centuries, when they were lavishly refurbished or rebuilt. But one by one they are celebrating their eight-hundredth, nine-hundredth, thousandth, even twelve-hundredth anniversaries. By contrast, almost everywhere in western Europe monasteries were eradicated either by the Reformation, by the French Revolution or under the aegis of Napoleon. Further east, in the Czech Republic for example, many lasted into the twentieth century but succumbed to communist regimes after the Second World War. The almost unique continuity of monastic life in many of the great Austrian foundations was breached only for a few years, during the Nazi regime. If the visitor knows that the Emperor Joseph II, as ruler of the Austrian Monarchy in the 1780s, is notorious for having carried through a drastic programme of Church reform which included the suppression of numerous monasteries, he will wonder how on earth these vast establishments came to survive.

Figures about Joseph's suppressions remained inconsistent and unreliable until Professor Peter Dickson published in 1987 his *Finance and Government under Maria Theresia 1740–1780*, followed by his article in the *Historical Journal* of 1993, 'Joseph II's Reshaping of the Austrian Church'. These two magisterial works have cleared up most of the uncertainties in the statistics. In the entire Austrian Monarchy, including the geographically separated provinces of Belgium and Lombardy, there were just over 2,000 religious houses when Joseph II succeeded his mother in 1780. In the lands that were then in the strict sense parts of Austria, that is, Upper and Lower Austria, Inner Austria, Tyrol and Vorarlberg, and Further Austria, monasteries held an especially important position. This area contained more than 500 houses, with altogether about 10,000 monks and over 1,000 nuns. As against these more than 11,000 regular clergy there were only about 6,500 secular, that is non-monastic, clergy. Monasteries owned nearly half of all Church land, which meant something like 20 per cent of all land. In most of these Austrian provinces, unlike other parts of the Monarchy except the Netherlands, the local representative assemblies or Estates were headed by a First Estate consisting entirely or largely of abbots of monasteries of ancient foundation. Bishops, of whom there were in any case very few, were not always included. The president of the First Estate of Lower Austria was the abbot of Melk, who, after the *Landmarschall*, the government's representative, was usually the most important member of the permanent sub-committee (*Landes-Ausschuss*) which conducted the business of the Estates between Diets. There is some force in the ancient catchphrase 'Österreich, Klöster-reich', which might be translated 'Austria, the monasteries' state'. During the 1780s, however, Joseph II directed a barrage of ordinances at the monasteries, and by 1790, when he died and and a halt was called, there remained in these provinces of Austria only 233 houses and 4,500 regular clergy.

This policy evoked both enthusiasm and indignation in its day, and is still highly controversial in Austria itself. But its results seem rather limited if they are set against the total suppressions carried out in France by 1792, and in Germany and nearly all of Italy by 1812. On the other hand, it was easily the most radical monastic policy enacted by any eighteenth-century Catholic government before the Revolu-tion. Dickson is not primarily concerned with the content of Joseph's ecclesiastical legislation nor with the philosophy behind it. He rightly points out that they have been much better studied than the matters he has examined, namely, Joseph's investigation and reorganisation of the Church in the central lands. As he says, the emperor's principal aims are well known: to subject the Church to state control in all save purely spiritual matters; to introduce legal toleration for the main Protestant churches and for Jews; to strengthen the episcopate; and to reshape 'the church away from its traditional emphasis on monasticism towards a more numerous, better educated, secular clergy'.[1]

While it is true that Joseph's policy has often been described, certain of its aspects have still not been adequately covered. In this chapter I shall consider some of them, using new or little-known material from the Vatican, Austrian and Hungarian archives. I shall concentrate on the following issues: the relationship between Maria Theresa's monastic policy and her son's; the involvement of monasteries in parochial work; hitherto unsuspected opposition to Joseph's policy at the highest level of the bureaucracy; and the impact of his legislation in Hungary, which was significantly different from its effect in Austria itself. The subject is so complex and the documentation so vast that I cannot pretend to deal exhaustively with any of these topics. What I hope to do is to open up some neglected themes and to show how much remains to be found out.

I

It was probably in 1750 that Maria Theresa dictated the first version of her political testament. This was just after she had forced through a reform of the constitution of her central lands, curbing the power of the Estates – and therefore of the great abbeys of Austria – in order to increase her revenue and army.[2] In this document she declared that the clergy of the German lands were in a good and flourishing condition and needed no more of the lavish assistance that they had been receiving from the state, or from her predecessors. In fact, she went on,

> they do not, alas! apply what they have as they should, and moreover, they constitute a heavy burden on the public. For no monastic House observes the limitations of its statutes, and many idlers are admitted; all this will call for a great remedy, which I propose to effect in good time and after due consideration.
>
> [But, she continued,] I except from such measures the Kingdom of Hungary, where much still remains to be done for religion, in which task I shall require the clergy there to cooperate, but not work with them alone, but concert chiefly with laymen on the principles to be followed, the chief aim of which must be to introduce seminaries, colleges, academies, hospitals for the sick and injured, conservatories (as in Italy) for unmarried women, for the better instruction of the young etc., taking careful pains to support and develop what is useful to the public, and not what profits the private advantage of the clergy, monks and nuns in any Province.[3]

This is an astonishing pronouncement coming from a young and devout monarch, still with a Jesuit confessor, and heiress to Charles VI who had yearned to complete a palace-monastery for himself by remodelling the ancient Augustinian house of Klosterneuburg.[4] It is deservedly a famous passage, and it has been asserted that from this utterance stems the whole gamut of Church legislation associated with her and with Joseph II, that what is known as Josephism or Josephinism actually derives from Maria Theresa's 'great remedy'.[5]

There are many difficulties about placing so much weight on this statement. The greatest is that, under examination, the programme, like the syntax, appears both incoherent and elusive. On the one hand, she says it is desirable that the Catholic religion should flourish and that the condition of the clergy should be good; on the other hand, *what is useful to the public* is a touchstone. She declares that monasteries should observe the limitations of their statutes and not admit idlers, but she does not condemn them in principle. She envisages different remedies for the central lands and for Hungary. It is with specific reference to Hungary that she makes one of her most radical statements, that she will require the clergy to co-operate with laymen in reform. But it sounds as though she thinks the Church in Hungary, unlike that in the central lands, needs *more* priests and *more* endowments. One cannot tell from her words what her concept of 'utility to the public' amounts to, or what her attitude is to monasteries of contemplative orders. The meaning of 'useful' can be almost infinitely variable. Even in Joseph II's reign, in 1781, one of his most trusted ministers, Count Hatzfeld, president of the Staatsrat, argued that contemplative orders ought to be regarded as contributing to *das allgemeine Beste* (the general advantage) through their prayers and worship.[6] It is virtually certain that Maria Theresa would have agreed with him.

If one takes down the nine volumes of Maria Theresa's published edicts, it is disconcerting to find that the third item, of early 1741, is a prohibition on erecting maypoles because it employs labour and wastes wood.[7] That might be an edict of Joseph's, though environmentalism seems here to take precedence over objections to superstition. Contrariwise, a month before he died, Joseph was taking great pains to ensure that the Catholic church founded by Joseph I in St Petersburg should be well supplied with silver, missals and vestments from dissolved monasteries, 'since [he said] it is highly desirable, indeed necessary, that I should give an example in supporting and glorifying my true religion, especially in foreign countries'.[8] He and his mother, for all their violent disputes, were not *diametrically* opposed to each other. Both wished in some sense to promote Roman Catholicism in their dominions. But many historians of the last fifty years, by urging that Joseph's measures derived directly from Maria Theresa's, have underrated the differences between them.

Despite what she said in the first version of her testament – no similar passage occurs in the second of 1756 – Maria Theresa did nothing concrete about general monastic reform until after 1765, when Joseph II succeeded his father and became Holy Roman Emperor and co-regent of the Austrian Monarchy. As emperor he had some rather ill-defined powers over the Church in the *Reich*. As co-regent he had no power in his own right, but much opportunity to put his views and influence policy. In a *Memorandum* of 1765 'on the defects of the present system and the most effectual means of remedying them', a document which is perhaps even more famous and notable than Maria Theresa's political testament, he set out his plans for the reform of the Monarchy. He devoted a section to the monasteries. He declares that they are too thriving for the good of the state. They ensnare people into taking vows who are too young to know what they are doing, thus depriving the state of the services of men of genius. He would raise the age of profession to twenty-five – that is a very big rise; it was legally sixteen for men, following the dictates of the Council of Trent. He would appoint a commission to investigate all monasteries, to reform them and use them 'for pious purposes which would be at the same time useful to the state, such as the education of children who, while becoming Christians, would become good subjects'. Perhaps one in twenty monasteries should be reformed, in order to distribute ecclesiastics more evenly over the country.

This pronouncement shows that Joseph had no thought of abolishing all monasteries, at least in 1765. To reform one in twenty is a very modest proposal. On the other hand, he spoke very ill of Catholic education, much of which was in monastic hands, and urged that it should be drastically reformed.[9]

At Maria Theresa's request, Prince Kaunitz, her chief minister, wrote a lengthy response, dated 18 February 1766, to the vast range of proposals in this *Memorandum*.[10] What he had to say on monasteries is unexpected – indeed, given his reputation as an Enlightened reformer of the Church, positively embarrassing. Maass, in his five indispensable volumes of documents on Josephism, whose thesis is that Kaunitz was the mastermind behind the movement, does not bring himself even to mention it;[11] and Dickson gives it only a reluctant footnote as evidence of Kaunitz's inconsistency.[12] The chancellor refutes the emperor's statements point by point. He questions whether there are too many monks in the German hereditary lands. There are only 23,000, he says – in fact this may be too high a figure.[13] He scoffs at the idea that they include thwarted geniuses. Most monks are virtually unemployable outside their houses, and there are too few benefices to go round in any case. The convents are performing a service by maintaining such people. Then he defends the usefulness of monasteries. Unless religious worship is to be curtailed, the monks' contribution to it is indispensable: 'It is true that there could be fewer monks if there were more secular priests. But it is not less true that the cost of priests is much higher than that of monks, for it is clear that three monks can live in a community on what it would be necessary to pay one priest living on his own.'

Among the assumptions behind this defence are, first, that the provision of parish priests is of prime concern to the state; secondly, that such provision is or ought to be the most important function of the Church, overriding all others; and thirdly, that monasteries have a vital role in this provision. Parish priests were considered to be central not only to strictly religious activity, as the Council of Trent had laid down, but also to the life of society as a whole, and to the state. Religious teaching, whether in church or in school, was seen as a first essential of education, and was expected to inculcate obedience and service to the state. How useful the parish clergy could be to the state was shown when Joseph compelled them to assist his reforms by ordering them to read certain of his edicts from the pulpit. The number of persons who thereby gained knowledge of his ordinances must have exceeded by hundreds of times the ordinary print-run of publications in this period.[14]

In countries other than the *Reich* and the Austrian Monarchy, monks were normally thought of as distinct from parish clergy. This separation was nowhere complete. Throughout the Catholic world, for example, the Premonstratensian Order exploited a unique papal privilege allowing it to supply parish clergy from its own ranks – 600 of them, for example, in France before the Revolution.[15] The rule of the Augustinian canons permitted them to work outside their monasteries. But in the German and Austrian lands other Orders did so too, in large numbers and as a normal practice – Franciscans, Benedictines and Cistercians for example. This point is seldom emphasised, and has sometimes not been grasped, by historians of the subject.[16] But, unless it is appreciated, neither Kaunitz's attitude to the monasteries in his memorandum, nor Joseph II's policy towards them, can be understood.

The Austrian duchies are the most striking case. In 1780 at least 20 per cent of all the land of Lower Austria was owned by monasteries, and more than 70 per cent of all clergy were monastic.[17] The Benedictine abbey of Melk, with an income of over 50,000 florins a year, supplied around twenty-five priests from its own numbers for the cure of souls in fourteen parishes.[18] In 1743 the Augustinian house of St Florian in Upper Austria, which was nearly as rich, had thirty-one of its canons, that is two-thirds of them, working out of the monastery in twenty-three parishes.[19] All large monasteries were also seminaries, and these clergy received their basic training in theology and philosophy in their houses. They did not necessarily go on to university, not even to the University of Salzburg, which was itself run by the Benedictines of St Peter's.[20]

Kaunitz, despite what he had said in replying to Joseph's *Memorandum* in 1766, began promoting monastic reform in the duchy of Milan, of which he was effectively the ruling minister, in 1767. He told Count Firmian, the governor there, that it would have to proceed step by step, because, first, it was necessary not to offend the religious sentiments of the sovereign, and, secondly, 'the number of monastic professions in Italy, though prodigious, is to some degree the result of the constitution of the country and of families'.[21] While Maria Theresa had to be humoured, pressure in the opposite direction from the new co-regent must have been a factor in Kaunitz's espousing monastic reform. An enquiry was set up, and in 1769 the process began of abolishing small convents. The same justification was put forward as Pope Innocent X had given in the mid-seventeenth century, that a house with fewer than twelve religious was not viable. A deal was then done by Maria Theresa's government with Pope Clement XIV under which small monasteries, rather than being straightforwardly dissolved, were united with others. The resulting rather limited profits were applied to parishes, hospitals and orphanages. By the death of Maria Theresa sixty-five out of 291 male monasteries had been suppressed in Lombardy, and the number of monks had fallen from 5,500 to 4,330. Only six out of 176 nunneries had gone, because the bishops fought for their retention. Monasteries had been suppressed mainly on the grounds that they were small, but with some regard to their 'uselessness' and to the possible utility of their buildings. These Italian measures are often treated as a trial run for the whole Monarchy, and this is true in the limited sense that any dissolutions constituted a precedent for other dissolutions. It is also true that much the same criteria were adopted in dissolving a rather similar proportion of the monasteries of Galicia soon after Austria acquired that province by the first partition of Poland in 1772. There 214 houses were reduced to 187, and 3,212 regulars to 2,895 by 1777.[22] But the situation in Lombardy was quite different from that in the German lands. Hardly any Italian monasteries were involved in parish provision, and they had no role in any form of Estates.

In 1770 Kaunitz emerged as a monastic reformer for the whole Monarchy. In this case he himself stated that he was partly influenced by the wishes of Joseph II. Kaunitz is now to be found vigorously arguing that the number of monks and nuns was 'far too high' and should be reduced by the state raising the age of profession to twenty-four. This should be done without papal authority or concurrence. It was clear, he said, that Protestant countries benefited from having fewer monks, and fewer celibates generally. Monasteries, because their property was inalienable, distorted the market in land. Monks are not necessary to Christianity – they are not to be found in the Church before the fourth century. Then he produced another telling calculation: 'A parish priest in the countryside with three chaplains or "co-operators" can provide worship and cure of souls for 4,000 persons.' If that is so, the same four clergymen can do as much in a town. Yet the density of clergy in Vienna is far higher than that. The position will be better in every way if there are fewer monks and priests but all have a genuine vocation.[23] He has certainly changed his tune since 1766, but he still assumes that many parish priests will be regulars. However, he insists that they must be educated not as they have been hitherto, but on the same basis as in the universities, according to a curriculum approved by the government. He does not yet propose that the training of priests be taken out of the hands of their monasteries altogether.

Maria Theresa agreed to raise the age of profession to twenty-four – not twenty-five, as appears in my *Joseph II* – and to imposing all kinds of often petty restrictions on monasteries, as to number of monks, reception of novices, education of priests, relations with superiors and foreign houses and so forth.[24] But she never appointed a commission of enquiry into them and she dissolved none in the

German lands or in Hungary – with the enormous exception of the Jesuits'.

In 1773 the Society of Jesus was completely suppressed in Maria Theresa's territories. This was a draconian measure, and of huge importance. I have dealt with it in Chapter 8, on 'Maria Theresa, Joseph II and the Suppression of the Jesuits', but it cannot be omitted here, especially as in this context some different points arise. Paradoxically, the story of the suppression of the Jesuits in the Austrian Monarchy reinforces the argument that Maria Theresa's policy – and even Joseph's – were not doctrinairely anti-monastic.[25]

At least until the late 1750s, the Jesuits were from many points of view the most powerful of all monastic orders in the Monarchy. Their houses were not so wealthy as the greater monasteries of the old Orders. They had no seats in the Estates. But, as the vanguard of the Counter-Reformation, they had acquired a near-monopoly of university education and the major role in secondary education. They played the chief part in the censorship of books and they supplied confessors to all members of the royal family.

In the 1750s Maria Theresa began to assail the monopolies and privileges of the Society. In 1759 they were deprived of their controlling position in the universities and the censorship, and in the following year the first non-Jesuit royal confessor was appointed. Whatever the long-term implications of these measures for the power of the Church, in the short run they were a victory both for the secular clergy as against the regulars, and for the old religious Orders as against the Jesuits. Theology could now, for example, be taught in universities by Benedictines, Augustinians and Dominicans, whose approach and tradition were different from the Jesuits'. When Maria Theresa chose a non-Jesuit confessor for herself in 1767, he was Ignaz Müller, provost of the Augustinian monastery of St Dorothea in Vienna. She came to believe that the moral teaching of the Jesuits was dangerous. In a certain sense she can even be classed as a Jansenist. She objected to certain aspects of baroque piety, she attached great importance to private devotions, and some of the religious books she recommended to her children were undoubtedly Jansenist.[26]

Meanwhile, much more drastic measures were being taken against the Jesuits in other Catholic countries. In 1765 they were expelled from France, as they had previously been from other Catholic countries. In the circumstances it is extraordinary that Joseph did not so much as mention the issue in his great *Memorandum* of that year, in which he discussed so many other matters; and nor did Kaunitz in his reply. Nor were the Jesuits considered in relation to the Italian monastic suppressions.[27]

In 1769–71 a great debate took place at the highest level about how a state educational system might be established in the Monarchy. The role of the Jesuits in education was so important that this was almost a debate about the Society. There were those who, like Count Pergen in a notorious paper of 1770, argued that all regular clergy should simply be debarred from any role in education because their influence was inevitably pernicious. But Maria Theresa, Joseph and Kaunitz, in a rare display of unanimity, all agreed that this was not a practical possibility. They concurred that there were nowhere near enough secular clergy, and especially secular clergy of calibre, to satisfy existing educational demands, let alone to man an expanded system. They went on to agree that, since it was necessary to go on using monks as teachers, it was essential to re-educate them so that they would not inculcate 'superstition' but would instead teach 'sane religion'. Contrary to what is commonly believed, Joseph and Kaunitz as well as – perhaps more than – Maria Theresa were admirers of the Jesuits, or at least of some of them and of some of what they did, especially in education and scholarship, and refused to assist actively the movement for their suppression. The rulers of Austria acquiesced in it eventually in order to please their Bourbon allies, who were determined to force the pope to suppress the Society completely. Joseph could of course see how the dissolution could be turned to advantage, provided that the Jesuits' property could be taken over by the state. A cartoon depicted him washing his hands and saying, 'I am innocent of the blood of this just Society'. But he believed that most of the criticisms made of their activities in other countries did not apply in the Monarchy.

The suppression meant the dissolution of 192 houses in Austria and Hungary. Afterwards, the rulers of Austria demanded permission from the pope to continue employing ex-Jesuits in education, where their services were held to be indispensable. Those who did not find new posts were given a pension. Other Catholic states were much less generous. In 1775 the empress gave remarkable testimony of her respect for Jesuit scholarship: she rejected the idea of forming a Vienna Academy on the grounds that she would become a laughing-stock, since nearly all those who could possibly be appointed to it were ex-Jesuits whom, in obedience to the pope, she had just turned out of their houses.[28]

So it was the pope and the other Catholic Powers who imposed on Maria Theresa and Joseph the suppression of the Jesuits. The only initiative she herself took in suppressing monasteries was the limited programme carried through in Lombardy and Galicia. On this basis it is hard to regard her actual legislation as amounting to the 'great remedy' which she spoke of in 1750 but never defined, or to the blueprint for Joseph's programme.

II

Within a few months of the death of Maria Theresa, Joseph set about serious reform of the monasteries in the Monarchy. It is worth stressing that he rarely offered as a justification the existence of abuses such as laxity, frivolity and cruelty in particular houses. He operated instead on general principles. He first abolished all the connections that existed between houses in his territories and superiors or monasteries in other states. Then, late in 1781, he decreed the suppression in the central lands of all purely contemplative monasteries which, being 'utterly and completely useless to their neighbours', 'could not be pleasing to God'. These were the houses of Orders such as the Carthusians whose rule and vows prohibited them from doing what Joseph saw as useful work.

He next turned to other Orders, intending that no monastery of any kind would be allowed to survive unless it performed a useful function. That meant, in Joseph's own first draft for the Council of State (Staatsrat), only educating youth or looking after sick persons. To these qualifying functions were added, after discussion, 'preaching, hearing confessions and attending deathbeds' and, later still, cure of souls.[29] In the summer of 1782 an Ecclesiastical Commission was established to implement this policy in the central lands and in Hungary. The emperor appointed as its chairman Freiherr von Kressel, declaring that under his direction he was confident the commission would produce 'in this business so near to my heart ... the best results for religion and the state'.[30] Thirty-two years after Maria Theresa had spoken in her political testament of applying a 'great remedy' to the Church, Joseph at last ordered a full survey of monasteries as part of an elaborate and detailed survey of all Church land. Pending its report, Joseph forbade monasteries to take any new novices. On 24 October 1783 a decree was issued that envisaged the establishment of new parishes wherever too many people were included within an existing parish or were too far away from an existing church. It was now within this context of improving the provision for the cure of souls that the fate of all monasteries was to be decided: 'Among monasteries, those will be retained which are necessary either to staff their own parishes or to assist the cure of souls, and for these houses an appropriate number of clergy will be laid down, enough to meet all contingencies. The other monasteries that are entirely unnecessary for the cure of souls will wither away [*gehen nach und nach ein*] ...' Monks were encouraged to leave their Order and become parish clergy or be pensioned. If they stayed in their Order, they might still become parish priests but otherwise would find themselves in the course of time moved, and brought together with members of other suppressed monasteries of their Order into one house until they died out. It must be emphasised that, unlike the initial dissolution of contemplative Orders, these measures were not, at least in principle, directed at entire Orders. Every single monastery was to be considered on its merits – a recipe for delay, uncertainty, ill feeling and inconsistency.[31]

The financial mechanics of the process were that the property of the suppressed houses, or the proceeds of its sale, was transferred to a Religious Fund, established early in 1782. Maria Theresa had set up a fund of the same name, but that was entirely devoted to converting Protestants to Catholicism.[32] The first charge on the new fund was the payment of pensions to the ejected monks and nuns who could not find employment. The emperor was especially hostile to nuns as almost wholly useless: they could not be priests, confessors or preachers, and few of them undertook charitable work. Most nunneries were therefore suppressed but, since former nuns were unlikely to find jobs, to pension them proved particularly costly. The second charge on the religious fund was the creation and endowment of the new parishes, parish clergy and parish churches.

How these measures worked in practice has not been fully studied, but Dr Ludwig Raber has written an excellent account of their impact on the Franciscan houses of Austria, with special reference to Lower Austria, in which he has published many of the original documents.[33] The Franciscan Order, of course, is a mendicant Order, which raises an important question not yet addressed: the emperor's attitude to begging. He would have liked to stop it altogether. He disapproved of it on principle, as obstructing market forces, discouraging people from working hard, and denying personal responsibility. He believed that the regularised mendicancy of the Orders imposed a special and unjustifiable burden on the poor. Further, he and his sympathisers thought that mendicant monks used improper spiritual inducements to extract alms, and that during their begging tours they preached superstition and bigotry. However, he was forced to admit that the monasteries of these Orders could not survive financially without some revenue additional to that supplied by their endowments. He was therefore compelled in the short run to make numerous exceptions to the prohibition on begging, and in the longer run to provide alternative revenue for the monks, confusingly known as pensions, further reducing the financial returns from his ecclesiastical measures.

There were sixteen Franciscan monasteries in Austria at the beginning of Joseph's reign. They were the largest single Order in the area. On the basis of the returns they made to the enquiry on ecclesiastical revenues and provision, the commission decided that thirteen of the sixteen should be suppressed, leaving only the three located in Vienna and its suburbs. These three were to supply parish priests from their own number, to house secular priests to whom some of the Franciscan monks would act as assistants in parish work, and to maintain a kind of reserve of clergy to stand in when incumbents were ill or absent or died. Perhaps the most striking detail to emerge from Raber's account is that the thirteen monasteries were not all suppressed at once. The bureaucracy pointed out that, under the terms of the emperor's edicts, this was impossible. In Raber's words,

> The priority was to make room in the monasteries by transferring the younger Fathers, and later the lay brothers, to the cure of souls or to other available posts. Thus a logical sequence was arrived at: monasteries were suppressed in order to procure personnel for the cure of souls, and monks were sent to parish work in order that monasteries could be dissolved.

The most that could be hoped for was to suppress one house a year, and that target was not always achieved. By the time Joseph died in February 1790, four of the thirteen houses had still not been dissolved, one saved by the intercession of the bishop of St Pölten, the others waiting their turn to be suppressed. The death of Joseph and the accession of Leopold II procured them a stay of execution. If this pattern was applicable to all Orders, it becomes easier to understand how Joseph's policy turned out to be less drastic in result than in intention. Some of the statistical uncertainties may spring from confusion between those houses that were actually suppressed and other houses that had been condemned but were not actually suppressed in time. This issue needs further research.

However, the policy of converting monks into parish clergy certainly achieved notable success with the Franciscans of Austria. Raber reports:

Between 1783 and 1790 were transferred to the cure of souls:

in the diocese of Linz	15 Fathers
in the diocese of St Pölten	55 Fathers
in the archdiocese of Vienna	107 Fathers
as army chaplains	4 Fathers
Total	181 Fathers

In Lower Austria there had been 325 Fathers in 1783. Clearly that figure is not calculated for the same area as those in the table, but it would appear that a very considerable proportion of all Franciscan priests – perhaps a half – became parish clergy.

Taking again the example of the Austrian duchies, according to Dickson's tables, 1,178 additional secular clergy, over and above the 6,500 recorded in 1780, were in post or in training in 1790 as a result of Joseph's suppressions. In the whole Monarchy, almost 5,000 secular clergy were added to the previous total.[34]

Suppression of monasteries and the creation of new parishes formed part of a much broader programme of Church reform. In 1783 all religious brotherhoods were dissolved – thousands of them, involving tens of thousands of lay persons. All seminaries run by bishops and monasteries were shut down, and it was decreed that all those training for the priesthood must go into the small number of new general seminaries established to teach the sort of theology and canon law that the regime approved. Not only begging, but also the giving of unsystematic charity, was condemned. All charity, or poor relief, was in future to be distributed by a single 'institution for the love of one's neighbour', relying on the confiscated funds of the brotherhoods and on contributions from the private sector.[35]

So far as the monasteries were concerned, it is important to understand that Joseph was not content with suppressing half of them outright. He did not leave the other half untouched. It was not only the dissolved monasteries whose funds were tapped. If a house had surplus revenue, the religious fund might take it without the house being dissolved. When an abbot died, Joseph generally forbade the monks to elect a successor. Instead, they were allowed to choose a prior to be the spiritual head of the institution on a three-year tenure, while an outsider, perhaps a lay man, was appointed to administer the temporalities to the benefit of the religious fund. This arrangement incidentally deprived the abbey of representation in the Estates. A house might be peremptorily ordered to create a new parish out of its existing benefices and to build a parish church out of its own revenues – as the Vienna Schottenstift was compelled to do with the church of St Laurenz in the eighth district of Vienna. According to a modern abbot, his predecessor in Joseph's reign, Benno Pointner,

> made a courageous stand against the Josephist pamphlets and also fought for the rights of the parishes, to which he sent at least half his priests for the cure of souls ... There was no avoiding the incorporation of more parishes into the foundation, so that the number of Schotten parishes reached 18 – a much too high number considering the heavy obligations associated with the foundation in Vienna. But perhaps that excessive burden was necessary in order to stave off the danger of the monastery's suppression by Joseph's administration or of the appointment of a so-called 'commendatory abbot' who would not have to belong to the Order.

Melk too now sent the majority of its monks into parishes. The Premonstratensian monastery of Geras raised the number of parishes it owned and serviced from ten to seventeen. Between 1782 and 1791 it spent 14,000 florins on four new priest-houses, eight schools and a new church.[36] This must have been the pattern in all the surviving houses, except for the few which had been allowed to exist because of their contribution to education and the care of the sick rather than because they provided parishes and clergy. Overall figures appear not to be available, but the increased provision of parish clergy by the remaining monasteries from the ranks of their own monks must have added substantially to the total number of those charged with the cure of souls, over and above those supplied by the religious fund. Doubtless these people would have been classed as regulars in the statistics.

With their young monks away at the general seminaries and their able-bodied priests working in parishes, monasteries found it difficult, if not impossible, to maintain a proper community life. Choral services were drastically cut down on the ground that, now that monks were required to be useful, all this singing, especially in the middle of the night, would be injurious to their health and therefore to the spiritual well-being of their flocks. Half the monasteries survived, it is true, but only as half-monasteries. In cases where it seemed to the government more convenient or economical, they were allowed to live on, but as depleted, cowed communities to be bullied, mulcted, scattered, and stripped of their traditions, of their independence and of their role in the Estates.[37]

III

In attempting to answer the question why Joseph allowed so many monasteries to survive, another part of the explanation must lie in the relations between the emperor and his civil servants. New light is thrown on this aspect of the problem, as on the whole story of Joseph's reign, by material in the despatches sent to Rome by the papal nuncios, Giuseppe Garampi down to 1785 and Giovanni Battista Caprara thereafter.[38] For ordinary purposes the despatches of nuncios are not as valuable for this as for earlier periods, when the pope was a militant player in international politics. But on religious questions, which in Joseph's reign bulked so large, the reports of Garampi and Caprara are far superior to those of other envoys. While 2,500 parish priests in Austria could be compelled to read the emperor's edicts from the pulpit, at least as many clergy may well have been happy to provide unsolicited information to the pope's representatives. Although some of their despatches have been published, many of them have been neglected by historians,[39] and they turn out to be wonderfully full.

Among their most interesting features are the strikingly different impressions that the two nuncios give of Joseph II's relationship with his officials. Garampi, who had been in Vienna during the last five years of Maria Theresa's reign, was emphatic that tremendous changes were occurring. Even before a single monastery had been suppressed, he talked of 'a crisis similar to that which the Church suffered in the sixteenth century'.

> All the regulars [he wrote] are so shaken that they not only carry out punctiliously the orders they receive but they actually go beyond the royal instructions ... I'm reminded at this juncture of the fatalism of the Turks who, unnerved by the fear that their monarchy is in decay,

calmly await its end, making no effort to prevent it, and excusing their supine inaction as what they call resignation to the divine will and to the inevitability of Fate.

He had no doubt at all that the emperor himself was the prime mover and that he was having to dragoon his officials into implementing his policy. Garampi informed Rome in July 1781, and again in November, that he could not square it with his conscience to administer the Easter sacrament to Joseph, the nuncio's traditional privilege, because his measures revealed him to be a Jansenist heretic. This suggestion clearly alarmed the pope and must have helped to induce him to make his famous journey to Vienna, where he arrived in time to administer communion personally to the emperor on Easter Day.[40]

One of the commonplaces of historians, without a single exception, is that the president of the ecclesiastical commission, Baron Kressel, said to have been a Freemason, was a zealous promoter of Church reform.[41] As we have seen, Joseph thought so too. But on 5 May 1783 Garampi, in one of his huge, especially confidential despatches sent by safe courier, reported a secret conversation with Kressel. The baron

> in no way concealed the torment he suffered [in carrying through these reforms]; but he added that ... despite his feelings he remains in his post, no longer with the hope of doing good, but merely of diminishing evil. He foresees that, if he gives it up, there are now too many capital enemies of the Church and blind flatterers of the sovereign who would weakly follow instantly every hasty idea or command he gives.

Kressel, while bitterly regretting the harm done to the Church, thinks he has succeeded in minimising its effects. 'He assured me that, once the emperor has adopted a principle, it is a waste of time to try to oppose it. The only thing to do is to bring up one by one the difficulties that make it awkward to carry out.' By this means, he said, he had succeeded in preventing Joseph carrying out his plan to put all clergy on fixed salaries, and had persuaded him that the best course was to leave them with their possessions and in control of them. He believes that anyone else would have acquiesced in Joseph's scheme of destroying all ecclesiastical foundations. Some of his colleagues, he said, 'professed a hatred of everything that is piety, church, order, hierarchy and monks'. He reckoned that 'the multiplication of parishes was a bottomless pit for which the funds would never suffice'.[42]

The nuncio can hardly have invented this conversation, surprising though it is, and Kressel would hardly have spoken in this foolhardy way if he had not felt passionately about these issues. Had Joseph known of Kressel's private views and of his contacts with the nuncio, far from expressing such confidence in him, he would surely have sacked him. But the obstruction Kressel describes himself as practising is uncannily like the sort of behaviour Joseph complained of among bureaucrats in his famous pastoral letter of December 1783.[43] The bitter disputes among his servants, and their secret undermining of his plans, go far to account for the dilution of his policies as they were translated into decrees.

On the other hand, as the nuncios realised with horror, there were also genuine radicals near the centre of power. Joseph von Sonnenfels, famous as professor of political economy, dramatic critic, official censor and Freemason, wrote confidently and rejoicingly, when the Jesuits were dissolved, that all other Orders would shortly follow.[44] Ignaz von Born, a noted metallurgist and an even more prominent Freemason than Sonnenfels, published in 1783 *Monachologia*, a satirical classification of monks on the Linnaean system, anticipating the extinction of all their species.[45] The progressive canonist, Johann Valentin Eybel, wrote not only *Was ist der Pabst?* [*What is the Pope?*], *Sieben Kapitel von Klosterleuten* [*Seven Chapters of Monks and Nuns*], and sundry other pamphlets highly critical of the traditional Church, but was also employed by Joseph II as ecclesiastical commissioner in Upper Austria, where he derived particular pleasure from ordering great abbots about and taking part in the formalities attending the suppression of monastic houses.[46]

Caprara was as certain as Garampi had been that it was Joseph who genuinely took the decisions. But he saw the emperor, for all that he abominated his measures, as the only bulwark against still worse changes. Joseph alone, he thought, stood in the way of the total abolition of clerical celibacy, which Eybel and others advocated. If Caprara both exaggerated the influence of the extremists and sometimes proved too optimistic about Joseph's attitudes, he was certainly right that the emperor's radicalism had its limits, and that a married clergy was beyond them.[47] Joseph undoubtedly saved some monasteries from suppression. Eybel kept on recommending that the great house of St Florian should be dissolved to endow the new bishopric of Linz. In the end the bishop was assigned some of the monastery's revenues and the provost's house in Linz for his palace.

But Joseph ordered Eybel never again to raise the question of suppressing the foundation. It was too useful as a provider of parish priests.[48] In Bohemia, the emperor was asked to suppress the rich Premonstratensian house at Strahov on the castle hill in Prague. It had just built itself a second 'philosophical' library to match its 'theological' library of the seventeenth century. In so doing it used bookcases and accommodated books from dissolved monasteries, and placed a bust of Joseph in the pediment of the new building. He declared the monastery too useful to destroy.[49] On the other hand, as late as 1789, the emperor agreed to suppress the major Cistercian monastery of Lilienfeld on the special ground that its spendthrift abbot had run it into debt. Since the religious fund was overstretched, Joseph's officials were always looking for excuses for dissolving juicy foundations.[50]

The emperor had travelled a long way since he had proposed to his mother in 1765 that one in twenty monasteries should be abolished. Evidence known to me does not settle the question whether by the end of his life he would have had any religious qualms about suppressing all monasteries. But he certainly still held the view that there were practical advantages in preserving some of them.

IV

In her testament of 1750 Maria Theresa had promised to give special treatment to Hungary, 'where much remains to be done for religion'. It is likely that she had in mind, first, that there remained many Protestants in Hungary – perhaps a quarter of the population – and that the campaign waged by the Catholic Church, with the support of the Habsburg dynasty, to convert them to Rome had so far achieved only partial success. Secondly, she must have known that the overall provision of Catholic parishes was thin. To try to remedy this lack, her father Charles VI had established in 1733 a fund to create new parishes. But after her death, while the population of Hungary was twice as large as that of the Austrian lands, there were one-and-a-half times as many Austrian as Hungarian clergy, and the total revenues of the Hungarian Church fell much below those of the Austrian. The provision was also very uneven. In the western and north-western counties the Church was strong and comparatively rich, in the rest of the country much less so. In two of the ten districts into which Joseph divided Hungary, his inspectors in 1786–87 credited the Church with a million florins of income, and four districts had over a thousand clergy. In four there were under five hundred clergy and Church income was under 300,000 florins. This variation arose partly because some of the strongholds of Protestantism lay in the east. But that itself had much more to do with the historical experience of the different regions of the country. The extreme west had experienced only rare Turkish incursions and was closely tied to Austria. An intervening area had been won back from the Turks immediately after the siege of Vienna of 1683. But the more easterly regions had come under the effective control of the Habsburgs only after the great Rákóczi revolt had been defeated in 1711. Here the Catholic Church was truly a missionary church. The central and western lands of the Monarchy had seen a massive rebuilding and refurbishing of churches and monasteries in the late seventeenth and early eighteenth centuries – by Italian standards a much delayed flowering of the Counter-Reformation. The Hungarian Counter-Reformation came even later, and Hungarian churches were mostly rebuilt from ruins or from scratch in the eighteenth century, and in a distinctly less opulent manner than to the west. Whereas the Austrian Church seems virtually to have stopped building and to have lost its missionary *élan* around 1750, the Hungarian Church was advancing and expanding right up to Joseph's accession.[51]

In Marczali's words:

> In the counties formerly occupied by the Turks, where there was scarcely any other foe to contend with except the havoc and destruction that had been wrought, and where the life not merely of the Catholic Church but of Western Christianity had become entirely extinct, the chief rôle among the champions of the Church was still played by the Franciscans ... their numbers continually grew in dimensions.[52]

In Hungary there were four times as many mendicants, mainly Franciscans, as endowed monks, whereas in Austria the mendicants outnumbered the non-mendicants by less than two to one. The ancient Orders that dominated Austria had only a few houses in Hungary, and their role in the Church was relatively insignificant. One of them, Benedictine Pannonhalma, celebrated its nine-hundredth anniversary in 1996, but in fact they had ceased to exist during the Turkish occupation and had to be refounded after the Turks had been driven out. The relative poverty and weakness of Hungarian monasteries overall is shown by the following table, based on Dickson's figures:[53]

TABLE 9.1 Monastic numbers and wealth in Lower Austria and Hungary

Area	Population (approx. million)	Mendicants	Endowed monks	Monastic revenue (approx. million florins)
Lower Austria	1	1,805	1,047	1.4
Hungary	8	3,736	988	1.2

So Maria Theresa was absolutely right that the religious situation in Hungary was markedly different from that in the central and western lands of the Monarchy. However, despite what she said in her testament of 1750, her legislation did not take much account of the difference. The most distinctive of her Hungarian Church measures, apart from those especially concerning the Greek Orthodox minority, was the establishment of three new bishoprics in 1777, though even that was paralleled in Bohemia.[54]

Joseph's approach was in some respects the opposite of his mother's. His travels had given him unique first-hand knowledge of the varied character of his dominions. But this only strengthened his determination to unite his disparate territories and to make them as uniform as possible. In his orders to the Hungarian authorities he regularly spoke of the need for *Gleichförmigkeit* in the Monarchy's legislation. His instructions about monastic reform were virtually identical for Hungary and the central lands, and Kressel's Ecclesiastical Commission, despite considerable Hungarian opposition, was placed in charge of both areas.[55] But the situation in Hungary was so unlike the position in Austria that identical policies, administered by the same men, produced significantly different results.

One perhaps unimportant difference was that the main group of suppressions, which in Austria began in 1783, did not start in Hungary until 1786–87, which was when the enquiry into the Church's revenues reported. Once the process had started, however, it seems to have proceeded rapidly. As always, it is difficult to establish precise figures for monastic suppressions. A major part of the problem is that the emperor's officials used varying definitions of Hungary, and it is not easy for historians to sort them out and decide between them. The most thorough study, a recently published article by Péter Bán, relying on a series of tables prepared for the Hungarian Diet of 1790–91, concludes that, in Hungary widely defined, there were 255 monasteries in 1782, *not including those of the Piarists, the Brothers of Mercy and the Basilians*. Out of the 255, 136 were dissolved and 119 survived.[56] To make the comparison with Lower Austria again, Dickson's calculations show that in 1790 the revenue of that province's monasteries was still almost a million florins, having been reduced by only a third since 1780. In Hungary total monastic revenue was in 1790 less than 600,000 florins, under half the total in 1780. However, both in Lower Austria and in Hungary the number of regulars in 1790 was about half the number in 1780.[57]

In total contrast to what happened in the German lands (and in Belgium), in Hungary only two of the eight Benedictine houses, and those not the richest, were spared, and all eight Premonstratensian houses were suppressed. Despite the prejudice of the emperor and his supporters against mendicant Orders, eighty-one out of 116 Franciscan houses and eleven out of nineteen Capuchin houses survived.[58] This difference between Hungary and other parts of the Monarchy has scarcely been noticed, let alone studied. Much more research is needed before a full analysis can be provided. But here is a tentative explanation. The abbots of the great Hungarian monasteries had places in the Diet, but they were few and unimportant compared with their Austrian counterparts. In Hungary the bishops, and especially the archbishop of Esztergom, dominated the First Estate.[59] However, this difference was of limited importance because Joseph had no intention of calling a Diet, whereas the Austrian Estates continued, if grudgingly, to work with his government. He deliberately flouted Hungarian susceptibilities, imposing his preferred policies regardless of opposition. It must be significant that, unlike in Austria, the monasteries he suppressed in Hungary were the rich ones. The Benedictine and Premonstratensian houses might be few, but they were on average *forty* times wealthier than Franciscan houses.[60] In the case of Pannonhalma at least, there was an inconclusive negotiation between the monastery and the government as to whether the monks would run a school in order to make their institution qualify as useful. It appears that even the Premonstratensians supplied few parish priests, but they surely could have supplied more.[61] Presumably, given the especially poor provision of clergy and the relatively low income of the Church in Hungary, the government simply could not finance the creation and maintenance of a satisfactory number of new parish clergy without taking over the revenues of the particularly wealthy monasteries. It was the Franciscans who had been conspicuous in parochial work before 1780, and it is to be presumed that they played an even greater role in it after Joseph II's reforms. Overall, the suppressions seem to have made it possible to supply 2,212 additional secular clergy for Hungary, a percentage increase much greater than elsewhere in the Monarchy.[62]

V

The policy of Joseph II towards the monasteries owed little to his mother's example. She took only limited measures against them, and much of what she did do – most importantly, the raising of the age of profession – was influenced by his views. There is no reason to think that she was hostile to contemplative monasteries as such, or to nunneries, two of Joseph's main targets. But his overriding concern was to improve parochial provision, either by dissolving monasteries and using the resulting funds to create new parishes and parish clergy, or by forcing surviving monasteries to make such provision themselves.

Both Garampi and Caprara may have been right in their differing estimates of the emperor's role in the 1780s. At the beginning of his sole reign he was goading a reluctant bureaucracy to drastic reform. By the end, many of the officials in charge of ecclesiastical matters were extremists whom he was reining in. The treatment meted out to the surviving monasteries showed little respect for their rules and traditions, and seemed to threaten the whole basis of monasticism. But, in the central lands at least, many of the major communities managed to maintain themselves after a fashion. When Joseph died in February 1790, it was still easy to muster the prescribed eight mitred abbots to accompany his corpse to the crypt of the Capuchins.[63]

By then the French Revolution had withdrawn state recognition from monastic vows and seized most Church lands. In the Monarchy, however, Joseph's successor Leopold inaugurated at almost the same time the opposite process of restoring the monasteries' position, abolishing the general seminaries and permitting the revival of theological training in the cloister, re-establishing Lilienfeld and allowing abbots to be elected. He seemed to agree in principle to the restoration of some Hungarian monasteries, but no action was taken.[64] In 1801 Francis I was finally persuaded to assist the revival of the old Orders in

Hungary, and in 1827 he permitted new foundations of contemplative Orders in his Empire.[65] Though he maintained Joseph's ecclesiastical position in most respects, here he diverged from it. Those monasteries that had been spared in Austria now enjoyed again the favour of the government, some of them were given an important role in higher education, and they could return to a monastic regimen closer to that of the period before 1770.

A book published in 1951 to celebrate the mere five-hundredth anniversary of the Franciscan Order in Austria contains this passage: 'Certainly parishes were imposed on us by necessity, for both under Joseph II and also under the Nazi persecution the acceptance of a parish was the last expedient to preserve the monastery from suppression ... [But] what originally happened under duress is also in the line of modern development, and it is possible to see here the hand of Providence.'[66]

Austrian monasteries play a larger role in parochial work than those of any other European country. This peculiarity, and the fact that Austria is the one state in Europe where a large number of ancient and splendid Catholic houses can boast a continuous existence from the middle ages into the twentieth century, are largely explained by the complex story of Joseph II's dealings with the monasteries.

Notes

This chapter first appeared in N. Aston (ed.), *Religious Change in Europe, 1650–1914. Essays for John McManners* (Oxford, 1997). A modified version, incorporating some new material, can be found in my *Prosperity and Plunder: European Catholic Monasteries in the Age of Revolution, 1650-1815* (Cambridge, 2003), ch. 8.

1 This essay follows from the discussion of monasteries and their reform in P. G. M. Dickson, *Finance and Government under Maria Theresia* (2 vols, Oxford, 1987), esp. vol. I, chs 4, 11 and pp. 103, 446, and 'Joseph II's Reshaping of the Austrian Church', *Historical Journal* [hereafter *HJ*], 36 (1993), pp. 89–114. Professor Dickson not only gave me copies of these works but has been unfailingly generous with help and advice over many years. He made most useful comments on an earlier draft of this chapter.

On the Estates see also H. Stradal, 'Die Prälatenkurie der österreichischen Landstände', *Anciens pays et assemblées d'états*, 53 (1970): 117–80.

The Austrian provinces of the eighteenth century include all of modern Austria except Salzburg and its region, which then made up an independent prince-archbishopric, and Burgenland, then a part of Hungary. On the other hand, part of the Tyrol and all of Further Austria are no longer Austrian territory.

There is no general survey of the history or place of monasteries in the Austrian Monarchy.

2 J. Kallbrunner (ed.), *Kaiserin Maria Theresias politisches Testament* (Vienna, 1952), has the best text of the testament. A. Ritter von Arneth, 'Zwei Denkschriften der Kaiserin Maria Theresias', *Archiv für österriechische Geschichte* [hereafter *AÖG*], XLVII (1871): 267–354, is more accessible. On the dates of the two versions see Dickson, *Finance and Government*, vol. II, p. 3n. On the constitutional reform, F. Walter, *Die theresianische Staatsreform von 1749* (Vienna, 1958).

3 Kallbrunner, *Kaiserin Maria Theresias politisches Testament*, p. 38.

4 D. Beales, *Joseph II. I: In the Shadow of Maria Theresa, 1741–1780* (Cambridge, 1987), p. 23.

5 See F. Maass, *Der Josephinismus. Quellen zu seiner Geschichte in Österreich, 1760–1850* (Fontes rerum austriacarum [FRA], 5 vols, Vienna, 1951–61), vol. I, pp. 5–9 and *Der Frühjosephinismus* (Vienna, 1969); E. Wangermann, *The Austrian Achievement, 1700–1800* (London, 1973), pp. 74–88.

6 C. Freiherr von Hock, *Der österreichischer Straatsrath* (Vienna, 1879), pp. 397–8.

7 *Sammlung aller k.k. Verordnungen und Gesetze vom Jahre 1740, bis 1780 ...* (9 vols, Vienna, 1787), vol. I, p. 6.

8 Hock, *Staatsrath*, p. 413.

9 A. Ritter von Arneth (ed.), *Maria Theresia und Joseph II. Ihre Correspondenz* (3 vols, Vienna, 1867–68), vol. III, pp. 348–51.

10 Kaunitz's response to Joseph's *Memorandum* was published in A. Beer, 'Denkschriften des Fürsten Wenzel Kaunitz-Rittberg', *AÖG*, XLVIII (1872). See esp. pp. 107–9.

11 See n.5 above. Maass does make one back-handed reference to the document in his article 'Vorbereitung und Anfänge des Josephinismus im amtlichen Schriftwechsel des Staatskanzlers ... mit ... Firmian, 1763 bis 1770', *Mitteilungen des österreichischen Staatsarchivs* [hereafter *MÖSA*], I (1948): 301.

12 Dickson, *HJ*, 36 (1993): 97n.

13 Ibid., 94ff.

14 Ibid., 97n. My calculation is as follows: in the Austrian duchies there were about 2,500 parishes. If we suppose that only 100 persons on average attended the main service at which these edicts were read out, 250,000 heard them in Austria alone.

15 J. de Viguerie (ed.), *La vocation religieuse et sacerdotale en France. XVII–XIX Siècles* (Angers, 1979), p. 52.

16 P. von Mitrofanov in *Joseph II.* (2 vols, Vienna, 1910) appears to miss this point, and even Dickson (see n.1 above) barely refers to it. It emerges clearly from such works as G. Winner, *Die Klosteraufhebungen in Niederösterreich und Wien* (Vienna, 1967); *Welt des Barock* (2 vols, Linz, 1986); *Josefinische Pfarrgründungen in Wien* (Historisches Museum der Stadt Wien, 1985); L. Raber, *Die österreichischen Franziskaner im Josefinismus* (Maria Enzersdorf, ?1983).

17 Dickson, *Finance and Government*, vol. I, p. 103 and *HJ* (1993): 95–8.

18 B. Ellegast, 'Vernunft und Glaube' in *900 Jahre Benediktiner in Melk* (Melk, 1989), p. 364, and data in the permanent exhibition on view at Melk.

19 F. Reisinger, 'Ein Herz und eine Seele in Gott', *Welt des Barock* (2 vols, Linz, 1986), vol. II, p. 326.

20 For the University of Salzburg, most recently, H. Klueting (ed.), *Katholische Aufklärung – Aufklärung im katholischen Deutschland* (Hamburg, 1993), esp. the essays of G. Heilingsetzer and L. Hammermayer.

21 C. Capra in D. Sella and C. Capra, *Il ducato di Milano dal 1535 al 1796* (vol. XI of *Storia d'Italia*, ed. G. Galasso, Turin, 1984), p. 398 (19 Nov. 1768). Kaunitz is presumably referring to the practice, widespread and generally accepted among the Italian landed classes, of placing surplus sons and (especially) daughters in monasteries.

22 Ibid., pp. 398–400, 497 for the whole paragraph. For Galicia, H. Glassl, *Das österreichische Einrichtungswerk in Galizien (1772–1790)* (Wiesbaden, 1975), pp. 135–40.

23 Maass, *Josephinismus*, vol. II, pp. 139–41.

24 See Beales, *Joseph II*, pp. 450–2 and the sources there cited. I owe thanks to Professor E. Wangermann for pointing out to me my mistake about the age of profession.

25 See pp. 214–20.

26 Beales, *Joseph II*, pp. 54, 60, 65–6, 81, 441–4. The classic treatment is G. Klingenstein, *Staatsverwaltung und kirchliche Autorität im 18. Jahrhundert* (Vienna, 1970). Cf. P. Hersche, 'War Maria Theresia eine Jansenistin?', *Österreich in Geschichte und Literatur*, 15 (1971): 14–25 and his important book, *Der Spätjansenismus in Österreich* (Vienna, 1977).

27 See nn.9 and 10 above.

28 For this and the previous paragraph Beales, *Joseph II*, pp. 455–64; Dickson, *Finance and Government*, vol. I, pp. 65–8. More recently, on education, J. V. H. Melton, *Absolutism and the Eighteenth-century Origins of Compulsory Schooling in Prussia and Austria* (Cambridge, 1988), esp. pp. 204–9. On Pergen, P. P. Bernard, *From the Enlightenment to the Police State: The Public Life of Johann Anton Pergen* (Urbana, 1991), esp. ch. 3. Franz A. J. Szabo, *Kaunitz and Enlightened Absolutism 1753–1780* (Cambridge, 1994), esp. pp. 241–7, supports this view of Kaunitz's attitude to the Jesuits. For the cartoon about Joseph, Winner, *Klosteraufhebungen*, p. 29.

29 For this and the previous paragraph Hock, *Staatsrath*, pp. 295–6.

30 Joseph to Kressel, 22 July 1782: H. Schlitter (ed.), *Pius VI. und Josef II.* (FRA XLVII/2, Vienna, 1894), pp. 147–8. Schlitter prints the draft instruction for the Ecclesiastical Commission on pp. 41–6.

31 *Sammlung der kaiserlichen-königlichen Landesfürstlichen Gesetze und Verordnungen in Publico-Ecclesiasticis vom Jahre 1782 bis 1783* (Vienna, 1784), pp. 109–13.

32 Hock, *Staatsrath*, p. 415.

33 For this and the next para., Raber, *Die österreichischen Franziskaner*, passim. The quotations come from pp. 139 and 236. See esp. p. 219. Dickson,

HJ (1993), draws attention to the importance of the distinction between mendicant and other Orders.

34 Dickson, *HJ* (1993): 105, 110.

35 A convenient account of the whole policy is E. Bradler-Rottmann, *Die Reformen Kaiser Josephs II.* (Göppingen, 1973), ch. VI. On brotherhoods, P. Ardaillou, 'Les confréries viennoises aux 17e et 18e siècles', *Revue d'histoire ecclésiastique*, LXXXVII (1992): 745–58.

36 J. Kellner (ed.), *Pfarre Sankt Lorenz am Schottenfeld 1786–1796* (St Pölten, 1986). H. Peichl, 'Die Schottenabtei in der Neuzeit' in F. Krones (ed.), *800 Jahre Schottenabtei* (Vienna, 1960), pp. 56–7. For Melk see Ellegast's article (n.18 above), pp. 362–4; for Geras, J. Ambrósy and A. J. Pfiffig, *Stift Geras und seine Kunstschätze* (St Pölten, 1989), p. 34.

37 See the accounts of Winner, Klosteraufhebungen, and R. Hittmair, *Der josefinische Klostersturm im Land ob der Enns* (Freiburg im Breisgau, 1907).

38 Archivio segreto vaticano: Nunziatura di Vienna [hereafter ASVNV], 179–84, 197A, 199–200. I am grateful to Mgr Charles Burns for much generous help during my work in the Vatican Archives.

39 H. Schlitter in *Die Reise des Papstes Pius VI nach Wien* and *Pius VI und Josef II* (FRA XLVII, Vienna, 1892, 1894) uses these files and gives extensive extracts from them, but it seems clear that many of the most confidential documents were not available to him. G. Soranzo, *Peregrinus apostolicus* (Milan, 1937) is rather fuller on the papal side. E. Kovács, *Der Pabst in Teutschland* (Munich, 1983) relies on these two works. T. Vanyó, *A bécsi pápai követség levéltárának iratai Magyarországról, 1611–1786* (Budapest, 1986) is largely confined to references to specifically Hungarian affairs. I am grateful to Professor István Tóth for the reference to Vanyó's book. Since I wrote this chapter Father Umberto Dell'Orto, with whom I had valuable conversations in Rome, has generously sent me a copy of his very important study, *La Nunziatura a Vienna di Giuseppe Garampi, 1776–1785* (Collectanea Archivi Vaticani, Vatican City, 1995).

40 ASVNV, 180, Garampi's despatches of 20 July and 18 November 1781.

41 E.g. E. Wangermann, *From Joseph II to the Jacobin Trials* (2nd edn, Oxford, 1969), p. 6; L. Bodi, *Tauwetter in Wien* (Frankfurt, 1977), p. 228.

42 ASVNV, 182, Garampi's despatch of 5 May 1783, section on 'Kroesel'.

43 *Joseph des Zweyten Erinnerung an seine Staatsbeamten, am Schlusse des 1783ten Jahres* (Vienna, [1783]).

44 *Sonnenfels gesammelte Schriften* (10 vols, Vienna, 1783–87), vol. VIII, pp. 329–30 (from *Deutsches Museum*, Apr. 1782).

45 The first edition was in Latin: *Joannis Physiophili Specimen Monachologiae methodo Linnaeana* (Augsburg, 1783).

46 See Bodi, *Tauwetter in Wien*, pp. 53, 125. Hittmair, *Der josefinische Klostersturm* is very informative about Eybel's activities in Upper Austria, and M. Brandl, *Der Kanonist Joseph Valentin Eybel (1741–1805): Sein Beitrag zur Aufklärung in Österreich* (Steyr, 1976) about his writings.

47 E.g. Caprara's despatch of 3 Aug. 1786 (ASVNV, 199). Cf. Dickson, *HJ* (1993): 97n.

48 Hittmair, *Der josefinische Klostersturm*, pp. 253–4.

49 Hock, *Staatsrath*, p. 407; F. and R. Malecek, *Strahov Praha* (Prague, ?1993). I owe the latter reference to Dr L. C. Van Dijck.

50 For supplying me with material about the case of Lilienfeld I am very grateful to Mag. E. Fattinger.

51 My main published sources on the Hungarian Church are Dickson, *Finance and Government*, vol. I, esp. ch. 4, and his article in *HJ* (1993); H. Marczali, *Hungary in the Eighteenth Century* (Cambridge, 1910), esp. ch. IV; B. K. Király, 'The Hungarian Church' in the maddeningly footnote-less collection, W. J. Callahan and D. Higgs, *Church and Society in Catholic Europe in the Eighteenth Century* (Cambridge, 1979); and L. Csóka, *Geschichte des benediktinischen Mönchtums in Ungarn* (Studia Hungarica, Munich, 1980), esp. pp. 312–64. For sources in the Hungarian National Archives see n.55 below – my comments on uneven provision derive from file C.107 of the Ecclesiastical Commission, reinforced by the graphic evidence in the remarkable articles of G. Tüskés and E. Knapp, esp. 'Österreichisch-ungarische interethnische Verbindungen im Spiegel des barockzeitlichen Wallfahrtwesens', *Bayerisches Jahrbuch für Volkskunde* (1990), pp. 1–42, and 'Bruderschaften in Ungarn im 17. und 18. Jahrhundert', ibid. (1992), pp. 1–23.

Many Hungarian scholars have helped me to understand better the differences between the Hungarian and Austrian churches. I should particularly like to thank here Professor D. Kosáry and Professor L. Péter.

52 Marczali, *Hungary in the Eighteenth Century*, p. 271.

53 From *Finance and Government*, vol. I, pp. 35 and 39, and *HJ* (1993): 98.

54 J. Tomko, *Die Errichtung der Diözesen Zips, Neusohl und Rosenau (1776) und das königliche Patronatsrecht in Ungarn* (Vienna, 1968). I owe this reference to Professor R. J. W. Evans.

55 These remarks are based partly on research in the Hungarian National Archives on the collections of Joseph's Normalia (A 58) and the papers of the Ecclesiastical Commission (C 70–107). Professor Éva Balázs made my work there possible, and I was greatly assisted by Dr Éva Hoós and Dr Márta Velladics, who unselfishly abstracted material for me and directed me to appropriate files. I owe special thanks too to the staff of the National Archives, who gave me help far beyond the call of duty.

56 P. Bán, 'Új adatok a szerzetesrendek II. József korabeli megszüntetéséröl', *Baranya*, III (1990–91): 61–71. The three Orders mentioned are excluded because none of their houses was dissolved. Dr Velladics very kindly supplied me with a photocopy of Bán's important article, since corrected in significant ways by her own work, still largely unpublished.

Dickson's figure of 117 Hungarian monasteries dissolved (*Finance and Government*, vol. I, p. 76) refers to a smaller definition of Hungary, but still including Croatia. His figure of 154 as the total number before dissolution (ibid., p. 446 and *HJ* [1993]: 114n.) is not comparable, since it excludes e.g. Croatia. M. von Schwartner, *Statistik des Königreiches Ungern* (2 vols, Budapest, 1809), vol. I, p. 171, gives a figure of 147 Hungarian monasteries spared by Joseph II, including Piarist houses.

57 Dickson, *HJ* (1993): 98, 108.

58 Bán, *Baranya* (1990): 61–2, 65–6.

59 Dr I. Szijártó informs me that only three abbots had seats in the Diet.

60 Bán, *Baranya* (1990): 68.

61 Cf. Csóka, *Geschichte des benediktinischen Mönchtums in Ungarn*, pp. 348–52, 262. The tables in C.107 (see n.55 above) give tiny figures for monks acting as parish clergy in Hungary before 1786 (cf. Dickson, *HJ* [1993]: 101, n.30, for figures for other provinces).

62 Dickson, *HJ* (1993): 105.

63 ASVNV, 200, Caprara's despatch of 22 Feb. 1790.

64 Winner, *Klosteraufhebungen*; Maass, *Josefinismus*, vol. IV, esp. pp. 3–13.

65 Maass, *Josefinismus*, vol. IV, 51; J. L. E. Graf von Barth-Barthenstein, *Das Ganze der österreichischen politischen Administration* (4 vols, Vienna, 1838–43), vol. II, p. 133. This of course helps to account for the fact, noted by Dickson (*HJ* [1993]: 114), that there were more Hungarian monasteries in 1847 than in 1780.

66 *500 Jahre Franziskaner der österreichischen Ordens-Provinz* (Vienna, 1951), p. 189. Cf. J. Hollnsteiner, 'Die Orden und Kongregationen in Österreich', in A. Hudal (ed.), *Der Katholizismus in Österreich* (Innsbruck, 1931), pp. 110–19.

The Origins of the Pope's Visit to Joseph II in 1782

No event of Joseph II's reign aroused more interest across Europe than the visit paid to him in Vienna by Pope Pius VI in the spring of 1782.[1] This was the first occasion since the middle ages when a reigning pope had left Italy. The visit, although the public was told more about it than about most diplomatic proceedings of the period, provoked intense curiosity and speculation at the time; and, despite the fact that many of the relevant archival sources have been published by historians, it remains in some respects mysterious still. Why the pope decided to make the journey, what if anything he agreed with Joseph, and what it achieved are all in some doubt. In this chapter I am concerned with the pope's reasons for going to Vienna.

It was always known of course, in general terms, that Pius had been provoked to make the journey by the early manifestations of Joseph's intention to reform the Catholic Church in his dominions unilaterally, and by the well justified fear that many more radical measures were to follow. By the time the pope wrote to the emperor saying that he wished to come to Vienna, in December 1781, the emperor had already enacted on his own authority many measures to which Rome objected. Early in the year a secret instruction had greatly relaxed the censorship, permitting the publication and circulation of many anticlerical and unorthodox works. He had begun issuing rescripts granting toleration to his non-Catholic subjects in some of his provinces. He had ordered monasteries to sever their links with superiors of their Orders based outside his dominions and had placed them instead under the authority of their local bishops. He had banned the publication and discussion of the bull *Unigenitus*, the highly controversial decree of 1713 that had stigmatised doctrines considered to be Jansenist. He had declared that no papal pronouncements were to be received and published in his lands without his prior permission. He had asserted his power as the lay sovereign to appoint to all ecclesiastical benefices in his lands, including Lombardy, over which the pope claimed special rights. It was known that he intended to suppress a number of monasteries, especially those that were purely contemplative.[2]

New light is thrown on the pope's motives for going to Vienna in unpublished and virtually unstudied despatches from the papal nuncio in Vienna, the future cardinal Giuseppe Garampi.

Garampi was a highly experienced diplomat, who had already spent periods as a papal representative in the Empire and as nuncio at Warsaw before coming to Vienna in 1776. He was also a scholar and archivist of note. His despatches have long been recognised as a major source by students of papal history. In particular, Hanns Schlitter used many of them and published a substantial selection from them in his standard work of 1892 on the pope's visit to Vienna. Giuseppe Soranzo's *Peregrinus apostolicus*, the fullest account of the pope's journey, published in 1937, largely depends on the nuncio's reports.

Most subsequent writers have relied on Schlitter and Soranzo for their knowledge of these documents. However, Garampi was a most conscientious envoy, and his voluminous reports deserve thorough study. They are revealing not only of his own attitude and of papal policy but also of many aspects of Josephism as it developed.[3] Special value attaches to the 'extraordinary' despatches that he sent from time to time by courier or by a trusted individual – despatches often of enormous length – which describe the situation in the Austrian Monarchy with exceptional frankness, amplitude and acuity. It would appear that these reports were not available to Schlitter and Soranzo.

I print below translations of parts of two of these extraordinary despatches, which reveal that Garampi repeatedly urged Rome to make a strong stand against the emperor's policies and especially against his apparently Jansenist views. Garampi himself insists that he will not be able in conscience to administer the sacrament to the emperor on Maundy Thursday 1782, as nuncios traditionally did and as Garampi himself had done in 1781. The Cardinal Secretary of State tried to argue him out of this position, but he would not budge. It is striking that, when Garampi repeated his threat, the pope's reply was to announce his intention of coming to Vienna himself. The hawkish stance of the nuncio surely goes a long way to account for the pope's ultimately rather hasty and surprising decision to depart from the practice of centuries. Had Garampi openly refused communion to the emperor over the question of *Unigenitus*, it would not have amounted to excommunication in the proper sense. But it would certainly have caused at least a tremendous furore and might well have led to the schism that the pope was determined to avoid. If the pope had made the public condemnation of Joseph's programme which Garampi recommended, a rift would have been hard to avoid.

In accordance with his policy of turning the other cheek to obstreperous lay rulers – the policy he pursued until at last he decided he had no alternative but to condemn the French Revolution's Civil Constitution of the Clergy in 1791 – the pope issued no public criticism of the emperor's policies. And he was himself in Vienna to administer the sacrament to Joseph II in a private chapel on Maundy Thursday 1782.

Garampi had remained in Vienna after all, to assist the pope during his visit. No one remarked on the fact that, while the pope was giving communion to the emperor, Garampi was celebrating High Mass in the Augustinian Court church nearby.[4]

Garampi's despatches, Archivio Segreto Vaticano, Nunziatura di Vienna 180

1 Garampi's despatch from Vienna to Pallavicini, Cardinal Secretary of State, 20 July 1781 (ciphered) (fol. 116v–119v)

Since the French Secretary has had to send a courier to Paris today, I take advantage of it, to give Your Excellency some more confidential information.

Y.E. will have gathered from my previous despatches how much worse the position of the Church and religion is becoming every day. As in civil, so also in religious matters, new and unexpected orders are being produced in great haste: there is no class of citizens that has not either already been harmed or is in fear and danger of being so.

All the monks and nuns are so shocked that they are not only obeying to the letter the orders that they receive, but they are even going beyond them. There is no doubtful case in which they dare to act without consulting the government; and indeed the latter acquires every day new motives and new excuses to proceed further. I am reminded in these circumstances of the fatalism of the Turks who, brought low by fear of the collapse of their empire, await it calmly and make no effort to stop it, excusing their feeble inaction by so-called resignation to the divine will and to the necessity of fate.

The bishops fear losing their temporalities, or being harassed by the departments, and so they invent reasons for optimism or prudence to justify acquiescing in everything, hoping that matters will be remedied in the distant future. Only those of Hungary have it in mind to raise some objections, chiefly on the bull *Unigenitus*. Most have done nothing but communicate the orders of the sovereign to their consistories for information, but up to now they haven't circulated them to the clergy. [Some of the bishops have even shown themselves pleased with the suppression of the bull.]

But of all these evils the greatest and most terrible is the licence of the press. Every day the most injurious and biased books against Catholic dogmas are introduced, and people are allowed to publish here all those hostile to the clergy, to the liturgy and to the discipline of the Church. [Two books favourable to the Church] have been strictly prohibited without investigation but merely on the basis of their titles. The solemn condemnation of Raynal's book[5] by the *parlement* of Paris is little regarded, and they allow the book to be published. Y.E. will see that such licence and libertinism amounts to a continuous mission and campaign against the Church; and an even more notable change follows from it, namely, that sermons and preachings by non-Catholics are heard in churches and in the squares.

So we have now reached a crisis similar or near to that which the Church suffered in the sixteenth century. All good people lament it; and however little effect they believe the pope's fatherly observations would have, they none the less wish the pope's voice to be heard, for their comfort, or at least to restrict the daily advance of corruption in other provinces and states of the Empire. They regret that the emperor's journey [to Belgium] has delayed any such remonstrances. It still seems that the pope could address himself to other princes of the Empire, both ecclesiastical and secular, perhaps by letters or by sending nuncios (as they did in the sixteenth century) or at least ... sufficiently accredited persons to prevent so far as possible the spread of the corruption of these states. Otherwise, silence or a purely private correspondence ... would undoubtedly be interpreted by the ill-disposed as acquiescence on the part of our lord the pope, and as indicating that he had no hope of being listened to or finding means to prevent such calamities.

I add as my private advice ... that, to give greater weight to the concerns expressed by the pope, it would be desirable that it should be known that all these matters were being dealt with by a special Congregation of chosen Cardinals ...

Would Y.E. please think, and consult our lord, about my own future conduct? Ought I to tolerate this situation and be patient, or should I make a point of stirring up the bishops and warning them? Up to now I haven't done so, and I only do it in a cautious way with those who are relatively friendly to me and are my confidants. If I alter my conduct, it will very soon become apparent. But if the coming negotiations yield no significant result and things continue to get worse, would it not perhaps be better for His Holiness himself to remove me from here, so as to give not only to these peoples and to this Court, but to the whole world, the clearest of indications of his disapproval? I also bring forward for consideration that, after the orders that have been given about the bull *Unigenitus*, I can no longer in conscience give Easter Communion to His Majesty, given the rules laid down in Benedict XIV's encyclical to the bishops of France.

2 Garampi's 'extraordinary despatch' of 18 November 1781, Vienna, carried by Niccolò Foscarini, the Venetian ambassador (partly ciphered)

[He cannot accept the argument put to him by the Secretary of State that the case of the French bishops was different.]

To avoid putting a point of such importance to the trial, since our lord approves none of the plans I put forward in my ciphered despatch of 20 July, I now propose a compromise, that is, for me to take leave from here from the beginning of Lent, on the pretext that I need to go and prepare for the visit of the Grand Duke and Duchess of Russia to [my estate of] Monte Fiascone, and return here in the summer. This would inconvenience me greatly, but far less than to lend myself to a sacrilege.

Notes

This chapter originally appeared under the title 'Nuncio Garampi Proposes to Excommunicate Joseph II, 1781' in a collection of documents with explanatory introductions in honour of Professor Éva Balázs: *Miscellanea fontium historiae europaeae*, ed. J. Kálmár (Budapest, 1997), pp. 252–7. I have translated and shortened the documents and extended the introduction, taking into account the very helpful criticisms of Professor Elisabeth Garms-Cornides and the appearance after I wrote the article of U. Dell'Orto, *La nunziatura a Vienna di Giuseppe Garampi, 1776–1785* (Vatican City, 1995). The author of this admirable book generously gave me a copy of it. Unlike Schlitter and Soranzo, he made use of the 'straordinari' despatches and, had his book been published earlier, I could not have claimed much novelty for my findings. However, they remain novel in English, and he does not attach so much importance as I do to Garampi's threats, veiled and overt.

1 The standard works on the visit are H. Schlitter (ed.), *Die Reise des Papstes Pius VI. nach Wien und sein Aufenthalt* (Vienna, 1892); G. Soranzo, *Peregrinus apostolicus* (Milan, 1937) and E. Kovács, *Der Pabst in Teutschland* (Vienna, 1983).

2 See Dell'Orto, *Garampi*, and F. Maass, *Der Josephinismus* (5 vols, Vienna, 1951–61), vol. II.

3 See also F. Dörrer, 'Der Schriftverkehr zwischen dem päpstliche Staatssekretariat und der apostolischer Nuntiatur Wien in der zweiten Hälfte des 18. Jahrhunderts', *Römische historische Mitteilungen*, 4 (1960/61): 63–246.

4 Dell'Orto, *Garampi*, p. 339.

5 This is G.-T. Raynal's famous *Histoire philosophique et politique des deux Indes*, of which the third, much extended version is dated 1780 and was available early in 1781. Much of it had actually been written by Diderot. It criticised (among other things) the missionary efforts of the Church in non-European lands. Joseph II dined in Raynal's company at Spa on the very day when this despatch was sent (Joseph to Marshal Lacy, 20 July 1781, Haus-, Hof- und Staatsarchiv, Vienna, Familien-Archiv, Sammelbände 72).

CHAPTER II

Was Joseph II an Enlightened Despot?

Joseph II died on 20 February 1790. He was buried in the Kapuzin-ergruft with much of the usual pomp, but in a sarcophagus totally unlike those of any of his predecessors. Absolutely plain, it silently continues, in death, the protest he made all his life against the baroque ostentation of his parents, still opulently relaxing on their overpowering tomb-chest nearby.[1]

As he himself said, it is difficult to imagine a more unhappy death. Twice a week, his desperate letters followed each other across the Alps to his brother Leopold in Tuscany. In pain and scarcely able to breathe, he believes himself 'the unhappiest mortal alive'; he has sacrificed everything to his 'fanaticism ... for the good of the state' and now sees his reputation in tatters and the Monarchy going to rack and ruin; his is a worse fate than that of the martyrs – living 'to suffer, and dishonoured':

> seeing that I am unfortunate in everything I undertake, the appalling ingratitude with which my good arrangements are received and I am treated – for there is now no conceivable insolence or curse that people do not allow themselves to utter about me publicly – all this makes me doubt myself, I no longer dare to have an opinion and put it into effect, I allow myself to be ruled by the advice of the ministers even when I don't think it's the best, since I dare not hold out for my own view and indeed I haven't the strength to impose it and argue for it.

Thus he renounced, under extreme duress, his absolutism – or should one call it despotism?[2]

Everyone, even the savagely critical Prussian envoys, had to admire the dignity, courage and fortitude Joseph displayed during his final illness, and the strength of will which enabled him to write generous farewell letters to friends and ministers in his last hours. But many people had longed for his death, which some thought a necessary condition of the very survival of the Monarchy. His rule had been widely regarded as a despotic aberration, and there were many, including most Belgians and Hungarians, who wanted it relegated – as Chancellor Kohl claimed to have consigned the DDR – to the footnotes of history.[3]

In fact, historians have remained fascinated by Joseph II and his experiment in government. I want to pursue the question most often asked about him: 'Was Joseph II an Enlightened despot?' In writing the first volume of my biography of Joseph II, which ends with the death of his mother Maria Theresa in 1780, I had no doubt that the question needed answering; but I had decided to leave a proper consideration of it to volume II, when I should have completed my work on the reforms of his sole reign during the 1780s. This I have not finished, and so I can give only a preliminary answer to the question. What has really provoked me to prepare such an answer is a review of my book by Professor William Doyle. In the course of the review (which was entirely fair, not to say generous) he wrote that I hedged the question whether Joseph was an Enlightened despot. He gave his own answer to the question: that the whole notion of Enlightened despotism was 'rusty', that to add the word 'Enlightened' in front of despotism 'now impedes more than it promotes historical understanding' and that in any case Maria Theresa was the greater revolutionary.[4] To the stimulus of these remarks should be added the recent appearance of a number of studies which breathe new life into the theme.[5]

I shall argue that the notion of Enlightened despotism or absolutism – and I think the use of 'despotism' is on balance preferable to that of 'absolutism' – is meaningful and valuable, and that Joseph's rule clearly belongs to this category. I have not space here to consider adequately the question whether Maria Theresa was the greater revolutionary. But it may put her activity in perspective to recall that her annual output of laws (excluding those for Hungary) averaged under a hundred, while Joseph's averaged 690.[6]

I am going to assume that when we speak of Enlightened absolutism or despotism we are thinking of a regime in which the ruler possesses or assumes the right to enact legislation without consent, exercises the right extensively and, in doing so, is influenced by 'the Enlightenment' as the term is used by historians of the eighteenth century – not by enlightenment in some more general sense. I am also going to assume that Enlightenment so used is itself a meaningful concept, a term denoting critical, rationalist, reformist opinion in the eighteenth century.

Problems of definition

It seems necessary first to deal with some general difficulties raised by the concept of Enlightened despotism. The first is the claim that the very notion of an Enlightened despot, or an Enlightened absolute monarch, is a contradiction in terms. This view derives support from a tradition of thought epitomised by Lord Acton's dictum: 'Power tends to corrupt, and absolute power corrupts absolutely.'[7] How could a necessarily corrupt despot possibly be Enlightened? Further, most American historians, Peter Gay at their head, and many historians from other English-speaking countries, nurtured as they are in a tradition of representative government unbroken since the middle ages, and aware that the American Revolution ranks as an aspect and achievement of the Enlightenment, see the movement as inherently associated with political liberty and parliamentary rule. Among great thinkers of the Enlightenment some, like Montesquieu and Rousseau, always agreed, and others like Diderot came to agree, that Enlightenment and despotism or absolutism were incompatible.[8]

My first response to this line of thinking would be that many examples can be found of absolute rulers who manifestly were not absolutely corrupt, such as Frederick the Great and Catherine the Great. Secondly I should reply that the Enlightenment was very various. Not infinitely various: I think all its representatives were critical of the extremer claims of Christian Churches and in favour of some measure of religious toleration, condemned some aspects of what were called superstition or fanaticism, supported some legal reform tending to greater uniformity, greater rationality or utility and greater fairness – similarly with economic reform – and also supported some mitigation of censorship. But economic policy, for example, was much debated among the Enlightened, some writers like the Physiocrats favouring free trade, others still adhering to forms of mercantilism. What was acceptable in the way of monarchical rule to the great majority of German representatives of the *Aufklärung* went far beyond what was acceptable to Montesquieu, Rousseau and Diderot and to English and American thinkers in general.[9] I would not maintain (and no sensible person would) that all Enlightened thinkers were ready to accept, still less justify, absolute monarchy. That would be absurd. But I would maintain that many were, and I shall shortly give chapter and verse.

The second principal objection is that the terms Enlightened despotism and despot, or their variant Enlightened absolutism, were not used in the period to which they are supposed to apply. Betty Behrens was particularly strict on this point.[10] My first answer to this point would be: So what? The fact that the term *ancien régime* cannot be found before 1788 quite rightly doesn't stop Doyle – any more than it stopped Behrens – from writing books with that title which are almost entirely devoted to periods before 1788.[11] Many indestructible historical concepts were invented after the period to which they refer, for example the Industrial Revolution, the middle ages – or indeed the Enlightenment itself, except in reference to Germany.

However, I should take as a second line of defence that the term 'Enlightened despot' – though not 'Enlightened despotism' – *can* be found in eighteenth-century writing. Incidentally, though the word 'absolute' had long been used to mean more or less 'untrammelled', the word 'absolutism' itself was not invented until the nineteenth century.[12] Further, I should argue that the *notion* of Enlightened despotism, as opposed to the precise term, was widespread in the eighteenth century.

This seems the appropriate place to consider a subsidiary difficulty, the significance of 'despotisme légal'. This is an important concept in Le Mercier de la Rivière's *L'ordre naturel et essentiel des sociétés politiques*, published in 1767. The notion has been taken to correspond with Enlightened despotism – or at least, according to Behrens, to be the only eighteenth-century usage that approximated to it.[13] Le Mercier's book was the collectively agreed political manifesto of the Physiocrats, whose main concern of course was with economics. It is one of those books that are much mentioned but little read. It claims that government, society and especially the economy are subject to laws which, like the laws of geometry, are indisputable and self-evident. They are the laws of the free market, but with agriculture treated as the only true productive activity. It is the business of the good ruler to put these laws into effect, or – according to one formulation – to get rid of the existing counter-productive laws and then sit back, do nothing and let the new laws operate. These laws may, by a play on words, be described, like Euclid's laws, as despotic. The concept 'despotisme légal' therefore does not imply, as is sometimes supposed, the vindication as lawful of what is normally understood by despotism. Far from acting wilfully or individually, the ruler who enacts Le Mercier's laws will have no discretion; he will be doing the self-evidently right thing, not what he likes but what is natural and essential.[14] True, there are certain affinities with the notion and practice of Enlightened despotism. On Diderot's recommendation, Catherine the Great summoned Le Mercier to St Petersburg to give her advice.[15] Some rulers, including Joseph II, showed their susceptibility to Enlightened theory by declaring their conviction that certain of the Physiocrats' economic principles, such as free trade in grain or the encouragement of private property in land, were ineluctably right.[16] The Natural Law on which German rulers relied as a justification for making the laws of their provinces uniform and more rational is not wholly unlike Le Mercier's geometric laws.[17] But the concept of Enlightened despotism, as normally understood, involves rulers exerting themselves to impose on their states, not an immutable set of laws, but a particular brand of Enlightenment, and admits that each state has specific problems in some ways different from those of other states. So 'despotisme légal' cannot be identified with Enlightened despotism.

In an invaluable article François Bluche has marshalled some of the best and earliest French instances of the usage 'Enlightened despot'. This is the most striking. In 1767, when discussing Le Mercier de la Rivière's notion of 'despotisme légal', Baron Grimm, editor of the *Correspondance littéraire*, wrote: 'It has been said that the rule of an ENLIGHTENED DESPOT, active, vigilant, wise and firm, was of all regimes the most desirable and most perfect, and this is a true saying; but it was important not to take it too far. I, too, passionately love such despots.'[18]

Even more notable is this quotation from the third edition of Raynal's *Histoire philosophique et politique du commerce et des établissements des Européens dans les deux Indes*, dated 1780: 'However you will hear it said that the most satisfactory government would be that of a just, firm, Enlightened despot. What a wild view!'[19] We now know that these are the words of Diderot. Coming from such a source, this remark would seem sufficient by itself to establish that a theory of Enlightened despotism was significant in French thought of the period. Moreover, he goes on to argue that the first Enlightened despot in a line of rulers is a great evil, the second worse still, and the third a terrible scourge. In other words, however much he condemns them, he accepts that Enlightened despots may exist. Indeed, it is clear that, earlier, Diderot had himself believed in the possibility of beneficent Enlightened despots. He denounced Frederick the Great, whom he had previously admired, in the unpublished *Pages contre un tyran* of 1771; but that he had not entirely abandoned hope is shown by his journey to Russia in 1773, undertaken with the idea of converting Catherine II, whom he considered to be unquestionably a despot, into a more enlightened ruler.[20]

Apart from the admittedly infrequent use of the phrase 'Enlightened despot' in the eighteenth century, there seems to me abundant evidence that many Enlightened thinkers had hopes of a ruler of this kind. Voltaire was the best known writer of all. He did not put all his eggs in one basket. He much admired the English constitution, where law was sovereign, and where the king was restricted (Voltaire claimed) to the point that he could do only good. He even showed sympathy with the democratic movement in Geneva. He at first welcomed the embrace of Frederick the Great, then escaped, disillusioned, from his clutches, but after an interval resumed a flattering correspondence with him. He was made historiographer royal by Louis XV in 1745 and supported the royal stance against the *parlements*. He eventually wrote what has been called the first social or not purely political and religious history, the *Essai sur les moeurs* (first edition, 1756). But he still maintained that great men had brought about most of the great changes of history, and wrote eulogistic biographies of Charles XII of Sweden, Louis XIV of France and (after the appearance of the *Essai*) Peter the Great. In the last years of his life he became the uncritical admirer and correspondent of Catherine II. He refused to accept what he considered Montesquieu's laboured distinction between despot and monarch, and much of what he wrote assumed the possibility of beneficent change from above by fiat of an Enlightened ruler. Lortholary's *Le mirage russe* mordantly catalogues the credulous expectations inspired by Catherine's rule in one *philosophe* after another.[21]

A less well-known author who addressed the problem directly was Giuseppe Gorani (1740–1819), an associate of the Verri brothers and Beccaria in Milan. In his book *Il vero dispotismo*, published in 1769, he pinned all his hopes of reform and improvement on a monarch possessed of despotic power, who would use it to abolish feudal and ecclesiastical abuses, vested interests, even property rights, and to introduce a rational economic system, freedom of expression and so on.[22] Here we have a dream of Utopia to be achieved through

Enlightened despotism. The efforts and visits of Joseph II helped to keep such attitudes alive in Lombardy. Pietro Verri himself wrote as late as 1781:

> In my opinion, subjects ought never to fear the power of the sovereign when he himself exercises it and doesn't surrender any essential part of it into other hands ... Only intermediate power is to be feared, and I think and feel that the best of all political systems will always be despotism, provided that the sovereign is active and in overall control and doesn't give up any portion of his sovereignty.[23]

More generally, it has to be remembered that the American dream had scarcely been invented by the time Voltaire died and had not come to fruition by the time Joseph succeeded his mother; that until the American colonies won their independence, no country had been the product of a revolution since the Dutch Republic; and that no country at all had a full-blown rational written constitution until the American revolt. Such republics as there were before then seemed backward and doomed, and such constitutions as existed seemed to make beneficent change almost impossible, as for example in Venice, Belgium and Hungary. The effective reforming law-givers of Europe were in fact the monarchs.

The third main difficulty lies in distinguishing the concepts 'despotism' and 'absolutism'.[24] Virtually everyone writing with awareness of serious political thinking – as opposed to just tossing off abusive remarks – regarded a despot as a ruler who possessed untrammelled power. At least in the second half of the eighteenth century, the word despot was generally pejorative and connoted the exercise of untrammelled power according to the whim and caprice of the ruler, perhaps as opposed to its exercise for the general good. Usage was much influenced by Montesquieu's novel distinction in *De l'esprit des lois* of 1748 between despotism and monarchy, a classification to which he attached great importance and which soon became almost universally known and widely, though not universally, accepted among writers and statesmen. In a monarchy, as he defined it, there must be a constitution of sorts, embodying both a law of succession and intermediary bodies such as *parlements* that the ruler had to consult over legislation. If these conditions were not satisfied, the state was a despotism. Hence, according to Montesquieu, Russia was a despotism and France a monarchy. However, Montesquieu recognised that examples of pure despotism or pure monarchy were hard to find.

What we call, but Montesquieu was very careful not to call, the pretensions of the French Crown to absolute power, for example to legislate without the consent of the *parlements*, were to be regarded as steps towards despotism. It is important to grasp that for Montesquieu despotism is a form of government characterised both by the nature of the constitution in the state concerned and by the behaviour of the ruler, which will necessarily be dictatorial, cruel and capricious; and that he deliberately avoided the word and concept '*absolu*' applied to power and government, wishing to identify it with despotic rule and thus discredit it.[25]

Jaucourt's article 'Monarchie' in the *Encyclopédie* avowedly follows Montesquieu, but his article 'Monarchie absolue' introduces – or, better, revives – an intermediate stage between monarchy and despotism: 'the origin and nature of absolute monarchy is limited by its very nature, by the intentions of those from whom the monarch derives it and by the fundamental laws of his state.'[26] Jaucourt's classification is close to that of Roger Mettam in his book, *Power and Faction in Louis XIV's France*. Mettam emphasises the limitations on Louis's power, both in practice and in theory, maintaining that the contemporary expression *la monarchie absolue* 'did not describe the system as it was presently constituted. It was rather a direction in which the royal ministers were hoping to proceed.' Even so, he contends, it was understood to mean the exercise of royal power 'for the greater good of the kingdom. Otherwise it was *monarchie arbitraire*.' *Monarchie arbitraire* corresponds with despotism.[27]

Montesquieu's distinction remains important in modern writing, although his notion of 'monarchy' has fallen into disuse. Some modern historians like Mousnier have used 'absolutism' in virtually the same sense as Montesquieu used 'monarchy', contrasting it with despotism. It must be recognised that most of these usages – of 'monarchy' by Montesquieu, of 'absolutism' among historians of France and even of *la monarchie absolue* in the *Encyclopédie* – fall short of other established notions of 'absolute monarchy' and 'absolutism'. Jean Bodin in his *Republic* of 1576 stated categorically: 'The principal mark of sovereign majesty and absolute power is the right to impose laws generally on all subjects regardless of their consent.'[28] This was what the Stuarts and Louis XIV were thought by many of their opponents to stand for. It is also more or less the position adopted in eighteenth-century Germany by many rulers and by the large body of writers who justified absolute government. The subjects, it was maintained, had surrendered all their rights to their ruler, who therefore had the right and power to make such laws as he thought proper without consent. It was held to be by far the best arrangement that sovereignty should be placed straightforwardly in the hands of the prince: he was much more likely than any group of people, or than all the people, to govern in the interests of the whole state and of all its population. It was his moral and Christian duty to act for the general good rather than for his private advantage. But his power was to be in no sense formally restricted. It was admitted that, if he acted arbitrarily, his absolute power degenerated into despotism. But absolutism as used by historians of Germany to describe this sort of government and the theory behind it, though still differentiated from despotism, clearly means something much nearer to it than Montesquieu's monarchy or Mousnier's absolutism, and as such reflects the differences between German and French reality.[29]

So there is a broad range or spectrum of meaning covered by the term 'absolutism'. The normal German usage of the word is compatible with the sort of conduct we have in mind when we speak of 'Enlightened despotism', the imposition of an Enlightened programme of reform by the ruler from above, on his own legislative authority, for the general good. Such activity is plainly irreconcilable with Montesquieu's monarchy and Mousnier's absolutism, both of which are conceived to be limited by intermediate powers, by fundamental laws and by ancient liberties and privileges varying from province to province, town to town and corporation to corporation. Under such a constitution, radical reform from above is inconceivable. As Jaucourt said: 'Monarchy is lost when a prince believes that he demonstrates his power better by changing the order of things than by accepting it.'[30]

To use the term 'Enlightened absolutism', then, does not make everything plain. Nor is despotism so clear-cut a concept as is often assumed. Bodin was not the only writer to distinguish between despotism and the still worse condition of tyranny.[31] Hobbes, on the contrary, maintained that sovereign, absolute, despotic and tyrannical all meant the same thing: 'for they that are discontented under monarchy, call it tyranny'.[32] Montesquieu's insistence that despotism is characterised both by the ruler's legislative sovereignty and by his capriciousness confuses the issue. But I still find it more satisfactory to use 'Enlightened despotism' for five reasons: because despotism unequivocally refers to a situation in which the ruler possesses the power to legislate without consent; because what needs to be expressed is something more drastic than French (and Stuart) absolutism as now commonly understood by historians; because it is a long-standing usage, especially in English but also in other languages; because, unlike absolutism, the term despotism was current in the eighteenth century and the usage 'Enlightened despot' has some eighteenth-century warrant; and because, whereas there is no personal noun cognate with absolutism, despot is cognate with despotism. But I employ the word despot, as did writers like Hobbes, Grimm, Gorani and Verri, with the understanding that he may use his untrammelled power not for his personal advantage but for the public good.

Joseph II as despot

I now come to the Austrian Monarchy and Joseph II. His education was firmly based on the theory of Natural Rights and Natural Laws, especially as taught by the German school, particularly Pufendorf. They cherished the idea of a wise and rational sovereign who would work for *'das allgemeine Beste'* ('the general best'), that is, to strengthen his state as against other states, to make its laws more rational and homogeneous, to promote the welfare of his subjects, perhaps to grant them all the same civil rights and to accord a certain measure of religious toleration. But the young prince was also firmly told that he must respect the various constitutions of the Monarchy's diverse provinces.[33]

Joseph said with Rousseau that education is everything. His own case goes far to disprove the claim. While he drank in the despotic aspects and implications of what he was taught, he rejected the constitutionalism. In his *Rêveries* of 1763 he horrified his mother by the intentions he revealed. His first basic aim was to secure 'the absolute power to be in a position to do all possible good for the state'. To this end he would seek to 'humble and impoverish the grandees'.

> This smacks of despotism, but without an absolute power ... to be in a position to do all the good which one is prevented from doing by the rules, statutes and oaths which the provinces believe to be their *palladium*, and which, sanely considered, turn only to their disadvantage, it is not possible for a state to be happy or for a sovereign to be able to do great things ... God keep me from wanting to break sworn oaths, but I believe we must work to convert the provinces and make them

see how useful the limited despotism [*despotisme lié*], which I propose, would be to them. To this end I should aim to make an agreement with the provinces, asking them [to yield to me] for ten years full power to do everything, without consulting them, for their own good.

While it is true that he talks in this passage of persuading rather than compelling the provinces to surrender despotic power to him for ten years, it seems clear that the only force of the word *lié* is to restrict the period of the despotism, not its scope.[34]

He appears to have remained faithful to this plan, at least in respect of Hungary. When he succeeded his mother in 1780, he refused to be crowned king of Hungary, which would have involved his swearing to uphold its constitution. Almost until he died, for over nine years, he acted as though he could exercise unlimited power there, introducing a welter of enactments which most Hungarians considered illegitimate because he was uncrowned and declined to summon a Diet. In the preface to a collection of his Hungarian laws published in 1788 the editor, Joseph Keresztury, stated that the emperor would soon be calling a Diet and would submit all his ordinances to it.[35] This was plainly not his intention then or earlier. When in 1784 his officials suggested that the decree making German, instead of Latin, the language of administration in Hungary needed the approval of the Diet, Joseph responded:

The chancellery could have saved itself the trouble of making the recent representation in which it urges the necessity of putting off until a diet [meets] the abolition of the Latin language in official business, because it's only a matter of language and not of substance and I am the last man to make soap bubbles into bullets.[36]

Only rebellion, his need for war supplies and finance, and his desperate illness, brought him to recognise the necessity of calling a Diet and submitting to a coronation – though he died before either could happen.[37]

In Belgium, for reasons not fully clear, he allowed deputies to take the necessary constitutional oaths on his behalf when he succeeded his mother.[38] Nevertheless, he introduced reforms that flouted the old constitutions. Rebellion in Brabant compelled him in 1787 to withdraw some of his measures; but, when his troops had restored order, he talked of treating the country as a conquered land, completely at his mercy. He then swept away the entire old constitution, informing the

Estates of Brabant a month before the fall of the Bastille: 'I do not need your consent for doing good.' No wonder that Belgian publicists compared him to Tiberius, Caligula, Nero, Caracalla, Alaric, Attila, Mahomet, Amurath, Machiavelli, Alva and Cromwell. By the time he renounced his personal rule, his armies had been driven out of nearly all his Belgian lands.[39]

On the spectrum of monarchical pretensions, his rule in Hungary and Belgium must plainly be located at the despotic end. It would be hard to claim and exercise more personal power than he did. We have seen that he did not scruple, in private, to recommend despotism by that name. On another occasion he suggested that he be made dictator.[40] All that was lacking to qualify him unequivocally as a despot by Montesquieu's definition was that his actions were evidently inspired by a conception of the public good rather than by mere caprice.

It is instructive to read what is said about his rule and the con-stitution of the Monarchy in a comprehensive *Essai sur la Monarchie Autrichienne et son état actuel (Essay on the Austrian Monarchy and its Present Condition)*, prepared for the Neapolitan government just after his death.[41] This document specifically addresses the question whether the Habsburgs are absolute or despotic rulers in the Monarchy. The answer given is: absolute, in every province. Admittedly the legislative power as well as the executive lies with the sovereign.

> It is necessary nevertheless to grasp that there is a great distance between the absolute monarch and the despotic monarch. [The latter is] a designation which is in no way appropriate to the sovereign of the hereditary lands, which these sovereigns would never wish to have, and which they have always held in horror.
>
> Despotic government recognises no laws but the mere will, and often the mere caprice, of the sovereign; while in monarchical govern-ment, even if absolute, the sovereign's will is subjected to councils, formalities, to privileges of estates, peoples, corporations and even individuals, and caprice can have no place.

Great stress is laid on the wisdom of his consulting with trusted ministers, respected by the people, who can 'enlighten him about so many things' and 'who countersign the laws after him'.

The *Essai*, however, betrays embarrassment on several fronts, two of which are of special interest here. On Hungary it describes the articles of the constitution 'tending to limit monarchical power' as being 'insufficiently clear' and alleges that the Diet meets only for a coronation, while admitting that the country has to be governed 'in accordance with the laws established by His Majesty and the general Diet'. On the reign of Joseph II, it does its best to associate as many of his policies as possible with his mother's and with the influence of 'this enlightened minister', Prince Kaunitz. But the writer has to acknowledge that Joseph did not always observe formalities and that: 'After the death of the Empress Queen, Prince Kaunitz stood out against several reforms that the late Emperor projected, and so strong was his opposition that the monarch used to consult him only rarely.'

I have not yet discovered who wrote this treatise nor in precisely what circumstances. It is obviously related to the visit of the Neapolitan Court to Vienna and to current plans for an alliance between Vienna and Naples; it clearly owes something to the Neapolitan minister, Sir John Acton, and also to the Marquis de Gallo, the Neapolitan ambassador in Vienna and the confidant of the Queen of Naples. It is by way of being a eulogy of Kaunitz's successes and an apology for his role under Joseph II; and it does its best to minimise the emperor's autocracy. No doubt its constitutionalism is designed to ape or gratify Leopold II, whose manifesto to the Belgians commending representative government was published in March 1790.[42] But what strikes the modern reader is that the *Essai*, even while underplaying the pretensions of Joseph, gives a surprisingly high estimate of the powers possessed by the Habsburgs, making it hard to distinguish their absolutism from despotism. As for Joseph, he made it clear that he regarded his officials as servants rather than advisers. He constantly complained that they were slow, incompetent and obstructive and that he had to draft despatches himself.[43] He was prepared to humiliate even the great Kaunitz. The emperor was in Russia during the early stages of the Brabant revolution in 1787. He had left Kaunitz to mind the shop in Vienna, but when the chancellor wrote recommending him to approve a document involving a concession to the rebels, Joseph returned it 'torn in pieces', with orders that it should be passed on to the administration in Brussels in that state. 'I am surprised', [he wrote], 'that the people of Brussels and the fanatics who stir them up haven't yet asked for my breeches, and that the government hasn't meanwhile given them assurances that I will send them on.' So much for consultation of ministers and observance of formalities by an absolute, not despotic, ruler![44]

Joseph's Enlightenment

Finally, were Joseph and his rule Enlightened? I have myself contributed a little to make it more difficult to answer this question. My
description of Joseph's education, based on the work of other scholars,
shows it to have been relatively unenlightened, innocent of almost
all the great works of the French Enlightenment except Voltaire's
Henriade and carefully selected portions of Montesquieu's *De l'esprit
des lois*, and apparently innocent too of Maria Theresa's own practical plans for quite radical administrative and ecclesiastical reform.[45]
I have also shown, or rediscovered, that many of the most famous
quotations attributed to Joseph were not in fact his. He did not say
(most notorious of all): 'I have made philosophy the legislator of my
empire.' He meant by philosophy, when he used it, metaphysics or
long-suffering; he did not accept the redefinition of the word by such
men as Voltaire which gave it a radical, anti-Catholic, critical sense. He
once said that he followed neither the ancient Greeks nor the modern
French.[46] He lacked two characteristics which, according to a recent
discussion by Günther Birtsch, are essential to ideal Enlightened rulers:
he wrote no theoretical tracts and he conducted no correspondences
with *philosophes*. But Birtsch's *Idealtyp* is manifestly tailor-made to fit
Frederick the Great.[47] It is certainly wrong to suppose that Joseph
was a disciple of the *philosophes*, who should in any case be regarded
as only one small, if very influential, group within the diversity of
the Enlightenment. But he was unquestionably associated with many
other aspects of the movement.

Many of Joseph's contemporaries thought him an exemplar and
promoter of the Enlightenment, quite radically understood; and his
behaviour, pronouncements and enactments often supported this view.
Voltaire was informed in 1769, on the authority of Grimm, that the
emperor was 'one of us'. In 1774 appeared *Le monarque accompli* by the
Swiss Protestant publicist, Lanjuinais, three volumes of unmitigated
and indiscriminate praise of Joseph as an ideal ruler who resembled
not only the most notable kings of France, especially Henri IV, but
also the most celebrated Roman emperors like Trajan and Marcus
Aurelius, who favoured toleration and understood *l'esprit philosophique*.
Voltaire docketed this effusion 'roast monarch'. In 1777 he visited
France, as was claimed, *en philosophe*; he spoke well of Diderot and
Raynal, and met D'Alembert, Lavoisier, Marmontel, Turgot and La
Harpe. In 1781 he dined at Spa with Grimm and Raynal.[48]

More important, after succeeding his mother he embarked on his well-known programme of reforms, introducing measures of religious toleration for Protestants and Jews, some personal liberties for serfs, a much looser censorship, the suppression of all purely contemplative and many other monasteries, and all religious brotherhoods, etc. One of his most active supporters, Gebler, a member of the Council of State, dared to tell Nicolai, the creator of the *Allgemeine deutsche Bibliothek*, the principal organ of the North German Protestant Enlightenment:

> For a man who thinks philosophically there is no more remarkable period than that which opened in 1781. Such a rapid change in the general way of thinking, reaching down to the common people, who put to shame many still obscurantist persons of higher classes, is to my knowledge without parallel. The just recently effected abolition of brotherhoods, of most so-called *Andachten* [special devotions] and all *Klosterpredigten* [sermons by monks] has finally given the last blow to superstition ... The freedom of the press, and still more the *freedom of reading* (for there is virtually no book that is not publicly on sale) bring with them much else ... Our monarch meanwhile pursues his way undeterred.[49]

In 1782 was published an authentic correspondence the emperor had been conducting with the elector of Trier, who had written to him complaining about his religious reforms. In these letters Joseph displayed a mocking knowledge of theology, scoffed at the infallibility of the pope, rejected some of his other claims, urged the futility of discussing the bull *Unigenitus* and defended the relaxation of the censorship.[50]

At the end of 1783 the emperor issued to all his officials what became known as his *Hirtenbrief* or 'pastoral letter', originally written in his own hand in French and soon published in several languages. These were some of its assertions:

> I have weakened the influences resulting from prejudices and old, deep-rooted habits by means of Enlightenment [*Aufklärung*], and combated them with proofs; I have tried to imbue every official of the state with the love I feel for the general weal and with zeal to serve it.
>
> Hence it necessarily follows that, in considering how to act, we should have no other purpose in our actions but the utility and good of the majority. Since there can be only one good, namely that which

interests the whole and the greatest number, and likewise all the
provinces of the Monarchy form only a single whole and thus can
have only one purpose, ... in all of them nationality and religion must
make no difference, and as brothers in one Monarchy all should set to
work equally in order to be useful to one another.

The monarch has been chosen by Providence (*die Vorsicht*) 'to serve
these millions of people' and 'must account to the state as a whole
and to each individual' for his use of taxes. This document, Joseph's
most elaborate public pronouncement of his views and aims, embodies many of the commonplaces of Radical Enlightenment: the desire
to weaken ingrained prejudices through *Aufklärung*; the zeal for the
service of the state and its people, for the *allgemeine Beste* and the
good of the greatest number; the intention to treat all provinces,
nations and religions equally; the acknowledgement of the monarch's
responsibility to every individual; and the substitution of Providence
for God as the justification of the monarch's position.[51] It received
widespread praise and was the inspiration, through its insistence that
officials be thoroughly acquainted with Joseph's ordinances, of the
numerous collections of his laws published during the latter part of
his reign.[52]

In the same year as the pastoral letter there appeared the most
elaborate and effective panegyric of his work, the *philosophische Roman,
Faustin, or the Philosophical Century* by Johann Pezzl. It achieved the
distinction, rare for a book written in German, of being translated
into French and published in France. The hero, Faustin, undergoes
experiences very reminiscent of Voltaire's Candide. But it is not
the philosophy of Leibniz that plays Faustin false; it is the conviction instilled into him by his teacher, represented as a priest, that
beneficent Enlightenment was now – since 1763, that is – advancing
unstoppably. For 'Each monarch vies with the others to promote
toleration, enlightenment [*Erleuchtung*] and freedom of thought in
his states, and to expel superstition, barbarism, fanaticism, stupidity,
chicanery and misery from his peoples.' This is the 'universal victory
of reason and humanity, it is the enlightened, philosophical century'.
But when Faustin and his tutor put this happy conviction to the test,
it is proved false in one country after another in Europe and America,
with disastrous results. One or other or both of them are beaten
up by workers who resent the abolition of feast-days; imprisoned
for possessing works by Voltaire, Helvetius, Bayle, Montesquieu,

Frederick the Great, etc.; attacked by a crowd which had gathered to watch the antics of the notorious exorcist, Gaßner; for criticising South German monasticism, driven to take refuge in Venice; there set on by bandits and banished for criticising the constitution; faced with a variety of similar problems in other parts of Italy, Spain and Portugal; disillusioned in France by the government's treatment of Voltaire's body; appalled by the Gordon riots and general intolerance in England; and, after having fled to America, sold as slaves. Hope rises again only when Faustin, after endless adventures, all of them based on genuine events of the period, reaches Prussia. There at last is to be found a 'crowned philosopher'. But even in Berlin a *Liederkrieg* (song war) is in progress about the right of a congregation to sing Paul Gerhardt's hymn *Nun ruhen alle Wälder*.[53] Only when Faustin finally gets to Vienna does he discover a place where Enlightenment is in full cry. Joseph's letters to the elector of Trier, Faustin considers the most notable contribution made to the debate between Church and State, or Empire and Papacy, since the days of Pope Gregory VII. The emperor's opening of the Augarten park to the whole people in 1775 is 'a monument to philosophy on the throne'. 'Joseph the Great', who is to be compared to Sesostris, to the first Chinese emperor, to Orpheus, Titus and Marcus Aurelius, has inaugurated 'the era of Enlightened southern Germany', 'the era of Joseph'; 1780 is 'the year of salvation'. So, unlike Candide's, Faustin's philosophy is ultimately vindicated – in Joseph's Vienna.[54]

Soon after this effusion appeared, the emperor began to get a worse press. No doubt this had much to do with his involvement in wars and attempted annexations, with his legislation of 1785 placing some limitations on Freemasonry in his dominions, and with signs of his withdrawal from the fullest implications of other measures like the toleration edicts. But it is common to exaggerate the extent of the disillusionment felt by men of the Enlightenment at the end of Joseph's reign.[55] On his death, the young Beethoven in Bonn set to music an ode about it, which contained these sentiments:

Recitative: A monster, its name Fanaticism, arose from the depths of Hell, stretched itself out between the earth and the sun, and all became night.

Aria: Then came Joseph, and with God's strength dragged the frenzied monster away ... and crushed its head. Then mankind rose into the light.[56]

If Joseph's public pronouncements and recognition by Enlightened writers are insufficient justification for calling him Enlightened, more can be adduced from his private utterances. In the *Rêveries*, written in 1763, he advocated making all official appointments on the sole ground of 'personal merit. If this principle is inviolably observed, what geniuses will not emerge, who are now lost in obscurity either through laziness or because they are oppressed by nobles!'[57] In the next year, even before the appearance of Beccaria's *Crimes and Punishments*, he cast doubt on the utility of the death penalty.[58] As soon as he became co-regent, he urged on his mother in a famous document a massive programme of change including the end of the censorship, wide religious toleration, and the raising of the minimum legal age at which binding monastic vows could be taken to twenty-five. This last proposal, of course, was designed in the long run to reduce drastically the number of monks and nuns. He had much to do with the enactment of this measure in 1770, and it was not his fault that the other reforms were delayed until after her death.[59]

He was no great reader, but it is clear that once he was free – or as free as his mother would let him be – to go into society, he became acquainted with up-to-date radical writings ignored in his education. His knowledge of Voltaire passed the acid test of conversation with Frederick the Great. He is known to have read a physiocratic periodical. He justified not seeking out the great *philosophes* during his visit to France on the ground that, once you had read them, to meet them would be disappointing. One of the women who knew him best claimed that he followed the doctrines of Holbach and Helvetius. This is plainly untrue, but could hardly have been said if he had been wholly ignorant of these authors.[60]

Two major difficulties stand in the way of his acceptance as an Enlightened ruler by Anglophone historiography. First, he was not anti-Catholic. He told his mother, in the midst of denouncing her refusal to tolerate Protestants, that he would give all he possessed if that would make all his subjects Catholic. He was convinced, and he persuaded the pope, that he was a faithful son of the Church.[61] But it was possible to be a Catholic by the standards of the late eighteenth century, if not by those of the first Vatican Council, while holding views highly critical of the claims of the pope and the state of the Church. From one point of view, a Catholic and Enlightened ruler had much more to do than a Protestant and Enlightened ruler. Frederick the Great inherited a measure of toleration, he had in his dominions so few monasteries that he could afford to leave them alone. On the other hand, Joseph's edict of toleration of 1781 went far beyond that of any Catholic state and stirred envy in many Protestant communities, such as the city of Hamburg. His toleration of the Jews, inspired though it was by ideas of assimilating them, was uniquely generous in its day. His relaxation of the censorship was considered astonishingly liberal.[62]

Secondly, many historians have felt uneasy because his reforms seem to be primarily directed towards obtaining more taxes and more soldiers for a bigger army that would obtain more territory. The problems of defence certainly obsessed Joseph. It was the business of every ruler to preserve his territories, and the Monarchy was exposed to attack on several fronts. He worked hard to win Bavaria whether by inheritance or exchange, and sought aggrandisement in the East. But, for what it's worth, his most radical and secret document, the *Rêveries*, is concerned with internal reform and defence, while Frederick's under the same title is full of schemes for aggrandisement. Joseph wrote in 1768, as though in reply to the very criticism that modern historians make:

> I am no more attached to the military than to finance. If I could be persuaded that the reduction of the army would be a real advantage, I would disband them this very day and make them labourers. But our circumstances are very far from permitting us to do anything like that. We must try always to combine the necessary security with the country's welfare.[63]

When he was reluctantly fighting the Turks in 1788, unsuccessfully leading his own troops in the inhospitable climates around the Danube, he wrote home to Kaunitz:

> Nothing is so easy as to propose that we should get together a couple of great armies, pass into enemy territory, provoke some important and decisive events by battles or sieges ...
>
> But ... in Serbia or Bosnia, provinces in any cases without resources and devastated, we would have twenty leagues of the finest country behind us ... which have cost immense sums to establish, ruined in a moment: neither the risk nor the advantage would be worth it. And by what right may even a Sovereign, whom his subjects pay to defend them, allow their lives to be lost and their possessions taken away, and abandon them purely to go and make some insignificant conquests or

to obtain futile advantages which resound only in the newspapers and in the opinion of the mass, while he would be diminishing the true capital of his state and weakening all its resources for years to come?

Kaunitz in reply cruelly reminded him of the more martial spirit of his mother.[64]

Belgium is a striking case, a province (or group of provinces) that Joseph wanted to exchange with Bavaria. It has often been claimed that this foreign policy aim dominated his approach to domestic reform in Belgium. But his programme proceeded on very similar lines to his programme on Lombardy, which he had no idea of giving up. When he decided to have a second try at exchanging Belgium in 1784 – surely a scheme of such overwhelming strategic advantage to the Monarchy that it should have been pursued regardless of financial benefit – he wasted precious weeks enquiring how the revenues of the two provinces compared and, learning that Belgium was supposed to yield more than Bavaria, made his task even more difficult by demanding more than just Bavaria in exchange for it. Further, so little did he appreciate the risks associated with domestic reform that his drastic measures of 1787 to remodel the Belgian administration were promulgated when only a handful of troops were stationed in the province. In all these cases he allowed the pursuit of internal reform and fiscal advantage to take precedence over considerations of foreign policy.[65]

Joseph, then, was both despotic and in many respects Enlightened. He would have liked to wield yet more despotic power and impose still more measures of an Enlightened character. When in the last months of his life he conceded the failure of his attempt at personal rule, he was surrendering also the hope of carrying further his programme of Enlightened reform in the Monarchy.

Notes

This is an expanded version of a lecture given in the Juridicum of the University of Vienna on 27 March 1990. I am grateful to Professor Grete Klingenstein and Professor Wilhelm Brauneder for their help and for making that occasion possible. Other organisations have heard variants of the piece and provided helpful comments on it, especially the Austrian Studies Conference of April 1989 at the University of Minnesota. I also owe thanks to Professor T. C. W. Blanning, Professor S. M. Dixon, Dr T. J. Hochstrasser, Professor L. Péter, Professor Ritchie Robertson, Professor H. M. Scott and Dr R. L. Wokler, but I should emphasise that they are not to be taken to agree with every part of my argument.

I have slightly modified the text, which was published in *Austrian Studies*, 2 (1991): 1–21, chiefly by removing the foreign-language quotations and improving the English versions.

1 M. Hawlik-van de Water, *Die Kapuzinergruft. Begräbnisstätte der Habsburger in Wien* (Vienna, 1987) gives details of the monuments, but does not explain why Joseph's is such a new departure.

2 *Joseph II. und Leopold von Toscana: Ihr Briefwechsel von 1781 bis 1790* [hereafter *JuL*], ed. A. Ritter von Arneth (2 vols, Vienna, 1872), vol. II, p. 303 (21 Dec. 1789), p. 304 (24 Dec.), p. 310 (14 Jan. 1790), p. 312 (21 Jan.).

3 The reports of the two Prussian envoys, Podewils and Jacobi, formerly in Zentrales Staatsarchiv, Merseburg, esp. 20 and 24 Feb. 1790 (Rep.96.154.J). Cf. F. Engel-Jánosi, 'Josephs II. Tod im Urteil der Zeitgenossen', *Mitteilungen des österreichischen Instituts für Geschichtsforschung* [hereafter *MIÖG*], 44 (1930): 324–46.

4 W. Doyle, *London Review of Books*, 19 May 1988, pp. 19–20. Cf. his later remarks in *The Times Higher Education Supplement*, 29 June 1990, reviewing Scott's collection (see next n.), in which he declares that Catherine II was the only Enlightened *despot* and Joseph II 'the most celebrated practitioner of Enlightened absolutism'.

5 Among the most important are: F. Venturi, *Settecento riformatore* (5 vols [7 tomes], Turin, 1969–2002), esp. vol. IV, tome 2, section VIII (pp. 615–779), on Joseph II generally, and vol. V, tome 1, section III (pp. 425–834), on Lombard reformers; C. Capra, 'Il Settecento', in D. Sella and C. Capra, *Il ducato di Milano dal 1535 al 1796* (vol. XI of *Storia d'Italia*, ed. G. Galasso, Turin, 1984), pp. 153–684; M. Bazzoli, *Il pensiero politico dell'assolutismo illuminato* (Florence, 1986); B. Köpeczi, A. Soboul, E. H. Balázs and D. Kosáry, *L'absolutisme éclairé* (Budapest, 1985); P. G. M. Dickson, *Finance and Government under Maria Theresia* (2 vols, Oxford, 1987); H. M. Scott (ed.), *Enlightened Absolutism* (London, 1990); G. Birtsch, 'Der Idealtyp des aufgeklärten Herrschers. Friedrich der Grose, Karl Friedrich von Baden und Joseph II. im Vergleich', *Aufklärung*, II (1987), pp. 9–47; V. Press, 'Kaiser Joseph II. – Reformer oder Despot?', in G. Vogler (ed.), *Europäische Herrscher. Ihre Rolle bei der Gestaltung von Politik und Gesellschaft vom. 16. bis um 18. Jahrhundert* (Weimar, 1988). I owe thanks to Professors Bazzoli, Dickson and Venturi, and to the editors of *L'absolutisme éclairé* for generously sending me copies of the volumes cited and to the late Professor G. R. Elton for lending me Press's article.

6 Dickson, *Finance and Government*, vol. I, pp. 318–19.

7 In Acton to Creighton, Apr. 1887 (L. Creighton, *Life and Letters of Mandell Creighton* [2 vols, London, 1906], vol. I, p. 372), with reference to popes and kings and in a sixteenth-century context.

8 It is perhaps sufficient to cite P. Gay, *The Enlightenment: An Interpretation* (2 vols, London, 1967–70), esp. vol. II, pp. 461–96.

9 To give references for the whole paragraph would mean providing a bibliography of the Enlightenment. For the differences in political outlook between Germans and others see esp. T. C. W. Blanning, *Reform and Revolution in Mainz, 1743–1803* (Cambridge, 1974), pp. 1–38.

10 C. B. A. Behrens, 'Enlightened Despotism', *Historical Journal*, XVIII (1975): 401–8.

11 W. Doyle, *The Ancien Régime* (London, 1986); C. B. A. Behrens, *The Ancien Régime* (London, 1967).

12 So it is universally stated. But Dr R. L. Wokler has generously drawn my attention to Diderot's use of 'despotisme … éclairé': *Oeuvres politiques*, ed. P. Vernière (Paris, 1963), p. 272.

13 Behrens, *Historical Journal* (1975): 401. Cf. K. O. von Aretin (ed.), *Der aufgeklärte Absolutismus* (Cologne, 1974), p. 11, and M. Cranston, *Philosophers and Pamphleteers: Political Theorists of the Enlightenment* (Oxford, 1986), pp. 112, 114. These authors all seem to me to have misunderstood Le Mercier's argument, as, I think, in a different way has Gay (*Enlightenment*, vol. II, pp. 494–6).

14 The best treatment remains G. Weulersse, *Le mouvement physiocratique en France* (2 vols, Paris, 1910). For other valuable discussions see H. Holldack, 'Der Physiokratismus und der absolute Monarchie', in Aretin, *Aufgeklärte Absolutismus*, pp. 137–62; Bazzoli, *Pensiero politico*, esp. ch. X.

15 I. de Madariaga, *Russia in the Age of Catherine the Great* (London, 1981), pp. 337, 627.

16 E.g. Joseph II to the duke of Courland, 2 Feb. 1781: 'les Terres ne fructifient jamais plus qu'entre les mains des Particuliers', Haus-, Hof- und Staatsarchiv, Vienna [hereafter HHSA], Handbilletenprotokolle, tom. V.

17 On the role of geometry in the thinking of German *Aufklärer*, especially Kaunitz, see G. Klingenstein, *Der Aufstieg des Hauses Kaunitz* (Göttingen, 1975), pp. 168–70, and H. Klueting, *Die Lehre von der Macht der Staaten* (Berlin, 1986), esp. pp. 26, 172, 228. Professor Klingenstein generously sent me a copy of Klueting's book.

18 F. Bluche, 'Sémantique du despotisme éclairé', *Revue historique de droit français et étranger*, 4th series, 56 (1978): 79–87, quotation from p. 86.

19 The third edition of Raynal's book seems to have become available only in 1781: Y. Benot, *Diderot, de l'Athéisme à l'Anticolonialisme* (Paris, 1981), p. 163. The quotation is from vol. X of the Peuchet edition of 1820, p. 52.

20 On the part played by Diderot in the composition of Raynal's book, and on the development of his political attitudes, see Benot, *Diderot*; H. Wolpe, *Raynal et sa Machine de Guerre* (Stanford, 1957); Denis Diderot, *Pensées détachées*, ed. G. Goggi (2 vols, Siena, 1976–77); A. Strugnell, *Diderot's Politics* (The Hague, 1973); and the characteristically elusive discussion in L. Krieger, *An Essay on the Theory of Enlightened Despotism* (Chicago, 1975), pp. 20–2, 86–7.

21 The classic account is P. Gay, *Voltaire's Politics* (London, 1959), from which I differ in emphasis. I should like to acknowledge the generosity of Clare College, acting through Professor T. J. Smiley, in giving me the late Mr C. W. Parkin's copy of this scarce volume. See Voltaire on Montesquieu's distinction in *L'A,B,C* (1768) and A. Lortholary, *Le mirage russe en France au XVIIIe siècle* (Paris, 1951).

22 On Gorani and his book, Venturi, *Settecento riformatore*, vol. V, tome 1,

esp. pp. 500–11; Bazzoli, *Pensiero politico*, pp. 95–9; C. Capra introducing G. Gorani, *Storia di Milano (1700–1796)*, ed. A. Tarchetti (Bari, 1989), esp. pp. ix–xi. Professor Capra kindly gave me a copy of this book, as also of his article cited in the next n.

23 Quoted in C. Capra, 'Alle origini del moderatismo e del giacobinismo in Lombardia: Pietro Verri e Pietro Custodi', *Studi storici* (1989): 876–7.

24 Among treatments of this distinction I have found especially useful Krieger, *Enlightened Despotism*; Bazzoli, *Pensiero politico*, esp. ch. III.

25 Uses of 'absolu' in *De l'esprit des lois* are at least very rare. Montesquieu does refer to 'les monarchies extrèmement absolues' in Book XIX, ch. XXVI. For interpretation of the work see M. Richter, *The Political Theory of Montesquieu* (Cambridge, 1977); R. Shackleton, *Montesquieu* (Oxford, 1961), esp. ch. XII.

26 The articles are conveniently reprinted in J. Lough (ed.), *The Encyclopédie of Diderot and D'Alembert: Selected Articles* (Cambridge, 1954), pp. 160–4.

27 R. Mettam, *Power and Faction in Louis XIV's France* (London, 1988), pp. 34–5.

28 J. Bodin, *Six Books of the Commonwealth*, ed. M. J. Tooley (Oxford, n.d.), p. 32; Q. Skinner, *The Foundations of Modern Political Thought* (2 vols, Cambridge, 1978), vol. II, pp. 284–9.

29 A valuable discussion of the issues raised in this paragraph is to be found in F. Hartung and R. Mousnier, 'Quelques problèmes concernant la monarchie absolue' in the proceedings of the X Congresso Internazionale di scienze storiche (Rome, 1955), *Relazioni*, vol. IV, pp. 1–55. Cf. for Germany G. Parry, 'Enlightened Government and Its Critics in Eighteenth-century Germany', *Historical Journal*, VI (1963): 178–92; T. J. Reed, 'Talking to Tyrants: Dialogues with Power in Eighteenth-Century Germany', *Historical Journal*, XXXIII (1990): 63–79.

30 Lough (ed.), *Encyclopédie: Selected Articles*, p. 163. I should add that Montesquieu's articles were found useful in certain respects by Enlightened despots. See Bazzoli, *Pensiero politico*, esp. pp. 54–8; P. Dukes (ed.), *Catherine the Great's Instruction (NAKAZ) to the Legislative Commission, 1767* (Newtonville, 1977), Introduction; I. de Madariaga, 'Catherine II and Enlightened Absolutism', 'Catherine II and the *Philosophes*' and 'Catherine II and Montesquieu' in her *Politics and Culture in Eighteenth-Century Russia* (London, 1998), pp. 195–261, reprints of earlier articles. Professor de Madariaga very kindly gave me a copy of this volume.

31 Bodin, *Six Books*, pp. 56–9.

32 T. Hobbes, *Leviathan*, ed. M. Oakeshott (Oxford, n.d.), pp. 121, 132–3. A further range of semantic difficulties arises in Russian: see I. de Madariaga, 'Autocracy and Sovereignty' in her *Politics and Culture*, pp. 40–56.

33 D. Beales, *Joseph II. I: In the Shadow of Maria Theresa, 1714–1780* (Cambridge, 1987), pp. 43–68.

34 See Chapter 6, 'Joseph's *Rêveries*'.

35 J. Keresztury, *Introductio in opus collectionis normalium constitutorum, quae regnante ... Josepho II. pro regno Hungariae ... condita sunt* (Vienna, 1788), part 2, p. 96.

36 HHSA, Staasrataktenprotokollen 1784, vol. III, no. 3602.

37 There is no satisfactory account of his Hungarian policies and his renunciation of them, at least in a generally accessible language. The best guide in English is É. H. Balázs, *Hungary and the Habsburgs, 1765–1800* (Budapest, 1997). See T. C. W. Blanning, *Joseph II* (London, 1994), pp. 112–16.

38 For Joseph and the Brabant revolution the best treatments available in English are W. W. Davis, *Joseph II: An Imperial Reformer for the Austrian Netherlands* (The Hague, 1974) and J. L. Polasky, *Revolution in Brussels, 1787–1793* (London, 1987), but neither has gone beyond the published sources for Joseph himself. See for the Belgian oaths my *Prosperity and Plunder* (Cambridge, 2003), pp. 210–24.

39 Beales, *Joseph II*, p. 5.

40 Ibid., p. 215.

41 I first encountered this striking document in the Austrian collection of the library of the University of Minnesota in Minneapolis (MS Z943.6 fEs 73) (p. 528). I later found another copy, apparently identical in text though not in pagination, in the Acton MSS, University Library, Cambridge. My quotations come from pp. 67–9, 73, 89, 216, 508 in the Minneapolis version.

42 I have still found no reference of any kind, contemporary or subsequent, to this not inconspicuous document. Its presence in the Acton collection guarantees its connection with the Neapolitan minister Acton. On p. 479 of the MS it is coyly stated: 'Je ne dirai rien du Marquis de Gallo ... parceque je suis partial.' Cf. for Austro-Neapolitan relations A. Wandruszka, *Leopold II.* (2 vols, Vienna, 1963–65), vol. II, pp. 213–19, 297–301; G. Nuzzo, *La monarchia delle Due Sicilie tra Ancien Régime e Rivoluzione* (Naples, 1972), which, though it has a chapter on Acton's policy, does not mention this document.

43 E.g. Joseph to Leopold, 7 Aug. 1782; 6 July 1787: *JuL*, vol. I, pp. 128–9; vol. II, pp. 213–19, 297–301.

44 Joseph to Kaunitz, 23–24 June 1787, from Leopol (HHSA, Vienna, Handbilletenprotokollen, vol. XI).

45 Beales, *Joseph II*, pp. 55–63.

46 See Chapter 5, 'The False Joseph II' and Chapter 3, 'Christians and *Philosophes*', above.

47 Birtsch, *Aufklärung* (1987).

48 My *Joseph II*, pp. 377–8, 393; cf. H. Wagner, 'Die Reise Josephs II. nach Frankreich 1777 und die Reformen in Österreich', in *Österreich und Europa. Festgabe für Hugo Hantsch zum 70. Geburtstag* (Vienna, 1965), pp. 221–46.

49 Gebler to Nicolai, 16 Nov. 1783: R. M. Werner (ed.), *Aus dem josephinischen Wien* (Berlin, 1888), p. 12.

50 They were republished in D. G. Mohnike, 'Briefwechsel Kaiser Josephs II. mit Clemens Wenzel, Churfürst von Trier', *Zeitschrift für die historische Theologie*, 4 (1834): 263–90.

51 One contemporary version was *Joseph des Zweyten Erinnering an seine Staatsbeamten, am Schlusse des 1783ten Jahres* (Vienna, [1784]). The original French MS is in HHSA, Staatskanzleivorträge 138 (1783).

52 Its inspiration is acknowledged in Keresztury, *Introductio*, Part I, p. iv; in [J. Kropatschek,] *Handbuch aller unter der Regierung des Kaiser Joseph des II. für die KK Erbländer ergangenen Verordnungen und Gesetze*, vol. I (Vienna, 1785), p. (i) and in J. N. Hempel-Kürsinger (ed.), *Alphabetisch-chronologische Übersicht der k.k. Gesetze ... vom ... 1741 bis ... 1821*, vol. I (1825), p. vii. Cf. p. 298 below.

53 The hymn is known in an English version as 'The duteous day now closeth'.

54 On *Faustin* see L. Bodi, *Tauwetter in Wien: Zur Prosa der österreichischen Aufklärung 1781–1795* (Vienna, 1975); M. Delon, 'Candide au service de Joseph II', in E. Bene (ed.), *Les Lumières en Hongrie, en Europe centrale et en Europe orientale. (Actes du 4me Colloque de Mátrafüred, 1978)*, pp. 61–6.

55 This seems to me true both of Bodi and of E. Wangermann, for example in *The Austrian Achievement, 1700–1800* (London, 1973), pp. 142–7, 157–66. A recent example is G. Ammerer, 'Provozierte Öffentlichkeit: Zensurerleichterung, Lesewut und die Folgen am Beispiel der Wiener Diskurse um den letzten Österreichischen Türkenkrieg (1788–1791)', in *Jahrbuch der Österr. Gesellschaft zur Erforschung des achtzehnten Jhdts*, 13 (1999), pp. 107–32, which shamelessly ignores evidence in the contrary sense, e.g. the enthusiasm for the capture of Belgrade. See Blanning, *Joseph II*, pp. 186–7.

56 *Ludwig van Beethoven's Werke. Serie 25: Supplement* (Leipzig, 1887), pp. 1–54.

57 See above, p. 171.

58 Beales, *Joseph II*, p. 237.

59 Ibid., pp. 164–76, 445–55. Twenty-four was the age stipulated.

60 Ibid., pp. 154–5, 317–18.

61 Ibid., p. 469. E. Kovacs, *Der Pabst in Teutschland* (Munich, 1983), p. 101.

62 J. Whaley, *Religious Toleration and Social Change in Hamburg, 1529–1819* (Cambridge, 1985), p. 146; J. Karniel, *Die Toleranzpolitik Kaiser Josephs II.* (Gerlingen, 1986); P. von Mitrofanov, *Joseph II. Seine politische und kulturelle Tätigkeit* (2 vols, Vienna, 1910), pp. 841–2.

63 Beales, *Joseph II*, p. 189 and chs 9 and 13.

64 Joseph to Kaunitz, 26 Aug. 1788: A. Beer (ed.), *Joseph II., Leopold II. und Kaunitz* (Vienna, 1873), pp. 307–9.

65 For a chronology of Italian Church legislation see F. Valsecchi, *L'assolutismo illuminato in Austria e in Lombardia* (2 vols, Bologna, 1931–34), vol. II, p. 238n. On the attempted exchange of 1784, P. P. Bernard, *Joseph II and Bavaria* (The Hague, 1965), chs X and XI. For the Belgian reforms, Davis, *Joseph II*, esp. ch. VII.

CHAPTER 12

Joseph II and Josephism

My objects in this chapter are to explain the meaning of Josephism and the origins of the term, to elucidate the relationship between Joseph II's work and Josephism and between Josephism and Enlightened absolutism or despotism, and finally to consider the varying impact of Josephism on the different peoples and provinces of the Austrian Monarchy.

The three most conspicuous instances of Enlightened absolutism are acknowledged to have been Frederick the Great's in Prussia, Catherine the Great's in Russia and Joseph II's in the Austrian Monarchy.[1] Notoriously, the first two rulers have been almost universally styled 'the Great', while Joseph has virtually never been so honoured.[2] Doubtless Frederick and Catherine owe their title to their huge military successes and territorial gains rather than to any other aspect of their rule, and its denial to Joseph reflects his relative military failure. On the other hand, the identification of Joseph's name with a programme or movement, 'Josephism', in German, *Josephinismus* – which is, I think, a unique distinction for a monarch – is objectively well justified by his reforms which, even if one takes into account only the measures of his sole reign, outclassed in number, range and rapidity those of Frederick and Catherine, and indeed those of any other practitioner of Enlightened absolutism. Though they seemed 'inconsequent' in detail and in execution, and many of them can be paralleled elsewhere, they were consistent enough, and in their ensemble characteristic enough, to warrant their being treated as distinctive and as a system.[3]

But are the reforms of his reign to be regarded as identical with Josephism? By no means. In the first place, many of his reforms amount to the continuation or extension of measures taken by his mother or the fruition of principles laid down during her reign. Even before 1761, when he began to participate regularly in decision-making, she imposed in 1748–49 the administrative and financial reforms for the central lands masterminded by Count Haugwitz, and

in 1759 important restrictions on the role of the Jesuits in education
and censorship promoted by Gerard van Swieten. Her so-called political testaments date from 1750 and 1756 and she endorsed Kaunitz's
invention of the Staatsrat in 1760.[4] After 1761, and more especially
after Joseph became emperor and co-regent in 1765, he played a
significant part in shaping policy. How significant a part is a matter
of dispute. To some extent it always will be, because, despite the
remarkable number of surviving letters between Maria Theresa and
Joseph, many of them extraordinarily revealing, we shall never know
what passed between them, or between each of them and Kaunitz,
in private. Both Joseph and Kaunitz, in their different styles, were
overweeningly vain, each constantly drawing attention to his own
wisdom, consistency and achievements. If one concentrates on the
papers composed by Kaunitz, elaborate, courtly, lucid and reasonable,
one is inclined to attribute the overwhelming influence to him.[5]
If one reads Joseph's curt, biting, impatient letters and his hectic,
fulminating, jumbled memoranda, although they so often complain
that his views are being ignored, it becomes clear that he was listened
to because he had to be – though he was never conceded anything
like the whole of what he demanded. Maria Theresa drew certain
lines which she would not permit to be crossed, about religious
toleration, about the treatment of Belgium and Hungary and about
the supersession of herself as ruler of the Monarchy. It must surely
be agreed by everyone that the government had between 1765 and
1780 taken some of the important steps in the history of Josephism,
and that the policy owed much to each of Maria Theresa, Joseph
and Kaunitz. But I think it must also be accepted that after 1780 the
number, range and radicalism of the measures enormously increased;
that they were now fully applied, as had not been the case before,
to Hungary and then to Belgium and Lombardy; and that, so far
as any monarch could, Joseph laid down the policy and made the
decisions himself.[6]

I

Before saying more about the 1780s, however, I want to consider
critically how the term 'Josephinismus' originated – a question to
which historians have given astonishingly little attention. The great
series *Geschichtliche Grundbegriffe* has shown the value of examining
the origin and historical development of the concepts employed by

historians. But, while 'Enlightenment' and 'Despotism' both appear in these volumes, and there is some though inadequate discussion of Enlightened absolutism, they give no help whatever on Josephism.[7] Rather surprisingly, none of the three major works on the subject, Winter's, Valjavec's and Maass's,[8] considers the origins of the term. The only important discussion of it known to me is that of Roger Bauer in his review of Maass's first four volumes published in 1958.[9] It is common for historians to write as though the term existed in the late eighteenth century,[10] but I believe he is right in concluding that it did not. As he says, the adjective '*josephinisch*' is used quite commonly in documents of the reign of Joseph II and thereafter, at least down to the 1850s, simply meaning 'of Joseph II' or 'of the time of Joseph II', without any content other than personal or chronological. So far as he could find, the use of the adjective with an ideological content began only in the 1830s, at the same time, he concludes, as the noun 'Josephinismus' was coined. No more recent writer appears to have found an earlier instance of these usages, with one possible exception that I shall cite shortly. Bauer's view is supported by the fact that, as Professor Dickson notes, the first example of the term 'Josephinismus' in Maass's vast collection of documents under that title does not appear until volume V, in a letter written in 1840 by Metternich. It is in French, and speaks of 'what is understood by Josephinism'.[11] Metternich's use of the form '*joséphinisme*', rather than the natural and already coined French form, '*joséphisme*', suggests that the term was by then established in German.[12] But it must still have been new and it seems not to have been commonly used. It is often lacking in places where one might expect to find it. I could not find the noun in Groß-Hoffinger's or Meynert's works on Joseph II, published in 1837 and 1862 respectively, or in Arneth's *Geschichte Maria Theresias* or in his autobiography.[13] Of course, I cannot be certain that I have not missed the word in skimming through works running to two, four and ten volumes, but I am at least certain that these authors did not use it regularly.

The history of the adjective is more complicated, not least because of the half-exception I mentioned, namely, that Johann Pezzl in his *Faustin*, originally published in 1783, wrote of 'a new era ... the era of Enlightened southern Germany, the Josephist era', to be dated from 1780. The year marks the 'victory of Reason and Humanity' and ought to be celebrated as the 'year of salvation, as the beginning of the Enlightened philosophical century, that future generations will celebrate with rejoicing and place in the records of the human race next the accession of Sesostris, Fohi, Orpheus, Antoninus and Marcus Aurelius'.[14] This seems like a bid on Pezzl's part to endow the adjective with ideological content. But it appears to be a unique instance in this period both of the form '*josephisch*' and of the adjective in any but a neutral sense. It is also, interestingly, an anticipation of Kant's celebrated christening of the age of Enlightenment in the following year as 'the age of Frederick'. '*Fritzisch*' – not '*fritzinisch*' – was used at the same period with at least a partisan significance, but I don't believe anyone has employed '*Fritzismus*'.[15]

How, then, were the terms '*Josephinismus*' and the ideological adjective '*josephinisch*' used when they were first employed, in the last years of the reign of Emperor Francis? Bauer quotes a despatch from the papal nuncio in Vienna, Ostini, of 1834, in which he says that 'Josephine teaching' (*l'insegnamento Gioseffino*) infects all the organs of Austrian government.[16] A young French priest, Charles Sainte-Foi, who had studied in Munich and was making a tour of Austria, probably in 1835, wrote in his journal: 'It was under [the Emperor Francis] ... that Josephist legislation was systematically brought into force'; and he talked of the 'baleful' effects in the Austrian provinces of '*le joséphisme*'.[17] When Metternich himself used the term in 1840, he was engaged in manoeuvring to repeal what was left of Joseph's Church legislation, at least in so far as it was now objectionable to the papacy. In the cited letter he was talking about rescinding Joseph's law of 1783 which introduced civil marriage. He wrote: 'reduced to its essence, Josephinism is only a ghost, which passed over a land intending to transform it, but succeeded only in causing a stir without creating anything'. He goes on to say, rather belying his statement that it is a phantom, that its pretensions are simply illegal, and its application – he seems to be thinking especially of the marriage law – leads to striking contradictions.[18] Robert Evans is evidently correct in suggesting that the noun was invented by clericals to describe the system they thought they were fighting.[19]

On the other side of the political and religious debate the noun is harder to find. But Groß-Hoffinger, for whom 'All that Austria is and can still be, it has become through Joseph', at least used the adjective in an ideological sense, talking in the final eulogistic peroration of his biography about 'Josephinist spirit, education, principles'.[20] His idea of what it meant to be '*josephinisch*' was of course distorted by his acceptance as genuine of the *Letters of Joseph II*, the so-called

'Constantinople letters', published in 1790, which represented the emperor as a *philosophe*.[21]

It is surely significant that both the noun and what I have called the ideological adjective arrived so late, more than forty years after Joseph's death, and as pejorative terms, and that they had reference to the position in the 1830s and 1840s and to the continued vigour of some of Joseph's legislation down to 1848 and beyond. And not only of his legislation. Metternich in his memoirs declares that it was the skilful obstruction of the bureaucracy, inspired by their ingrained Josephinist attitudes, which frustrated his attempt to abolish what he calls the absurd legislation of Joseph II on religion. Ignaz Beidtel, too, saw the civil service, to which he belonged, as the last redoubt of the emperor's ecclesiastical principles.[22]

Historians using the concept 'Josephism' must, it seems to me, accept that it includes the phenomenon which it was invented to describe, namely the persistence of some of Joseph II's legislation and attitudes – perhaps even the strengthening of these attitudes within the government service – into the reigns of Francis and Ferdinand. All three of the major writers on the theme, Winter, Valjavec and Maass, rightly extend their discussion into this period. This point has a corollary that is important for my argument. It follows that Josephism ought not to be regarded as straightforwardly identical with Enlightened absolutism. Francis was certainly a pillar of the Josephism of the 1830s, and in at least one respect would seem to have gone beyond his uncle's position. I think it is now widely accepted that Maria Theresa, Joseph and Kaunitz, although they had worked to reduce the power of the Jesuits, were all genuinely reluctant to see the Society suppressed by the pope in 1773. This is a rare instance where Professor Franz Szabo and I agree. After the event the two rulers and their chancellor were all determined to make full use of the talents of ex-Jesuits, and Joseph appointed several of them as tutors to Francis.[23] But it was with great difficulty that Francis was persuaded to allow a few exiled Jesuits back from Russia in 1820, and then only into Galicia, and all the efforts of Metternich and the ultramontane party could not get them allowed into the rest of the Monarchy over the opposition of the emperor and the bureaucracy.[24] This opposition is a manifestation of the Josephism which the term was invented to describe, but surely Francis himself cannot be regarded as a representative of Enlightened absolutism.

II

Let us now return to the 1780s, or the period from roughly 1748 to 1792, and look at Josephism as commonly understood nowadays, the mainly domestic and reforming policies of Joseph II and, where applicable, of his mother, his brother Leopold (emperor from 1790 to 1792) and Kaunitz. There are several respects in which Josephism so understood is distinctive as compared with the other major examples of Enlightened absolutism.

First, it was concerned to an exceptional extent with ecclesiastical and religious matters, understood in a broad sense. If in the 1830s the religious element loomed too large in retrospect, it had always been of the highest importance. Some historians, in their laudable efforts to treat Enlightenment and Enlightened absolutism as Europe-wide phenomena, seem to me to be in danger of underrating the ineluctable differences between Protestant and Catholic countries. For example, on the one hand some English historians emphasise that in the eighteenth century the country, with its entrenched and privileged Anglican Establishment, was a confessional state, analogous, they say, to the Catholic Church in Gallican France.[25] On the other hand, attempts have been made to show that Maria Theresa's personal large-heartedness amounted to genuine religious toleration. In one particularly desperate attempt on these lines, Count Karl von Zinzendorf – a risky case to take anyway, since he had to convert to Catholicism in order to pursue a career in the Austrian service – is said to have experienced non-Catholic worship in that well-known Presbyterian institution, the Viennese Schottenstift.[26] It is certainly true that in all European countries a Christian Church or Churches dominated education at all levels. In all countries one Church was established. In no European country did anything like the separation of Church and state, and virtual religious freedom, exist as it did in the United States after 1789 and in some of its constituent states earlier. In at least one largely Catholic country, Poland, Protestants and their worship had legal status.[27] Something similar was found in parts of Germany and parts of the Austrian Monarchy, chiefly Hungary and Transylvania. But Protestants did not have legal status in most other parts of the Monarchy before 1781, or in other Catholic states. Moreover, no Protestant country had 40 per cent of its land owned by the Church, as in Lower Austria, or even more as in Bavaria; or 20 per cent of the land owned by monasteries, as in Lower Austria, and again much more than that in Bavaria – I need hardly say that no Protestant country contained more than a tiny handful of usually half-secularised monasteries. In no Protestant country did large areas form part of dioceses whose bishop was based outside the territory, as was true to a wholly exceptional extent in the Austrian duchies. Of course, in no Protestant country was it necessary to pay attention to the religious decrees of a foreign sovereign, or the decrees of foreign superiors of religious Orders. In virtually no Protestant country were there any Jesuits at all, whereas in Catholic countries before the 1750s they were more or less monopolistic censors, professors and royal confessors. So far as I know, in no Protestant country were all bishops nobles, as in France and the Empire. In Catholic countries the Enlightenment, including the Catholic Enlightenment, had to address these matters as of the highest priority. In Protestant countries these problems did not exist.[28] In this context Orthodox Russia, with its more or less apolitical Church, came nearer to Protestant than Catholic countries. If these were insufficient reasons for the prominence of ecclesiastical issues in Josephism, there was the additional *Sonderweg* for the Austrian Monarchy that three successive rulers, Maria Theresa, Joseph II and Leopold II, were virtually amateur theologians. It has been plausibly argued that Maria Theresa was a Jansenist – she certainly came close.[29] The papal nuncio thought Joseph II was one, and Joseph certainly bandied theology in his published correspondence with the elector of Trier in 1781.[30] He believed, following Febronius, that it was his duty as ruler to reform the Church, and he told the pope, with a self-assurance breath-taking even for him:

> Without needing to search the texts of Holy Scripture or the Fathers of the Church, I have within me a voice that tells me what, as legislator and protector of religion, it is appropriate for me to do or leave undone; and this voice, with the aid of divine grace and the honest and just character that I know I possess, cannot lead me into error.[31]

The pope was not accepted as infallible, but Joseph claimed so to be. Finally, Leopold II – though he denied being a Jansenist or having supported Jansenism when asked the straight question by abbot Gerbert of St Blasien after he had succeeded his brother in Vienna – had certainly looked like one as he gave his blessing to some of the projects of bishop Scipione de' Ricci in Tuscany.[32]

III

Secondly, Josephism, at least as embodied in Joseph II, was peculiar in that it was more radical in its reformism, and I believe – though I know this is a controversial position – more despotic, both in theory and in practice, than either Frederick's or Catherine's regime. As for Frederick, it is true that he had no prime minister and no principal adviser, answered all major despatches himself, had a genuinely large part in internal regulation, treated his ministers and civil servants with contempt – and possessed a ferociously disciplined army which dominated the state. But in his numerous writings he was very fond of distinguishing absolute from despotic rule and always aligned himself with the former. When he took control of new provinces, he respected their old boundaries and allowed them some individuality. He upheld the nobility as a necessary support of his regime and hence did very little to assist the serfs. By comparison with Joseph, he introduced many fewer legislative changes.[33] Catherine ranked as a despot in the categorisation of Montesquieu and most contemporaries because, first, she was a usurper whose rule was made possible by the fact that Russia had no law of succession and, secondly, her power as sovereign was constitutionally untrammelled. But she was desperately anxious to shed the image of the despot, explicitly called herself absolute and not despotic, in 1766 summoned the extraordinary Legislative Commission of 630 representatives to advise her – it is quite inconceivable that either Joseph or Frederick would have done that – established 'intermediary bodies' between the ruler and the subject, as required by Montesquieu, and claimed always to wait on the development of opinion before trying to impose reform. She too was absolutely dependent on the nobility and deliberately extended their rights and privileges.[34] Joseph, on the other hand, although he liked to criticise the 'despotism' of the pope and of subordinate officials, famously urged in 1763 that a *despotisme lié* be imposed on the provinces – 'lié' meaning 'not restricted in any way other than by a time-limit of ten years'.[35] He did not blench at the word, to which some more notable thinkers than he were also at roughly the same time imparting a favourable sense: most famously, Grimm and Diderot, but more pertinently some of Joseph's Lombard subjects, who were developing a theory of benevolent, philosophical or Enlightened despotism. Count Giuseppe Gorani published in 1770 *Il vero dispotismo* (*The true despotism*). Despotism, he says, has been universally condemned as a monstrous government. He defines it as the operation of

> that will which acts on its own without consulting others, which includes in itself the entire legislative and executive power, which by virtue of the strongest attraction joins and attracts to itself all the vigour and wide-ranging powers of the sovereign, the prince, the government and the whole state, so that the movement of the entire political machine depends on his movement ... Though above the laws, which he can create and destroy at his pleasure, he can through his absolute will arrive at laws as good or better than those existing, which generally and in most countries may be thoroughly bad.

This, he asserts, can yield 'a kind of despotism which ought to result in utility to the public' and a 'total reform'.[36]

Count Pietro Verri, who had given Cesare Beccaria substantial help in writing his *Dei delitti e delle pene* (*Crimes and Punishments*) of 1764 and then, as an official of the government of Lombardy, had urged on Joseph's attempt to remodel its administration in 1769–71, declared in 1781:

> In my opinion, subjects ought never to fear the power of the sovereign when he himself exercises it and doesn't surrender any essential part of it into other hands ... Only intermediate power is to be feared, and I think and feel that the best of all political systems will always be despotism, provided that the sovereign is active and in overall control and doesn't give up any portion of his sovereignty.[37]

Such views also found support from the bitter pen of Simon Linguet, who was notorious for his defence of slavery as a necessary support to a civilised and Enlightened elite. He said that he preferred to all other forms of government,

> for the happiness of the people, that is the most numerous and weak-est part of a nation, [the form] that we improperly stigmatise with the odious name of despotism, namely, the one in which there are no intermediaries between the prince and his subjects powerful enough to stifle the complaints of the latter and to fetter the influence of the former.

It is no surprise that Joseph employed Linguet to defend his policies, especially his foreign policy, in articles and pamphlets, and gave him a title of nobility.[38]

Rather than rely on modern work or on well-known documents, I will illustrate the extremism – and the 'system' – of Joseph's aims and methods from his brother Leopold's *Report on the Journey and Stay ... in Vienna in July 1784*.[39] Parts of this extraordinary document of over 600 pages were drawn upon by Wandruszka in his biography of Leopold,[40] but most of it seems never to have been used. By this date the emperor had irrevocably decided not to remarry, and therefore thought of Leopold as his probable successor and Leopold's son Francis as his ultimate heir; and it was the purpose of Leopold's journey from Florence to bring his son to be educated under Joseph's eye and for both of them to be primed about the state of the Monarchy and the emperor's plans. Leopold's immense *Report*, despite its characteristically jaundiced attitude, was essentially a factual *aide-mémoire* recording what he had learned, from observation and in long conversations with Joseph himself and with the principal officials, about the situation and policies which he might at any moment inherit. It must have been from Joseph's own mouth that Leopold derived his knowledge of what he calls 'the true views of the Court of Vienna in the present system', and so this document almost rivals Frederick the Great's *Rêveries* as a statement of the emperor's secret long-term aims. Some of them are well known, most have been suspected, but not quite all; and this document supplies authoritative evidence for them. It also reveals the depth of the rift between Joseph and Leopold, and hence the difference between what might be called their versions of Josephism.

The emperor, Leopold writes, intends always to have the army and treasury in a condition to be ready for any attack and to sustain war for one campaign. This is twice stated to be the first aim, but other aims are treated as independent, not as arising directly out of the military need or as subordinate to it. Joseph further intends

> to introduce in all his lands an entirely uniform system, identical in all the provinces of the Monarchy [except Italy and Belgium] and hence abolishing every convention, concordat, statutes and privileges of every province, and every privilege or exemption existing in the state, and every distinction of persons even if it is associated with duties; to this end he aims to abolish all Estates, titles ... deputies, privileges, diets etc.[41]

So far as Hungary is concerned, he intends never to call the Diet again and has given instructions that his orders concerning Hungary are to be carried into effect immediately and without prior consultation, 'directly and arbitrarily', and that no attention is to be paid to any protests made against them.[42] He is also going to abolish the Council of State, which according to Leopold produces reports that are 'either insipid or remit the question to the emperor's opinion, without ever saying anything that elucidates the matter'.[43] Joseph has indicated that he does not want nobles at the head of departments.[44] He will abolish serfdom and commute the services for money.[45] All religious practices not found in the primitive Church will be abolished, all friars and nuns will be suppressed, and all clergy turned into salaried officials.[46] Elementary education is to be expanded, but 'higher studies, universities, colleges, building enterprises, manufactures, roads, draining of marshes, navigation, the making of canals, trading projects etc. etc., are objects which the government, with its current principles, intends to do nothing towards, nor even hear them talked about'.[47]

One learns with dismay that even in the University of Vienna there is not deemed to be a single professor of repute. Externally, Joseph is engaged in trying to exchange Bavaria with Belgium, and expects to secure Salzburg as part of the bargain. He still regards the recovery of Silesia as essential, wishes also to regain Belgrade and the lands once held around it, and to obtain from Venice, when it can be compensated from the lands of the Ottoman Empire, the Dalmatian coast.[48] As part of the expected benefits of the Bavarian exchange he will acquire 'the city of Regensburg, and suppress the Imperial Diet on the pretext that no appropriate city can be found for it, thus effectively abolishing it'.[49]

Leopold acknowledges in his *Report* that Joseph 'has good intentions and works night and day', and has done good work in army affairs, and in funding provision for the sick from his own resources.[50] Leopold approves the principle of some of his other measures, such as the suppressions of monasteries, while criticising the manner of their enforcement.[51] The great task imposed on Count Karl von Zinzendorf, of establishing a uniform taxation system on the basis of a new land survey, is 'just, useful and advantageous for the country', but is grossly defective because, for example, it takes account only of cultivable land; it is, moreover, being obstructed by all other officials, and it would in any case need '30 years, 20 millions, and 2 or 3000 people' to do the job properly.[52] Leopold records that everyone lived in fear of the emperor, and the whole public is discontented, except for the common people whom Joseph flatters. The officials all display 'discouragement, degradation, ill humour and ill will' because their conditions of work have worsened and they are constantly receiving orders and counter-orders, being told to get things done more quickly than is possible, being sent letters containing 'very strong and humiliating threats' which go into their files; and they have recently been subjected to the published criticism, largely unfair, of the emperor's 'pastoral letter' [*Hirtenbrief*]. The result is that they

> do nothing but complain, and either don't execute the orders they receive or execute them badly, or only in appearance, or they pass on the orders they receive to the provinces without troubling whether they will be carried out, giving no or confused explanations to the inferior departments that ask for them, or address them directly to the emperor. They let the public know in advance what the government intends to do, presenting it in the worst colours and attributing to the government the worst motives.

They boast freely in public that 'the emperor thinks he can do everything without their assistance, and that he alone should have the credit for everything that succeeds, but that they will show him that without them he can do nothing'.[53] Even Leopold's secret agents, though, had not discovered the clinching evidence that Baron Kressel, the trusted head of the ecclesiastical commission, had told the papal nuncio he was working to obstruct Joseph's aims in every possible way.[54]

Joseph is aware of the discontent of officials and public, and troubled by it. He can no longer go into any company without hearing criticism of his policies. 'It is to be feared that, having no one to whom he can talk freely, he will at some time or another, in disgust, let affairs take their course, as the officials want, and take less interest in them, which is what the heads of department desire, taking pride in wishing to reduce him to this point.' This is only a particularly strong statement of well-known criticisms, but it comes with special force from a ruler and an heir writing for himself alone and secretly, and it is striking that Leopold thinks matters have reached such a low state by the middle of 1784, a year before what is often said to be the caesura of the reign, when the pamphlet *Unwahrscheinlichkeiten* was published and Freemasonry was restricted – and three years before the appearance of *Warum wird Kaiser Joseph von seinem Volke nicht beliebt?* [*Why is Emperor Joseph not loved by his people?*].[55]

Most of the criticisms of Joseph's regime in Leopold's *Relazione* are ascribed to others, but he states as his own opinions that the censorship has been too much relaxed and that the police is inadequate. He comes out strongly against the policy of administrative standardisation, and says of the Hungarian constitution that, despite certain defects, it 'has the greatest advantages in general, superior to all the others in the Monarchy'. As for the early attempts to introduce the new system into Lombardy, 'given the nature of the country, the nation and the legislation, it is completely impossible and could not succeed'. For Leopold, these policies were despotic and unacceptable.[56]

It is notorious that, at the end of the reign, Kaunitz lamented 'that despotic obstinacy has reduced this fine Monarchy to the state it is in'.[57] The bitterest dispute had concerned Joseph's policy towards his Belgian provinces from 1786 onwards. Having failed to effect the Bavarian exchange, Joseph extended the policy of provincial homogenisation to the Netherlands. When rebellion followed in the spring of 1787 and the governors-general caved into the demands of the dissidents, Joseph was far away in Russia while Kaunitz had been left in charge at home. The chancellor wrote to the emperor telling him he agreed with the governors-general and sending conciliatory drafts for Joseph to sign. Joseph replied from Lemberg:

> I am surprised that the people of Brussels and the fanatics who stir them up haven't yet asked for my breeches, and that the government hasn't meanwhile given them assurances that I will send them on. [The signatures you ask for would not be wrung from me by the prospect of certain death.] You will send the document which would have dishonoured me torn in pieces, as it deserves, back to the Government … Whoever dares to speak to me in this fashion is neither the friend of Joseph nor of the emperor.[58]

Philipp Cobenzl, Kaunitz's deputy, was horrified by Joseph's refusal to accept Kaunitz's advice:

> *One letter* is enough to calm everything down and prevent civil war, with its incalculable consequences. How can one hesitate? What will people say of him in his states? What will be said of him throughout Europe? It will be said of him that he counts as nothing the ruin of his provinces, the fate of his servants, the miseries of war, the blood of his subjects, when it's a question of backing him whether he is right or wrong. What will be said of the minister who without any delay executes the orders that his master gives him in a fit of temper? What do

you risk by waiting at least until the emperor is a bit calmer? Anyone who advises him to yield to the torrent, he says, is not his friend; and for my part I should not regard myself as his good and faithful servant if I gave in to his reasoning.

Cobenzl says he will 'sacrifice everything' rather than act on these decisions. Kaunitz replied that he had said all this and more to Joseph, and the only result had been to produce a decision diametrically opposed to his advice, couched in very disobliging terms. He'd deferred acting on the emperor's explicit orders for almost forty-eight hours. 'I cannot allow myself to delay longer; and it will be for him, not me, to answer for the outcome before God and men.'[59] This is the extreme case, when Kaunitz, who had had the principal voice in policy-making since Joseph was a child, who was head of the Belgian department and who had been explicitly left in charge in Vienna while Joseph was away in Russia, acknowledged that the will of the ruler, though all the official advice is against him, must prevail. It is significant that this confrontation occurred over domestic and not over foreign policy.

When Joseph was dying, at the beginning of February 1790, Leopold issued a manifesto dissociating himself from Joseph's despotic views and proclaiming his belief in constitutional government. In so doing he was not simply making a desperate throw to save the cohesion of the Monarchy; he was revealing his long-held beliefs. A year after Leopold ascended the throne, Zinzendorf, who had become thoroughly disillisuioned with Joseph in his last years, wrote in his diary: 'What changes in principles and assumptions and decisions since then! Everything used to be directed towards concentration, uniformity; [now] everything is directed towards dispersion, diversity. It used to be all despotic monarchy, now it is all an anarchy of provincial Estates.'[60]

IV

Josephism, then, understood as Joseph's policy and activity during his sole reign, was exceptionally radical and despotic. It is frequently claimed by modern historians, and was claimed at the time in different words, that absolutism must always rest on the collaboration of ruler, ministers and aristocracy, and hence is very far from despotism.[61] Haugwitz and Kaunitz are classic instances of the readiness of some nobles to further the cause of absolutism. It was certainly the policy of Leopold II to collaborate with the numerous privileged bodies in his dominions. But Joseph was ready – according to Leopold, actually yearned – to dispense with aristocratic co-operation. He refused for several years to take account of opposition in Hungary and Belgium, and he set the nobility at defiance in his serfdom and taxation patent of 1789. By the end of his reign he had completely alienated the most loyal and reformist of his noble supporters. If a readiness to co-operate with the nobility is a qualification for Enlightened absolutism, then Joseph's regime did not deserve that title, but rather that of Enlightened despotism.

The most easy-going monarch will offend some nobles. On the other hand, aristocratic opposition, even when it reaches the point of rebellion, so long as the monarchical principle is accepted, has to offer some terms of co-operation with the ruler. But Kaunitz, as he himself recognised, was not a typical member of his order. Maria Theresa, it should be remembered, though she has left behind her an image of motherly and harmonious co-operation with her peoples and the nobility, had overridden strong aristocratic opposition by royal diktat to carry through the Haugwitz reforms, and in 1777 appeared ready again to override it in order to mitigate the condition of the serfs.[62] The fate of Joseph's regime suggests strongly that it was a necessary condition of the *success* of Enlightened absolutism, at least in a large and civilized country, that the ruler should *normally* enact only such reforms as ministers of repute and a sizeable portion of the aristocracy would support. But it seems to me gratuitous to *define* Enlightened absolutism as collaboration with the nobility and then try to show that Joseph's regime fitted into that definition. It didn't.

V

Joseph used to speak of patriotism and of encouraging that feeling among his subjects, and he and his assistants appealed to love of the fatherland, especially during the Turkish war at the end of his reign. The capture of Belgrade late in 1789 certainly unleashed patriotic demonstrations.[63] But, as for example Robert Evans and Moritz Csáky have shown, the attempt to create a quasi-national consciousness for the whole sprawling Monarchy was inevitably much less successful than Joseph's unwitting evocation of individual provincial nationalisms within his envisaged *Gesamtstaat*.[64]

Hungary is the one country he ruled which has refused to acknowledge him as sovereign, because he had declined to be crowned. Hence his Hungarian laws were, technically at least, null and void and were so treated after 1790. But of course not everything could be unscrambled. None of the monasteries he suppressed in Hungary was re-established until after 1802. And he had certainly given encouragement to Protestant culture and self-awareness by his toleration edict, which was retained.[65] The imposition of German as the language of government, instead of Latin, which was decreed just before Leopold's visit to Vienna, helped to arouse Hungarian national consciousness and the cultivation of the old language, although it was of course the return of Latin, not the use of Hungarian, that the Diet demanded in 1790. In Belgium, too, where observers had thought that Flemish was slowly disappearing, suddenly, in 1788, in the midst of Joseph's assault on the constitutions of the ten provinces, Verlooy published the first vindication of the language.[66]

However, nationalist movements were not all reactions against Joseph's work. The emperor seems, like many of his contemporaries, to have been simply unable to appreciate intense national feeling, or to see it as a threat. It is hard to imagine that he could have understood Rousseau's proposals for nurturing national feeling in Poland, if he had known of them. Yet in fact his activity and methods gave much positive encouragement to the revival and regularisation of languages which had previously had low status. In Transylvania Joseph's determination to treat all his subjects equally, together with his measure of religious toleration for the Greek Orthodox, led to the limitation of the privileges of the three existing so-called nations, Saxons, Szeklers and Magyars, and the awakening of the Orthodox Romanians' political consciousness. In their petition to Leopold, the *Supplex libellus valachorum* of 1790, they wrote (in Latin of course):

It was acknowledged finally by that blessed emperor of eternal
memory, the all-just and almighty Emperor Joseph the Second who
understood the pure and simple rights both of man and of the citizen,
who realised the injustice and oppression, who saw with his own
eyes and was fully persuaded that the Romanian nation was far more
numerous than the others in the province and of great use, both in
times of peace and of war; that is why, in his desire to carry out his
task as an all-just prince, and restore to the citizens their rights in order
to prevent discord and disagreement between the nations, overlooking

all the prejudices of those who were opposed, often decided, with great mercy, that in the future, wiping out completely any unjust discrimination of inequality, the Romanians, even irrespective of their nation and religion, should fully enjoy the same rights and benefits as the other peoples in this Principality, and since they are charged with equal tasks, they should be granted equal rights and benefits.[67]

I once did some work in the archives of the Hungarian Sanitäts-Hofkommission. Joseph's ever-active government, both before and after the imposition of German, circulated to its subjects, free of charge, little printed booklets on how to deal with urgent practical problems: fires, grain diseases, diseases of sheep and cattle, Danube floods and so forth. The administration was charged to make and distribute translations in the vernacular languages. The lists varied, but one of them consisted of seven languages apart from Latin and German, namely, Hungarian, 'schlovakisch' (Slovak), 'illirisch' (Illyrian), 'wallachisch' (Romanian), 'raitzisch' (Serbian), 'ruthenisch' (Ruthenian/Ukrainian) and 'kroatisch' (Croat).[68] Some of these pamphlets must be among the earliest modern texts in their languages.

VI

Joseph had tried to pursue a whole series of potentially conflicting aims at one and the same time, virtually, it seems, without a sense of priorities. He wanted to be despotic while lacking the means to enforce his will. His handling of his subordinates was disagreeable and counter-productive. Hence many of his projects were not fulfilled, or only partially achieved. But what he did succeed in imposing, together with what his mother had sanctioned – and it must always be remembered too that Leopold was as discriminating as circumstances permitted in what he allowed to subsist of their measures – sooner or later won over most civil servants to his policies, and even many clergy, as shown by their hostility to the repeal of his ecclesiastical legislation in the *Vormärz*. And it left an ineffaceable, if dubious, memory of radicalism and populism which liberals and other reformers could exploit in 1848 and afterwards.[69] Josephism certainly created a great deal of stir, not always in the directions intended. But it was no more a phantom than Italy, that other political force which Metternich contemptuously dismissed, was a mere geographical expression.

Notes

This chapter is a translation of my article 'Joseph II und der Josephinismus', in H. Reinalter and H. Klueting (eds), *Der aufgeklärte Absolutismus im europäischen Vergleich* (Vienna, 2002), pp. 35–54. It is becoming commoner to find the form 'Josephinism' used in English, but I prefer the natural English 'Josephism' to the quasi-German 'Josephinism'.

1 The two most useful surveys are K. O. Freiherr von Aretin (ed.), *Der aufgeklärte Absolutismus* (Cologne, 1974) and H. M. Scott (ed.), *Enlightened Absolutism* (London, 1990).

2 Attempts were made to designate Joseph 'the Great', e.g. K. A. Schimmer, *Kaiser Joseph. Biographische Skizzen ...* (2nd edn, Vienna, 1845), p. vii.

3 It is a particular pleasure to cite in support of these points the most recent book on the emperor, by my friend and colleague T. C. W. Blanning (*Joseph II* [London, 1994]), who began work on the emperor some years before I did and has advised and helped me continuously ever since, and read and commented on an earlier draft of this chapter. See also H. Klueting (ed.), *Der Josephinismus* (Darmstadt, 1995). P. von Mitrofanov, *Joseph II.: seine politische und kulturelle Tätigkeit* (2 vols, Vienna, 1910) remains the best extended treatment.

4 Among the many historians who have made major original contributions to these themes I would like to single out Professor Grete Klingenstein, esp. in her *Staatsverwaltung und kirchliche Autorität im 18. Jahrhundert* (Vienna, 1970) and Professor Peter Dickson, esp. in his masterly *Finance and Government under Maria Theresia* (2 vols, Oxford, 1987).

5 I am of course thinking here of the admirable work of Professor Franz Szabo, *Kaunitz and Enlightened Absolutism 1753–1780* (Cambridge, 1994).

6 Cf. Blanning, *Joseph II*, passim.

7 O. Brunner, W. Conze and R. Koselleck (eds), *Geschichtliche Grundbegriffe* (8 vols, Stuttgart, 1972–97).

8 E. Winter, *Der Josefinismus und seine Geschichte* (Brünn, 1943; rev. edn, Berlin, 1962); F. Valjavec, *Der Josephinismus. Zur geistigen Entwicklung Osterreichs im achtzehnten und neunzehnten Jahrhundert* (2nd edn, Munich, 1945); F. Maass (ed.), *Der Josephinismus. Quellen zu seiner Geschichte in Österreich, 1760–1850* (5 vols, Vienna, 1951–61).

9 R. Bauer, 'Le Joséphisme', *Critique*, XIV (1958): 622–39. This article is the basis of this and the two following paragraphs.

10 Elisabeth Kovács has maintained this in a number of places, e.g. in the article on 'Giuseppinismo' in the *Dizionario dell'Istituto dei Maestri Perfetti* and in her chapter 'Katholische Aufklärung und Josephinismus: Neue Forschungen und Fragestellungen', in H. Klueting (ed.), *Katholische Aufklärung – Aufklärung im katholischen Deutschland* (Hamburg, 1993), esp. p. 248. Grete Klingenstein makes the same claim in the recent *Dizionario dell'Illuminismo*. These statements would carry more conviction if they were supported by even a single example of the use of the word 'Josephinismus' in the eighteenth century.

11 Metternich to Lützow, Austrian ambassador in Rome, in Maass, *Josefinismus*, vol. V, p. 565, referred to in Dickson, *Finance and Government under Maria Theresia*, vol. I, p. 59n.

12 Cf. Bauer, *Critique* (1958): 623, n.5.

13 A. J. Groß-Hoffinger, *Leben- und Regierungsgeschichte Josephs des Zweiten* (4 vols, Stuttgart, 1837), consulted in the 2nd edn of 1842. H. Meynert, *Kaiser Joseph II* (Vienna, 1862); A. Ritter von Arneth, *Geschichte Maria Theresias* (10 vols, Vienna, 1863–79) and *Aus meinem Leben* (2 vols, Vienna, 1891–92).

14 On *Faustin* see L. Bodi, *Tauwetter in Wien* (Vienna, 1977), pp. 184–91; and Chapter 11, 'Was Joseph II an Enlightened Despot?'. The crucial passages are printed in Klueting, *Der Josephinismus*, pp. 310–15. Intriguingly, Frederick the Great came near this usage in the very first days of Joseph's sole reign, when he referred to 'ce nouveau gouvernement Joséphin' (to Finckenstein, 6 Dec. 1780: *Politische Correspondenz*, vol. 45 [Berlin, 1937], p. 92).

15 See Goethe, *Dichtung und Wahrheit*. I owe these points to Dr Thomas Biskup, who generously translated the article into German.

16 Bauer, however, confuses Ostini with Orsini.

17 C. Sainte-Foi, *Souvenirs de Jeunesse 1828–35*, ed. C. Latreille (Paris, 1911), pp. 427, 437, cited in Bauer, *Critique* (1958): 625nn.

18 Maass, *Josefinismus*, vol. V, p. 565.

19 R. J. W. Evans, 'Josephinism. "Austrianness" and the Revolution of 1848', in R. Robertson and E. Timms (eds), *Austrian Enlightenment, Austrian Studies, II* (1991), pp. 145–60. A. J. Reinerman, *Austria and the Papacy in the Age of Metternich*, vol. II: *Revolution and Reaction, 1830–1838* (Washington, DC, 1989), uses 'Josephism' and its derivatives without any enquiry whatever into their origins or into contemporary usage, but in ch. IX, dealing with Ostini's negotiations, and its footnotes he quotes (in translation) a few uses of the adjective.

20 Evans in Robertson and Timms (eds), *Austrian Enlightenment*, p. 147; Groß-Hoffinger, *Leben- und Regierungsgeschichte*, vol. III, pp. 602–3.

21 See Chapter 5, 'The False Joseph II'.

22 Metternich's letter of 27 Apr. 1850 in his *Mémoires*, ed. R. von Metternich-Winneburg (8 vols, Paris, 1880–84), vol. III, p. 313; for Beidtel, and for a more profound account of the attitudes of the bureaucracy, see W. Heindl, *Gehorsame Rebellen: Bürokratie und Beamte in Österreich, 1780 bis 1848* (Vienna, 1990), esp. p. 37.

23 See D. Beales, *Joseph II. I: In the Shadow of Maria Theresa, 1741–1780* (Cambridge, 1987), pp. 460–4; Szabo, *Kaunitz*, pp. 241–7; H. Haberzettl, *Die Stellung der Exjesuiten im Politik und Kulturleben Osterreichs zu Ende des 18. Jahrhunderts* (Vienna, 1973); W.C. Langsam, *Francis the Good: The Education of an Emperor, 1768–1792* (New York, 1949).

24 A. J. Reinerman, 'The Return of the Jesuits to the Austrian Empire and the Decline of Josephism', *Catholic Historical Review*, LII (1966): 372–90.

25 See J. C. D. Clark's controversial but highly influential *English Society, 1688–1832* (Cambridge, 1985).

26 See the article of C. Lebeau, cited in n.61 below. The Schottenkirche is a Benedictine abbey.

27 See for the United States esp. the work of H. F. May, e.g. 'The Christian Enlightenment in America', *Miscellanea historiae ecclesiasticae*, VI (1987): 319–29. The volume contains many other valuable relevant pieces, particularly on the situation in Poland.

28 A similar case is made in K. O. von Aretin, 'Der Josephinismus und das Problem des katholischen aufgeklärten Absolutismus', in G. Plaschka and G. Klingenstein, *Österreich im Europa der Aufklärung* (2 vols, Vienna, 1985), pp. 508–24. My figures for percentages of Church lands come from P. G. M. Dickson, 'Joseph II's Reshaping of the Austrian Church', *Historical Journal*, XXXVI (1993): 89–114.

29 P. Hersche, 'War Maria Theresia eine Jansenistin?', *Österreich in Geschichte und Literatur*, XV (1971): 14–25.

30 See the extracts from Garampi's despatches reproduced in Ch. 10 above, pp. 258–60. The correspondence between Joseph and the elector of Trier was published in 1782 and in G. Mohnike, 'Briefwechsel zwischen Kaiser Joseph dem Zweiten und Clemens Wezeslaus, Churfürsten von Trier', *Zeitschrift für historische Theologie*, IV (1834).

31 Quoted by Professor Carlo Capra, who has given me much help on these matters, in D. Sella and C. Capra, *Il ducato di Milano dal 1535 al 1796* (Turin, 1984), p. 493.

32 Caprara's despatch to Rome, 21 July 1790, Archivio segreto vaticano, Nunziatura di Vienna, 200. Cf. Wandruszka, *Leopold II.*, vol. II, pp. 111–39.

33 Cf. P. Baumgart, 'Wie absolut war der preußische Absolutismus?', in M. Schlenke (ed.), *Preußen: Beiträge zu einer politischen Kultur* (Hamburg, 1981), pp. 89–105.

34 I. de Madariaga, *Russia in the Age of Catherine the Great* (London, 1981), esp. ch. 9. P. Dukes (ed.), *Catherine the Great's Instruction to the Legislative Commission, 1767* (Newtonville, 1977).

35 See Chapter 6, 'Joseph II's Rêveries'.

36 G. Gorani, *Il vero dispotismo* (2 vols, 'London', 1770), pp. 6–7, 35. See my discussion on pp. 51–2, 267–8.

37 Quoted in C. Capra, 'Alle origini del moderatismo e del giacobinismo in Lombardia: Pietro Verri e Pietro Custodi', *Studi storici* (1989): 876–7.

38 Quoted in A. Lortholary, *Le mirage russe en France au XVIIIe siècle* (Paris, 1951), p. 138. See D. G. Levy, *The Ideas and Careers of Simon-Nicolas-Henri Linguet* (London, 1980), esp. pp. 225–39.

39 Haus-, Hof und Staatsarchiv, Vienna [hereafter HHSA], Familien-Akten 16 [hereafter *Relazione*].

40 Wandruszka, *Leopold II.*, vol. II., pp. 82–100.

41 *Relazione*, pp. 363–4.

42 Ibid., pp. 252–3, 262–3.

43 Ibid., pp. 74–6.

44 Ibid., p. 387.

45 Ibid., p. 372.

46 Ibid., pp. 369–70.

47 Ibid., pp. 372–3.

48 Ibid., pp. 340–50.

49 Ibid., p. 346.

50 Ibid., pp. 79–96, 191–214.

51 Ibid., pp. 148–9, 155–62.

52 Ibid., pp. 117–28. Cf. P. G. M. Dickson, 'Monarchy and Bureaucracy in Late Eighteenth-Century Austria', *English Historical Review* (1995): 323–67.

53 *Relazione*, pp. 337–83. Cf. Heindl, *Gehorsame Rebellen*.

54 See Chapter 9, 'Joseph II and the Monasteries of Austria and Hungary'.

55 *Relazione*, pp. 400–2. See Bodi, *Tauwetter in Wien*, ch. 5 and pp. 365–7.

56 *Relazione*, esp. pp. 250–1, 278–9.

57 Kaunitz to Mercy, 6 Jan. 1790 (A. R. von Arneth and J. Flammermont, *Correspondance secrète du comte de Mercy-Argenteau avec l'empereur Joseph II et le prince de Kaunitz* [2 vols, Paris, 1891], vol. II, pp. 291–2).

58 HHSA, Handbilleteprotokollen, vol. XI, Joseph to Kaunitz, postscript dated 24 June 1787 from Lemberg attached to letter dated 23rd from Leopol.

59 These letters are in HHSA, Große Correspondenz, 406. They were quoted in H. Schlitter, *Die Regierung Josephs II. in den österreichischen Niederlanden* (part I [but no other published], Vienna, 1900), p. 104.

60 I owe this reference to the generosity of Dr Dorothea Link. For Leopold's manifesto see Wandruszka, *Leopold II.*, vol. II.

61 For a recent rather strident statement of this view see C. Lebeau, 'Le "gouvernement des excellents et des meilleurs". Aristocratie et pouvoir dans la Monarchie des Habsbourg, 1748–1790', *Revue de la Bibliothèque nationale de France*, I (1994): 17–26. The argument was put in the *Essai sur la monarchie autrichienne et son état actuel*, a MS of over 400 pages evidently prepared for the Neapolitan government in 1790, after Joseph's death, with the deliberate intention of erasing the memory of his methods. See my article in *Austrian Studies* II (1991): 10–11, 20.

62 See e.g. Beales, *Joseph II*, pp. 54–5, 354–8.

63 Blanning, *Joseph II*, pp. 186–7 and the references he cites.

64 E.g. R. J. W. Evans, 'Joseph II and Nationality in the Habsburg Lands', in Scott (ed.), *Enlightened Absolutism*, pp. 209–19; M. Csáky, *Von der Aufklärung zum Liberalismus: Studien zum Frühliberalismus in Ungarn* (Vienna, 1981).

65 See for a stimulating survey E. Balázs, *Hungary and the Habsburgs 1765–1800: An Experiment in Enlightened Absolutism* (Budapest, 1997).

66 J. Van den Broeck, *J. B. C. Verlooy* (Antwerp, 1980).

67 D. Prodan, *Supplex libellus valachorum* (Bucharest, 1971), p. 462.

68 Hungarian State Archives, Budapest: C66, Dep. Sanitatis, Normalia 490 and 491. The particular list of languages refers to translations of a work on

liver disease in sheep (491, 1787). An earlier example (Joseph to Pálffy, 29 May 1784, 490) referred to *Anzeige der Mittel die Ungesundheit derjenigen Wohnungen zu vermindern, welche die Uiberschwemmungen ausgesetzt gewesen*, by M. Cadet de Vaux, head of health provision in Paris.

69 See above, pp. 289–91 and F. Engel-Jánosi, 'Kaiser Josef II. in der Wiener Bewegung des Jahres 1848', *Mitteilungen des Vereins für Geschichte der Stadt Wien* XI (1931): 53–72.

Select Bibliography of Works in English

(Place of publication London unless otherwise stated)

General books on the eighteenth century

General books which cover Europe and place it in a wider context include A. Cobban (ed.), *The Eighteenth Century* (1969); W. L. Dorn, *Competition for Empire, 1740–63* (1940) and L. Gershoy, *From Despotism to Revolution, 1763–1789* (1944) in the series *The Rise of Modern Europe*, ed. W. L. Langer; R. R. Palmer, *The Age of the Democratic Revolution: A Political History of Europe and America, 1760–1800* (2 vols, Princeton, 1959, very useful, although his overall thesis is dubious); F. Venturi, *The End of the Old Regime in Europe* (2 vols covering 1776–89, translations of parts of Venturi's magisterial *Settecento riformatore* [5 vols, 7 tomes, Turin, 1969–2002]) and T. C. W. Blanning (ed.), *The Eighteenth Century* (Oxford, 2000), a volume of the *Short Oxford History of Europe*.

General histories of eighteenth-century Europe include W. Doyle, *The Old European Order, 1660–1800* (Oxford, 1978); E. N. Williams, *The Ancient Regime in Europe* (1970).

Inter-state relations

For general treatments, see D. McKay and H. M. Scott, *The Rise of the Great Powers, 1648–1815* (1983) and the brilliant and controversial P. W. Schroeder, *The Transformation of European Politics, 1763–1848* (Oxford, 1994). For the period of Joseph II, D. Beales, *Joseph II, I: In the Shadow of Maria Theresa, 1741–80* (Cambridge, 1987); T. C. W. Blanning, *The French Revolutionary Wars, 1787–1802* (1996, wider than its title suggests); I. de Madariaga, 'The Secret Austro-Russian Treaty of 1781', *Slavonic Review*, 38 (1959): 114–45; K. A. Roider, *Austria's Eastern Question, 1700–1800* (Princeton, 1982); H. M. Scott, *The Emergence of the Great Powers, 1756–1775* (Cambridge, 2001).

Enlightened absolutism / despotism

Among comparative studies are H. M. Scott (ed.), *Enlightened Absolutism* (1991); B. Behrens, *Society, Government and the Enlightenment: The Experiences of Eighteenth-century France and Prussia* (1985). On Russia S. M. Dixon, *The Modernisation of Russia, 1676–1825* (Cambridge, 1999); I. de Madariaga, *Russia in the Age of Catherine the Great* (1981) and *Politics and Culture in Eighteenth-century Russia* (1998). On Austria and Prussia see 'Germany' below.

The Enlightenment

The best introductory treatment is D. Outram, *The Enlightenment* (Cambridge, 1995). The two classic studies are E. Cassirer, *The Philosophy of the Enlightenment* (Princeton, 1951) and P. Gay, *The Enlightenment: An Interpretation* (2 vols, 1967, 1970). Other particularly valuable works are M. Cranston, *Philosophers and Pamphleteers: Political Theorists of the Enlightenment* (Oxford, 1986); R. Darnton's three books: *The Literary Underground of the Old Regime in France* (1982), *The Business of Enlightenment: A Publishing History of the Encyclopédie* (1979) and *The Forbidden Best-sellers of Pre-Revolutionary France* (1996); H. Dieckmann, *Le Philosophe: Texts and Interpretation* (St Louis, 1948); J. McManners, *Death and the Enlightenment* (Oxford, 1981); R. Porter and M. Teich, *The Enlightenment in National Context* (Cambridge, 1981).

Culture and society

This section of course overlaps with that on the Enlightenment. T. C. W. Blanning, *The Culture of Power and the Power of Culture: Old Regime Europe, 1660–1789* (Oxford, 2002) is the pre-eminent English-language study of the nature, growth and impact of the 'public sphere'. See also R. Chartier, *The Cultural Uses of Print in Early Modern France* (Princeton, 1987) and *The Cultural Origins of the French Revolution* (1991). On the role of Courts J. Adamson (ed.), *The Princely Courts of Europe, 1500–1750* (1999); J. Duindam, *Vienna and Versailles: The Courts of Europe's Dynastic Rivals, 1550–1780* (Cambridge, 2003).

On the *visual arts* A. Blunt (ed.), *Baroque and Rococo: Architecture and Decoration* (1978); R. Toman (ed.), *Baroque: Architecture, Sculpture, Painting* (Cologne, 1998).

For *music* N. Zaslaw (ed.), *The Classical Era* (1989). More specifically on Mozart and his background V. Braunbehrens, *Mozart in Vienna* (Oxford, 1991); O. E. Deutsch, *Mozart: A Documentary Biography* (London 1966) and its supplement, C. Eisen (ed.), *New Mozart Documents* (1991); H. C. Robbins Landon, *Haydn: Chronicle and Works* (5 vols, reprinted 1994); J. Rosselli, *The Life of Mozart* (Cambridge, 1998).

The Churches and religion in society and politics

W. R. Ward, *Christianity under the Ancien Régime* (Cambridge, 1999) is the best overall survey. On Catholicism O. Chadwick, *The Popes and European Revolution* (Oxford, 1981); R. P.-C. Hsia, *The World of Catholic Renewal, 1540–1770*; L. Châtellier, *The Europe of the Devout* (Cambridge, 1987) and *The Religion of the Poor* (Cambridge, 1997); D. Beales, *Prosperity and Plunder: European Catholic Monasteries in the Age of Revolution, 1650–1815* (Cambridge, 2003).

Works on Germany and the Austrian Monarchy

General works on *Germany* include J. Gagliardo, *Germany under the Old Regime* (1991); E. Sagarra, *A Social History of Germany, 1648–1914* (1977); J. J. Sheehan, *German History, 1770–1866* (Oxford, 1989); P. H. Wilson, *The Holy Roman Empire, 1495–1806* (1999). Important monographs include T. C. W. Blanning, *Reform and Revolution in Mainz (1743–1803)* (Cambridge, 1974); M. R. Forster, *Catholic Revival in the Age of the Baroque: Religious Identity in Southwest Germany, 1550–1750* (Cambridge, 2001). On *Prussia* (as well as Scott, *Enlightened Absolutism* and Behrens, *Society, Government and the Enlightenment*) P. G. Dwyer (ed.), *The Rise of Prussia, 1700–1830* (2000); T. Schieder, *Frederick the Great* (2000).

On the *Austrian Monarchy*, especially under Maria Theresa and Joseph II, the most useful survey is C. Ingrao, *The Habsburg Monarchy, 1618–1815* (Cambridge, 1994), but the following all make particular contributions: P. S. Fichtner, *The Habsburg Monarchy, 1490–1848* (2003, succinct); R. A. Kann, *History of the Habsburg Empire, 1526–1918* (Berkeley, 1974); C. A. Macartney, *The Habsburg Empire, 1790–1918* (1968, has a chapter on Joseph II, is especially knowledgeable on Hungary); R. Okey, *The Habsburg Monarchy c.1765–1918* (2001), V.-L. Tapié, *The Rise and Fall of the Habsburg Monarchy* (1971, strong on baroque and Bohemia). R. J. W. Evans, *The Making of the Habsburg Monarchy, 1550–1700* (Oxford, 1979) is a brilliant and immensely learned social, cultural and religious survey, reaching well into the eighteenth century. C. A. Macartney (ed.), *The Habsburg and Hohenzollern Dynasties in the Seventeenth and Eighteenth Centuries* (1970) provides a valuable collection of translated documents concerning the Austrian Monarchy and Prussia.

Of works concentrating on the eighteenth century E. Wangermann, *The Austrian Achievement, 1700–1800* (1973, well illustrated) focuses on Josephism, especially under Maria Theresa. M. Hochedlinger, *Austria's Wars of Emergence, 1683–1797* (2003) puts wars and the army firmly back into the picture, as C. Duffy, *The Army of Maria Theresa* (1977) had done for 1740–80. P. G. M. Dickson, *Finance and Government under Maria Theresia* (2 vols, Oxford, 1987) is chiefly concerned with government and administration, economics and finance but throws light on almost every aspect of the period, incidentally correcting much of what previous scholars had written. His three articles, each worth more than many a monograph, illuminate important aspects of Joseph II's reign: 'Joseph II's Reshaping of the Austrian Church', *Historical Journal*, 36 (1993): 89–114; 'Joseph II's Hungarian Land Survey', *English Historical Review*, CVI (1991): 611–34; 'Monarchy and Bureaucracy in Late Eighteenth-Century Austria', ibid., CX (1995): 323–67. F. A. J. Szabo, *Kaunitz and Enlightened Absolutism, 1753–80* (Cambridge, 1994) supplies a good account of the minister's work in internal affairs (excluding Belgium) but omits foreign policy, his chief preoccupation.

Much of R. A. Kann, *A Study in Austrian Intellectual History* (New York, 1960) is devoted to the thought of Josef Sonnenfels, 1732–1817, an important thinker, writer, teacher and civil servant under Maria Theresa and Joseph II. R. Robertson and E. Timms (eds), *The Austrian Enlightenment and Its Aftermath* (=*Austrian Studies* II [1991]), is a useful collection.

Other books relevant to more than one area of the Monarchy are: three by P. P. Bernard: *Jesuits and Jacobins: Enlightenment and Enlightened Despotism in Austria* (1971); *The Limits of Enlightenment: Joseph II and the Law* (1979); *From the Enlightenment to the Police State: The Public Life of Johann Anton Pergen* (Urbana, 1991); C. H. O'Brien, 'Ideas of Religious Toleration at the Time of Joseph II', *Transactions of the American Philosophical Society*, 59, 7 (1969); H. E. Strakosch, *State Absolutism and the Rule of Law* (Sydney, 1967); E. Wangermann, *From Joseph II to the Jacobin Trials* (2nd edn, Oxford, 1969). The position of the Jews is considered in W. O. McCagg, *A History of Habsburg Jews,*

1670–1918 (Bloomington, 1992) and D. Sorkin, *The Transformation of German Jewry, 1780–1840* (Oxford, 1987).

Among *biographies of monarchs* the best on Maria Theresa remains E. Crankshaw's (1969), though it is not always reliable. Probably the best picture of her personality and contribution can be gathered from the combination of Beales, *Joseph II* and A. Fraser, *Marie Antoinette* (2001). T. C. W. Blanning, *Joseph II* (1994) holds the field for the 1780s.

Individual provinces/regions of the Monarchy are discussed in the following works:

The Austrian provinces: G. Klingenstein, 'The Meanings of "Austria" and "Austrian" in the Eighteenth Century', in R. Oresko et al., *Royal and Republican Sovereignty in Early Modern Europe* (Cambridge, 1997), pp. 423–78.

Bohemia and Moravia: R. J. Kerner, *Bohemia in the Eighteenth Century* (1932); P. Shore, *The Eagle and the Cross: Jesuits in Late Baroque Prague* (St Louis, 2002); W. E. Wright, *Serf, Seigneur, and Sovereign: Agrarian Reform in Eighteenth-century Bohemia* (Minneapolis, 1966); H. Freudenberger, *The Industrialization of a Central European City: Brno and the Fine Woollen Industry in the 18th Century* (Edington, 1977).

Hungary: E. H. Balázs, *Hungary and the Habsburgs, 1765–1800* (Budapest, 1997); B. K. Király, *Hungary in the Late Eighteenth Century* (1969); D. Kosáry, *Culture and Society in Eighteenth-Century Hungary* (Budapest, 1987); H. Marczali, *Hungary in the Eighteenth Century* (Cambridge, 1910).

Italian provinces: D. Carpanetto and G. Ricuperati, *Italy in the Age of Reason, 1685–1789* (1987); D. M. Klang, *Tax Reform in Eighteenth-century Lombardy* (New York, 1977); F. Venturi, *Italy and the Enlightenment* (ed. S. J. Woolf, London, 1972).

Netherlands: J. Craeybeckx, 'The Brabant Revolution: A Conservative Revolt in a Backward Country?', *Acta historiae neerlandica*, 4 (1970): 49–83; W. W. Davis, *Joseph II: An Imperial Reformer for the Austrian Netherlands* (The Hague, 1974); J. Polasky, *Revolution in Brussels, 1787–1793* (1987).

Transylvania: D. Prodan, *Supplex libellus valachorum* (Bucharest, 1971).

Tyrol: M. J. Levy, *Governance and Grievance: Habsburg Policy and Italian Tyrol in the Eighteenth Century* (W. Lafayette, 1988).

Index

63–9, 263; and inoculation, 19,
185; and Jansenism, ch. 8, 293;
and Josephism, 287–8, 292;
and Leopold II, 160, 162; and
monasteries, 200, 211, 229–37,
249; and *Rêveries*, 158–9, 160, 161,
164; and serfdom, 199, 301; and
toleration, 14, 200, 292
Maria Theresa, Archduchess, Joseph
II's daughter (1762–70), 183
Marie Antoinette, queen of France
1774–93, 93, 121, 128, 161, 208
Marie Christine, Archduchess, 199
Marmontel, Jean-François, author of
Bélisaire (1767), 40, 75, 275
marriage, civil, 15, 290; of clergy, 244
Marx, Marxism, 7, 9
mathematics, 28–9, 70, 73
Maulbertsch, fresco painter, 80
Max(imilian) Franz, archduke,
elector-archbishop of Cologne
from 1784, 68, 92–3, 123, 128, 196
Max Joseph, elector of Bavaria
(d. 1777), 195
maypoles, 230
Mazarin, cardinal, 45
Melk, Benedictine Abbey, 99–100,
227, 228, 233, 241
mendicant Orders of monks and
nuns, 212, 238–40, 246–9
Mercier, Louis-Sébastien, 41–2
Mercy-Argenteau, comte de, Austrian
ambassador to France, 68, 76
Mesmer, 81
metaphysics, 28–32, 37, 42, 45, 61,
65, 70, 72, 75
Metternich, Prince, Austrian
chancellor, 4, 289–91, 303
Meusel, Professor J. G., 135, 139
Meyer(n), Friedrich von, 103
Meynert, Hermann, historian, 135,
289
Migazzi, Count, cardinal-archbishop
of Vienna and bishop of Vác, 215,
216, 218
Milan, duchy of, 10, 34, 52, 92, 193;
benefices in, 256–7; government
of, 165, 167, 172, 176, 212, 233,

281, 288, 296; monastic reform in,
233–4, 236, 237
Mitrofanov, Paul von, historian, 122,
134
Modena, duke of, 94
monasteries, monks and nuns, 1, 3,
4, 9, 22–3, 74, 78–9, 94, 99, chs
8–9, 278, 292–3; contemplative
Orders, 40, 237–8; in Austria and
Hungary, 213, ch. 9; Joseph II's
attitude to, 117–19, 125, 142–3,
211, 228, 231, 237–45, 256, 297;
his suppressions of, 98, ch. 9, 276;
parochial work, ch. 9; *see also*
Jesuits, Kaunitz, Leopold II, Maria
Theresa, mendicant Orders
Montesquieu, author of *De l'esprit
des lois* (1748), 8, 39, 46–7,
53–4, 55, 64–5, 75, 106, 217, 264,
267–70, 275, 277, 294
Montmorin, French minister, 126,
128
Moravia, 10, 15, 78
Moslems, attitudes to, 104–6, 116
Mousnier, R., historian, 269, 270
Mouzay, *curé* of, 81
Mozart, Leopold, 92, 100
Mozart, Wolfgang Amadeus, 3, ch.
4; as Freemason, 99–103; and
Catholicism, 99–100; and the
war of 1788–91, 103–6, 107–10;
his politics, 98–9; his works:
dedications, 93–4; texts, 100–10;
Ave Verum Corpus, 106; C minor
Mass, 94; German dances, 93;
'Jupiter' symphony, 99, 104;
masonic works, 99, 101–3; *Ascanio
in Alba*, 92–3; *La clemenza di Tito*,
94, 106; *Così fan tutte*, 97; *Don
Giovanni*, 93, 97; *Die Entführung*,
94–6; *La finta semplice*, 96; *The
Impresario*, 97; *Lucio Silla*, 94; *The
Magic Flute*, 99, 141; *The Marriage
of Figaro*, 93, 96–7; *Mitridate*, 94;
Il rè pastore, 93; song *Beim Auszug
in das Feld*, 104–10
Müller, Ignaz, provost of the
Augustinian house of St